Brazilian Multinationals

Since the 1950s, subsidiaries of the most prestigious foreign multinationals have played a key role in Brazilian economic development, thus creating a very competitive domestic market. On top of this, government interventions in the last few decades have been inconsistent and contradictory, resulting in a series of economic crises. Only the most resilient Brazilian firms have been able to survive and prosper in this challenging environment. This book analyzes a variety of leading Brazilian multinationals and examines their competences and competitive strategies in a variety of different settings. It develops an innovative analytical framework based on international business, international operations management, and international human resources management. This framework is then applied not only to Brazilian multinationals, but also to firms from Latin America, Russia, India, and China. Thus, the book provides novel insights into the rise of Brazilian multinationals and the increasingly important role played by emerging economy multinationals in the global economy.

AFONSO FLEURY is Professor of Technology, Work, and Organization in the Production Engineering Department of the University of Sao Paulo. He has been a research fellow at the Institute of Development Studies (UK), the Tokyo Institute of Technology (Japan), École Nationale des Ponts et Chaussés (France), and the Institute for Manufacturing, University of Cambridge (UK). He is currently an associate editor of the Journal of Manufacturing Technology Management and Vice-President (Americas) of the Production and Operations Management Society.

MARIA TEREZA LEME FLEURY is the Dean of the School of Business Administration of Fundacao Getulio Vargas, in Sao Paulo and former Dean of the School of Economics, Business Administration, and Accountancy of the University of Sao Paulo. Her publications cover areas such as strategy and competence management, human resources management, management of organisational culture, and labor relations. She was Visiting Professor at ESSEC (France) and at the Institute for Manufacturing, University of Cambridge, as well as a research fellow at the Institute of Development Studies (UK) and the Institute for Developing Economies (Tokyo). She is currently Director of ANPAD (Brazilian Academy of Management).

Brazilian Multinationals

Competences for Internationalization

AFONSO FLEURY

AND

MARIA TEREZA LEME FLEURY

CAMBRIDGE
UNIVERSITY PRESS

CAMBRIDGE UNIVERSITY PRESS
Cambridge, New York, Melbourne, Madrid, Cape Town, Singapore,
São Paulo, Delhi, Dubai, Tokyo, Mexico City

Cambridge University Press
The Edinburgh Building, Cambridge CB2 8RU, UK

Published in the United States of America by Cambridge University Press, New York

www.cambridge.org
Information on this title: www.cambridge.org/9780521519489

First published 2011

Printed in the United Kingdom at the University Press, Cambridge

A catalogue record for this publication is available from the British Library

Library of Congress Cataloguing in Publication data
Fleury, Afonso (Afonso Carlos Correa), 1947–
    Brazilian Multinationals : Competences for Internationalization / Afonso Fleury,
    Maria Tereza Leme Fleury.
      p.   cm
    Includes bibliographical references and index.
    ISBN 978-0-521-51948-9
    1. International business enterprises – Brazil.   2. International business
    enterprises – Developing countries.   I. Fleury, Maria Tereza Leme.   II. Title.
    HD2834.F54 2011
    338.8′898101724–dc22
    2010045706

ISBN 978-0-521-51948-9 Hardback

To our grandchildren, Marina, Leonardo and Gabriela,
who will surf the waves of the new world,
and to our sons, Andre, Fernando and Pedro, and
  daughters-in-law,
who are teaching the children the art and science of sailing
  through rough waters.

Contents

Figures

xii

Tables

Boxes

Acknowledgments

We have been studying multinational enterprises for several decades. As we live in Brazil, we mainly research their subsidiaries within the local operating and institutional context.

The research project on Brazilian multinationals and their management models that gave rise to this book, however, is more recent. It began in 2006, with the support of two Brazilian agencies: CNPq – Conselho Nacional de Desenvolvimento Científico e Tecnológico (the National Scientific and Technological Development Council) and FAPESP – Fundação de Amparo à Pesquisa do Estado de São Paulo (the Research Foundation of the State of São Paulo). Our home institutions, namely, the Departments of Production Engineering and of Business Administration of the University of São Paulo, and the School of Business Administration of Fundação Getulio Vargas, granted the conditions for the achievement of our objectives as well.

Our project matured at Cambridge University, where we were visiting researchers at the Institute for Manufacturing (IFM) in 2007, thanks to our dialogues with the researchers of various institutes. We are particularly grateful to Mike Gregory and Yongjian Shi, of the IfM, and to Peter Williamson and Eden Yin, of the Judge Business School.

In Birmingham, John Child and Susana Rodrigues, of the Business School, were always points of reference for our work, while David Bennett, at Aston University, added important contributions from his experiences in Asian countries.

Raphie Kaplinsky, John Humphrey, and Hubert Schmitz of the Institute of Development Studies (IDS) in Brighton continued to be important interlocutors, even though Brazil was no longer being covered by IDS studies.

Two distinguished scholars from the international business area were of great help for us to penetrate the meanders of this fascinating field of knowledge: John Dunning and John Stopford. Dunning welcomed us, with his generosity and interest, into the heart of the

Academy of International Business, while Stopford, who is well aware of Brazilian reality within the context of the global economy, offered us precious advice.

In the United States, we owe special thanks to Ravi Ramamurti, of Northeastern University, for the projects with which he entrusted us and for the invariably constructive dialogues. We would also like to thank Alvaro Cuervo-Cazurra for his insights into multilatinas.

A group of Brazilian researchers shared our journey. Moacir de Miranda Oliveira Junior and Felipe Borini conducted with us several of the activities described in this book. Our colleagues Angela Rocha, Betânia Tanure, Miguel Caldas, Thomas Wood, Alvaro Cyrino, and Eduardo Vasconcellos contributed with their knowledge and experience on different topics related to Brazilian firms and internationalization issues.

The doctoral students Fernanda Ribeiro, Germano Glufke Reis, Eduardo Pinheiro, Erika Barcellos, Dinorá Floriani, and Natacha Bortóia da Silva provided us with important insights during the journey.

We are grateful to Paula Parish, from Cambridge University Press, who acknowledged the value of publishing a book on Brazilian multinationals and guided us toward that aim. We also want to thank the three anonymous reviewers engaged by Cambridge University Press for their valuable comments.

We dedicate this book to our sons, André, Fernando, and Pedro, who not only encouraged us, but also gave us unwavering and interested support.

Introduction

The first Brazilian who ventured into international activities and defended the project of Brazil becoming an international player was the Baron of Maua, Irineu Evangelista de Souza, who lived from 1813 to 1889. From humble origins, he rose by his own merit and initiative. A trip to England in 1840 was crucial for the formation of his global mindset and entrepreneurial project. Returning to Rio de Janeiro, he bought a small foundry which became a major shipyard. Using material produced by this foundry, he was responsible for the installation of the piped water system in Rio de Janeiro. In April 1854, he inaugurated the railroad connecting the Rio to Petropolis, in the presence of Emperor Dom Pedro II, who heralded him as Baron. In 1855, along with other investors, he formed Maua, MacGregor & Cia, a financial institution with branches in London, Paris, New York, Buenos Aires, and Montevideo. His wealth in 1867 reached a sum that was 20 percent higher than Brazil's governmental budget. It is estimated that his fortune would be equivalent to $60 billion today.

Maua allied entrepreneurship and international vision to competences related to technology, finance, and marketing. The institutional context, however, was not favorable to him. Brazil was an agro-export economy, just liberated from Portuguese colonial rule, and slavery still persisted. Resistance to his ideas was fierce.

One hundred years later, the Baron of Maua became a symbol of entrepreneurship, as a precursor to better working conditions, investment in technology, internationalization, and multilateralism.

In the last two decades, the emergence of Brazilian multinationals fulfilled the vision of the Baron of Maua: Brazil as a player on the international context. Today, a number of Brazilian multinationals stand out as leading global players: Embraer (aircraft), Companhia Vale do Rio Doce (mining), Petrobras (oil and gas), and Gerdau (steel), among others. Overall, the number of Brazilian multinationals has risen significantly since the early 1990s and particularly since 2000.

Actually, the internationalization of Brazilian corporations is part of a large process whereby multinationals from emerging economies began to play an increasingly important role in the global economy. It was not until 2005 that *Fortune 500* included corporations from emerging countries in its ranking. If only those from Brazil, Russia, India, and China (the BRICs) are counted, they were twenty-seven in 2005, thirty-five in 2006, thirty-nine in 2007, forty-six in 2008, and fifty-eight in 2009. China accounted for the largest share; Brazil had three in 2005 and six in 2009. Since 2005, the Boston Consulting Group has produced a report on the "100 New Global Challengers" that, in 2009, included thirty-six enterprises from China, twenty from India, fourteen from Brazil, six from Russia, and seven from Mexico, the remaining seventeen coming from nine other countries. Those numbers provide the initial insights into the argument that companies that were considered laggards, working in less developed contexts, began to challenge the leaders.

Year	Some examples of rising emerging country multinationals
2003	Lenovo acquires IBM's PC division
2005	Brazilian Vale acquires International Nickel Company (INCO) becoming the world's largest producer
2006	Indian Mittal acquires Arcelor to become the world's largest steel producer
2008	Indian Tata launches the revolutionary Nano car
	South African Brewery (SAB) Miller, and AB INBEV (a merger of Belgian Interbrew and Brazilian AMBEV) become world leaders in the beverage industry
2009	Brazilian JBS Friboi becomes the world's largest meat producer

The impacts of the expansion of multinationals from emerging countries raised issues such as: why do they internationalize, where do they move to, how do they move, and what will be the impact on international production and trade?

The explanatory power of the classical theories on internationalization was challenged and more focused theoretical approaches started to be developed. The approach adopted for this book seeks to establish an interface between those two streams of literature because it is based on the following interdependent assumptions:

(a) the propensity to internationalize increases whenever there are changes in the paradigms that guide production organization at the global level, thereby creating "windows of opportunity" and "waves of internationalization"; and

(b) seizing those opportunities is connected with the organizational competences and managerial styles developed by firms while competing in the global industries and interacting with their national, or local, environments, respectively.

For example, consider the unforeseen acquisition of Jaguar/Land Rover by Tata Motors. *The Economist* (March 29, 2008: 82) analyzes the issue under the title "Now what?" The question is pertinent. However, to answer it adequately it is not sufficient to look at Tata's resources, competences, and managerial style, which are gradually being considered as India's icon for competitiveness in the new global economy. It is as important as well to understand why Ford agreed to let it go and why, previously, Jaguar and Land Rover were sold to Ford.

The above assumptions will outline the analytical framework, to be applied first and foremost to the case of Brazil. The analysis of Brazilian firms focuses first on their genesis and evolution, especially in the interplay between them and the multinationals that established operations in Brazil throughout the twentieth century. Then it looks at the development of Brazilian multinationals regarding internationalization: the decision process which led them to establish operations abroad and their approaches to the management of foreign subsidiaries. This allows us to sketch an emerging Brazilian model of international management.

The subsequent application of the analytical framework to the study of multinationals from other emerging countries reveals that Brazilian firms' process of internationalization has specific characteristics that contrast not only with the internationalization dynamics of firms from other emerging countries, but also with classic multinationals, the so-called early movers.

Therefore, the book aims to provide:

- an analytical framework to be used to study the internationalization of firms as well as as a tool for providing support for the implementation of internationalization strategies in firms and institutions;
- a comparative analysis of the paths taken by multinationals from different emerging economies, where the local influences of the

different cultural, political, and economic environments play a fundamental role.

The book is organized into two parts. The first part aims to develop the analytical framework for the study of the internationalization process of companies from emerging countries. The second part is devoted to the study of Brazilian multinationals and comparative analyses with multinationals from other emerging countries such as China, India, Russia, and other countries in Latin America.

The first part starts with a chapter on globalization and internationalization. In this book, globalization is seen as a socio-political process involving countries and institutions, while internationalization is considered as a purposeful decision taken by an organization. In Chapter 1 that distinction is further developed and exemplified. Indicators of globalization and internationalization are presented and critically analyzed. The final section introduces emerging countries and discusses the roles that they played, currently play, and are expected to play in regards to globalization and internationalization.

Chapter 2 outlines the overarching analytical framework. Our perspective will take the firm as its basic unit of analysis, but will also highlight the context in which the company operates. In other words, it regards the firm as an open system in permanent interaction with its environment. We assume that the decisions of internationalization are related to the company's positioning in regards to the opportunities and threats that arise in the national and international environments, and its ability to anticipate and react to them. This, in turn, stems from the organizational competences developed by the company and its management style.

That perspective is derived from the resource-based view of the firm and builds, particularly, on the works of authors who developed concepts and models to explain what competence-based competition is. Therefore, in Chapter 2, an introduction to the resource-based view of the firm is followed by the proposition of a framework to look at how firms develop competences in their dynamic interrelationship with the competitive environment, either national or international.

At firm level, the development of management styles is primarily influenced by the national or local environment. We assume that the socio-political and cultural dimensions, as well as the country's or region's factor endowment, are the most relevant dimensions of the national or local environment in the shaping of managerial styles.

Therefore, the analytical framework takes organizational competences and management style as the key determinants of a firm's strategy in general and internationalization strategy in particular. Organizational competences are primarily driven by the firm's competitive environment while management style is primarily influenced by the firm's national or local environment.

Understanding the dynamic interplay among those dimensions is crucial for the study of emerging country multinationals. The main finding revealed in this book relates to the developing organizational competences and managerial styles derived from their founding, growth, and success in their respective countries, which provided the conditions for them to follow particular internationalization paths and develop winning strategies.

In Chapter 3 we look at "early-movers and the earliest internationalization theories." During 1950–70 three blocks of countries coexisted: the so-called first world (the industrially advanced countries), the second world (the countries behind the Iron Curtain), and the third world (the other countries, considered underdeveloped at the time). It was a time when conditions for corporations from advanced countries to expand internationally were enticing.

The pioneering theories conceptualized the firm as an economic agent, and modeled their rationale through the firms' inclination to engage in foreign direct investment (FDI). A variant approach, based on the behavioral theory of the firm, developed by the Nordic school, is also a product of those times. Those theories created the mainstream for international business studies.

We revisit and update these theories to identify commonalities in relation to the analytical framework used in this book. Moreover, we set the ground for the shift that has happened in recent times, when a set of factors, to be addressed in Chapter 4, changed the competitive landscape for the early-movers and created the conditions for the emergence of multinationals from emerging countries. During the first wave of internationalization, third world countries were essentially receivers of FDI and hosts to the subsidiaries of multinational enterprises (MNEs) of the aforementioned countries.

Chapter 4 analyzes the second wave of internationalization in the 1970s and 1980s. That was triggered by changes in the market regime worldwide. Until the 1970s, most markets operated according to the "seller's law": since demand was greater than supply, producers established their rules and procedures and imposed them upon consumers. That was the rationale followed by the early-movers because, in the period that followed the second world war, there was a widespread need to create the capacity to produce goods and services. However, in the 1970s, there was a radical shift in certain markets because increased production capacity caused supply to exceed demand. Markets started to operate under the "buyers' law": power shifted to consumers, and quality became the main strategic concern. The Japanese industry was the first to operate according to this new rationale. To do so, Japanese corporations created a distinct management model which prioritized a new set of competences under a particular management style. That allowed Japan to catch up with the most advanced countries. Korea soon followed, and the competitive landscape was profoundly modified. At the same time, the initial attempts of corporations from third world countries to internationalize were observed. The results were far more modest.

In Chapter 5 we look at productive globalization, the restructuring of Western MNEs and the rise of MNEs from emerging countries. Political, social, and technological shifts in the 1970s and 1980s redefined the characteristics of the operating global environment. At the micro level of Western world corporations, profound changes were undertaken to absorb and upgrade the newly revealed best-practices of the Japanese management model's thus counterbalancing the competitive power of Asian corporations. Those factors led Western countries and their multinationals to undertake a set of changes in terms of competitive positioning which received the broad denomination of productive restructuring.

New concepts such as focusing, outsourcing, offshoring, fragmentation, and modularization became corporate reorganization guideposts. Production systems became increasingly complex, while firms took on specialized and complementary roles in global production networks. The classic multinationals (early-movers) started focusing on highly value-adding activities and outsourced those with lower value-adding potential (generally routine activities and/or commodities producing). In other words, leading firms developed new management models, combining new profiles of competences and management styles. They abandoned and/or outsourced other types of organizational competences. This made it possible not only for new firms to enter but also generated windows of opportunity for firms from emerging countries.

Thus, Chapter 5 has three objectives. The first, of a descriptive nature, emphasizes the changes which took place in American and European MNEs as of 1980. The second objective is to present a summary of the new management models developed by those companies to remain competitive in the new global economy. That includes how the companies were internally restructured and how this impacted the organization of their international activities. The third objective is to demonstrate how changes within MNEs from developed countries opened space for new multinational companies from emerging countries. With that, the analytical framework for the study of multinationals from emerging countries is complete.

Brazil is the focus in the three chapters that follow. Initially, Brazil's political, economic, and social development, from the colonial period until the 1980s, is summarized, in order to put the emergence of its MNEs into context. Brazil performed differently in each of the internationalization waves. During the first wave, in the 1950s and 1960s, Brazil was essentially a receiver of FDI, playing host to new subsidiaries of foreign MNEs. During the second wave, in the late 1970s and early 1980s, isolated and unsuccessful attempts of native Brazilian firms to move into international markets took place. Finally, in the third wave, in the 1990s and 2000s, Brazil is producing an effective internationalization movement.

Chapter 6 highlights the interplay, as from the early twentieth century, of Brazilian firms and MNE subsidiaries, all of which had to operate within a complex institutional context whose main feature was uncertainty and discontinuity. It is within this context that Brazilian companies are born and evolve, i.e., in competition with the subsidiaries of foreign MNEs, to then grow into Brazilian MNEs.

Chapter 7 looks at the recent evolution of Brazil and the rise of Brazilian multinationals. In the early 1990s, productive restructuring in Brazil was particularly complex and exceptionally demanding for the corporations. Traditional industrial groups and leading enterprises disappeared; important state-owned enterprises were fully privatized. Nevertheless, the competitive environment thus instated generated a selection process that revealed which Brazilian enterprises were able to develop management competences in order to survive and prosper and which were not. The leading Brazilian firms began to converge to a sort of Brazilian managerial model. This was the setting in which the internationalization of Brazilian firms grew and became solid.

This chapter first describes the context of production restructuring in the period 1990–2008. That is followed by a section on the resurgence of the movement of Brazilian firms to the foreign countries, starting with Mercosul. Then an overall view of Brazilian multinationals is presented. The section closes with the outcome of a survey which reveals the main features of the internationalization process of Brazilian enterprises and the way in which they are managing their subsidiaries abroad. This allows the identification of a sort of Brazilian model of international management.

Chapter 8 presents the cases of the most outstanding Brazilian multinationals. Nineteen were chosen to illustrate the international presence of Brazilian multinationals belonging to different classes of corporations. State-owned, recently privatized, and private were distinguished. Within the private corporations group, agribusiness, manufacturing (from eight different industrial sectors), engineering services, specialized services, information technology (IT) products and services and born globals were analyzed on their own merits. A short text precedes each case to contextualize it within the national and international environments.

Latin America comprises very distinct national environments nurtured from common roots. Despite being parts of Iberian empires, heterogeneity and lack of integration are the key characteristics of the region. Interestingly, Argentina was one of the most developed countries in the turn of the twentieth century; Argentinean MNEs spread throughout Latin America. However, after a second attempt during the 1980s, the current standing of multilatinas is relatively modest. Chapter 9 analyzes the evolution of multilatinas, the multinationals from other Latin American countries – Argentina, Chile, and Mexico, in particular. It starts with a short section on the economic development of Latin America. That is followed by the analysis of the transition that started in the 1990s, when they opened themselves up to international markets, which brought different outcomes for different Latin American countries. Then, the multilatinas are presented and the sources of international competitiveness are discussed. The comparative analysis reveals how the national environments influenced their internationalization process and provides information for hypotheses regarding the sustainability of their internationalization strategies.

The content of Chapter 10, the multinationals from China, India, Russia, and South Africa, highlights a different comparative track. In the case of the multilatinas, comparisons to the Brazilian case allowed us to advance the influence of national environments over internationalization strategies and performance. When China, India, and Russia are considered, the comparative analysis must emphasize how those countries are creating conditions for becoming world leaders in certain industries.

Chapter 10 begins with a broad view of Asia and its recent economic development, as a background for the introduction of the Indian and Chinese cases. Each of these is then analyzed in terms of recent economic development, country specific advantages and disadvantages, and profiles of outstanding multinationals. Short case studies about these multinationals are used to outline the main characteristics of the internationalization process. Due to its specific features, the case of Russia is taken separately.

In the concluding chapter, we first retrieve and consolidate the analytical framework. We illustrate its applicability by revisiting some of the most illustrative examples. We then synthesize the findings of Brazilian multinationals as well as the main points that arose in the comparison with multinationals from other emerging countries. The final section establishes some conjectures about the sustainability of multinationals from emerging countries and suggests future work.

PART I

Developing *the analytical framework and contextualizing the phenomenon*

1 | Globalization and internationalization: the perspective of emerging countries

Let Fame with wonder name the Greek no more,
What lands he saw, what toils at sea he bore;
Nor more the Trojan's wand'ring voyage boast,
What storms he brav'd on many a perilous coast:
No more let Rome exult in Trajan's name,
Nor Eastern conquests Ammon's pride proclaim;
A nobler hero's deeds demand my lays

(Camões, *The Lusiads*, as translated by W. J. Mickle in the eighteenth century)

1.1 Those who go to sea prepare on land

The Portuguese navigations, sung by Luiz de Camões in his poem *The Lusiads*, significantly expanded the world as it was known in the fifteenth and sixteenth centuries. They are part of the globalization process, which should not be seen as a recent phenomenon, given that since humankind's earliest days, man has been venturing into new territories.

What caused the Iberian globalization project to stand out was not only its geographic, economic, and cultural scope, but the preparation process that preceded it. In the fourteenth and fifteenth centuries, the School of Sagres was a cornerstone for the whole venture. It was there that the project was conceived and planned, under the leadership of the bastard king D. João I, of his English wife Phillipa of Lancaster, who modernized the Portuguese court, and of their children and aides, not to speak of the heroes in the battles against the Spaniards and the Moors, all of whom played a relevant role.

In the book *Sagres, a revolução estratégica* (Sagres, the strategic revolution), by Luiz Fernando Pinto, the project of Portuguese maritime expansion is described, showing that ancient Portuguese partnership with the sea implied in the development of competences such as:

- craftsmanship for working with stone and timber, which resulted in naval competences and in the construction of the Iberian caravel, whose advantage was its sail surface, twice as big as that of similar ships, which lent greater speed and enabled it to tack against the wind;
- obtaining financing, whether from the religious orders, the kings' personal fortunes, other financers or the yield of each expedition (from the sale of slaves, piracy, and plunder);
- selecting and training fishermen and pirates, benefiting from the learnings inherited from the Roman legions that had controlled the Iberian Peninsula;
- developing technology in terms of navigation instruments and charts that indicated the islands in the Atlantic.

Iberian entrepreneurship, in a successful globalization project of the fifteenth and sixteenth centuries, resulted in Vasco da Gama discovering the route to the Indies, in Pedro Alvares Cabral discovering Brazil, and in Christopher Columbus discovering the Americas.

In 1494, Portugal and Spain signed the Treaty of Tordesillas, splitting the world in two; at first, the Atlantic, known as the Ocean Sea because the Europeans were unaware of the Pacific's existence at the time, was divided. Years later, as they set up establishments in the Orient, the Tordesillas meridian also became the element that partitioned the lands of the Indies.

The history of how Portugal, until then an inexpressive country on the world scene, overflowed into the sea, shows how the globalization phenomenon can involve different players at several historical moments.

From those times to our days, the dynamics of globalization went through several stages, with periods in which borders were more tightly closed and others in which they were more permeable. There are even some who feel that the present day world is less globalized than in the nineteenth century. The most recent phase is characterized by the rising importance, when it comes to the world's political and economic relations, of a group of some twenty nations known as emerging countries.

It is the overflow process of these countries into a world order already globalized and orchestrated by developed nations that forms the backdrop for this chapter. The emergence of new global players in this process, i.e., the internationalization of firms from these countries, is also addressed.

Thus, the aim of this chapter is to present the concepts of globalization and internationalization. It is not our intent to embrace ideological positions in this debate, but merely to point out the various points of view and arguments, providing a conceptual overview and a brief coverage of historical periods in terms of globalization. This allows one to outline the setting of the restructuring of the global systems for the production of goods and services in which the new multinational enterprises (MNEs) of the emerging countries play their roles, as important actors. It is within a rising context of globalized economic activity that the arena and the circumstances that enable these firms to arise are being created.

1.2 Globalization: the interconnected world

1.2.1 What is globalization?

As a subject of study, the globalization phenomenon has been analyzed from a range of different perspectives: anthropological, economic, social, cultural, and political. It is a polemic issue. Among those who have been poring over it for the last decades, there are some whose evaluation is positive and others who point out its negative impact. By casting light upon the different facets of the process, they provide data and information in support of one or the other of these points of view.

Globalization is the process whereby interconnections and interdependences in the many fields of human activities are gradually increasing. There are many ways to augment interconnections and to create interdependences. Currently, the Internet is the best example, in that it increasingly involves everything and everyone all over the world.

Theodore Levitt, a renowned marketing author, commented in the early 1980s that "the globalization of markets creates opportunities for firms to offer globally standardized products that are advanced, functional, reliable and low priced" (Levitt, 1983: 93). This is not exactly what happened later, but this warning was important for the conduct of companies' international strategies.

Peter Dicken, in *Globalshift*, his 1992 book, stressed economic flows and defined globalization as "a shift in traditional patterns of international production, investment, and trade" (Dicken, 1992).

Keniche Ohmae, on the other hand, saw the reduction of barriers to commercial and financial flows as the chief factor. For him, globalization meant "the absence of borders and barriers to trade among nations" (Ohmae, 1995).

Therefore, the ultimate aim of globalization is the creation of a single world market for labor, capital, goods, and services. However, to date, we are far from achieving this, so authors tend to highlight the acceleration of the unification of the world's markets. Berger (2005: 9), in proposing the notion that "globalization is the acceleration of the processes in the international economy and in domestic economies that operate toward unifying world markets," reminds us that this process also affects domestic markets.

The definitions above, however, make no mention of the globalization agents. In other words, globalization can also be seen in relation to the ambitions and actions of key global actors. Furthermore, globalization is the outcome of technological advances and of the natural curiosity of the human species, fuelled by increasingly cheap and sophisticated communication systems.

Building on Kaplinski's definition (2005: 12), we assume that "Globalization is a complex and multidimensional process that can be viewed through a variety of lenses. It is a process in which the barriers to cross-border flows are being reduced, not just for financial, economic and material flows, but also for the diffusion of knowledge, information, belief systems, ideas and values." Thus, new environmental conditions arise for those organizations and institutions that pursue influence and global acknowledgment, whether of a political, religious, cultural, or economic nature.

Box 1.1 Shakespeare and globalization

In London, a group of artists that included William Shakespeare created the Globe Theatre. The name seems to have been chosen deliberately: "It was at the theatre, noted Thomas Platter, a Swiss tourist who visited England and saw plays there in 1599, that the English pass their time, learning at the play what is happening abroad" (Shapiro, 2005: xv).

Table 1.1 *Financial indicators, 1980–2007*

Financial indicators	1980	1985	1990	1995	2000	2005	2007
Daily currency exchange turnover, % world GDP[a]	0.7	1.3	3.8	5.6	6.8	4.6	6.6
Cross-border bank loan stock, % world GDP[b]	13.9	19.9	34.3	33.1	37.6	39.1	n/a

Source: Guillén (2007).
[a] Data are for 1979, 1984, 1989, 1995, 1998, 2004, and 2006.
[b] Data are for 1981, 1986, 1991, 1995, 2000, and 2005.

1.2.2 The indicators of globalization in recent times

In order to characterize what globalization has been in recent times, it is important to understand its phases and how they are concatenated. To understand the pace of globalization one must define indicators and measure them.

Chesnais (1995) and Baumann (1996) identified three stages in the recent period of globalization. The first was financial globalization, initiated in the 1970s. Two important drivers were the deregulation of financial markets and the rapid advances in computing and telecommunication technologies. Money started circulating far faster.

The first indicator in Table 1.1 (daily currency exchange turnover) shows the total of all the currencies from all countries converted into the currencies of other countries as a percentage of global gross domestic product (GDP, defined as the total value of all completed goods and services produced in the world in one year). This figure was modest in 1980, but rose to almost 7% before the market crisis of 2000, when it dropped; this was followed by a gradual recovery up to 2007. The second indicator shows that the stock of cross-border bank loans also posted significant growth: from 13.9% of global GDP in 1980 to almost 40% in 2006.

The second stage was commercial globalization, which became stronger in the 1980s as a result of the reduction of barriers to international trade, and thanks to the development of transportation technologies, especially the maritime container. Raw materials and finished products began moving much faster.

The first three indicators in Table 1.2 show that international trade (measured by exports plus imports of goods and services) increased 46% more than world GDP from 1980 to 2007. The growth of the emerging countries' share of international trade is impressive: 149% versus 26% for the developed countries.

The fourth indicator (exports of foreign affiliates as a percentage of world exports) shows intracompany international trade, i.e., exports among the subsidiaries of multinationals in different countries. Since 1980, this figure has mirrored the growth of international trade. It was affected quite strongly by productive globalization, which will be discussed next.

Finally, the group of three indicators at the bottom of the table disregards the flow of goods and services, focusing instead on the international flow of direct investment in production activities. More specifically, it evaluates the stock of inward foreign direct investment (IFDI) in relation to global GDP. It provides a measure of how much investment in production in a given country was financed by other countries. The added indicator reflects considerable growth, from 6.7% to 27.9% of GDP, which, in turn, also rose. One can also see that foreign investments in developed countries grew proportionally more than foreign investments in emerging countries. In other words, although the IFDI in emerging countries increased significantly, as we will see further on, IFDI in developed countries grew even more, which reveals that investment priorities changed, although not radically, in the recent past.

After financial and commercial globalization, the third stage was the globalization of production, when production and operation systems became organized according to a globally integrated production rationale. The MNE became the main agent of this process. In other words, the location where things were produced and the way in which they were delivered began to change.

The upper section of Table 1.3 reflects the growth of the flows into investment in production, as measured by foreign direct investment (FDI), connected with MNEs' activities. "The recent upsurge in FDI reflects a greater level of cross-border mergers and acquisitions (M&As), especially among developed countries. It also reflects

Table 1.2 *Economic indicators, 1980–2007*

Economic indicators	1980	1985	1990	1995	2000	2005	2007
Exports + imports of goods & services, % world GDP	39.0	38.7	38.3	42.0	50.0	54.1	56.9[a]
Developed countries, % GDP	39.0	39.9	38.1	40.5	48.2	49.6	49.4[a]
Developing countries, % GDP	33.0	32.6	39.3	48.3	57.2	63.5	82.2[a]
Exports of foreign affiliates, % total world exports	n/a	31.9	27.5	32.3	33.3[b]	33.3	33.3
Inward foreign direct investment stock, % world GDP	6.7	8.4	9.3	10.3	18.3	22.7	27.9
Developed countries, % GDP	4.9	6.2	8.2	8.9	16.3	21.4	27.2
Developing countries, % GDP	12.6	16.4	14.8	16.6	26.2	27.0	29.8

Source: Guillén (2007).
[a] 1998. [b] 2006

higher growth rates in some developed countries as well as strong economic performance in many developing and transition economies" (UNCTAD, 2006: xvii). The 2007 figures are approximately twenty times greater than those from 1982, both in terms of flows and of stocks. The apparent imbalance between FDI inflows and outflows

Table 1.3 *Selected indicators of FDI and international production,*
1982–2007

Item	Value at current prices ($bn)			
	1982	1990	2006	2007
FDI outflows	27	239	1.323	1.997
FDI outward stock	579	1.785	12.756	15.602
Exports of goods and non-factor services	2.395	4.417	14.848	17.138
Cross-border M&As	n/a	200	1.118	1.637
Sales of foreign affiliates	2.741	6.126	25.844	31.197
Gross product of foreign affiliates	676	1.501	5.049	6.029
Total assets of foreign affiliates	2.206	6.036	55.818	68.716
Exports of foreign affiliates	688	1.523	4.950	5.714
Employment of foreign affiliates (000s)	21.524	25.103	70.003	81.615

Source: UNCTAD, based on its FDI/TNC database (www.unctad.org); UNCTAD, GlobStat; IMF, *International Financial Statistics*, June 2008.

shown in the table is merely the result of an accounting problem (Aykut and Goldstein, 2008).

   The table's lower section shows the operational details of production globalization. MNEs resorted strongly to M&As as a means of reorganizing their global production activities, by concentrating on certain lines of business and divesting others. The table shows that

Table 1.4 *Communication indicators, 1980–2007*

Comunication indicators	1980	1985	1990	1995	2000	2005	2007
Internet users, % world population	n/a	n/a	0.1	0.8	6.5	16.2	21.8
Developed countries, % population	n/a	n/a	0.3	4.0	32.9	62.4	67.7
Developing countries, % population	n/a	n/a	0.0	0.1	1.7	8.2	13.0
International calls, minutes per capita	n/a	n/a	7.1[a]	11.1	19.5	28.0	27.7[b]

Source: Guillén (2007).
[a] 1991. [b] 2006.

cross-border M&As, which were not very relevant up to the 1980s, grew sixfold from 1990 to 2006. Meanwhile, MNEs reorganized their activities by redefining the role of their subsidiaries. The staff at subsidiaries grew threefold, from 1990 to 2006, whereas sales increased fourfold, gross sales increased more than threefold and exports from subsidiaries also grew threefold, leading us to conclude that the performance of subsidiaries improved substantially.

This set of figures provides a clear indication of how production activities were reconfigured into the so-called "productive globalization" process, which paved the way for the participation of emerging countries. In other words, the very fast expansion of the global trade in manufactured goods was fuelled by the systematic reduction of trade barriers, all of which led to the establishment of global production networks. As production capabilities grew in many parts of the world, production was increasingly undertaken by locally owned firms, benefiting from the global mobility of finance.

Other indicators may be used to reveal globalization's facets. Internet access is another good indicator of globalization (see Table 1.4). Although access is still limited and controlled in some countries, the rise in the number of internauts is remarkable. Moreover, the means of

Table 1.5 *Demographic indicators, 1980–2007*

Demographic indicators	1980	1985	1990	1995	2000	2005	2007
Stock of international migrants, % world population	2.2	2.3	3.0	2.9	2.9	3.0	n/a

Source: Guillén (2007).

communication (forums, chats, blogs, etc.) created international virtual communities and social networks, evidencing the rising scale of interconnectivity among people. There is also a huge potential for the growth of this communication tool, given that only some 14 percent of the world's population uses the Internet. However, Dadi Perlmutter, Director of Intel's Mobility Group, estimates that the number of devices linked to the Internet will grow by a factor of ten from 2008 to 2015, when some fifteen billion access devices are expected to be linked to the web (*O Estado de São Paulo*, August 15, 2008, p. L1). Given that in developed countries more than half of the population uses the Internet, whereas in emerging countries this ratio is under 10 percent, the Internet's expansion is bound to involve the latter group of countries primarily.

On the demographic front, migrations did not play a major role, being restricted by the policies of each country. The cases of India and China, characterized by strong diaspora movements, are exceptions to this rule (see Table 1.5).

On the institutional front, the most important indicator concerns international institutions. The intergovernmental organizations in operation dropped by about 27%, while non-governmental organizations (NGOs) increased by about 73% from 1980 to 2005. What explains this is that many countries, during this period, went through political reforms that reduced the role of the state in several economic activities. Meanwhile, the activities of the so-called third sector developed enormously.

More than ten years ago, Baumann (1996) and Chesnais (1996) foretold that the fourth stage of globalization would concern the institutional plane. In other words, after the globalization of finance, commerce, and production, it would be necessary to regulate how

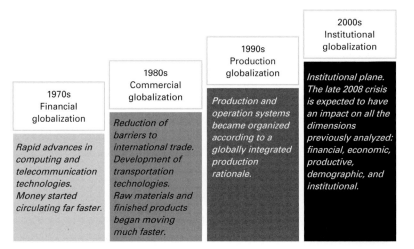

Figure 1.1 Globalization phases

transactions take place in this new globalized arena. This is the challenge the world faces, because unlike domestic markets, which tend to have the support of domestic regulating institutions and domestic policies, economic globalization rests on frail underpinnings: "there is no global antitrust authority, no ultimate global lender, no global overseeing agency, no global security network and, naturally, no global democracy. In other words, global markets have weak governance and therefore scarce popular legitimacy" (Dani Rodrik, "A morte do consenso da globalização" [The death of the globalization concensus], *Valor*, July 14, 2008, p. A15).

The late 2008 crisis is expected to have an impact on all the dimensions previously analyzed: financial, economic, productive, demographic, and institutional. We will deal with them in due course in this book, as they arise.

In sum, the globalization phenomenon, despite different analyses and interpretations, has been changing the nature of the world. In trying to evaluate whether "globalization is civilizing, destructive or feeble," Guillen (2001: 255) concludes that "[it] is neither a monolithic nor an inevitable phenomenon. Its impact varies across countries, societal sectors, and time. It is contradictory, discontinuous and haphazard ... [However] it begs to be engaged, comprised, given form." Figure 1.1 depicts the way in which the globalization process is accelerating in current times.

1.3 Internationalization: the multinational as an agent of globalization

Internationalization is a phenomenon specifically connected with the agents, i.e., the social actors that take part in the globalization process. They can be private-sector enterprises or government-owned companies, governmental and supra-governmental institutions, and non-governmental organizations. This book will focus on MNEs, although it will frequently refer to the other actors as well.

1.3.1 The generations of multinational enterprises

The first modern MNE is considered to be the Dutch East India Company, established in 1602. Other enterprises that succeeded the old colonial firms became important MNEs, in the nineteenth century. That was the case of Imperial Chemicals in England, Siemens in Germany, and Saint-Gobain, a French glassmaker that claims to have been the first corporation to establish a foreign factory, back in 1853, "moving beyond the confines of France, into Mannheim, Germany" (Hamon, 1988: 73). Thus, European enterprises were the first to manage international spillovers.

In the early twentieth century, it was the turn of the American firms to go international. The earliest American MNEs developed large-scale production of standardized products, such as Singer (sewing machines) and the automakers (in particular General Motors (GM) and Ford). The golden age of the American MNEs was the period immediately following the second world war, when they led their industries and became role models.

In the 1980s, the Japanese companies internationalized strongly, both influencing and being influenced by Korean firms. However, it was as of 1990, during the production globalization stage, that MNEs were truly transformed, becoming the chief globalization agents.

If in the 1960s and 1970s MNEs' activities were suspiciously accepted, gradually the situation turned around and, with globalization well under way and moving ahead at high speed, MNEs became the "drivers of progress." A statement by Dunning (1993: 26) clearly explains the reason for the change: "the key elements of contemporary economic growth – the so-called created assets, such as technology, intellectual capital, experience and learning, organizational competence – are not only becoming more mobile across national borders, but are increasingly installed in the systems of transnational companies. [Consequently] the local governments, which in the past established rules for the entry of foreign capital and for the operation of multinational companies, are deeply preoccupied in attracting foreign investments by creating a local infrastructure capable of leveraging the competitiveness of the subsidiaries installed there vis-a-vis global competition."

Concurrently, the emerging countries were trying to improve their macroeconomic circumstances. These improvements encompassed endogenous issues (the population's purchasing power as well as their degree of education and urbanization, to mention only two hugely important indicators) and the pursuit of integration with international markets.

As the emerging countries started becoming successful in this undertaking, the first result was the growth of domestic demand, which enabled local companies to expand.

As of the 1990s, as a consequence of the reduction of barriers to international trade and the growth of MNEs' mobility after their restructuring processes, firms from the emerging countries started facing stronger competition in their local markets, while enjoying the enhanced possibility of joining international production networks, thanks to outsourcing and offshoring systems. Enterprises successful during this period eventually became the national champions and the potential candidates to the position of new multinationals.

1.3.2 What characterizes a multinational enterprise?

James March, one of the chief authorities in the field of organizations, commented in his lectures at Stanford University that an "organization (in the sense of company, firm)" can be understood as a primitive concept, i.e., one established by intuition, that becomes necessary by comparison, distinction, exemplification, experience. In other words, there is an intrinsic difficulty to define what is and what is not a company, although we all know, intuitively, what it is. In the case of MNEs, this difficulty is greater and there is no consensus regarding the concept.

Some authors try to establish clear differentiation criteria, such as Hill (2008), who proposes: "A MNE is any business that has productive activities in two or more countries." There are authors, nevertheless, who consider that producing abroad is not a prerequisite and admit that other forms of international activity, such as sales offices or distribution centers abroad, are sufficient to classify an enterprise as a multinational.

Dunning, one of the pioneers in the development of the field of international business, proposes that "A multinational or transnational enterprise is an enterprise that engages in foreign direct investment (FDI) and owns or, in some way, controls value-added activities in more than one country" (Dunning and Lundan, 2008: 3). For him, this would be the threshold definition of an MNE because it is widely accepted in academic and business circles, by data-collecting agencies, and by most national governments and supra-national entities.

For Rugman and Verbecke (2001: 238), "The MNE is a differentiated network of dispersed operations, with a configuration of competences and capabilities that cannot be controlled fully through hierarchical decisions about Foreign Direct Investment taken by the corporate headquarters."

To our aims, the key features that characterize a company as a multinational are:

- a network of dispersed operations;
- a configuration of competences; and
- an internationalization strategy involving FDI.

However, the degree of internationalization, evidently, does differ from firm to firm. The *World Investment Report (WIR)*, 2006 published by the United Nations Conference for Trade and Development (UNCTAD), estimated that there were some 77,000 MNEs that controlled approximately 800,000 subsidiaries worldwide, and 72 million jobs. Clearly, some are more internationalized than others.

Several sets of indicators have been proposed, to measure the extent to which firms are internationalized.

1.3.3 Indices and indicators of internationalization

The internationalization index most commonly used is the Transnationality Index (TNI), devised by UNCTAD. It is comprised of the following indicators:

- production: assets abroad/total assets;
- sales: sales abroad/total sales;
- resources: personnel abroad/total personnel.

In general, these figures are relatively difficult to obtain, as they involve definition, appropriation, and totaling issues. The production indicator, presumably the most important for one to assess the degree of internationalization, is gauged using asset value, an indirect measure that is difficult to interpret.

TNI yields a picture of each firm's international branch at a given point in time. The comparison of the indicators of the firms in a given industry or from a given country leads to the rankings published by different institutions.

Table 1.6 shows the list of the firms with the highest degree of internationalization, according to UNCTAD (2008).

The table has an interesting composition, as it brings together firms that process natural resources, enterprises that provide services pertaining to the information and knowledge society, and food and beverage companies. Hutchison Whampoa, considered the most internationalized firm from the emerging countries, ranks tenth.

If we prepare a list based on foreign assets, however, the picture is different (see Table 1.7). Except for Vodafone, which ranks seventh on both lists, the names are different and, in a way, more familiar. One should note that the TNI of these firms is noticeably smaller, revealing specific internationalization strategies.

The TNI results form a snapshot of a firm's position at a given point in time. It enables a comparative analysis relative to other firms in the same industry or even in the same country. However, if one takes a reading year after year, changes and discontinuities that are difficult to interpret appear constantly.

To overcome this difficulty, a research group from Erasmus University in Rotterdam, the Netherlands, analyzed the internationalization paths "of the 300 largest non-financial firms worldwide in 1995 plus the top 50 largest firms from a selection of the most important investor countries worldwide: the US, Japan, UK, France, Germany and the Netherlands." The firms were chosen based on UNCTAD's WIR ranking for 1995, but the research group analyzed the evolution of their internationalization indicators from 1990 to 2004. Six different types of internationalization trajectories were identified (see Table 1.8).

Table 1.6 *Firms with the highest degree of internationalization ranked by TNI*

Ranking by:

TNI*	Foreign assets	II**	Corporation	Home economy	Industry
1	92	58	Barrick Gold Corp.	Canada	Gold mining
2	37	15	Xstrata plc	United Kingdom	Mining and quarrying
3	48	12	Linde AG	Germany	Industrial trucks, tractors, trailers
4	77	14	Pernod Ricard SA	France	Beverages
5	68	67	WPP Group plc	United Kingdom	Business services
6	67	1	Liberty Global Inc.	United States	Telecommunications
7	7	99	Vodafone Group plc	United Kingdom	Telecommunications
8	46	44	Philips Electronics	Netherlands	Electrical and electronic
9	23	7	Nestlé SA	Switzerland	Food and beverages
10	22	11	Hutchison Whampoa	Hong Kong, China	Diversifed

Source: UNCTAD, 2008

* TNI, the Transnationality Index, is calculated as the average of the following three ratios: foreign assets to total assets, foreign sales to total sales, and foreign employment to total employment.

** II, the Internationalization Index, is calculated as the number of foreign affiliates divided by the number of all affiliates (note: affiliates counted in this table refer only to majority-owned affiliates).

Table 1.7 *Firms with the highest degree of internationalization ranked by total foreign assets*

Ranking by:

Foreign assets	TNI*	II**	Corporation	Home economy	Industry
1	71	54	General Electric	United States	Electrical and electronic equipment
2	14	68	British Petroleum Company	United Kingdom	Petroleum expl./ref./distr.
3	87	93	Toyota Motor Corporation	Japan	Motor vehicles
4	34	79	Royal Dutch/Shell Group	United Kingdom, Netherlands	Petroleum expl./ref./distr.
5	40	35	Exxonmobil Corporation	United States	Petroleum expl./ref./distr.
6	78	64	Ford Motor Company	United States	Motor vehicles
7	7	99	Vodafone Group	United Kingdom	Telecommunications
8	26	51	Total	France	Petroleum expl./ref./distr.
9	96	36	Electricite De France	France	Electricity, gas and water
10	92	18	Wal-Mart Stores	United States	Retail

Source: UNCTAD, 2008

* TNI, the Transnationality Index, is calculated as the average of the following three ratios: foreign assets to total assets, foreign sales to total sales, and foreign employment to total employment.

** II, the Internationalization Index, is calculated as the number of foreign affiliates divided by the number of all affiliates (note: affiliates counted in this table refer only to majority-owned affiliates).

Table 1.8 *A classification of internationalization trajectories of MNEs and examples*

Strong expansion	Strong, gradual, and not clustered in time	France Telecom
Comprehensive	Highest level and steady increase	Dow
Stable – volatile	No clear pattern for expansion and reduction	Otto Versand
Clustered	Expansion and stability clustered in time	Thyssen Krupp
Home-oriented	Very slow international expansion	Safeway
Home-reoriented	Reduction of international activities	British American Tobacco

Source: Fortanier and vanTulder, 2007.

The main point to highlight is that even the largest and most successful MNEs experience different internationalization paths and paces. Not all of them adopt strategies that are strong, gradual, and not clustered in time.

1.3.4 *Global or regional multinationals?*

Some authors, among whom Alan Rugman from Indiana University stands out, feel that "global" is an unsuitable description when it comes to enterprises: according to them there is no such thing as a "global enterprise." For Rugman, the idea of regionalization is a better way of understanding MNEs' movements.

Rugman analyzed the MNEs from the list of the world's 500 largest enterprises, as compiled by *Fortune* magazine. He organized them according to their area of origin, classifying them into one of the regions of this triad: North America, Europe, and the Pacific Basin. He then defined those with at least 20 percent of their sales in each one of these regions as "global companies." He concluded that "the world's largest 500 firms operate predominantly on an intra-regional basis, not globally, and this picture is consistent over time" (Rugman, 2008: 89).

It is a fact that when any enterprise goes international, it must face the so-called "liability of foreignness," i.e., the cost of undertaking social, political, and economic risks when venturing into unfamiliar markets. Thus, companies have a strong tendency to first expand into the immediately surrounding regions, before expanding into regions that are further away.

1.4 The globalization and internationalization of emerging country enterprises

1.4.1 The changes in patterns of investment flows

Developed countries' investments in other developed countries (i.e., North–North investments) have always been the greatest. Most of the research into international business up to the 1970s describes the experiences of American companies investing in Europe and vice-versa. However, as of that decade, the North–South investments (those made by developed countries in search of opportunities in emerging countries) became prominent. Among Brazil, Russia, India, and China (known as the BRIC countries), Brazil stands out as a major receiver since the late 1950s.

Box 1.2 Developed, developing, or emerging countries: basic definitions

We assume that there is no established convention for the designation of "developed" and "developing" countries. In common practice, Japan in Asia, Canada and the United States in North America, and the countries in Western Europe are considered "developed." A transition or transitional economy refers to a country that is changing from a centrally planned economy to a free market. The term emerging country or emerging economy is used to describe a nation's social or business activity that is undergoing a process of rapid growth and industrialization. At present, there are approximately twenty-eight emerging markets in the world. The BRICs (Brazil, Russia, India, and China) are considered the most influential group of emerging countries.

As of the 1980s, regional FDI from emerging countries, i.e., South–South investments, started rising hesitantly. Argentina, Brazil,

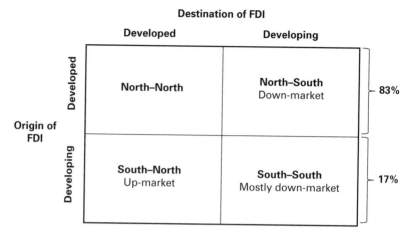

Figure 1.2 Origin and destination of foreign direct investment (FDI)
Source: Ramamurti and Singh (2009: 113).

Hong Kong, India, South Korea, Singapore, and Taiwan led this movement (Lall, 1983). As of the 1990s, relevant FDI started to be sourced from countries such as Egypt, Chile, China, Mexico, Malaysia, and South Africa, among others (Aykut and Goldstein, 2008). Figure 1.2, due to Ramamurti and Singh (2008), shows the share of outward foreign direct investment (OFDI) originated in developed and developing countries and its destination.

UNCTAD's *WIR* suggests that South–South FDI has been growing rapidly over the last fifteen years. Together, the emerging countries accounted for 13 percent of FDI in 2005, whereas in 1990 this figure stood at about 7 percent (Aykut and Goldstein, 2008). Since 2003, the growth rate of FDI from emerging countries exceeded the FDI sourced by enterprises from developed countries (UNCTAD, 2005)

However, the bulk of South–South FDI (excluding offshore financial centers) is intraregional in nature:

In fact, during the period 2002–2004, intra-Asian annual average flows amounted to an estimated $48 billion, or more than four-fifths of all flows. Intraregional FDI accounted for almost half of total flows to Asia, and was particularly pronounced between and within East Asia and South-East Asia. Intra-Asian investment accounted for one-fifth of the stock of total FDI in this subregion. The second largest stream of FDI within the group of developing countries was intraregional investment within Latin America, mainly driven by investors in Argentina, Brazil, and Mexico.

Intraregional flows within Africa were an estimated $2 billion during 2002–2004, reflecting, in particular, South African FDI in the rest of the continent. (UNCTAD, 2006: 117)

The fourth stream of FDI, the one that has been studied the least, concerns the investments made by emerging country MNEs in developed countries (South–North). The increase in this type of investment is recent, dating back only to the 1990s. In international business literature, South–North investments were regarded as an anomaly until recently. However, since 2000, South–North transactions have grown quickly: the value of South–North M&As (excluding transactions involving offshore centers) rose from $9 billion in 2003 to $43 billion in 2005 (UNCTAD, 2006: 108).

For emerging countries, the subject of this book, that shift had an enormous impact, especially regarding their inclusion in global production networks, as we shall see in the next section.

1.4.2 The BRICs and other emerging economies

Goldman Sachs's Global Economics Paper no. 99 *Dreaming with BRICs*, dated October 2003, coined the BRIC acronym and had an impact on world development. The statement that "over the next 50 years, Brazil, Russia, India, and China – the BRIC economies – could become a much larger force in the world economy … If things go right, in less than 40 years, the BRIC economies together could be larger than the G6 in US dollar terms" (Wilson and Purushothaman, 2003) turned out to be a self-fulfilling prophecy. Somehow, this report clearly and objectively identified a developing situation that had been in the making for roughly twenty years. As of the 1980s, the emerging countries began playing an important role in global expansion.

Since the turn of the century, the BRICs started to be seen as the world economy's greatest drivers, accounting for roughly two-thirds of its growth, as shown in Table 1.9.

The greater relevance of emerging and developing economies as a group is a product of the current decade to some extent. Although the Asian economies have acquired greater substance since the late 1970s – with a brief gap in 1997–8 – and the economic upsurge of China and India predates the 2000s, it was only in the second

Table 1.9 *World and region growth estimates for selected countries, 2008–10 (%)*

	2008	2009	2010
World	3.7	3.7	4.8
Advanced economies	1.3	1.3	2.7
United States	0.5	0.6	2.9
Eurozone	1.4	1.2	2.1
Japan	1.4	1.5	1.7
Emerging and developing economies	6.7	6.6	7.1
Emerging Asia	8.2	8.4	9.1
Latin America and the Caribbean	4.4	3.6	4.4
Africa	6.3	6.4	6.4

Source: International Monetary Fund (IMF), April 2008; Frischtak, 2008.

half of the 2000s that the growth of the emerging and developing countries became generalized, driven by exports and, progressively, by their domestic markets. Concurrently, the price of agricultural commodities, minerals, and energy-generating products rose substantially in real terms, giving rise to a shock in regard to the terms of exchange of the exporting countries, which consisted largely of developing economies. As a result, the current account positions of these countries became stronger, as they advanced from having deficits to achieving substantial surpluses (see Table 1.10).

The new current account position and the policies adopted to contain the sharp rise in the value of their currencies led many of these countries to increase their reserves and to become exporters of capital. One of the ways in which this was accomplished, among others, was by setting up sovereign funds that, by the end of 2007, held more than US$3.5 trillion in assets. Another way was by FDI.

One can argue that the dynamics of FDI largely reflect both the rising weight of exports in these economies and the fact that firms are also undergoing the process of becoming more mature and of joining global trade networks, as well as the international flows of financing. Thus, one observes that in the two groups of countries – developed

Table 1.10 *Trade growth and current account position: 1991–2000, 2000–5, 2006, and 2007*

	1991–2000	2000–5	2006	2007
World exports (growth %)	6.9	5.7	10.1	9.2
High-income countries	6.9	4.3	9.2	8.2
Developing countries	6.8	10.4	12.7	12.0
Current Account (% of GDP)				
High-income countries	–0.1	–0.8	–1.1	–0.7
Developing countries	–1.5	1.4	3.6	3.1

Source: World Bank, *Global Economic Prospects, 2008*; Frischtak, 2008.

and developing – the importance of the flow of foreign investments rose in the most recent year (2006), as compared to the 1990–2000 average.

Undoubtedly, the participation of the Asian countries, especially of China, is more important to explain these results than is the case of other regions, such as Latin America and Brazil in particular. "The regional distribution of OFDI from emerging markets has undergone a dramatic change over the past twenty-five years. In particular, the role of Latin America and the Caribbean versus Asia as dominant home of the region has been reversed: the former accounted for two-thirds of OFDI stock of emerging markets in 1980, a share that declined to one-quarter in 2005; over the same period, the share of Asia rose from nearly one-quarter to almost two-thirds in 2005" (Sauvant, 2008: 6).

1.4.3 Emerging country multinationals

Ramamurti (2004) distinguishes two groups of multinationals from emerging countries. The first emerged during the import-substitution period and consisted basically of exporters to lower income countries. These firms were forced to restructure due to economic liberalization and only some of them accomplished this successfully. The second group includes a new generation of emerging country multinationals that have blossomed in the context of open markets and global competition: "Today's thriving emerging country multinationals seem to target the much larger market of rich countries than the small markets of other developing countries."

In today's global economy, the multinationals from emerging countries are more than niche players, as they lead several industries, such as mining (BHP-Billington from Australia, and Vale, from Brazil), steel (Arcelor-Mittal from India), beverages (AB-Inbev from Brazil and Belgium, and SAB-Miller from South Africa), oil and gas (Gazprom from Russia), and cement (CEMEX from Mexico), among others. In some cases, certain sectors in developed countries are controlled by multinationals from the emerging countries. Tenaris from Argentina, and Gerdau from Brazil, for instance, are the largest producers of drawn steel pipes for the US building industry.

Table 1.11, produced by UNCTAD (2008), presents the largest non-financial MNEs from emerging countries. We observe that the classification of emerging economies is broad, including Korea and separating China from Taiwan and Hong Kong. The ranking by foreign assets reveals differences when the TNI is used as the index to classify the firms. Three Brazilian multinationals are mentioned: Petrobras, Vale, and Gerdau.

The number of new Brazilian multinationals is rising. Although there are no official figures, we estimate that by 2010 there were more than eighty Brazilian multinationals operating all over the world. Six of them were listed by *Fortune* magazine among the world's 500 largest enterprises. The Boston Consulting Group (2009) listed fourteen Brazilian companies among the 100 new global challengers. For Ernst & Young (2009), the large Brazilian companies improved their standing in the ranking of the 300 largest companies in the world and were among those whose value increased the most in the first half of 2009.

The rapid advance of multinationals from emerging economies took policy makers, managers, and researchers, among others, by surprise. Firms previously regarded as laggards, operating in less developed contexts, now challenged the global leaders. This phenomenon raised new questions: might MNEs from emerging countries have different characteristics from those of the classic multinationals? What factors

Table 1.11 *The top fifty non-financial MNEs from emerging countries ranked by foreign assets, 2006*

Ranking by:

Foreign assets	TNI*	II**	Corporation	Home economy	Industry
1	18	9	Hutchison Whampoa Ltd.	Hong Kong, China	Diversified
2	88	94	Petronas	Malaysia	Petroleum expl./ref./distr.
3	53	11	Samsung Electronics	Republic of Korea	Electrical and electronic
4	21	4	CEMEX SA	Mexico	Cement
5	86	32	Hyundai Motor Company	Republic of Korea	Motor vehicles
6	33	3	Singtel Ltd.	Singapore	Telecommunications
7	92	86	CITIC Group	China	Diversified
8	65	10	Formosa Plastic Group	Taiwan, China	Chemicals
9	28	18	Jardine Matheson Holdings Ltd.	Hong Kong, China	Diversified
10	57	74	LG Corp.	Republic of Korea	Electrical and electronic
11	73	66	Companhia Vale do Rio Doce	Brazil	Mining and quarrying
12	94	88	Petrobras	Brazil	Petroleum expl./ref./distr.
13	69	73	China Ocean Shipping Group	China	Transport and storage
14	54	54	América Móvil	Mexico	Telecommunications
15	89	56	Petróleos De Venezuela	Venezuela	Petroleum expl./ref./distr.
16	50	8	Mobile Telecommunications	Kuwait	Telecommunications
17	41	85	Capitaland Limited	Singapore	Real Estate
18	45	15	Hon Hai Precision Industries	Taiwan, China	Electrical and electronic
19	80	65	China State Construction Engineering	China	Construction

Table 1.11 *(cont.)*

Ranking by:					
Foreign assets	TNI*	II**	Corporation	Home economy	Industry
20	67	5	Kia Motors	Republic of Korea	Motor vehicles
21	100	90	China National Petroleum	China	Petroleum expl./ref./distr.
22	72	82	New World Development Co., Ltd.	Hong Kong, China	Diversified
23	77	68	CLP Holdings	Hong Kong, China	Electricity, gas, and water
24	90	40	Telefonos De Mexico	Mexico	Telecommunications
25	87	47	Sasol Ltd.	South Africa	Industrial chemicals
26	55	77	Sinochem Corp.	China	Petroleum expl./ref./distr.
27	59	76	YTL Corp.	Malaysia	Utilities
28	37	25	Star Cruises	Hong Kong, China	Transport
29	66	7	Taiwan Semiconductor Manufacturing	Taiwan, China	Computer and related businesses
30	68	53	Quanta Computer Inc.	Taiwan, China	Computer and related businesses
31	32	30	Orient Overseas International	Hong Kong, China	Transport and storage
32	96	93	Oil And Natural Gas	India	Petroleum and natural gas
33	17	48	Shangri-La Asia Limited	Hong Kong, China	Hotels
34	49	24	Hynix Semiconductor Inc.	Republic of Korea	Electrical and electronic
35	43	12	Flextronics International	Singapore	Electrical and electronic

	TNI*	II**	Company	Economy	Industry
36	71	45	United Microelectronics Corporation	Taiwan, China	Electrical and electronic
37	24	58	China Resources Enterprises	Hong Kong, China	Petroleum expl./ref./distr.
38	11	6	China Merchants Holdings International	Hong Kong, China	Diversified
39	47	46	Metalurgica Gerdau SA	Brazil	Metals and metal products
40	30	19	Sappi Ltd.	South Africa	Paper
41	62	39	MTN Group Ltd.	South Africa	Telecommunications
42	8	49	Guangdong Investment Ltd.	Hong Kong, China	Diversified
43	83	84	Genting	Malaysia	Hotels
44	12	79	Galaxy Entertainment Group Ltd.	Hong Kong, China	Leisure
45	35	59	Orascom Construction	Egypt	Construction
46	51	2	Steinhoff International Holdings	South Africa	Domestic appliances
47	84	95	FEMSA-Fomento Economico Mexicano	Mexico	Food and beverages
48	27	29	Acer Inc.	Taiwan, China	Electrical and electronic
49	58	43	Lenovo Group	China	Computer and related businesses
50	64	78	Keppel Corporation Ltd.	Singapore	Diversified

Source: UNCTAD, 2008.

* TNI, the Transnationality Index, is calculated as the average of the following three ratios: foreign assets to total assets, foreign sales to total sales, and foreign employment to total employment.

** II, the Internationalization Index, is calculated as the number of foreign affiliates divided by the number of all affiliates (note: affiliates counted in this table refer only to majority-owned affiliates).

might explain their competitiveness in the global markets? These questions gave rise to new approaches that tried to capture the shared characteristics of the new MNEs.

This book aims to answer the aforementioned questions where Brazilian MNEs are concerned.

2 | *The analytical framework: the multinational as a network of competences*

2.1 Lenses, sieves, and molds in internationalization studies

The Iberian globalization project mentioned in the preceding chapter influenced strategic planning and the development of competences over the course of almost one century. The success of this undertaking turned the Iberian countries into the chief global benchmark reference of the fifteenth and sixteenth centuries.

These days, when we are faced with the successful internationalization of emerging countries' firms, certain questions arise again:

- How can one comprehend their internationalization process?
- How can one explain the strategy and organization of these multinational enterprises (MNEs)?

The different dimensions of the internationalization phenomenon led to the development of different approaches designed to produce answers for these questions; however, these approaches cast light upon certain points while disregarding others.

There are approaches that focus on international financial investments as the chief strategy indicator, whereas others try to understand corporate decision-makers' behavior. Another range of approaches attempts to study how factors external to the firm, especially those of an institutional nature, drove companies to become international. Each approach generates its own theories and models.

"Models, theories, conceptual frameworks and paradigms are all terms that help to organize thinking and action: they give differential priority as well as structure to ideas and practices" commented Warr (1980). They are built using lenses, sieves, and molds.

Like the approaches mentioned above, our perspective will take the firm as its basic unit of analysis, but will also highlight the context in which the company operates. In other words, it regards the firm as an open system in permanent interaction with its environment.

Sieves allow certain items to pass but disallow others; a mold selects some things over others thereby rearranging these elements. Whereas some theories resort to sieves that allow information on foreign direct investment (FDI) or management behavior to pass, ours identifies the firm's competences as a critical component of competitiveness in the domestic and international environments.

Finally, conceptual molds give shape to thinking, establishing systems of meaning and creating familiar patterns that enable manipulation and work. The conceptual molds that we will use are those proposed by the so-called resource-based view of the firm. They will enable us to articulate a competence-based approach with the issue of MNEs' strategy and organization.

Furthermore, as our study will conduct comparative analyses among the distinct types of MNEs from different countries, it will be important to focus on organizational competences and management styles. Although the two dimensions are interdependent, the distinction is necessary because they are related to attributes of different natures. As Child (2005: 6) states, management style depends on a firm's history, home country, and reputation; it reveals the enterprise's character and identity.

Both management style and organizational competences are influenced by the external environment. However, whereas the latter are influenced primarily by competition in product/markets, the former is strongly linked to the cultural and institutional factors that are typical of a country or a region.

Figure 2.1 outlines the analytical framework, the elements of which will be discussed in the subsequent sections. It will provide a technical language system, a set of interpretative principles and important benchmarks for guiding thought on internationalization, possible to be internalized in such a way that those interested can easily communicate with each other, share a common evaluative structure and routinely frame research questions and possible ways of finding answers.

2.2 Organizational competences as a strategic resource of firms

2.2.1 The roots of the competence-based approach

The organizational competence concept is the key notion for building our framework. Its theoretical roots lie in the resource-based view of

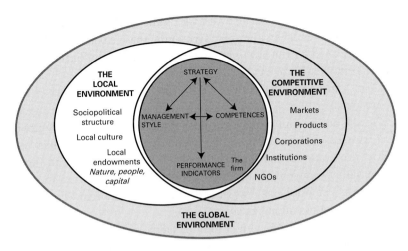

Figure 2.1 The analytical framework

the firm (RBV), the chief contribution to the field of strategic management of which is the integration of several lines of research from the fields of economics, organizational theory, industrial organization, and strategy. RBV can be seen as an excellent starting point for analyzing enterprises' strengths and weaknesses (thus dealing with the demand side as a factor that is exogenous to the firm), whereas the strategic positioning viewpoint, such as the framework proposed by Michael Porter, highlights the analysis of opportunities and threats, with only limited reflection on whether the company's resources can respond to pressures from the environment.

Edith Penrose's work from the late 1950s (Penrose, 1959) led to the development of the key RBV concepts, such as resources, organizational competences, and essential competences, among others. Though she did not concern herself directly with internationalization, the company model she presented is fundamental for one to properly understand the evolution of multinational enterprises.

Edith Penrose analyzed the process of company growth mainly in regard to the firm's internal trade-offs: what an enterprise is, what its characteristics are, and what its boundaries are. We selected five arguments that subsidize our developments:

(1) On the firm as an administrative unit with boundaries: "The economic function of a firm is assumed simply to be that of acquiring and organizing human and other resources in order profitably to supply goods and services to the market" (Penrose, 1959: xx).

Therefore, it must be regarded as a collection of resources bundled together by an administrative framework. Its boundaries are determined by the administrative coordination and authoritative communication areas.

(2) On productive resources and the services derived from resources: "... it is never *resources* themselves that are the inputs in the production process but only the *services* that the resources can render. Resources can be defined independently of their use while services cannot be. The term 'service' implies a specific joint activity or purpose" (Penrose, 1959: 25, emphasis from the original). The notion of "services derived from resources" was later associated to competences.

(3) On objective and experiential knowledge: objective knowledge is independent of particular individuals or groups and can be transmitted by documents. Experience, however, cannot be transmitted in this way: "Experience ... develops an increasing knowledge of the possibilities for action and the ways in which the action can be taken by the firm. This increase in knowledge not only causes the productive opportunity of a firm to change ... but it also contributes to the uniqueness of the opportunity of each individual firm" (Penrose, 1959: 53). Therefore, Penrose touched upon the issue of tacit and explicit knowledge. Later, both the notion of experiential knowledge and of uniqueness of opportunity came to be seen as an intrinsic attribute of core competences.

(4) On economies of size and economies of expansion: Penrose identifies several endogenous pressures for enterprise growth. One of them derives from enterprises producing not only products, but also knowledge. And knowledge increases a firm's production capacity. In Penrose's words: "... the process by which experience is gained is properly treated as a process [for] creating new productive services available to the firm" (Penrose, 1959: 48). Hence, Penrose's theory is a learning theory of the firm.

(5) On growth: Penrose understands growth as an indication that management resources are being used to develop new systems. "In the long run the profitability, survival and growth of the firm ... depend on the ability of the firm to establish one or more wide and relatively impregnable 'bases' from which it can adapt and extend its operations in an uncertain, changing and competitive world. It is not the scale of production nor even, within limits, the size of

the firm, that are important considerations, but rather the nature of the basic position that it is able to establish for itself" (Penrose, 1959: 137).

"The necessity of maintaining 'impregnable bases' or 'defenses in depth' implies that firms will be forced to specialize; consequently, opportunities will open up in the 'interstices' for smaller firms." Thus, for Penrose, interstices emerge because the rate of growth of any firm is limited and no firm can take advantage of all opportunities for expansion (Penrose, 1959: 222). When opportunities for expansion increase faster than they can be seized by large firms, interstices develop which can be filled by small firms, some of which will eventually become large firms themselves" (Best, 1990: 129).

The idea that firms are obliged to specialize leads to the concept of focusing, a key element of strategic positioning, to be later introduced, while the idea of interstices is associated with the niches that are opened for the emergence of new players, including firms from emerging countries.

After Penrose, the RBV resurged in the mid-1980s, thanks to the works of Wernerfelt (1984) and Rumelt (1994), but within a different context that included competitiveness, a novel concern. Penrose's model had to be revised from a strategizing perspective. Wernerfelt argued for the need to move away from analyses that emphasized external forces, products, and markets, toward focusing on the specific set of resources that were the source of the firm's long-term profitability. This should result in a "resource positioning strategy," in contrast to Porter's "industry position strategy." Rumelt advocated the idea that firms should concern themselves less with creating barriers to market entry and more with protecting their specific critical resources.

The RBV admits that competitive advantages derive from the firm's specific resources, which are scarce and superior in use than those of other enterprises. Therefore, an enterprise has a competitive advantage if it is able to create more economic value than a marginal (breakeven) competitor in its product market, through superior differentiation and/or lower costs.

Using marginal competitors as a comparison benchmark implies that a competitive advantage may be held by several or even most firms in a given industry and suggests that there may be several different routes to competitive performance. An enterprise can conceivably establish a competitive advantage even when it is not the best performer across all dimensions.

In other words, "the RBV postulates that enterprises with superior systems, structures and people are more profitable not because they invest in barriers to the entry of other companies or because they offer unique products, but rather because they appropriate the revenues from the firm's specific resources ... As Teece already stated back in 1982, 'diversification is less of a response to the structural imperfections of markets and more of an organizational mechanism for capturing earnings that are made achievable by the enterprise's specific assets' " (Proença, 1998: 107).

Thus, the RBV is about efficiency, in the sense of generating greater benefits per unit of resource, which is the essence of efficient production. But the RBV also concerns efficient adaptation. This is the interpretation of authors such as Teece *et al.* (1997), who developed the concept of dynamic capabilities, i.e., those competences that cannot be regarded as a stock of resources, but only as mobilized resources, permanently in motion and undergoing development (Teece *et al.*, 1997).

The RBV approach focuses on the enterprise level, whereas the approaches centered on other levels (industry, business groups, etc.) ascribe performance results more directly to external factors, such as market structure, institutional factors or strategic interactions. "Understanding RBV as a resource-level and enterprise-level analytical tool is critical for comprehending exactly what phenomena it can explain and what it cannot. RBV is not a substitute for industry-level analytical tools such as 5-forces analysis and game theory" (Peteraff and Barney, 2003).

2.2.2 Competence and resource are different

On the organizational front, the concept of resources and competences has other dimensions. Durand (1998) proposes an interesting analogy: "in medieval times, alchemists tried to transform metals into gold; today, managers and firms try to transform resources and assets into profit. Organizations require a new type of alchemy. We will call it 'competence'." According to Hamel and Heene (1994: 3), "The core competence perspective is simply an additional lens through which to view issues of competitiveness and firm performance."

Mills *et al.* (2002: 9) resume the expression "coordinating resources" to review the concept of competence. According to them, the distinction between competence and resource is crucial: "A resource is something that the organization has, or to which it has access, even if this access is temporary... a competence is the skill required to do something ... a competence is built from a set of 'blocks' called resources." (Mills *et al.*, 2002: 9–14).

Mills *et al.* define competence as a "way to write how well (or not) a company performs the necessary activities." They state that the enterprise has strength ("muscle") or great competence if it is able to outdo most of its competitors with regard to a competitive factor that consumers value. Thus, competence becomes a variable factor rather than an attribute, because the issue at hand is not whether or not a given enterprise possesses it, but to what extent this competence is found in this firm.

For Mills *et al.*, each competence is built from a series of bricks called resources. Combined resources generate competences that prop each other up, providing support for those competences that clients perceive. Thus, competitive advantage has the shape of a pyramid, formed by those organizational competences that generate the benefits that the clients value. The enterprise's performance results from the quality and the coordination of its resources.

2.2.3 *Core competences as competitive advantage*

In the late 1980s, Prahalad and Hamel contributed substantially to this debate when they proposed the concept of **core competences**. They defined competence as "a set of skills and technologies that allows an enterprise to offer superior benefit to its clients." The **core** competences, according to them, are those that meet three criteria: offering real benefits to consumers, being difficult to imitate, and providing access to different markets. In other words, a company has several organizational competences, found in different areas; of these, only some are essential, i.e., those that set the company apart and that guarantee a sustainable competitive advantage relative to other organizations. A core competence either adds to the value that clients perceive, or helps to reduce cost. However, although all essential competences are sources of competitive advantage, not all competitive advantages are core competences (Prahalad and Hamel, 1990: 237).

To identify an enterprise's core competences, one must understand why the firm achieves superior results and what the unique capabilities underpinning these results are. Rumelt (1994) ascribed the following attributes to core competences:

- Corporate scope: the competences underpin several of the corporation's products and businesses and are not the property of any single individual or area.
- Stability across time: products are the momentary expression of core competences, which are more stable and evolve more slowly than products.
- Learning by doing: competences are acquired or enhanced through operational work and day-to-day management; the more one invests in their development, the greater their differentiation vs. competitors.
- Competitive locus: competition based on products and markets is the superficial expression of deeper competition based on competences; at present, competition primarily concerns competences, rather than products and services.

However, the core competences that ensure the firm has an advantage today may become an obstacle in the future by inhibiting innovation. The nature of a core competence must be dynamic, rather than inflexible, especially in complex and changing environments. "Dynamism concerns the capacity to renovate competences, so as to achieve congruence with the changing business environment; certain innovative responses are required when market timing is critical, the pace of technological change is fast, and the nature of future competition and of the markets is hard to assess" (Teece *et al.*, 1997: 5, 515).

2.2.4 *Mapping core competences*

In order to identify organizational and core competences, criteria and methods had to be developed. It is important to recall the classic book *Industrial Organisation* by Joanne Woodward (1965). She considered that every enterprise must perform activities related to three different functions: operations (manufacturing), product development, and sales and marketing. In her field research, Woodward found that according to the type of product and market – engineering

Table 2.1 *Core competence typologies*

Woodward (1965)	Hamel (1994)	Fleury and Fleury (2000)
Manufacturing	Integrity-related competences	Production
Engineering	Functionality-related competences	Product development
Marketing	Market access competences	Marketing

firms, mass production, and continuous process production – one of the three functions became more strategic and consequently "powerful." Therefore, she unintentionally provided an early insight into the core competences in different types of firms.

More recently, Hamel (1994) suggested that it is useful to distinguish between three broad types of competences: (a) market-access competences: management of brand, sales and marketing, distribution and logistics, technical support, etc. In other words, all those skills that help to bridge the gap between a firm and its customers; (b) integrity-related competences: quality, cycle-time management, just-in-time inventory management, and similar elements, which allow the firm to do things more quickly, flexibly, or reliably than competitors; and (c) functionality-related competences: skills that enable the firm to invest its services or products with a unique functionality, which lends the product distinctive customer benefits, rather than just making it incrementally better. Clearly, integrity-related competences are associated with the extended view of manufacturing whereas functionality-related competences are associated with activities that usually fall under the label of product design and innovation; as for market access competences, they reflect customer orientation.

This approach was also employed by Fleury and Fleury (2000). In their book, core competences are connected with one of the three core functions of any enterprise: production, product development, and marketing. The other functions (such as finance and human resources management) are supportive functions.

The three approaches are summarized in Table 2.1. Each approach suggests that the identification of core competences at firm level starts with a typology consisting of three elements, which in practice

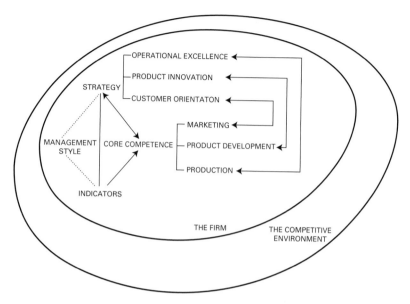

Figure 2.2 The core competence–strategic positioning relationship

correspond to each other, and that one must determine which of the three is the most strategic for the organization.

2.2.5 Core competences and competence-based strategic positioning

An organization's competitiveness is determined by the dynamic inter-relation between its organizational competences, the prioritization of its core competences, and competitive strategy. Thus, the organizational approach of the RBV suggests that the process of strategy formulation and competence development forms a feedback circle, which is illustrated in Figure 2.2.

Following the preceding section's typologies of core competences, one can ask whether there are typical competitive strategies or competence-based strategic positionings related to each type of competence profile. Using the terminology proposed by Treacy and Wiersema (1995), we assume that there are three different strategies whereby companies compete in the market: operational excellence, product innovation, and customer orientation; they are connected directly with production, product development, and marketing as core competences, respectively, as depicted in Figure 2.2. That dynamic relationship between core competence and competitive strategy is clarified below.

Production as core competence ⇔ operational excellence as strategy

The aim of a firm whose core competence lies in production is to achieve operating excellence by offering the market a product or service that optimizes the price/quality relation. Scale and standardization are major determinants of competitiveness.

Production – of goods and services – includes the entire logistical cycle: purchasing, production, and distribution. It is the competence in which the firm must excel to remain competitive. The development of competences in the other two areas – product development and marketing – aims at strengthening the performance of the first.

Product development is supportive to the production function's needs, focusing on process innovation and incremental product innovation, instead of breakthrough type of innovation. This is typical of the automobile industry, for example.

As for marketing, its main role is "getting customers to adapt to the operationally excellent company's way of doing business or convince the market that the price/quality relation provided is optimal" (Treacy and Wiersema, 1995). Thus, the enterprise focuses on mass marketing, seeking to influence overall market trends in favor of those products in which the firm has operational excellence.

"Superior operations effectiveness not only serves but buttresses a company's existing competitive position, but, when based on competences that are embedded in the company's people and operating processes, it is inherently difficult to imitate. For this reason, it can provide the basis for a sustainable competitive advantage, even when the company adopts the same competitive position as one or more of its competitors" (Hayes and Upton, 1998: 9).

In this category, the role models consist of those enterprises most often referred to in the operations management field: the automakers in general, more specifically Ford in the past and Toyota at present. In the electronics industry, Dell is an example of a firm that became world leader after breakthrough innovation in the operational model. In the services sector, Wal-Mart is the enterprise most often mentioned.

Product development as core competence ⇔ product innovation as strategy

Firms whose strategy is product innovation ensure their economic success by systematically launching radically new products in the market, usually by making the current ones obsolete. They survive and prosper as a result of the high profitability they enjoy for as long as they maintain a monopolistic market position (Abernathy and Utterback, 1975).

Firms that compete through product innovation invest continuously in the creation of radically new product concepts for defined market segments. Their core competence lies in research and development.

The technology management literature is inspired by the firms that compete on a product innovation strategy. From the early twentieth century until recently, Dupont was a role model, and its breakthrough innovation of synthetic fibers was the key example. Today, Intel is, perhaps, the new role model. In general, science- and technology-intensive industries, such as those in information technology (IT: telecommunications, computers and the Internet), as well as in biotechnology or biomedical enterprises (life sciences) belong to this category.

When a firm competes on product innovation, the role of production is different. The most important requirement is fast process development and the implementation of new production systems soon after a new product has been designed. What matters is the efficient transition from an "idea" to production on an industrial scale, what is called scaling-up or ramping-up, as well as efficient scaling-down and product discontinuing when the product is replaced. That is different from firms that compete on operating excellence, which develop competences for the management of relatively stable production processes.

The marketing function also has different characteristics from the previous case, since the company has to prepare markets and educate potential customers for the new products that will arise, thus increasing the propensity to purchase innovative products. Marketing competences rely on technical arguments to convince early-adopters.

Marketing as core competence ⇔ customer orientation as strategy

Firms that compete following a customer orientation strategy are concerned with serving specific clients by establishing a dedicated type of relationship. Marketing becomes the most important function for the development of specific solutions and systems that are customized to

Table 2.2 *Core competences and strategic positioning*

Competitive strategy	Core competence		
	Production	Product development	Marketing
Operational excellence	**World class**	Incremental innovations	Marketing for mass markets
Product innovation	Scale-up, primary production, and scale-down	**Radical innovations** (breakthrough)	Technical marketing
Customer-oriented	Agility, flexibility	Development of specific systems and solutions	**Services marketing**

the needs of the clients. Firms then become not only acquainted with their clients, but also develop close relationships with specific clients to understand current and future needs.

IBM used to be seen as this strategy's role model (Wheelwright and Hayes, 1985). Caterpillar was also considered a "customer intimacy" case (Treacy and Wiersema, 1995: 126). Their profitability resulted from the premium price that they were able to charge their customers for their dedicated services.

Even when firms deliver a product, their most important operation is the service they render. To this end, these enterprises acquire an in-depth understanding of their client and its business. Consequently, marketing becomes the critical function, leading product development and production. Product development is oriented toward the specific needs of each client; breakthrough innovation is not a concern. Production is primarily responsive and flexible, or agile, vis-a-vis the clients' needs.

In sum, the dynamic relationship between a firm's core competences and its strategic positioning is represented in Table 2.2.

2.3 How local environments influence competence-based competition

The environment can be defined as anything that surrounds a system and influences its performance. Therefore, the business environment is anything that surrounds the business organization, affecting its competences, strategies, and performance. Consequently the local environment in different countries creates different environments for local firms.

> Firms originating in different countries draw from a different set of factor endowments, cultural traits, and sociopolitical infrastructure, which give them unique competitive advantages when compared with firms originating in countries that are less hospitable in those areas.
>
> (Sethi and Elango, 1999: 285)

The authors apply this approach on a macro level, arguing that nations engender competitive advantage through a combination of factors endowment, unique cultural traits, and deliberate policy options. In this context, these three factors are related with economic and physical resources and industrial capabilities, cultural values and institutional norms, and national government's economic and industrial policies, respectively. By articulating these three factors, country-based competitive advantages can be built.

The same approach can be used at the micro level, the level of the firm. The three country of origin effects affect competence-based competition differently. The factors endowment affect the resources to which the local firms can gain access. The cultural traits influence companies' organizational culture. And the sociopolitical infrastructure, through institutions and the competition regime, influences the management systems and the managers' mindset.

2.3.1 How local factors endowment influence competence formation at firm level

Leo (1994: 47) argues that the features of the firm's home country influence the way in which competences are developed. The author goes as far as proposing the notion of country competences: "The connection between organizational competences and country specific competences is prominent: there is a mutual interaction between the resources of the firm and the resources of the environment."

The relation between local factors endowment and competence development has Japan as one of the best examples, as will be argued in Chapter 4. Being devoid of natural endowments, the country invested heavily in people in order to develop internationally competitive, home-grown, corporations.

Evidently, that relation holds true regardless of the country being considered. For example, the US has had a longstanding comparative advantage in technology and entrepreneurship, which influences competence-building in every American firm. Indian firms developed differently to Brazilian firms, based on the value they ascribe to education plus an abundance of highly skilled workers.

As this is one of the guidelines for the development of this book, the next chapters will cover this subject in more detail.

2.3.2 How cultural traits influence management style and competence-based competition

A company's management style reveals its character and identity; it reflects the firm's culture and its DNA. On the other hand, it is also influenced by the country's culture or place of origin.

The concept of culture was introduced into management sciences in the late 1960s. The process whereby European and American companies became MNEs, expanding their operations to other continents, led them to reproduce their management practices in order to gain competitive advantages, in countries other than their own, through cheap labor, new markets, or proximity to raw materials, among other elements. However, though they sought to reproduce their home practices as closely as possible, outcomes were rarely compatible. In general, managers faced problems they did not have to deal with in the MNE's home country. That is why the first notions about culture used by management were similar to those employed to define national culture.

The development of the concept of organizational culture was quite polemic, contrary to what occurred with other theoretical constructs, such as organizational climate for example. The concept of culture is "borrowed" from the basic social sciences – mainly anthropology and sociology, as well as from psychology.

In anthropology, the symbolic dimension is capable of integrating the elements of social practice. The concern that guides anthropological research is to reveal the habits of societies other than Western society. In such "different" societies, the sharing of a set of meanings about the world is handed down from generation to generation and confers legitimacy to the ruling social order.

Culture is always a collective phenomenon; it is shared by people who live or have lived in the same specific social environment. Hofstede, one of the main references for culture studies, states that these are the unwritten rules of the social game, the software of the mind that sets apart the members of one group from the members of another group.

In the model proposed by that author (Hofstede and Hofstede, 2005), values are represented by strong sentiments, with positive or negative extremes, such as good and bad, normal and abnormal, dirty and clean, secure and insecure, or pretty and ugly. The values are learnt from an early age, in the first ten years of a person's life, and change very little thereafter. Practices, however, are learnt and forgotten throughout life.

In an organization, people with different values may learn similar practices; organizational culture, according to this author, is rooted in the practices learnt and shared within a person's workplace (Hofstede and Hofstede, 2005). Hofstede further recommends that in other countries, firms should adopt management behaviors different from those of its country of origin, because management policies should conform with other spheres of people's lives in society, spheres that are beyond the organizational environment (for example, human resources management policies).

Hofstede identified four independent dimensions of culture, which he referred to as: "distance from power," "individualism versus collectivism," "masculinity versus femininity," and "uncertainty avoidance." In subsequent studies, his team developed a fifth independent dimension referred to as "Confucius dynamics," which looks at the opposition between short-term and long-term orientation and was used to partially explain the success of Asian economies in the last few decades.

Schein, another renowned author in the field of organizational culture, has a view that differs somewhat from that of Hofstede. He believes that firms develop such strong cultures of their own that the latter overcome the local context surrounding them: "organizational culture is a set of basic assumptions that a group has devised, discovered or developed about learning how to deal with external adaptation problems and that have worked sufficiently well to be considered valid and taught to new members as the right way to perceive, think and feel in relation to these problems" (Schein, 2001). He sees culture as a dynamic model that is learnt, transmitted, and modified; he understands that the concept is broad enough to be applied to small groups, such as work teams, or large groups, such as organizations.

Schein states that employees working at a formal and bureaucratic company may share values and basic assumptions that are much like those of an informal and horizontally structured company. That is why studies about organizational culture should not be limited to the observation of visible artifacts, but need to include interaction with members of an organization for the understanding of their true meaning. Even explanations given by members of an organization are insufficient, as there are assumptions that are deemed to be so obvious that people and groups are not aware of them. These assumptions influence the entire process of interaction between the members of a company, without them even realizing it most of the time. Thus, members of the group may act according to principles that they consider to be so self-evident and correct (deep truths) that they scarcely question them or grasp their basis or justification.

The debate among the different lines that discuss organizational culture raised the need to develop a conceptual proposal that, using Schein's conception as a starting point, would incorporate the political dimension inherent to such a phenomenon. In doing so, Fleury (1989) mentions that organizational culture can be conceived as a set of basic values and assumptions, expressed by symbolic elements that, in their capacity to ascribe meaning and construct organizational identity, act both as a communication and consensus element and render power relationships instrumental/express/manifest.

Thus, an organization's management style is influenced by local cultural factors, i.e., those linked to the firm's home country, as well as by its own cultural patterns that are woven within the organization by its members; these, during the course of the firm's history, share common values and visions concerning how best to conduct the firm's business.

2.3.3 How the socio-political structure influences management styles and systems

Institutions are "social, economic and political bodies that articulate and maintain widely observed norms and rules" (Child and Tse: 2001: 6). The understanding that institutions matter is hardly novel or controversial.

Table 2.3 WEF's *twelve pillars of competitiveness*

Basic requirements	• Institutions • Infrastructure • Macroeconomic stability • Health and primary education
Efficiency enhancers	• Higher education and training • Goods market efficiency • Labor market efficiency • Financial market sophistication • Technological readiness • Market size
Innovation and sophistication factors	• Business sophistication • Innovation development

Source: WEF (2009)

In the early 1990s, Kogut (1991: 33) had already identified differences in country competences among different countries due to differences in their institutions: "Countries differ in their underlying 'organizing principles' of work and these principles develop within the confines of a trajectory. These principles diffuse within an inter-industry network of firms, which, though differing in their products and markets, share common heuristics concerning how their economic activities are organized."

Nonetheless, the incorporation of the institutional dimension into the analyses of internationalization is recent. For Peng (2009: 257), "[Douglas] North's metaphor on institutions as being 'the rule of the game' has expanded the scope of international business strategy research, in order to account for aspects related to the dimensions of national context, culture, government, transactions and social interactions."

This author highlights the studies about emerging countries in connection with recognizing the value of the institutional dimension for one's understanding of internationalization processes: "as researchers increasingly probe into emerging economies whose institutions differ significantly from those of developed economies, there is an increasing appreciation that formal and informal institutions, commonly known as the rule of the game, significantly shape the strategy and performance of firms – both domestic and foreign – in emerging economies" (Peng *et al.*, 2008: 921).

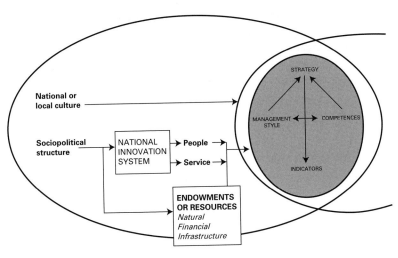

Figure 2.3 The influence of local environment

In practice, perhaps the best example of an approach involving the institutional dimensions, as stated by the authors above, is the work of the World Economic Forum (WEF), which defines "competitiveness as the set of institutions, policies and factors that determine the level of productivity of a country" (WEF, 2009: 7). For WEF, productivity, in the sense of creating a sustainable level of prosperity, rests on twelve pillars, as shown in Table 2.3.

Evidently, we will not go into an in-depth analysis of this, but only state the importance of the institutional dimension, which will be revisited in other chapters.

2.3.4 *The local environment and competence-based competition*

Figure 2.3 depicts the dimensions that were prioritized for the analysis of the environment's influence on competence-based competitiveness. It prioritizes and organizes several concepts that have been presented already, and outlines the eventual relations that might arise among them.

Local culture and policies shape the resources that influence firms in the development of their competences. In particular, local culture influences management style. The National Innovation System (Nelson, 1993) is in theory an institution similar to the National

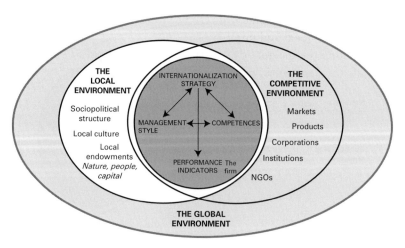

Figure 2.4 Internationalization strategy

Knowledge Development System, as dubbed by Rugman and Verbecke (2001: 240). This system supplies the firm with human resources and a varied set of services, from technical to advisory. Public policies establish the rules and procedures for access to and use of resources (natural, financial, and infrastructural).

2.4 The analytical framework of the book

As we saw in the preceding chapter, our study conceptualizes MNEs as:

- a network of dispersed operations;
- configurations of competences;
- having an internationalization strategy involving FDI.

Synthesizing the development presented in this chapter, Figure 2.4 retrieves the structure of the analytical framework, initially depicted in Figure 2.1, and introduces internationalization as the issue addressed within this book.

Our analysis plan proposes that the firm's strategy, in particular its internationalization strategy, results from the dynamic relations between the management style and the organizational competences that arise in response to the opportunities and threats posed by both the competitive environment (local and international) and the environment itself (local and international).

Resuming the metaphor of lenses, sieves, and molds, the application of this framework, even though it generates relevant knowledge from the academic and the practical standpoints, is unable to capture the full complexity of internationalization processes. However, as we will see during the course of this book, it is particularly well-suited for the study of emerging country multinationals.

3 | *The first wave: early-movers and the earliest internationalization theories*

3.1 Internationalizing under enticing conditions

Competence and competition are two sides of the same coin. With no competition, the development of competences tends to be feeble.

The earliest theories on the internationalization of firms were based on a global scene in which three blocks of countries coexisted: the so-called first world (the industrially advanced countries), the second world (the countries behind the iron curtain), and the third world (the other countries, considered underdeveloped at the time).

At that time, there was a worldwide need to create the capacity to produce goods and services. Although competition did exist, it was different from what it has become in modern times. For the major firms from first world countries, especially from the United States, the circumstances surrounding their international expansion were enticing. These were the firms that were at the core of the studies that gave rise to the pioneering international business theories. This, for instance, was the case of Caterpillar, mentioned in Box 3.1.

Box 3.1 Caterpillar's expansion after the second world war

"Caterpillar had started the war as an American company with no overseas plants and small but significant export sales. Six years later, the Caterpillar name would be known throughout the world, carried by American combat engineers and SEABEES [Construction Battalions (CBs) of the US Navy]. A combination of the reputation Caterpillar would earn in the harsh conditions of combat and the acute need for tools to rebuild two shattered continents would transform a postwar Caterpillar into the multinational company that it is today. After World War II, Caterpillar launched a period of unparalleled growth." from http://ohe.cat.com; retrieved on September 11, 2009.

The question that then arose was: why do companies (from the advanced countries) become international? The adopted viewpoints conceptualized the firm as an economic agent, while the rationale underlying internationalization was studied based on firms' inclination to engage in foreign direct investment (FDI). These theories generated the mainstream content of the international business discipline.

The aim of this chapter is to revisit these early internationalization theories, to provide examples for them, in order to show that the competence concept "was already there," although not explicitly. To this end, we shall begin by putting the development of multinational enterprises (MNEs) from developed countries into context, highlighting how organizational competences were built and how they already played a major role in the internationalization processes. At the same time, we will provide examples that illustrate how these competences helped to set up and expand subsidiaries in the countries now regarded as emerging nations. All examples are related to the internationalization of automobile manufacturers from developed countries toward Brazil.

3.2 The earliest multinationals: from the nineteenth century up to the second world war

3.2.1 From the colonial enterprises to the manufacturing multinationals

The second half of the nineteenth century, when the precepts of the modern industrial organization started consolidating, witnessed the birth of MNEs.

Though there were firms active on the international front before this time, it would be anachronistic to use the word "multinational" to refer to the transactions conducted by the merchants of different origins or even by the sovereign regions that preceded the modern idea of the nation-state, according to Jones (2005: 16). The West India Company and other similar enterprises (such as the Hudson's Bay Company and the Royal African Company) held a monopoly of trading rights that had been granted to them by the governments of their home countries. One can regard them as "protomultinationals," as they were the first organizations to conduct business on a large scale outside their countries of origin. They were also powerful regional integration agents.

As mentioned in Chapter 1, part of these colonial enterprises later became large MNEs, such as Imperial Chemicals (from England), Siemens (from Germany), and the glassmaker Saint-Gobain (from France). At that time, the issue of competitiveness among firms of different nationalities first emerged. For instance, in the case of Saint-Gobain, Hamon (1988) claims that it was the first corporation to establish a foreign factory, in 1853, "moving beyond the confines of France, into Mannheim, Germany, to combat increased international competition and counter the expansionist ambitions of the Belgian glassworks."

The more significant international investments were originated in Western Europe and England. "Certain European companies already maintained large multinational operations before World War II, in part as a legacy of colonialism. Oil companies such as Royal Dutch/ Shell and British Petroleum, electronics firms such as Philips, and food-processing companies such as Unilever are prime examples" (Ruigrok and van Tulder, 1995: 128).

After 1880, MNEs grew quickly in number and size, thanks to the discovery and exploitation of natural resources, and to agricultural production outside the home countries of these firms (Jones, 2005: 20). Encouraged by the progress of transportation technologies, especially by sea, MNEs also began operating in less developed countries, such as Brazil.

Box 3.2 The São João Del Rey Mining Company: a nineteenth-century mining enterprise in Brazil

"The company was formed in 1830 by a small number of investors, to lease and operate mines in [the province of] Minas Gerais, Brazil. The London board of Directors met bimonthly to discuss company business, and there was a small clerical staff in the head office. The chief operating officer in Brazil was known as the Superintendent who headed the mining operations. In Brazil, supervisory positions were held by British nationals, while lower level labor was undertaken by slaves (until 1882) and free Brazilians. By 1913, the company operated the deepest mine in the world, employing over 2,500 workers, including 150 European expatriates, and was the producer of the vast majority of Brazil's gold, acquired large real estate holdings, built hydroelectric plants and operated a private electric railway."

Extracted from Jones (2005: 46)

However, the most important element at the dawn of the twentieth century was the international expansion of American enterprises, based on an innovative model of industrial organization. Michael Best (1990: 30) identifies a rupture in the underpinnings of competition and concludes that "the slow decline of manufacturing based on craftsmanship [the system that European firms tended to resort to at the time] was not caused by restrictive working practices, high or low wages, or managerial failure. Rather, it was the failure to adapt to the principles of production and organization of the new competition of the day" [embraced by the American firms]. The author concludes: "the New Competition at that time was American Big Business and the Old Competition was market-coordinated, vertically specialized industrial enterprises" (Best, 1990: 7).

3.2.2 *The expansion of American manufacturing MNEs*

The mass production organizational model was born in the United States, specifically in the Connecticut River Valley metalworking industry district and in the Springfield Armory, around 1820. In this area of Massachusetts, a new production system was developed at the request of the US Army, based on the concept of interchangeable parts: the weapons ceased to be products handcrafted as a single unit, but were now assembled and maintained from identical components, a system that enabled replacing parts. This newfangled method was promptly embraced by the Colt guns factory and the Singer sewing machine plant.

The American System of Manufacturing was introduced to the world at the Crystal Palace Exhibition in London in 1851. "Leading English engineers and military men were startled by what they observed because of the revolutionary production methods that were implied" (Best, 1990: 29).

This competitive advantage led Colt to set up a subsidiary in London in 1853 and Singer to start operating in Scotland in 1857. "By 1901, US companies maintained around fifty overseas manufacturing operations. By 1913, this number had risen to 116, of which almost half were located in Canada and the UK" (Dicken, 1986: 58).

Henry Ford and Frederick Taylor were the men who, in the first decade of the twentieth century, truly consolidated the rationale underlying the American System of Manufacturing. In 1911, Taylor published *The Principles of Scientific Management* and in 1913 Ford opened the River Rouge plant, the first to resort to assembly lines and conveyor belts. The theory and practice of the American System of Manufacturing were widely acknowledged and became international.

The dissemination of the model was universal. Taylor's work dictated the basis of so-called industrial engineering, which influenced the format of industrial organization in all segments. His book, *The Principles of Scientific Management,* was translated into virtually all languages, including Russian. Stalin voiced his great admiration for Taylor's work and appointed comrade Stakanov to translate it; as a result, American Taylorism was disseminated in Russia under the name of Stakanovism.

The Ford production model soon became fashionable worldwide. For decades, the Ford plant in River Rouge was a role model for other companies, including those that did not belong to the metallurgical or mechanical industries. Nevertheless, it is important to stress that the Ford model extrapolates the technical dimension, dictating principles that concern the economic, social, and political planes:

Perhaps the most important effect of the postwar liberalization of international trade flows was that European industries were exposed to the micro-Fordist organization of production on which the US hegemony rested. The micro-Fordist concept of control was based on the introduction of mass-production techniques and on a stringent division of labor, within large and vertically integrated firms, and a simultaneous increase of wages and consumption. With the liberalization of international trade, the principles of Fordism and its regulatory setting themselves internationalized. (Ruigrok and van Tulder (1995: 124)

Box 3.3 Fordism in Brazil

Ford Motor Company began operating in Brazil in 1919, with a small truck assembly line. However, the Brazilian industrialization process was heavily influenced, from its very inception, by the Fordist model. In 1930, the Institute for Organization Development and Work Rationalization was established in São Paulo to disseminate Taylor's and Ford's principles and practices.

As a result of the onset of the first world war, MNEs' activity diminished. Most European investments were put on hold. Barriers to population mobility were raised, as were the barriers to investment and trade. Many economies that had been growing at the time, such as Canada, Australia, Brazil, and India, began investing in manufacturing concerns as part of an import substitution movement, driven by the difficulty of carrying out transactions in the international market. Additionally, the 1929 crisis added substantially to these external difficulties; from the 1930s to the 1940s, growth and new foreign investment levels were insignificant.

From the 1950s to the 1970s, however, economic globalization surged strongly. During this time, trade barriers and foreign exchange controls were reduced, especially between the United States and Western Europe. FDI and international investment flows were now controlled by governments, thanks to the tools built into the Bretton Woods system. The United States emerged as a hegemonic power and the US dollar became the currency of the world's reserves. Meanwhile, China, Russia, and other communist countries chose not to join the global capitalist game and several other developing nations also put up their barriers.

With the rising importance of MNEs for the reconstruction of the global economy, the generation of theories about internationalization and international management became increasingly relevant, while American companies effectively became the role model, taking over production leadership on the global scene.

3.3 The pioneering theories: economic reasons to internationalize

The increased visibility of the MNE phenomenon and the hegemonic presence of American companies led to the formulation of theories developed from different points of view, ranging from those underscored by a Marxist approach, which identified the internationalization movement with the expansion of the capitalist system, to those that embraced a corporate approach, trying to understand which elements explained the decision to invest abroad.

The latter seek answers to this question: why do companies make foreign direct investments? American firms were the subject of this research, mainly. The answers pointed to two variables: market power and technological leadership.

3.3.1 The prospect of oligopolistic market power

Stephen Hymer developed his doctoral thesis at Massachusetts Institute of Technology (MIT), in 1966, looking for answers to this question: "Why do (American) enterprises prefer to make foreign direct investments instead of making indirect investments (or portfolio investments)?"

Otherwise stated, Hymer's motivation for his research was dissatisfaction with the prior theories about international investment flows, as these theories did not distinguish between portfolio investments and direct investments in production abroad. Hymer stated that FDI involved the transfer of a package of resources (technology, management skills, entrepreneurship, and so on) and not just finance capital. Additionally, FDI involved no change in the ownership of resources or rights transferred, whereas indirect investment, which was transacted through the market, did require such a change. That is why Hymer is regarded as the author of the first modern theory about the international operations of large firms.

Hymer's work concluded that for firms to own and control foreign value-added facilities, they must possess some form of innovation, cost, financial, or marketing advantage of a proprietary nature and that this advantage must be sufficient to outweigh the disadvantages of competing with home-grown firms in the country of production (the "liability of foreignness"). Dunning and Lundan (2008: 84) consider the use of monopolistic advantage to be inadequate to characterize those cases, because "ownership advantages may arise from the ability of firms to improve the allocation of resources or organize transactions more efficiently than markets."

For Ietto-Gillies (2005: 62), "Hymer's demarcation criterion between FDI and portfolio investment is *control*. Direct investment gives the firm control [and increased market power] over business activities abroad; portfolio investment does not."

Nevertheless, direct production abroad involves risks and the added expenses that go with the liability of foreignness: the acquisition of information and communications, the less advantageous conditions granted by local governments, the costs, the exchange rate fluctuation risks, and so on. The benefits of FDI consist of turning to practical account the specific advantages that the firm can profitably exploit abroad and the elimination of conflicts vis-a-vis competitors in regard to foreign markets.

In sum, Hymer answered the question: "Why do large monopolistic and oligopolistic enterprises become international?" However, in his arguments the assumption that FDI would involve the transfer of a package of resources (skills included) brings in concerns about the competence transfer.

Box 3.4 The automotive multinationals in Brazil

The establishment of the automotive industry in Brazil is an interesting example. In the 1950s, the economic development plan contemplated accelerating the country's industrialization by getting durable consumer goods manufacturers to establish themselves in Brazil, in particular automotive and white goods industries. The executive group appointed to conduct this process tried to attract major international companies, which negotiated favorable terms in order to establish their subsidiaries in the country, demanding also that these terms be extended to their original suppliers, thus enabling the latter to establish themselves close by. The local industrial groups were only involved in the financial negotiations, as shareholders.

3.3.2 *Technological leadership as the driver of internationalization*

The "product life cycle" theory put forth by Raymond Vernon in 1966 consolidated a number of prior developments proposed by American authors; these dealt with productivity differentials and internationalization issues, based on technology and entrepreneurship as explanatory factors, both of which were cultural characteristics known to be strong in the United States.

The authors who preceded Vernon had already highlighted the following points, according to Ietto-Gillies (2005: 69):

- technological advantages lead to competitive advantages;
- technological advantages are likely to be cumulative for various reasons, including dynamic economies of scale, learning-by-doing and a tendency to accumulate inventions;

- competitive advantages change during the product's stages: a country that has an advantage in the innovative phase of the product is unlikely to maintain that advantage once the product reaches its maturity;
- imitation effects – in terms of demand and production – are very relevant and likely to be stronger in countries with high incomes; and
- the mechanisms and speed of imitation in production are linked to the market structure in which firms operate.

Vernon (1966) built the "product life cycle" theory to explain what these points meant for American firms in terms of their decision to internationalize: a product is first conceived and developed in the US, since this is where the most favorable conditions are to be found. It is produced in the US in its early stages. However, as demand for the product grows and it reaches maturity, the product becomes increasingly standardized. This calls for production processes that are capital and labor-intensive. At this stage, imitation becomes easier, competition tends to increase and cost-cutting becomes necessary. This may lead to a strategy of relocating production to developing countries.

Box 3.5 The first cars produced in Brazil (or was Vernon right?)

Until the 1950s, the Brazilian subsidiaries of Ford and General Motors (GM) only assembled buses and trucks made with imported components. After the establishment of the local automotive regime, the first cars produced in Brazil were the Volkswagen Beetle, launched in 1955 but produced in Germany since the 1930s, the DKW Vemag F-91, launched in 1956 (with a two-stroke engine, licensed for production by Auto Union), the Simca Chambord, launched in 1958 (a Ford France design from the 1940s that was then produced by the French company Simca), and the Renault Dauphine, launched in 1959 (manufactured under license using a project that dated back to 1956). The first GM automobile was only launched in 1968 (the Opala, an offshoot of the Opel line), the same being true of the Fords (the Galaxy and the Maverick were launched after they were discontinued in the US). This product policy only changed in the early 1990s, when the country drastically reduced its commercial barriers. In response to the ensuing clamor from the auto industry's subsidiaries, the then President of Brazil replied: "But you're only capable of making carts!"

Although Vernon's theory was highly relevant for subsequent development in the US (Abernathy and Utterback, 1975), it has been heavily criticized.

Some authors feel that the model is too simplistic and deterministic. Others comment that even if the technology and entrepreneurship variables were relevant, the behavior of American firms regarding internationalization might also be interpreted as a response to the prevailing characteristics of the changing US institutional and market environment, because "in the 1960s, at the societal level, the very foundation of Fordism, the combined rise of productivity and consumption, came under siege ... The intuitive reaction of core US firms was to flee from their increasingly adversarial domestic bargaining arena, by setting up subsidiaries and transferring part of their production processes abroad, in particular to Canada and the EC" (Ruigrok and van Tulder, 1995: 125).

A study that investigated whether the product cycle theory applied to Swedish enterprises concluded that it did not. The chief explanation for this was the difference in the size of the domestic markets: the US had large markets within which domestic enterprises could advance along the product cycle, whereas Sweden had a small domestic market, which obliged Swedish firms to internationalize in order to advance along the product cycle.

In other words, for historical reasons, the US in general and American firms in particular had distinguishing competences in the technological and entrepreneurial areas, even in relation to other developed countries. Thus, Vernon's model can explain the case of American companies very well, but works rather less satisfactorily when it is used to analyze other countries' enterprises.

It is interesting to note that Vernon's theory highlights organizational competences (corporate and technological) as key drivers in its explanation of internationalization movements. In this case, technological competence coupled with innovation is strategic (i.e., a core competence) and must therefore remain at headquarters, whereas production competence is routine or tactical and thus can be exported.

3.3.3 The choice between markets and hierarchy: the internalization theory

In 1980, Alfred Chandler, one of the most renowned authors in the area of strategy and structure, on the basis of his research into American enterprises, concluded that "the modern industrial enterprise did not grow by producing something new or by producing it in a different way; it grew by adding new units of production and distribution, by adding sales and purchasing offices, by adding facilities for producing raw and semi-finished materials, by obtaining shipping lines, railroad cars, pipelines and other transportation units, and even by building research laboratories" (quoted in Dunning and Lundan, 2008: 156). In other words, firms increasingly took on organizational functions previously born by the market, reducing, for instance, the licensing agreements.

Having first identified this trend, Buckley and Casson (1976: 36) related it with the then emerging theory of transaction costs, in order to study the reasons why firms became international. In discussing markets versus hierarchies, they proposed that firms tend to internalize flows within the enterprise, whenever the transaction costs are more favorable.

The initial research question they proposed was: "In a multi-plant firm, bringing under common ownership and control several interdependent activities linked by flows of intermediate products, why should interdependent activities be coordinated internally by the management of a firm, rather than externally, by market forces?"

It is interesting to note that the issue of markets or hierarchies was already being dealt with in other disciplines, such as operations management, in which there was a discussion on whether the issue of "make or buy" was critical for enterprise strategy.

However, Buckley and Casson's approach is broader, in that they assume that "the intermediate products are sometimes ordinary semi-processed materials passed from one industry to another, but more often are types of knowledge and expertise embodied in patents, human capital, etc. Efficient coordination of business activities requires a complete set of markets in the intermediate products" (1976: 33). Thus, it is the internalization of markets for intermediate products among major MNEs that characterizes the internalization theory of internationalization.

This approach had strong repercussions within the academic field, as Rugman (1981: 9) stated: "As long as a multinational enterprise implies in internalization across national boundaries, the theory of internalization becomes the modern theory of the multinational."

Nevertheless, the internalization theory was strongly criticized, to the point of eliciting self-criticism from its main authors, since there are methodological and empirical problems affecting it. The criticism ranged from objections to the assumptions that the authors used as their starting point to the issue of the variables and indicators that should have been used (Ietto-Gillies, 2005: 106–109).

Still, the main criticism was that, as time went by, what was actually observed was a rising tendency toward externalization rather than a rising degree of internalization. Chandler's phrase, which opens this section, was voiced at a point of inflection, when the management model employed by Western companies, and by the American ones in particular, collapsed under the eyes of the world, which witnessed the appearance of the Japanese management model as a new paradigm. Externalization is one of the main tenets of this model, as we shall see in the next chapter.

3.3.4 *The eclectic paradigm of international production*

John Dunning was one of the pioneers in the field of international business and his production was vast. However, two of his constructs stand out in particular.

The first is a typology that relates to the drivers or strategic intents of a company that has gone international and the types of foreign production. With this typology, the author tries to answer the following question: "Why become international?"

Dunning (1993) identifies four types of foreign production: (1) resource seeking (the subsidiary seeks access to the resources available in the host country); (2) market seeking (the subsidiary tries to exploit local markets from its operations in the host countries); (3) efficiency seeking (the local subsidiary plays a role in the rationalization of the international production process); and (4) asset seeking (the local subsidiary incorporates competences and strategic assets geared toward innovation).

The eclectic paradigm of international production deals primarily with the "how" aspect, rather than with the "why" aspect, of internationalization. It was first published in 1977. Since then, Dunning has been expanding and refining this framework, labeled the "eclectic paradigm":

The eclectic paradigm seeks to offer a general framework for determining the extent and pattern of both foreign-owned production undertaken by a country's own enterprises, and that of domestic production owned or controlled by foreign enterprises ... it does not purport to be a theory of the MNE *per se* ... nor a theory of foreign direct investment ... It prescribes a conceptual framework for explaining "what is," rather than "what should be," the level and structure of the foreign value activities of enterprises. Dunning and Lundan (2008: 95; italics in the original)

The set of factors that can be chosen for this explanation is organized into three blocks: ownership-specific advantages, location-specific advantages and internalization-specific advantages, as shown in Box 3.6.

Box 3.6 The main tenets of the eclectic paradigm (extracted from Dunning and Lundan, 2008: 99–100)

The level and structure of a firm's foreign value-added activities will depend on:

(1) The extent to which it possesses unique and sustainable ownership-specific (O) advantages vis-a-vis firms of other nationalities in serving particular markets or groups of markets. These O advantages largely take the form of a privileged possession of, or access to, intangible assets, including institutions, and those which arise as a result of the common governance and coordination of related cross-border, value-added activities.

(2) Assuming that condition (1) is satisfied, the extent to which the enterprise perceives it to be in its best interest to add value to its O advantages, rather than sell them, or their right of use, to independent foreign firms. These advantages are called market internalization advantages (I).

(3) Assuming that conditions (1) and (2) are satisfied, the extent to which the global interests of the enterprise are served by creating, accessing, or utilizing its O advantages abroad. The spatial distribution of location-bound resources, capabilities,

and resources is assumed to be uneven; hence, it confers a competitive advantage upon the countries that possess them over those that do not.

(4) Given the configuration of ownership, location, and internalization (OLI) advantages of a particular firm, the extent to which a firm believes that foreign production is consistent with the long-term objectives of the stakeholders and the institutions underpinning its managerial and organizational strategy.

In practice, we can look upon the eclectic paradigm as a relation of determinants of enterprise internationalization, extracted from the different internationalization theories and reorganized, and then expanded thanks to the studies conducted by the author. Using the concepts presented at the beginning of Chapter 2, the theories are models and the eclectic paradigm is a framework, based on which we can derive different theories or explanatory models.

Box 3.7 The eclectic paradigm and the establishment of the automotive industry in Brazil

The establishment of the Brazilian auto industry also exemplifies the eclectic paradigm. We can assume that back in the 1950s, several of the world's enterprises enjoyed an ownership advantage, consolidated in a design for an automobile and its respective production process. Some of these firms became interested in the Brazilian market, but the way in which the strategy of each of them evolved was different. Volkswagen (VW), the symbol of these years, played by the rules of the game: it set up a subsidiary, brought its Beetle project along and built a plant, the design of which was similar to that of the factories in the Ruhr region. By doing so, VW was able to enjoy the location advantages that the market and the Brazilian government provided at the time and the OLI dimensions became quite evident. On the other hand, DKW (at that time part of Auto Union, which is now Audi) decided to license its project to Vemag, a Brazilian manufacturer. In other words, DKW resorted to its O-advantage, but did not internalize it, choosing instead to resort to market mechanisms. The way in which DKW and Vemag split the L-advantages is not known.

Simca was a different case because the government of the state of Minas Gerais enticed it to invest in Brazil by granting the firm a set of location advantages. However, during the course of setting up its subsidiary, Simca discovered that only three of its suppliers were established in Minas Gerais, whereas 975 were in the state of São Paulo. This drove the firm to change the site of its subsidiary to the town of São Bernardo, in the São Paulo metropolitan area, directly in front of Volkswagen. In other words, we have here an example of how different combinations of L advantages and I advantages can affect a firm's internationalization strategy.

3.4 Internationalization as a learning process: the Nordic school

The emergence of the Nordic school of internationalization and the development of the Uppsala model turned out to be an extremely important variation of the economics-based internationalization models.

While still in the 1960s, Sune Carlson, from the University of Uppsala, Sweden, launched a program of research into international business, because of:

- Swedish industry's strong dependence on international markets for its own growth;
- the European economic integration proposal of the 1950s; and
- American firms' aggressive entry into the European market.

The first research project tried to identify the possible differences between working in the domestic market versus the international market. When interviewing executives from Swedish firms and their subsidiaries, the researchers identified differences between what the theories postulated and the firms' reality.

As already mentioned, Vernon's product cycle theory did not explain Swedish firms' internationalization because: (a) the domestic market was small and therefore the companies, unlike their American counterparts, were unable to progress along the product cycle and move into the maturity stages prior to becoming international; (b) the Swedish standards and consumption habits were different from the American ones; and (c) Vernon's theory stressed organizational competences in products and processes, whereas the Swedish enterprises ascribed greater importance to the competences that concerned their relations with the market. Two especially relevant issues emerged: the choice of the countries to which the firms extended their international activities and how the subsidiaries were managed.

The interpretation of the empirical data led to a new framework to explain the internationalization process of Nordic enterprises. Rather than conceptualizing internationalization as the outcome of rational economic decision-making processes, the group pursued a point of view based on organizational processes, keeping the enterprise as the basic unit of analysis. The theories that formed the cornerstone of the Nordic school's approach were *The theory of growth of the firm*, by Edith Penrose (1959), which we discussed in the preceding chapter, and *A behavioral theory of the firm*, by Richard Cyert and James March (1963).

Penrose (1959), in her pioneering work, defined the firm as an administrative unit with boundaries, comprised of productive resources and the services of resources, where objective knowledge is distinct from experiential knowledge. Thus, company growth should be closely tied to the acquisition of knowledge; this is presumably an evolving process that is based on the firm's accrued experiences.

Cyert's and March's book sought to model the reality of enterprises' decision-making processes. According to them, given the difficulty and the cost involved in obtaining information plus the time pressures on decision-making, the decision-making process is normally "satisficing" (a portmanteau word that blends "satisfy" and "suffice") and seldom optimizing. Additionally, Cyert and March felt that firms should not be regarded as a number of bureaucratic hierarchies but as coalitions of groups, or relationship networks with multiple interests, that can be converging or conflicting, and that learn to develop rules and procedures to work within bounded rationality conditions. Thus, it is fundamental to develop the ability to learn from experience.

As far back as the 1970s, the research under way at the University of Uppsala yielded its first model of Swedish enterprise internationalization, now based on the theories of the aforementioned authors.

It was found that when the domestic market is saturated, resulting in the reduction of opportunities to the point of hindering company growth, new sites for expansion should be sought. If vertical expansion is discarded due to uncertainty or insufficient profitability, the way to go is normally to expand geographically. As the alternatives for new sites involve greater uncertainties than known sites, expansion will target the locations that are more similar to those in which the firm already runs operations. From this point of view, the internationalization process is seen as a sequence of incremental steps that benefit the firm by providing successive learning along all the stages of growing commitment to foreign markets.

Thus, the Nordic school's theory focuses less on "why internationalize?" and more on "how to internationalize." This theory is based on concepts that were then new: a sequence of international modi operandi, commitment to international markets, and psychic distance.

The theory states that enterprises first seek an arm's-length involvement with international markets, through direct exports, for instance. Thereafter, the firm expands its knowledge, steps up its commitment and changes its modus operandi until it grows into setting up subsidiaries abroad.

The question underlying such behavior, the one which is modeled by the sequential steps proposition, is: how can a firm's foreign operations be controlled in a situation where there is a lack of knowledge about foreign markets? Here, the concept of experiential knowledge comes into play, or rather, learning about foreign markets through one's own operations in such markets. For the Nordic school's researchers, objective knowledge is not enough, as Penrose had already noted. As experiential knowledge can only be developed and accrued by individuals, the importance of front-line managers and of the ways in which the company's groups and people relate to each other becomes prominent, if the firm is to attain consistent decisions.

To the extent that the firm expands its knowledge about a given market and country, it can raise its level of commitment. However, a high degree of uncertainty invariably envelops the very first entry. This uncertainty is measured by the psychic difference, as a manifestation of ignorance about a foreign country. Entry into markets that are increasingly more far removed presumably takes place as the firm acquires experience with foreign operations.

Psychic distance is defined on the basis of the set of factors that can interfere with the flow of information between countries and it involves: geographical distance, differences in political, economic and social development, educational levels, language, culture, political systems, and institutions, among other factors. The researchers prepared a list of countries ranked according to their psychic

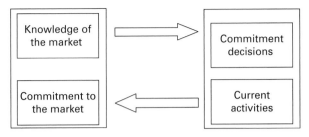

Figure 3.1 The Uppsala internationalization model
Source: Blomstermo and Sharma (2003: 22).

distance from Sweden. They concluded that firms seemed heavily inclined to make their initial investments in countries such as Denmark, Norway, Finland, and Western Germany, i.e., nations with a low psychic distance from Sweden. Consequently, it was inferred that psychic distance interferes with the process of selecting foreign markets, especially when the firm is in the early stages of internationalization.

The behavioral internationalization process model is dynamic in the sense that the outcome of one decision regarding foreign market entry is the input for the subsequent decision. Johanson and Vahlne (1977) identified two basic mechanisms in this model: state and change (Figure 3.1). State, which explains the subsequent internationalization, is the present state of the internationalization process of a firm and includes market knowledge and market commitment. Market knowledge is divided into objective knowledge and experiential knowledge. Experiential knowledge is inversely related to uncertainty and is the model's most critical factor. Market commitment comprises the amount of resources committed and the degree of commitment abroad. The more specific the resources are to a market or country, the greater the commitment. Regarding increased commitment, there are two effects: the economic one (the production scale in the foreign country) and the uncertainty-related one (increased interaction and integration with the local environment).

Change relates to commitment decisions and current activities. Commitment decisions are decisions to commit resources to foreign operations. These decisions are made by managers on the basis of their perceptions of problems and opportunities in the market abroad. Perceptions of problems and opportunities are aspects of experiential knowledge. Current activities are the daily work. Repetition of current activities is a valuable source of experience, which can be transformed into experiential knowledge.

One important step, according to Johanson and Vahlne (2003), was ascribing greater importance to the concepts of knowledge and commitment, leaving the concepts of decision and information in a secondary position. The concepts of experiential knowledge and psychic distance, besides being fundamental for the model's construction, are current to this day.

A lot of criticism of the Upsalla model has been voiced, questioning the determinism of the internationalization sequence, and the possibility of firms skipping stages or of being globally born enterprises. The researchers refuted this criticism, commenting that they had not intended to build a prescriptive method. The proposed concepts, however, remain up-to-date and are relevant both for researchers and practitioners.

3.5 Were competences already there?

The preceding overview reveals a key period in the history of globalization and internationalization, when MNEs decoded their role and conquered their arenas. This was the period during which they became the subject of investigation per se and that provided the input for the pioneering internationalization theories.

In all of them, we can find references to competences, in more or less explicit manners. Of the aforementioned theories, the one with the feeblest references to competences is Hymer's market power theory. In all the others, the reference is more evident.

In answering the question: "Why do (large monopolistic and oligopolistic) enterprises prefer to make foreign direct investments instead of making portfolio investments?" Hymer referred to the fact that FDI involves the transfer of resources, including skills. Perhaps we can say that, as an issue, it had a minor priority in the decision to internationalize because the large monopolistic and oligopolistic firms of that time already had a consolidated position in the market, based on competence differentiation relative to their competitors. This would be true especially if compared to the competences built by third world country firms at that time. In addition, the internationalizing firm was expected to develop competences in the host country to overcome the liability of foreignness. Therefore, we can say that the issue of competences was already there.

The internalization theory addresses competences indirectly. Every time a firm internalizes an activity, it must develop in-house competences. Every time it externalizes the said activity, it is buying competences in the market. As we have stressed, this is about "make or buy," one of the most critical decisions in any firm. The transaction costs analysis does deal with this dimension, albeit implicitly.

The product life cycle theory, however, explicitly mentions the competences issue. Indeed, the chief competitive differential of American companies was technology and entrepreneurship and they established the dynamics of internationalization.

Dunning's "Eclectic paradigm," (1980) from its earliest versions, under the heading "Intangible assets in ownership competitive advantage," gives one to understand that there is such a thing as a competences dimension, so much so that, in its later versions, the "Eclectic paradigm" actually mentions competences as a competitive advantage.

Finally, the Nordic school's approach addresses the competences issue from a new angle. It harbors the notion that the set of competences needed to operate efficiently in foreign countries is not the same as required in the countries of origin. The transfer of competences cannot be automatic. Thus, the gradual movement, the effort to learn by developing experiential knowledge, enables the construction of competences that are better suited to the host country's circumstances, while it perfects the dynamic capacities required to step up the internationalization process.

However, the strategic relevance of organizational competences becomes truly evident in the second internationalization wave, the subject of the next chapter.

4 | *The second wave: Japan and third world countries move abroad*

4.1 New fleets sail into international waters

In an article that has become a classic, Prahalad and Hamel (1990), to exemplify the meaning of "strategic intent," describe how Komatsu, the Japanese heavy equipment enterprise, organized itself in order to catch up with and overtake Caterpillar, an icon of the first wave of internationalization and, so far, unquestionable leader in global markets. The authors highlighted that to create strategic intent, Komatsu instituted a logo that consisted of a C within a circle. This was spread all over the firm to convey the idea that the strategy was to "encircle Caterpillar." As things turned out, Komatsu was highly successful.

The late 1970s and the 1980s were rich in unforeseen events such as this. Probably, the first of these materialized on the social front. May 1968 symbolized social unrest that extended to several countries, Brazil included. On the economic front, financial globalization became stronger, as previously mentioned. However, on the corporate front, two especially weighty events led to structural changes. The first and most visible consisted of the two oil crises, in 1973 and in 1978. The second, subtler and more gradual, was a change in market regimes.

Up to the 1970s, the market regime could be classified as a seller's market. As demand exceeded supply, what was produced was consumed. Thus, producers were the party setting the rules. Corporations' chief challenge was to expand their production capacity. They could achieve this horizontally, by increasing their range of products, or vertically, by internalizing functions carried out via market mechanisms, provided they had the funds for it. The requirements of competition were still attenuated by firms' comfortable circumstances.

The status quo started to change as of the "oil crisis" of the late 1970s. As new international players entered the market (in particular the Japanese enterprises, followed by those from Korea and other

Asian countries), supply increased more than demand and gradually it became evident that, in certain segments, overcapacity was increasing. Clients and consumers started "dictating the market rules," thus turning the markets into buyer's markets. Quality, in the sense of winning over consumers by identifying their needs and excelling in terms of products and services, emerged as the cornerstone of corporate competitiveness. Increasingly, enterprises became "customer oriented." The Japanese were the first to operate in accordance with this newfangled requirement; their productive model created a paradigm shift and provided an alternative to the Fordist model, allowing Japan to catch up with the most advanced countries.

This change of direction altered the rationale underlying international competition and made room for the entry of new multinational enterprises (MNEs). The Japanese companies made the most of this new internationalization wave, followed by those from Korea. However, the MNEs from what was then known as the third world countries also attempted to take advantage of this opportunity. Enterprises from Argentina, Brazil, India, and Hong Kong, among other countries, pursued internationalization, though achieving far more modest results.

Thus, the second internationalization wave was conducted largely by Japanese firms. It is important to revisit their development and internationalization history, because Japan is an example of how a country in a highly unfavorable situation in the post-war period defined and implemented a successful trajectory for itself, surfing a new internationalization wave.

Japanese development revealed new research themes because, contrary to the assumptions of internationalization theories discussed in the previous chapter, Japanese companies lacked the power of oligopolies and were known neither for their entrepreneurial characteristics nor for their technological leadership. In addition, they showed that externalization was preferable to internalization. Thus, they set the direction for the productive restructuring that took place in the 1980s and 1990s in Western countries and their enterprises.

Concerning the theme of this book, Brazil and the MNEs from other emerging countries, the case of Japan provides clues about why they were unsuccessful in that second internationalization wave. However, those countries and corporations learnt a lot from the

Japanese experience. It was one of the chief elements that explain their success in the third internationalization wave, especially in the case of Brazil.

4.2 The rise of Japanese multinationals

4.2.1 Japan: emerging as an industrial power

Despite Japan's ancient tradition as an industrialized country, its emergence as a global player only materialized in the 1970s and 1980s, so that recent literature regards it as a "late industrializer."

To Westerners, Japanese industry's rising competitive power was initially seen as a product of local conditions: "the Japanese are different." The acknowledgment of Japan's new international standing was achieved only after Japanese subsidiaries in the US, using American workers and applying the Japanese productive model (Watanabe, 2007) began performing better than their local competitors.

The remarkable thing about Japan's upsurge is the trajectory of the country and its firms in terms of preparing their entry into international markets. The catching-up began soon after the end of the second world war. Three stages were clearly identified: learning on the shop-floor (1945 to 1964), linking markets to the production process (1964 to 1973), and consolidating the Japanese productive model (1973 to 1990). The 1990s, regarded as a lost decade where the country's economy is concerned, brought significant changes to this Japanese model (Aoki, 2007).

In their internationalization process, Japanese firms try to transfer their organizational approach, since it provides them with a competitive advantage: "When they set up their factories abroad, Japanese manufacturers usually try to transplant key elements of the so-called Japanese Management Model (JMM), which is their mainstay in global competition" (Watanabe, 2007). That was clearly the case of Japanese subsidiaries in the US, where the first criterion for deciding on the location of a greenfield plant was that it be in a non-unionized area.

Additionally, the emergence of Japanese MNEs raised the bar for all corporations that were already in international markets, as well as for those that intended to become global players, by establishing new productivity standards.

4.2.2 *Japanese economic recovery after the second world war*

After the second world war, Japan had to rebuild its industry. It had an industrial base centered on the war effort as a starting point, but this was first flattened and then tutored by the allied occupation forces.

The period between the two great wars was underscored by a strong power conflict among the representatives of government, especially among those connected with the Ministry of Trade and Commerce, on one hand, and the *zaibatsu,* the large industrial groups belonging to traditional families, on the other. The *zaibatsu* resisted modernization and poor productivity had strongly influenced the war's outcome.

Once the war was over, however, the occupying forces intervened directly and radically in Japanese industry. One of the most polemic points was the application of US-style antitrust laws, with a view to breaking up the *zaibatsu.* Meanwhile, the occupying forces organized a major program for the development of small and medium-sized enterprises (SMEs), thereby renovating business leaderships.

This strategy was abruptly reversed when the Korean War broke out, as Americans then became dependent on the Japanese industrial base to prop up their war effort. The outcome of this unplanned process was that:

- the *zaibatsu* were reorganized under the tutelage of banks and trading companies, giving rise to the *kigyo shudan,* their current name (Fruin, 1992);
- efforts to renew the corporate system by creating SMEs were maintained and intensified;
- the Ministry of International Trade and Industry (MITI, the successor of the former Ministry of Industry and Trade), emerged as the driver of Japanese (re)industrialization, wielding vast power, with influence or control over a large number of industrial policy mechanisms, such as:
  - rates and quotas;
  - foreign exchange rates;
  - the allocation of resources of both government banks and private-sector banks;
  - technology transfers;
  - cartel laws; and
  - the creation of combined public sector/private sector enterprises.

As the occupying forces were gradually phased out, MITI started to exert its driving role in the (re)industrialization process. From 1950 to 1965, industrial policy was essentially geared toward the reactivation of Japan's industrial complex through funding coupled with performance targets established by planning processes. From the corporate standpoint, the challenge consisted of rebuilding the production systems and finding a new positioning for products and markets. From the government viewpoint, the issue was how to reorganize the entire industrial system.

On the corporate front, a strong learning process was unleashed, aimed at absorbing from the westerners, in particular from the Americans, the knowledge seen as relevant in order to catch up. These efforts involved traditional means, such as licensing contracts, reverse engineering, etc. But they also involved more unusual methods, such as industrial espionage and an unaligned position where patents and intellectual property were concerned.

This process was articulated and supported by governmental institutions, on the macro level, and by a set of associations, on the intermediate level. Three directives guided these efforts:

- the policy of being a good follower;
- monitored technology transfers; and
- investment and divestment strategies.

The first directive concerned the posture of Japanese companies of admitting they were not world leaders and, "respectfully," pursuing the position of competent and diligent followers, thirsty to learn from the masters, i.e., from more advanced countries and enterprises. The Toyota case illustrates this argument. Its inspiration came from the American automotive industry, the world's most advanced; so it tried to learn from it, in particular from Ford, to then pursue the optimum solution for its own reality.

According to Japanese views, the good follower strategy can be analyzed from two different angles. The first is the market-related and short-term angle and two cases illustrate it clearly: Japanese watches and cameras. The watches, in particular those of the Seiko brand, were copies of the best European watches, more specifically of Rolexes. They were mechanical devices that were not a "quality" brand as such; however, they were inexpensive and soon became highly successful. In the case of cameras, Yashica developed products based on cameras with the finest reputation, such as Leika and Rolleiflex, and started marketing cameras that "though not as good, were cheaper." With these products, Japanese industry carved niches in the international markets, making its own growth possible. The second is the long-term and essentially technological angle: through these products, Japanese industry learnt and developed technological know-how in strategic fields: fine mechanics, in the case of watches, and optics, in the case of cameras. The concurrent concern about short-term market decisions and long-term technological strategy lent direction and consistency, and hence power, to Japanese industry during the economic recovery period.

The second directive concerned the way in which MITI conducted the country's industrial policy and built up its own legitimacy through its competence in helping Japanese industry develop and overcome crises. MITI, among other things, was responsible for technology transfers through licensing agreements. In order to put pressure on Japanese enterprises, this ministry established very strict rules for authorizing agreements and their renovation: a Japanese firm would be barred from renewing technology transfer agreements unless it marketed an improved version of whatever it had been licensed to produce by the time the preceding agreement expired. In the case of the auto industry, for instance, "MITI encouraged and supervised the Nissan agreement with Austin (the English company), which went into effect in 1952, to assemble, and later to manufacture, the Austin A40 in Japan. Nissan relied on this arrangement to develop its production capacity and, when the agreement came to its end in 1959, Nissan launched the Cedric, a clone of the Austin A40" (Best, 1990: 186).

MITI's action did not consist merely of passive normalization: it was also actively engaged in inducing companies to embrace certain actions and in balancing the domestic market's competitive circumstances, which it named "healthy competition." From the point of view of international trade, only companies that had proven to be competitive at home were allowed to launch themselves into foreign markets. To be given an export certificate, the companies had to fulfill several Japan Industrial Standards – JIS requirements. JIS operated as a technical ally of MITI and its requirements were designed to ensure that Japanese export products met high quality standards, capable of adding value to the inscription "Made in Japan." Likewise, JIS set quality standards for all foreign products marketed within Japan.

The third directive concerned the matter of investing and divesting. Japanese firms, as a result of the way in which they were structured, had a high degree of flexibility when it came to entering and exiting different business areas. After the second world war, the most important industrial segments were the so-called light industries (textiles, foodstuffs, personal care products), which were fast superseded by heavy industry (chemicals, steel products), which in turn were supplanted by high added value manufacturing (automobiles, home appliance). This mobility, the outcome of an orientation toward non-specialization, enabled Japanese industry as a whole to speedily reposition itself strategically in relation to the constant changes of the international arena.

Several mechanisms were put into action to safeguard this flexibility. The structure of Japan's corporate system was one of them, as we will see further on. The government upheld an ongoing process of prospecting future scenarios, conducted in conjunction with enterprises, and requiring that the latter invest a certain percentage of their research and development budgets in fields that were not directly related to their chief areas of activity, so as to maintain the prospecting of alternative businesses permanently afloat.

Following a period in which it supported companies in exchange for production performance improvements, MITI redesigned its policies, in the light of the new competitive context that emerged after 1964. Concerned that the deregulation of foreign trade policies might give rise to a flood of foreign products, especially those made by US corporations, which might put the local, smaller, and more vulnerable firms at risk, MITI embraced a policy of fostering Japanese firms' production concentration and scale growth, encouraging mergers and acquisitions, as well as establishing reserves for strategic products and markets.

The business world viewed MITI's determinations with great resistance; this was particularly the case of the SMEs, which rejected merger proposals and resisted the formation of cartels. The unforeseen outcome was that this resistance gave rise to a strong relationship between business people. To put into practice the MITI directive of reserving certain strategic niches, they had to organize themselves into groups and engage in integrated strategic planning, with a view to justifying, fundamentally, which products should be imported and which should not.

Thus, if in the preceding phase MITI aimed at getting companies to individually recover their technological capabilities, in the second process unleashed by it the firms learned to communicate, to prospect future markets jointly and to identify the fields of knowledge that might warrant regulation.

4.2.3 The JMM as a competitive advantage

As of the 1970s, Japan emerged as a new global industrial power, underpinned by new organizational standards, in line with a new productive model: "A productive model emerges periodically when firms achieve a set of internally coherent and externally appropriate technical, organizational, management and social devices and practices which enable them to deal effectively with uncertainties related to the product market and worker behavior" (Tolliday *et al.*, 1999: 6).

Actually, three aspects of the JMM must be highlighted:

- the Japanese enterprise system;
- the Japanese management system; and
- the Japanese industrial relations system.

Among the countless studies that have discussed the management system of Japanese firms, the viewpoint of Masahiko Aoki (1990) had a lot of impact and generated a broad rethinking of the types of industrial organization.

Aoki opens his proposal listing the different explanatory approaches to Japanese economic success: the *Kanban* system and other manufacturing practices, a non-hierarchical mechanism of operations coordination, the nature of the companies' internal hierarchy, the manpower training and labor relations system, the bonus system, and the financial strategies based on banks and the banking system, among others.

The key question to him is: "Might the Japanese productive model's features result from a national culture, or is it a rationale to face the challenge of competition in globalized markets?" (Aoki, 1990: 2).

Aoki's core argument is the counterpoint between the horizontal coordination model found in Japanese firms, i.e., the J-mode (the Japanese way of doing things), and the Western companies' essentially vertical type of coordination, which he called the H-mode (the hierarchical way of doing things).

The H-mode, typical of American firms, is characterized by an organization based essentially on the hierarchical separation of tasks and functions, resulting in Taylorist features. To illustrate this point, Aoki works with three examples: production scheduling and control in the automotive industry, quality control in the steel industry, and new product development in the computer industry. In the three cases, Aoki found that all the planning activities are invariably allocated to departments of the highest hierarchical level. As a result, the functions define, in detail, the nature and order of the operations to be conducted, under a strict division of labor system. The means for dealing with unforeseen events and uncertainties are also planned: intermediary inventories, mobile teams for substitution, etc. The outcome of this organizational choice is that "the lessons from the experience of managing unforeseen or random events can only come to be used by the planning sectors in the subsequent round."

The characteristics of the Japanese firms' J-mode are the exact opposite: the coordination among the operating units is essentially horizontal. The planning determined at the highest levels is no more than an overarching framework based on which the operating units structure their activities in an integrated manner, relying essentially on current information from the work context. Thus, the horizontal coordination process is responsible for learning dynamics that are far faster and stronger at the production process level, providing Japanese firms with speedier and more flexible response standards, besides safeguarding organizational integrity and the efficacy of the decision-making processes.

The dynamics of intercompany relations in Japan was named "the Japanese enterprise system" by Fruin (1992). This author's argument is that Japan's industrial organization was invented, starting in the mid-nineteenth century, through a process of organizational learning. Fruin defined the Japanese enterprise system as "an interorganizational system of business coordination. It is based on strategic interaction and on the alignment of three basic forms of industrial organization: the plant, the firm and the inter-company network. High productivity, functional specialization and production flexibility are the intrinsic characteristics of this system, which set the Japanese enterprise system apart from all others."

The relations that began developing among the different institutions were essentially based on complementary interests and resources. For instance, while still in the early twentieth century, a trading company such as Mitsui was better placed than a textile firm to get quotations in the international markets for the price of raw cotton, finished products and looms. The trading company's opportunity cost was far lower, thanks to its many offices abroad: as far back as 1901, Mitsui already had offices in eight countries. A trading company, however, was able to provide far more than merely information: it could handle storage, forwarding, customs clearances, etc.

In the early twentieth century, the very fast pace of economic growth led a large number of firms to progress and to increase their sales, profits, sizes, and complexity. Nevertheless, the companies faced restrictions in terms of bank loans and joining the stock market. The existing management capacity was too limited to be able to deal simultaneously and effectively with the creation of new methods of financial and accounting control, the improvement of technological know-how, and the development of human resources and materials. Managers were available only in limited numbers and they were unused to running large, complex organizations:

This being the case, the Japanese companies did what they could; in other words, they specialized. Manufacturers focused on product lines, commercial firms tried to extend their services and marketing channels, and all firms looked sideways to establish connections that might make the expansion of their business feasible without incurring in the costs that such growth would imply in, if undertaken alone. A system of companies started to materialize, but slowly and gradually, at first. Fruin (1992: 119)

A very important idea that must be taken into account if one is to understand the Japanese enterprise system is that of "permeable boundaries." Despite a certain segmentation of the economic groups (the *zaibatsu*) and even a certain rivalry among them, when a process of cooperation is underway among Japanese enterprises, everything can move between the institutions involved: money, information, people, materials, etc. For example, it was a common practice among a single group's firms to transfer budget funds from the companies that performed well to those that had faced problems, subject to its being agreed that this was strategic. The transfer of people and information among enterprises was also common.

The intercompany networks can be roughly classified into three types: horizontal clusters of firms from different industries and sectors, which the Japanese dubbed *kigyo shudan* (the current name of the *zaibatsu* structure), and which comprise six main groups: Mitsubishi, Mitsui, Sumitomo, Fuyo, Sanwa, and DKB; vertical clusters of gradually smaller enterprises dominated by the large companies at the top (the *keiretsu*), such as Toyota; and ad hoc clusters (like a taskforce), in which the enterprises act in a coordinated fashion to perform activities of limited duration. A single firm may very well be involved in all these different types of enterprise arrangements.

As institutional evolution occurs, the permeable boundaries interlinking plants, enterprises and interorganizational networks lead to different standards of organizational interdependence. For instance, the Toyota Motor Corporation and Matsushita Electric Industrial Company lean toward the model of intercompany networks; in other words, most of their production and distribution is parceled out among dozens or even hundreds of subsidiaries. Kao and Canon are strong examples of firms that internalized most of the organizational functions into a single structure. However, Hitachi, Mitsubishi Heavy Industry, and Kyowa Hakko are organized primarily as focused plants. Even so, these firms and most large enterprises do have competences in all the functional areas, and it was the interdependent and integrated management of these competences that lent strength to the Japanese enterprise model.

Moreover, this pattern of intercompany interrelations gave rise to a different type of technological innovation: "the Japanese innovation pattern evolved from process innovation to system innovation, with an associated organizational change from a mechanical system to an organic network" (Imai, 1992: 225). In other words, the most typical feature of Japanese innovation is that it implies in the involvement and cooperation of several companies from different industrial segments. Kodama (1985: 2) named this "technological fusion," as opposed to the American pattern of technological breakthrough, and he exemplified it: "The typical example of breakthrough innovation is the discovery of the transistor, whereas mechatronics [the combination of mechanical and electronics engineering] is an example of technological fusion." Thus, Japanese industry's technological fusion results in the gradual development of several firms, whereas the breakthrough type of innovation contributes to the radical growth of a single specific enterprise.

4.2.4 Changes as of the 1990s

The 1990s brought significant change to Japan. On the economic front, the bursting of the financial and real estate market bubble went hand in hand with a change on the political front, as the Liberal Democratic Party (LDP) rose to power. Many refer to this period as the lost decade because of wealth loss, poor growth, and diminishing numbers of secure life-long jobs, not to speak of the downturn in Japan's self-esteem.

Aoki (2007: 1) argues that "underlying the apparent depression, competition among firms became keener during the period and management responses to the challenge of deflationary pressures, as well as the rise of industrial China, the IT revolution and so on ... steadily differentiated the better performers from the laggards and losers in the industry." Among the chief changes of recent times, the author highlights those that took place on the political plane. Although the LDP returned to power, its continuity came into question and alliances with a range of interest groups drove changes in the traditional J-mode and in the dynamics of inter-company relations.

In the late 1990s, Fujitsu was the first large Japanese corporation to abandon the traditional seniority-based pay system, replacing it with performance-based payment.

Many of the large enterprises such as Matsushita and Sony underwent major restructuring, abandoning traditional Japanese management practices. For instance, they cut the number of permanent employees by transferring them to subsidiaries, besides implementing staff downsizing and early retirement plans. The core workforce, managed according to the Japanese employment system, was thus reduced substantially. From 1995 to 2005, the number of regular employees sank by 4.1 million whereas the temporary employee category swelled by 6.5 million.

The Corporate Code Reform passed in 2002 forced Japanese companies to choose between two board structure alternatives: the American model, with independent sub-committees (auditing the appointment of management and its pay), or the traditional system, modified through the incorporation of a semi-independent audit committee. By 2005, sixty of Japan's largest firms had embraced the American system. The listed companies started being evaluated by the capital market. On the other hand, the management of the large corporations became far more aware of potential take-over threats.

Meanwhile, the injection of government funds into faltering enterprises became the target of rising criticism; the financial system's restructuring started to be conducted by the private sector: foreign-owned equity and bank-related corporate revival funds replaced commercial banks as major players in reorganizing the financially depressed firms.

4.2.5 The internationalization of Japanese companies

Japan resumed foreign direct investment (FDI) in 1951, following the San Francisco Peace Conference. Starting in the 1980s and up to 1997, its enterprises dramatically expanded their internationalization, despite the bursting of the economic bubble in 1991. However, from 1997 to 2003, Japanese firms' outward foreign direct investment (OFDI) slipped back to its 1986 level approximately (Chang and Delios, 2006; UNCTAD, 2008). "In 1999, 123 countries or regions were host sites for Japanese foreign investments. There were 19,030 Japanese subsidiaries, 3,733 of which were in the US." (Beamish *et al.*, 2001).

By late March 2005, the stock of OFDI had exceeded US$915 billion. North America and Europe accounted for 62 percent of this total, whereas the share of Asia and Latin America reached about 18 percent and 13 percent, respectively (Table 4.1). Asia's rising participation after the mid-1980s reflects the increased pace of investment in China.

Japanese direct investment in China began in 1979, following the announcement of the open market policy. By the spring of 2005, however, China had already become the second largest host country, after Indonesia, with an accrued total of US$ 31.5 billion. Nevertheless, the data in the tables underestimate the magnitude of Japanese investments in China. First, because many Japanese enterprises invest in China via Hong Kong and Taiwan, resorting to the knowledge of their branches where language, cultural traditions, information networks, and commercial skills are concerned. Second, because they have been transferring factories from other parts of Asia and from the US to China as part of their global business strategy.

The most internationalized sectors of Japanese industry are the electronics and automotive ones. Matsushita is the most internationalized

Table 4.1 Japanese FDI by fiscal year, 1951–2004

Period	All regions (US$ m)	Developed regions (%)			Developing regions (%)		
		North America	Europe	Oceania	Asia	Latin America	Other
1951–2004	915,707	37.9	24.1	4.7	17.7	13.1	2.5
1951–70	3,577	25.5	17.9	7.9	21.1	15.9	11.9
1971–80	32,920	27.0	11.6	6.8	27.6	17.0	9.9
1981–5	47,152	36.4	13.9	3.6	20.4	20.1	5.6
1986–90	227,157	48.1	21.1	6.1	12.4	10.9	1.4
1991–5	204,270	43.9	19.2	5.9	14.6	9.1	0.7
1996–2000	261,842	35.5	31.8	2.6	16.7	11.6	1.8
2001–4	140,791	21.7	36.7	3.3	19.8	17.9	0.6

Source: Watanabe, 2007.

Japanese enterprise, followed by Honda. The third is NEC, the second most important firm in the electronic sector, followed by Toyota, Toshiba, and Mitsubishi Electric, in fourth, fifth, and sixth places, respectively. The destination of these firms' investments is Asia and the US, mostly.

Of the 75 Asian firms among the worlds' 500 largest, 64 are Japanese. The study produced by Collinson and Rugman (2008) concluded that these companies' FDI has a regional profile, centering mainly on Asia:

Only one firm out of the 64 has more than 50% of its assets located outside Asia. Honda, with 31% of its assets located in Japan, over 55% in North America, just over 7% in Europe and 5% in Asia, can be considered a host-oriented firm in asset terms. Yet the global and bi-regional firms in terms of their sales among the 64 Japanese firms – Toyota, Sony, Nissan, Canon, and Bridgestone – all have over 50% of their assets in Asia. Overall, the 64 Japanese firms listed have an average of just 22% of their assets outside Japan and an average of 83% of their assets in Asia. Collinson and Rugman (2008: 218)

In their internationalization process, Japanese firms try to uphold their competitive advantages, including their management model: "When they set up their factories abroad, Japanese manufacturers usually try to transplant key elements of the so-called Japanese Management Model, which is their mainstay in global competition" (Watanabe, 2007). This was clearly designed after the initial investments in US greenfield sites, where the first criterion for the location decision was for the site to be in a non-unionized area. This entry strategy had obvious drivers, but it often ran into operating problems, as had been the case of Ford in its internationalization process many decades before.

First, it is a system that depends on tacit knowledge, demanding expatriates for proper implementation. Second, it calls for qualified workers at the host country, employees who can accept the principles on which the Japanese productive mode is based. Even if these two conditions are met, the communication problems remain.

The internationalization of Japanese enterprises was studied quite a lot, in particular regarding automotive companies, through the International Motor Vehicle Program (IMVP) and the Groupe d'Etudes et Recherche pour l'Industrie et les Salariés d'Automobile (GERPISA), a European-based auto industry research group, with different results. The main product of the IMVP work was the 1990 book *The machine that changed the world*, which critically analyzed the Japanese productive model and, excluding its characteristics of a cultural nature, created a new overarching organizational model called the lean production model (Womack *et al.*, 1990).

As for GERPISA, it discussed how the Japanese subsidiaries were organized in their host countries. The core concept underlying the analyses was "hybridization." Recognizing that successful pure transfers of productive models are very rare and that even a direct transplant cannot simply replicate the parent, "hybridization occurs when firms try to make principles or models drawn from one social and economic space compatible with the constraints and opportunities of another" (Tolliday *et al.*, 1998: 6; Westney, 2001: 636).

The case of Toyota, of great relevance, is explained as follows:

> The transplant project [to the USA] was the result of an all-out effort to condense the essence of its manufacturing capability and to transfer it to a new context. Many Toyota managers initially doubted the transferability of the Toyota system outside of the Japanese context, and it was only after the hesitant involvement in the NUMMI joint venture with General Motors [in Oakland, California] that they plunged alone into a high profile transplant project. In doing so, Toyota went through an intense learning experience to understand its own system in order to be able to transplant it. Mishina (1998: 112)

The internationalization of Japanese enterprises toward developing countries is slightly different. For instance, Watanabe (2007) analyzes Japanese subsidiaries in China and India, highlighting that in both countries their efforts were supported by their host governments, which encouraged the inflow not only of advanced hardware technology but also of production and quality control techniques. Unlike other developing countries, however, China and India have many old machinery factories, sometimes dating back to the pre-second world war period. Consequently, Japanese multinationals were often obliged to spend considerable time and energy rationalizing their partners' and suppliers' production facilities and work organization before introducing their own production methods.

To aid this transfer process, companies often get support from technical cooperation programs of the Japanese Government, such as the Association for Overseas Technical Scholarship (AOTS). With this, "the system-level home country effects ... [leading to] systemic cooperation encouraged Japanese firms to enter certain foreign locations, especially favoring Asia, and helped to provide an infrastructure that allowed them to maintain their 'Japanese-ness'" (Westney, 2001: 635).

4.2.6 The internationalization of the JMM

Japan's emergence, underpinned by a new and original productive model, had a massive impact on all production systems worldwide. In the 1994 book, *Global Japanization*, Williams *et al.* declared: "Japanese manufacturing now has the same international status as American manufacturing in the first half of the century; its factories are sites of international pilgrimage and its manufacturing practices are objects of emulation." Even in the industrial relations sphere, the Japanese strongly influenced the way in which industry operates worldwide (Cole, 1989).

Japanese management practices were initially considered to be locally ingrained. They then gained remarkable attention from scholars and business people in the 1980s. Even if the collapse of the Japanese economy, in the 1990s, led to a decline in Japan's popularity as a role model, the practical impact of the JMM is still growing. For example, the westernization of the basic concepts of the Japanese production system through the lean production model, popularized in the book *The machine that changed the world* (Womack *et al.*, 1990) is still in its dissemination stage. Having first been absorbed by the manufacturing industry, it then spread to the process service industries.

It seems plausible to state that the resurgence of the resource-based view of the firm (RBV, mentioned in Chapter 2), was influenced by Japanese success. For instance, Prahalad and Hamel's works were inspired by Japanese firms in terms of "core competences" and "strategic intent" (Prahalad and Hamel, 1990). In the case of Brazil, after their unsuccessful attempt to internationalize in the 1980s, Japanese MNEs became a new role model, as we shall see.

4.3 The emergence of Korean multinationals

4.3.1 The characteristics of Korean industrialization

Despite the rising presence of Korean brands in virtually all market segments in most countries and the expansion of Korean firms' subsidiaries even in advanced nations, Korea is still in a kind of intermediary position. It is a high-income member of the Organization for Economic Cooperation and Development (OECD) and classified as an advanced country by both the United State's Central Intelligence Agency (CIA) and the International Monetary Fund (IMF). Nonetheless, many still put Korea in the group of emerging countries.

The Korean industry followed a path that was a hybrid between the Japanese and the Western styles: strong governmental policies to catch-up followed by internationalization, picking-up winners as large conglomerates, and disciplined monitoring. On the other hand, the Korean management model was deeply influenced by the American tradition blended with traces of the local culture.

By the end of the 1980s, Alice Amsden (1989: 9) provided an important comparative analysis of Korean industrialization in relation to that of other developing countries. Her main arguments were the following:

(1) In the countries that were late industrializers, the state intervenes through subsidies to modify the relative prices and thus stimulate economic activity; in Korea, in exchange for subsidies, the state imposed performance standards upon private-sector firms.

(2) The expansion agent in all late industrializers is the modern industrial enterprise; in Korea, it takes the form of conglomerates with diversified businesses, called *chaebols*. Their magnitude and diversity is comparable to that of the Japanese *zeibatsu*. A *chaebol* is a Korean business group. It encompasses many subsidiary firms under the same name. "Chaebol originally meant money clique in Chinese and was used to refer to a group with a vast fortune" (Chang, 2003: 9).

(3) The engineers are the key personages in the late-industrializing countries, since they are the agents of the transfer of technology from abroad; in Korea, engineers had an exceptional performance because society invested heavily in their education right from elementary school.

(4) The late industrializers had an exceptionally well-educated work force relative to the early industrializers.

Amsden (1989: 14) notes that:

government discipline and the emerging large conglomerates were interactive. The large conglomerates (*chaebols*) consolidated their domain little by little, responding to exceptional stimuli in terms of exports, R&D or new product launches. The leading enterprises were rewarded with authorization to expand, which further increased their size. In recognition of their entry into areas that involved challenges and risks, the government rewarded entrants with other licenses for working in more profitable sectors, which resulted in the rising diversification of industrial conglomerates.

A study of the 108 largest Korean *chaebols* revealed a direct relation between their business volume and their diversification strategies. Whereas the larger *chaebols* generally pursued a growth strategy based on unrelated products, the smaller ones had a dominant product line (Chang, 2003: 9).

4.3.2 The internationalization of Korean firms

The internationalization of Korean firms took off between 1990 and 1996, when investments abroad outdid foreign investments in Korea's domestic market.

The year of 1994 was an inflection point where the internationalization of the Korean economy is concerned, thanks to the Kim Youn Sam administration establishing a policy called *segyehwa*. This determined that all social, political, economic, and cultural sectors had to become internationally competitive (Masiero, 2003). However, as a result of the Asian economic crisis, Korean OFDI slowed down somewhat, given that the emerging Asian economies had been the favorite destination.

In 1998, Kim Dae Jung became the head of a government that inherited the effects of the Asian crisis from the preceding administration and implemented a number of measures with the help of the IMF. One of the chief ones was to restructure the indebted *chaebols* and the financial sector. After the negotiation of the debt and the transfer of assets among the five main *chaebols* of key industries, a new cycle of economic and *chaebol* expansion began. In 1999, Korean gross domestic product (GDP) grew by 10.89% and, in 2000, by 8.81%. This was due to increased exports, the main products of which were semiconductors, computers, and communication equipment. Moreover, domestic demand also rose, indicating the end of the recession.

The recovery of Korean OFDI occurred soon after the early years of the 2000s, so much so that, in 2003, Korean enterprises reached

Table 4.2 *Korea – FDI flows, by region and economy, 2005–7 (US$ m)*

	2005	2006	2007
FDI inflows	7,055	4,881	2,628
FDI outflows	4,298	8,127	15,276

Source: UNCTAD (2008).

Table 4.3 *Entries by South Korean firms by region*

Region	Number of entries	Date of earliest entry	Mean date of entry
Asia	1,011	1981	1996
North America	284	1980	1995
Western Europe	117	1980	1995
South America	77	1981	1995
Eastern Europe	44	1989	1997
Australasia	27	1987	1994
Africa	19	1988	1995
Middle East	5	1994	1997

Source: Chang and Delios (2006: 35).

their highest level of OFDI since the 1990s. In the subsequent years, growth was also noteworthy, as Table 4.2 shows.

In terms of investment destination, Asia received some 64% of OFDI, followed by North America, with 18%, and Western Europe, with 7%. The Korean firms focused most of their FDI on the emerging economies of Asia, South America, and Eastern Europe, contrary to the Japanese firms, which mainly targeted the developed Europe (21%) and North America (50%) (Chang and Delios, 2006). These authors counted 1,587 subsidiaries of Korean enterprises worldwide (Table 4.3).

The most internationalized Korean firms are those in the electronics industry. If we rank order them, starting with those with the largest investments abroad, we have: first, LG Electronics; second, Samsung Electronics; and fourth, Daewoo Electronics. The third most internationalized firm is Daewoo Motor (Chang and Delios, 2006). However,

Table 4.4 *Korea – number of cross-border mergers and acquisitions, seller/purchaser, 2005–8*

	2005	2006	2007	2008[a]
Seller	41	44	30	20
Purchaser	32	56	56	29

Source: UNCTAD (2008).
[a] Jan–Jun.

in 2001, General Motors (GM) acquired most of the Daewoo assets (some 67%), forming GM Daewoo. The remaining 33% are held by the Korean Development Bank and other Korean entrepreneurs. China is the main destination of LG and Samsung investments. In terms of the number of countries with subsidiaries, Samsung ranks first, operating in thirty-two countries, followed by LG, in twenty-four, and KIA Motors, in eleven.

The expansion pattern of these firms in other countries generally consists of, first, maintaining a strong exporting orientation; this is followed by FDI, to support the growth of exports. Greenfield investments have become the most common type since the 1990s, but the number of mergers and acquisitions (Table 4.4) has also grown in recent years (Chang and Delios, 2006).

4.3.3 Korea: technology-driven internationalization

In sum, in macroeconomic terms, Korea grew substantially in recent years and managed to quickly overcome the Asian crisis. One can say that Korea's growth since the 1970s is the outcome of the government's sequence of development policies. The focus of industrial policy is currently telecommunications, a field in which Korean firms stand as world leaders.

What sets Korea apart from other developing nations is that ongoing government support for a small group of industrial conglomerates was indeed provided in exchange for exceptional performance, as measured by production management and operations, rather than by financial indicators.

4.4 The internationalization attempts of firms from third world countries

4.4.1 *The spread of third world MNEs in the early 1980s*

The phenomenon of developing countries' enterprises investing overseas is not entirely novel. For instance, Argentina offered scattered examples of this by the early1900s.

However, in the late 1970s and early 1980s, "the number of foreign ventures by genuinely indigenous firms from a wide range of developing countries ... increased dramatically [although] this is not predicted by the normal postulates of international or development economics" (Lall, 1983: 1) At least two-thirds of this outbound investment went to other developing countries, as South–South investment.

An initial interpretation of this phenomenon was provided by Louis Wells. His argument began with the notion that while multinationals from developed countries have been especially likely to seize on products, processes, or marketing techniques that appeal to a high-income market or save skilled labor, the markets of the developing countries, however, remain quite apart from those of the industrialized countries. The differences seem to lead to identifiable types of innovations by firms in the developing countries. The argument in this study is that when they go to other developing countries, the innovative multinationals from emerging countries have found that their differences provide an edge over potential local competitors and over multinationals from advanced countries. According to Wells (1982), these advantages are essentially related with competences developed for small production runs using low cost labor.

The 1983 book by Lall, *The new multinationals: the spread of third-world enterprises*, briefly recovers what this period consisted of in regard to three countries, Argentina, Brazil, and India, and discusses the appropriateness of Wells' argument.

Argentina is considered a pioneer among developing countries when it comes to internationalization. From 1900 to 1930, the firms that led this process were Alpargatas (textiles, headed primarily toward Brazil), Bunge y Born (foodstuffs, textiles and chemicals, also headed toward Brazil) and SIAM di Tella. In 1928, the Argentine manufacturer SIAM di Tella established a subsidiary in Brazil to produce gasoline pumps. At about the same time, the company set up manufacturing projects in Chile and Uruguay and commercial offices in New York and London (Wells, 1982: 1). According to Katz and Kosakoff (1983: 165), at that time, those firms truly ran "model factories" by international standards.

The second period, from 1969 to 1980, involved a different group of companies from different industrial segments, including petroleum exploration and extraction, foodstuffs, paper and publishing, pharmaceuticals, and wine. The expansion of Argentinean enterprises favored Latin America. The other countries that hosted Argentinean investments were Spain (publishing), Italy (foodstuffs), and the US (oils and fats). However, the entire movement had very little significance for the local economy and even less for the total Latin American economy: "Total accrued FDI over a 15-year period barely comes to 0.5% of one year's industrial exports" (Katz and Kosakoff, 1983: 145).

The (non-financial) Brazilian MNEs were still at a rather incipient stage where the number of firms is concerned and as a percentage of the total value of exports. Construction and engineering firms predominated. Manufacturing firms were moving at a much slower pace. The cases of the manufacturing firms identified at that time (Caloi, a bicycle manufacturer, Securit, a supplier of metal office furnishings, and Gradiente, an electronic appliances producer) were short-lived in terms of international operations. Other cases, such as MetalLeve (auto parts) and Tigre (building materials with a plant in Paraguay) lasted longer.

As for the Indian MNEs, in the early 1980s:

> there were over 100 Indian enterprises or business groups engaged in foreign operations. Some are relatively small enterprises that have drifted into overseas investment by dint of historical accident or due to the peculiar temperament of the entrepreneur concerned. Some are medium-to-large specialized firms that have gone international to exploit their accumulated knowledge of a given activity. And some are parts of enormous conglomerate business houses that have gone abroad as a conscious strategy of group diversification and growth. Lall (1983: 31)

India's investments abroad were quite concentrated in three groups: the Birla Group ("a metals powerhouse"), the Thapar Group (various businesses; textile-led internationalization), and the Tata Group. The three groups accounted for 40 percent of total investment abroad. The affiliates were located in neighboring countries and more than 60 percent of them were very small-scale operations. Lall identified thirteen ventures that were quite respectable in comparison with affiliates of the "real" MNEs in the small host countries frequented by Indian firms.

4.4.2 The catch-up efforts during the 1980s

The weaknesses revealed by the results above drove the emerging countries and their firms to engage in considerable catch-up efforts, in order to establish a sustainable competitive presence in the international arena. Three aspects must be highlighted: technological upgrading, management upgrading, and policy-making.

As had been the case of Japan, but on a different scale and with different intensity, the developing or third world countries invested in technology catch-up. Whereas previously research into technology in the third world focused largely on issues related to the transfer and choice of technology from abroad, in the 1980s, attempts were made to understand how imported technology was assimilated and adjusted to suit local circumstances, and how technological improvements were brought about.

Lall (1992: 166) declares that "a number of 'unconventional' approaches to the issues of technology in developing countries have arisen. These have assigned a central role to indigenous technological efforts in mastering new technologies, adapting them to local conditions, improving upon them, disseminating them within the economy and exploiting them overseas through the growth of manufactured exports."

The author analyzes firm-level technological capabilities (FTC) as well as national technological capabilities: "these are not simply the sum of thousands of individual firm-level capabilities developed in isolation. Because of externalities and interlinkages, there is likely to be synergy between individual FTCs" (Lall, 1992: 169). At the country level, capabilities were grouped under three headings: physical investment, human capital, and technological effort. Here, the author analyzes how they were influenced by incentives (of a macro-economic nature, competition related, or derived from market factors) and institutions.

In the case of Latin America, a program of studies about the technological capacity of firms in different industries (steel, pulp and paper, machinery, etc.) in the 1980s concluded that the operating conditions of these enterprises were entirely different from those found in developed countries. This led the local firms to operate using highly idiosyncratic technologies and to invest in rather unusual training programs. The size of the markets, the complexity of vertical integration, and the outsourcing difficulties (all of which could not be solely ascribed to the lack of materials and to the profile of the local manpower), as well as the impact of government policies, called for a large-scale, in-depth learning process.

The assessment of Desai (1984: 260) concerning India is similar. Meanwhile, Russia, within its political and economic regime, developed cutting-edge know-how in certain sectors, such as in the aerospace industry. As for China, its case is different, as we will discuss in Chapter 10.

These efforts were crucial for firms to face up to the technical barriers to internationalization that had been raised by the developed countries to replace and complement tariff barriers, since the early 1980s:

Local industrial locations are increasingly tied into two dimensions of global governance that are ignored by the established discourses on the world economy. These two global governance structures are instrumental in shaping the development dynamics and scopes of action. First, regions are increasingly integrated in global value chains often marked by networks and other forms of private governance. Second, global technical, social, and ecological standards are becoming increasingly important in world trade. Messner (2004: 5)

Thus, the evolution of third world countries' technological capabilities followed a certain path and had a certain timing, both of which were different from those experienced by Japan and Korea. Nevertheless, these capabilities were eventually acquired and became one of the pillars of the internationalization of their firms.

Concerning management upgrading, global acknowledgment of the Japanese production model shattered the hegemony of the Fordist model as the sole efficient way of organizing a firm, and unveiled new prospects for developing country enterprises.

At the same time, the intrinsic difficulty of transferring and adopting the JMM drove firms to really look for and develop their own style of management. In this process, they made ample use of the Japanese organization techniques, creating specific and unique management models, adjusted to the reality of their respective countries.

For instance, the dissemination of the Japanese techniques in Brazil was extremely fast. As far back as 1982, the number of active quality control circles in the country's firms was already the second largest in the world, only trailing behind Japan itself. The National Quality Award was instituted almost at the same time as the Malcolm Baldridge Award in the United States. The major Brazilian firms, especially those that were state-owned at the time (Petrobras, Companhia Vale do Rio Doce, and Embraer, among others) would come to be quality disseminators in the country.

Finally, it is important to note that in each emerging country a key date marked an inflection in the adopted model, redirecting the efforts to achieve economic and industrial development. China's economic reform, including changes in the ownership and governance of its enterprises, dates back to the late 1970s. In India, the striking event was its new industrial policy, released in July 1991, which imprinted a new shape upon the local economy. A particularly important fact was the demise of the "license raj," a system of licenses that had been in place since independence and that made the state an omnipresent party that intervened in all economic activities. In Brazil, this special date was the beginning of 1991, when protectionist barriers fell along with subsidy mechanisms, and when the ports were opened to international trade. These subjects will be resumed and developed in later chapters.

4.5 Lessons learnt from successful internationalization in the 1980s

This second internationalization wave was enormously important for all the dimensions of the study and practice of internationalization.

Japan and Korea showed:

- the feasibility of autochthonous industrial development based on local firms, capable of doing without foreign MNEs to drive the development process, and able to compete with them in international markets and in their home countries; although these home-grown enterprises lacked the marketplace muscle of the MNEs, they overcame the early-movers in their home territories, even in industries that developed countries considered proprietary;

- the importance of government support or of synergy between the macro, meso, and micro plans for project success;
- the possibility of developing internationally competitive enterprises in unendowed countries; and
- that technological leadership is not an essential factor for internationalization.

The shared features, which in this case could be classified as country-specific advantages, are the cultural and political factors, government support, and qualified human resources. These are the cornerstones of firm-specific advantages.

Furthermore, Japan revealed a new organizational model, that propounded externalization rather than internalization. Japanese MNEs emerged as the bearers of a new micro, meso, and macro organization. The Korean ones were not as detached, but with tenacity and discipline the Korean MNEs were put on the map.

Meanwhile, Brazilian MNEs, as well as most of the other third world country MNEs, paid dearly for their lack of competitive strengths and flaws related to the absence of organizational competences and global mindsets. It took another round of catching-up and restructuring for the emerging countries to breed multinationals with a strong foothold in the international markets.

5 On the threshold of the third wave: productive globalization and new multinationals

5.1 Pioneering fleets reequip and change route in increasingly contested waters

In the early 1990s, some companies which had been the role model for the development of management were facing a profound crisis; among them General Motors (GM), Sears and IBM. "GM, at the end of the 1980s, set a new record for the amount of money lost by a corporation in one year, and then it broke its own record in the following year. While other factors contributed to this disaster, GM's long, painful decline through the 1980s was mostly due to the mismatch of its organizational design choices." (Roberts, 2004: 40). Sears, which together with GM was one of the role models for America in the 1960s (Chandler, 1962), started divesting itself of many non-retail divisions, which were creating a burden on the company's bottom line. In 1993, it stopped producing its general merchandise catalog because of sinking sales and profits. In 1990, IBM, the "big blue", also faced a financial turmoil. The turnaround required a sort of shock therapy, with an outsider coming from Nabisco, a biscuit and cracker manufacturer, assuming as new chief executive officer (CEO). He produced a successful revolution in the company's organizational culture, leading IBM toward a new global market positioning. In summary, the changes which had been occurring in the global context challenged the existing management models, demanding their restructuring. Following the same trend, governments of developed countries had to reassess their development policies, prospecting which would be the future industries in order to support companies and help build a competitive edge. This broad revision and repositioning movement of countries and corporations was called productive restructuring.

This chapter has three objectives. The first, of a descriptive nature, emphasizes the changes which took place in American and European multinational enterprises (MNEs) as of 1980. The second objective is to synthesize how these companies searched for new management models in order to remain competitive in the new global economy. We initially highlight how the companies were internally restructured and how this impacted the organization of their international activities. The third objective is to demonstrate how changes within MNEs from developed countries opened space for new multinational companies in emerging countries.

5.2 Productive globalization and organizational restructuring

5.2.1 Early-movers search for new management models

When the changes in the global scene formerly mentioned spread to the developed countries, the first reaction from their corporations, especially from American companies, was to reinforce the technological dimension of their competitive strategies by exploring the then new and exciting microelectronics technologies. GM, for instance, invested US$84 billion in factory automation projects in the 1980s. GE defined its strategy as "supplier of factories of the future" and made a number of acquisitions, including Calma, one of the largest and most promising industrial automation companies. Following suit, the company built its highly automated factory, touted as the next generation in manufacturing. The prototype robotic facility never took off and has since been sold as office space.

Fiat built two new plants in southern Italy to produce cars which were "hand-built by robots," but they never became operational. At the same time, FIAT chose a Brazilian subsidiary to run experiments with as yet unknown Japanese management techniques. Results in the Brazilian operation were favorable and later on proved to be of importance to the company's survival and global restructuring, which followed.

With the questioning of former role models, new ones started being identified: Disney, Apple, 3M, McDonalds (Peters and Waterman, 1982); Ford, Xerox (Dertouzos *et al.*, 1989), Asea Brown Boveri, International Service System, 3M (Ghoshal and Bartlett, 1997), among others.

The automation investment debacle, the growing presence of Japanese companies in the international arena, and the characteristics observed in new role models, led to the conclusion that the solution for the crisis lay in restructuring organizations before adopting new technologies. In-depth diagnoses and suggestions to indicate which path should be followed by the MNEs from developed countries during their restructuring process depended on the perspective adopted by analysts and decision-makers.

First in the US, then in France, think tanks emerged to ponder how to behave in light of the changing environment and the growing Asian threat. Among the reports generated by such groups, those with greater impact were: *"Made in America: regaining the productive edge"* (Dertouzos 1989) and *"Made in France"* (Coriat 1993). They diagnosed the reasons behind productivity losses in these countries and proposed a series of measures to make these economies gain competitiveness and counteract "Made in Japan."

The creation of the Massachusetts Institute of Technology (MIT) Commission on Industrial Competitiveness, which prepared the report, *Made in America* was justified on this basis: "Late in 1986 the MIT convened its first commission on a major national issue since World War II. We did this to address a decline in US industrial performance perceived to be so serious as to threaten the nation's economic future." (Dertouzos *et al.*, 1989: ix). The study conducted by the MIT commission focused on eight sectors deemed to be "core" industries, among them automotive, machinery and tooling, semiconductors and chemicals. By and large, the diagnoses were incisive; for instance, the American automotive industry which "for 40 years was a system that worked brilliantly, works no more. The Japanese found a better way." (Dertouzos *et al.*, 1989: 19). For the capital-goods industry the assessment was also bleak: "It is not possible to be a world-class manufacturing [nation] without world class tools. Yet, the American machine tool industry is dissolving" (Dertouzos *et al.*, 1989: 20).

The propositions generated by this commission were strongly influenced by the Japanese Management Model (JMM), as shown in Table 5.1. These recommendations meant a significant shift from the Fordist model. The underlying competences for the companies' competitive strategies would have to be considerably altered.

Other analysts assumed that technology was the most relevant facet to explain the crisis and the need for change. Using Schumpeter's approach and the long economic cycles model, they explained that the crisis stemmed from the saturation of technologies based on fossil fuels

Table 5.1 *Guidelines proposed by the MIT Commission on Industrial Competitiveness (1988)*

Switch to the new fundamentals of manufacturing	Simultaneous improvement in cost, quality, and delivery
	Staying closer to the customer
	Closer relationships with suppliers
	Using technology for strategic advantage
	Flatter and less compartmentalized organizations
	Innovative human resources policies

Cultivating a new economic citizenship in the workforce
Blending cooperation and individualism
Learning to live in the world economy
Providing for the future

Source: Dertouzos *et al.*, 1989.

used by products and mechanisms with low energy efficiency coupled to the worn-out Fordist model of industrial organization. Promoting the recovery of economic activities into a virtuous circle would entail the pervasive use of microelectronics technology (non-polluting and low-energy-use heartland technologies) and the dissemination of a new entrepreneurship model including the collective entrepreneur. This argument strengthened the sunrise industries to the detriment of the sunset industries. Sunset industries of the future would be the mature, low-growth industries, like shoes, textiles, steel, and others. In contrast, sunrise industries would be younger, high-growth industries, like computers, consumer electronics, semiconductors, and digital equipment.

Finally, some propositions blended technology and organization. The most radical one was upheld by Hammer and Champy, in "*Reengineering the corporation: a manifesto for business revolution,*" a classic from 1994. The authors' argument was: "America's business problem is that it is entering the twenty-first century with companies designed during the nineteenth century." Reengineering was the radical redesign of a company's processes, organization, and culture, abandoning the most basic notions on which the modern organization is founded: the division of labor, the need for elaborate controls, and the managerial hierarchy, because those would no longer work in a world of global competition and unrelenting change. The authors introduced the notion of process orientation, of concentrating on and rethinking end-to-end activities which create value for customers. The business processes were to be conceived from a "blank sheet" (thus abandoning any past experience in regards to the organizational design), utilizing as much as possible the emerging information technologies.

As such, in the 1990s, the developed country multinationals started a deep restructuring process which encompassed their international operations and led them to rethink their production systems and organizational designs. As of this period, an intense phase of experimentation has been witnessed, with companies developing organizational models in accordance with circumstances and resources. Although final results differ greatly, some of the principles followed by the companies can be detailed, as will follow in coming sections.

The emergence of the Japanese Management Model had profound impacts, not only on the practical level of organizations' headquarters from developed countries, but also on the international management strategies and models. "Given that the MNE theory from the 1960s and 1970s strongly emphasized product innovation as the key firm-specific advantage with which a company could expand abroad, [one must admit] how much the Japanese firms' ability to ground a competitive advantage on process innovations and the organization of work changed our models of multinational enterprise – and indeed our models of strategy – in the 1980s and 1990s" (Westney, 2001: 628).

The development of new management models in Western corporations considered three perspectives of the restructuring process: upstream restructuring, that is, how companies rethought and reorganized activities related to obtaining required inputs; downstream restructuring, that is, how companies rethought and reorganized activities related to clients and markets; and indicators restructuring, that is, how companies reconceptualized their performance indicators. This process redefined their architecture of competences, which shall conclude this section.

5.2.2 Upstream restructuring: focusing, partnering, and outsourcing

The term "focused factory," was introduced in a 1974 *Harvard Business Review* article authored by Wickham Skinner. Responding to what the popular press called a "productivity crisis," he advised that to compete effectively, firms had to focus the entire manufacturing system on a limited task that is precisely defined by the company's strategy, technological competences, and economic resources. Skinner urged manufacturers to learn to focus each plant on a limited, concise, manageable set of products, technologies, volumes, and markets. He also encouraged firms to learn to structure basic manufacturing strategies and supporting services so that they focus on one, specific, manufacturing task instead of upon many inconsistent, conflicting or implicit tasks. In other words, focus and externalize rather than internalize to expand.

Two decades went by before Skinner's proposition was accepted by the companies. It seems fair to say that the escalation of the productivity crisis in the 1980s, the debacle of the automation projects and the demonstration effect of Japanese companies were the main factors which changed the mindset of Western executives.

GE's case is once again illustrative (Figure 5.1). The left column shows the acquisitions made during the 1980s, a period in which the company was diversifying its portfolio. The right column shows the divestitures during the 1990s, from which a large share involves acquisitions from the previous period, demonstrating a new market positioning based on core competences.

In practice, what was at stake was how to deal with the basic production decision: make-or-buy? The focused factory prioritizes making whatever is associated to the company's core competence and/or whatever adds more value. A supplementary factor to this decision-making is: who is going to be the supplier for the items no longer produced within the company's facilities? As a consequence, partnering and outsourcing practices emerged, once again influenced by the Japanese Management Model.

Business alliances are partnerships in which two or more companies invest their resources but maintain their individual strategic autonomy. Therefore, alliances include negotiations between partners of similar size and/or leverage, addressing specific products or markets. There are numerous types of alliances, from technology transfer agreements to complex joint ventures. The international business literature gave high priority to this subject; the book *Alliance advantage: the art of creating value through partnerships*, by Doz and Hamel (1998), is one of the most representative of that trend.

MAJOR ACQUISITIONS ($21 billion total)	MAJOR DIVESTITURES ($11 billion total)
• Calma (CAD/CAM equipment) • RCA (NBC Television, aerospace, electronics) • Intersil (semiconductors) • Employers Reinsurance Corp. • Decimus (computer leasing) • Kidder, Peabody (investment banking) • Polaris (aircraft leasing) • Genstar (container leasing) • Thomson/CGR (medical equipment) • Gelco (portable building leasing) • Borg-Warner Chemicals (plastics) • Montgomery Ward Credit (credit cards) • Roper (appliances) • Penske Leasing (truck leasing) • Financial Guaranty Insurance Co. • Thungsram (ligth bulbs) • Burton Group Financial Services • Travelers Mortgage (mortgage services) • Thorn Ligthting (light bulbs) • Financial News Network (cable network) • Chase Manhattan Leasing • Itel Containers (container leasing) • Harrods/House of Fraser Credit Cards	• Calma (CAD/CAM equipment) • RCA Globcomm International • GE Solid State (semiconductors) • Central Air Conditioning • Pathfinder Mines • Broadcasting Properties (non-RCA TV and radio stations) • Utah International (mining) • Housewares (small appliances) • Family Financial Services • RCA Records • Nacolah Life Insurance (RCAs) • Coronet Carpets (RCAs) • Consumer Electronics (TV sets) • Carboloy (industrial cutting tools) • NBC Radio Networks • Roper Outdoor Lawn Equipment • Ladd Petroleum (oil exploration and refining) • RCA Columbia Home Vídeo • Auto Auctions (auctions of used cars)

Figure 5.1 GE's investments in the 1980s and divestitures in the 1990s
Source: Bartlett and Wozhi (2005: 98).

Outsourcing was a practice widely used in the 1990s. Prevailing wisdom dictates that those who can best do a job are specialists. Hence, "the shift from economic reasoning that sponsored the self-sufficient large organization, through the internalization of transnational requirements, led to the resurgence of outsourcing" (Kakabadse and Kakabadse, 2002: 190). The values involved in outsourcing are huge, as shown by Table 5.2.

Asian countries are the primary choice for offshoring strategies, especially in the manufacturing and infotech industries.

5.2.3 Downstream restructuring: servitization and productization

Servitization is a recently coined term, which aims at describing a movement that may be connected to customer-oriented strategic positioning. In times of global competition, companies find that they are

Table 5.2 *Outsourcing ... a twenty-first century phenomenon (estimated values involved in offshoring according to industry)*

Logistics and procurement	$179 billion	Includes just-in-time shipping, parts purchasing, and after-sales repairs
Manufacturing	$170 billion	Contract production of everything from electronics to medical devices
Infotech	$90 billion	Software development, tech support, website design, IT infrastructure
Customer care	$41 billion	Call centers for tech support, air bookings, bill collection, etc.
Human resources	$13 billion	Includes payroll administration, benefits, and training programs
Engineering	$27 billon	Testing and design of electronics, chips, machinery, car parts, etc.
Analytics	$12 billion	Includes markets research, financial analysis, and risk calculation
Finance and accounting	$14 billion	Includes accounts payable, billing and financial and tax statements

Source: Engardio (2006).

rarely able to remain as pure manufacturing firms if they are to survive in developed economies. Instead, they have to move beyond manufacturing and offer services and solutions, delivered through their products. Since virtually every product today has a service component to it, the servitization of products means that companies seek to increase the service offer.

Recent technological developments – especially in data capture and information processing – are enabling firms to develop new business models, exploring the potential of information technology (IT) products. For example, Rolls-Royce Aerospace no longer sells aero engines, it offers a "TotalCare Solution", whereby customers buy the capability the engines deliver – "power by the hour." Rolls-Royce retains responsibility for risk and maintenance, generating revenues by making the engine available for use. Other traditional "manufacturing" firms, such as IBM, have fundamentally reinvented themselves as service businesses, moving away from the production of hardware to offer business solutions. Others have integrated service operations with traditional manufacturing. For example, BP and Shell both manufacture oil, yet they also run extensive retail service operations.

Meanwhile, the so-called pure service providers, such as banks, retail and others, for different reasons, have faced increasingly competitive environments. Consequently, they started to adopt approaches and techniques developed for manufacturing firms to increase productivity. For example, lean techniques, which were developed for auto manufacturing systems, are currently applied in banks, hospitals, commerce, etc. Banks now offer their services as products and product managers are responsible for portfolios of products. Sometimes this is called the productization of services.

Zarifian (2001: 69) foresees the emergence of an "industrial production of service model," that is, the production of a service which incorporates in its technologies, social organization, and performance criteria, principles which are similar to those found in a large industry, however modified according to the specific features of the service sector. Therefore, the old dichotomy between product and service is being replaced by a service–product continuum.

5.2.4 *Indicators restructuring: financialization*

Still during the 1990s, the value concept stood out in companies' practices and academics' analyses. Expressions such as "add value" and "generate value" started to be used in people's and organizations' day-to-day activities. This resulted in changes in how companies defined objectives, structured activities, calculated their performance indicators, and communicated to stakeholders. In the operational field, a

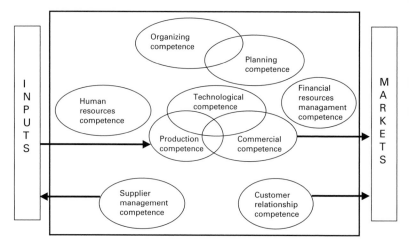

Figure 5.2 The generic competences of a firm

whole set of new methods and techniques started to prevail, beginning by the activity-based costing up to the balanced scorecard (BSC).

Nevertheless, other authors, such as Capelli (2009: 9), admit that the emphasis placed on financial indicators revealed a new economic order, the so-called financialization, which replaced the Fordist model:

A further evolution of the USA [business] model in the 1990s centered on the goal of securing greater importance for profit as the primary goal of business, in contrast to earlier "stakeholder" models, which asserted that business had many stakeholders other than shareholders and that the interest of these different stakeholders had to be balanced. This new approach became known as "financialization" because of this emphasis on financial goals and the pursuit of shareholder value.

5.2.5 A new architecture of organizational competences

The new characteristics desired by companies from developed countries allow us to identify nine different generic competences of a firm (Figure 5.2).

These competences are organized in four blocks (Table 5.3). The first block encompasses the two key competences needed in formulating, implementing, and managing the business model: the planning and organizing competences. A business model is a framework

Table 5.3 *The profile of corporations' organizational competences*

Business model	Planning competence	Establish and implement business strategies; core function: planning
	Organizing competence	Establish and implement management systems; core function: organizing
Operations	Technological competence	Add value to products and processes; core functions: research and development and engineering
	Production competence	Do things (goods and services); core functions: production and logistics
	Commercial competence	Deliver (goods and services); core function: sales
Support	Human resources management (HRM) competence	Capture, develop, and compensate human resources; core function: HRM
	Financial competence	Resource allocation and investment; core function: finance
Market relationships	Customer relationship management (CRM) competence	Bring the company close to its customers; core function: marketing (market intelligence)
	Supply chain management (SCM) competence	Implement and manage a network of suppliers; core functions: purchasing and inbound logistics

for creating economic, social, and/or other forms of value. In the most basic sense, a business model is the method of doing business by which a company can sustain itself, that is, generate revenue. The term business model is thus used for a broad range of informal and formal descriptions to represent core aspects of a business, including purpose, offerings, strategies, infrastructure, organizational structures, trading practices, and operational processes and policies. The business model spells out how a company makes money by specifying where it is positioned in the value chain. The planning and organizing competences are the most deeply related to the business model.

The second block includes the competences related to the realization of any product or service life cycle, namely, product (and service) development, production, and sales.

The third block covers the support functions to other competences and is in charge of screening, identifying, internalizing, adapting, and making available the best practices needed for efficient performance in each of the other competences. It includes the financial management and human resources management competences.

Finally, the fourth block reflects the technological and organizational changes made during the productive restructuring period and includes supply chain management as a competence to organize and manage upstream activities and customer relationship management for downstream activities. The supply chain management (SCM) competence, one of the key features of the Japanese management model, gradually became ingrained in the management approach of every firm. The customer relationship management (CRM) competence is associated with the implementation of the servitization and productization approaches in the interface of the firm with its clients.

5.3 New international management models: the multinational as a network of competences

The changes which occurred in the headquarters clearly impacted how these companies reshaped their international activities. Three aspects must be addressed: the headquarter–subsidiary relationship, the international management models, and the development of global production networks.

5.3.1 Subsidiaries recognized as sources of competences

The changes in the headquarter–subsidiary relationships may be ascribed to the crisis faced by headquarters, to the changes implemented by headquarters to overcome the crisis, and, as previously mentioned, possibly to the good performance of subsidiaries even through the crisis. Brazilian subsidiaries, for example, contributed remarkably to the global performance of automotive companies.

Prior to productive restructuring, subsidiaries operated in a relatively autonomous pattern and their organizational structures usually replicated the organizational functions that were found at the headquarters. Porter (1986) characterized those subsidiaries as multidomestic. Then things began to change.

In a longitudinal study carried out in the 1990s (Fleury, 1999), we observed that Brazilian subsidiaries had their relationship with the headquarters modified in many ways. Some became essentially "operational arms" since they kept only manufacturing operations and lost the more strategic, value-adding functions (such as research and development), which were reallocated to the headquarters. These were the tactics adopted by multinationals in the chemical industry, for instance. There were other subsidiaries that kept a relative autonomy regarding design activities and financial investments, as was the case of the automotive industry subsidiaries. Finally, a third group had their role as centers of competences, product developers, and best practice disseminators reinforced. Those were the cases of Siemens and Asea Brown Boveri (ABB) in hydraulic power systems, where the subsidiaries gained a more focused role.

The decisions on focusing, partnering, and outsourcing, as well as the shifts aimed to productization and servitization started to affect the role of subsidiaries. In the chemical industry, for instance, traditional producers such as BASF and Hoechst changed the profile of their product portfolio by focusing on specialty types of products because China and Turkey began producing the same type of commodity fibers they were producing at a more competitive price. Having abandoned the production of those products, both firms decided to sell their Brazilian plants to local entrepreneurs and, from then on, began selling the services required for the efficient and continuous operation of those and other plants in South America.

The greater diversity of functions the subsidiaries started performing and the different types of relationship with the headquarters led authors to realize that subsidiaries had become recognized as self-purposeful units: "In the literature the terms subsidiary 'strategy' and subsidiary 'role' are often used interchangeably but the distinction is more than semantic. Role suggests a deterministic process whereby the subsidiary fulfills its 'imposed' function; strategy suggests a higher degree of freedom on the part of the subsidiary management to define its own destiny" (Birkinshaw and Morrison, 1995).

Typologies of subsidiaries were then produced. Birkinshaw and Morrison (1995) proposed a threefold classification: local implementer, specialized contributor, and world mandate. Ferdows (1997) identified six types: offshore, source, server, outpost, contributor, and lead plant. The generic roles differed in two dimensions: the competence available in the subsidiary and the importance of the local environment where the subsidiary operates to the overall strategy of the MNE.

The variables which define the headquarter–subsidiary relationship were gradually identified and conceptualized. They are introduced in Table 5.4.

The first three variables are a prerogative of the headquarters; the last three are characteristics of the subsidiary. Competitive environment and business network refer to the subsidiary dynamics with components of the local environment. Initiative may be understood to be a result of this set of factors affecting performance plus a component associated to the specific management style.

5.3.2 Competences development and transfer within the MNE network

A competence developed in one unit – headquarter or subsidiary – may be transferable, or not, to other units, thus multiplying the competitiveness of the multinational as a whole. Using a typology proposed by Rugman and Verbecke (2001), we will categorize organizational competences as local, non-local, and specific.

Non-local competences are those created and developed in one unit and transferred to other units around the world. If one subsidiary is able to replicate a competence developed in the headquarters of an automobile manufacturer, for example, that is a non-local

Table 5.4 *Variables which define the type of headquarter–subsidiary relationship*

Autonomy	The degree of freedom that the subsidiary has in order to make decisions recognized by the headquarters.
Integration	The way in which organizational systems and procedures involve both headquarters and subsidiaries; communication is the key dimension.
Entrepreneurial orientation	General positive attitude at headquarters regarding new business opportunities being created and led by the subsidiary; involves trust and social capital.
Competitive environment	Countries with a strong competitive context are more favorable for local or global initiatives due to local factors, especially for the exploitation of market niches.
Business network	Relationships with business partners such as suppliers, financial and research institutions. The greater the embeddedness of a subsidiary in the foreign country networks, the greater the possibility of gaining access to resources capable of assuring the development of local or global initiatives.
Initiative	A discrete and proactive undertaking, that advances a new way for the corporation to use and expand its resources; an enterprising behavior that might be not encouraged by the headquarters.

Source: Borini *et al.*, (2009).

competence. The opposite may also happen, that is, a competence created and developed in a subsidiary is transferred to other multinational subsidiaries, or even to the headquarters. This would be the case of a subsidiary located in a highly competitive environment that is able to develop competence in prospecting customers that is superior to the level existing in other units and transfer that competence to them.

Other competences carry only local value. For example, the headquarters may develop some kind of competence that is irrelevant to the subsidiaries, because the competence is exclusively regional. The competence in human resources management is an example usually mentioned. Therefore, the multinational has a local competence when the headquarters and the subsidiaries develop strictly local competences instead of global ones.

Finally, it may happen that a subsidiary or the headquarters develop a competence that would be extremely useful for other units, but due to the specifics of such competence, its transfer is unfeasible. These are the so-called specific competences. The transferability, or not, of the Japanese Management Model is a good example. It is a model that was developed for the Japanese context, with peculiarities related to culture, religion, and the company's background. Even Japanese subsidiaries found difficulties in replicating the headquarters' model.

Therefore, the question of transference is essential to distinguishing the specific from the non-local competence, both potentially applied worldwide. However, only the second of those would be suitable for transfer.

5.3.3 The MNE as a network of competences: new international management models

The first multinationals chose to organize their international activities either in one single international division, or in divisions per products, or else per geographical regions. Stopford and Wells (1972) stated that the choice would depend on two factors: foreign product diversity and foreign sales. Later, a third factor was identified, namely the percentage of foreign manufacturing. In any case, the idea was that the subsidiaries' network structure and operation was defined by the headquarters.

Table 5.5 *International management models*

Type	Key features
Multidomestic	Autonomous subsidiaries; high responsiveness to local demands.
Global	Build cost advantages through centralized global scale operations.
Transnational	Exploit knowledge and competences through worldwide diffusion and adaptation.
Metanational	Speed in combining knowledge from different parts of the world and roll out the results throughout the world.

Sources: Bartlett and Ghoshal, 1998; Doz *et al.*, 2001.

As of the mid-1980s, new MNE organization logic is identified. Based on longitudinal studies of renowned global companies such as GE and Procter & Gamble, it was observed that the adopted organizational architecture became the one that best adjusts to the corporation's international strategy, which should respond both to pressures for local responsiveness and to pressures for global integration. ABB, led by Pierce Barnevik, was the most-mentioned role model in studies about multinationals during the early 1990s.

These studies lead to the identification of international management models, as presented in Table 5.5.

In the *multidomestic model*, subsidiaries have to serve their local markets in a differentiated way and there is little integration with the headquarters. This implies the existence of competences in subsidiaries that will guarantee a competitive edge to face local competition. Subsidiaries act as isolated companies that may receive investment from the parent company if their performance meets or exceeds expectations. Due to elevated autonomy and low integration between subsidiaries and headquarters, and among the subsidiaries themselves, competences developed in subsidiaries are exclusive, that is, they are not transferred.

Low integration does not allow headquarters or other subsidiaries to recognize the potential of competences developed locally. In cases where this potential is recognized, the autonomy and the low level of value-sharing between subsidiary and headquarters or among subsidiaries hinder the competence transfer to other units. Even if these challenges are overcome, high levels of involvement in the local market may be an obstacle to competence transfer, as market conditions (partnerships, customer behavior, and competitors' standards) are not identical.

On the other hand, in the *global model,* competence transfer follows a unidirectional path, from center to periphery. Strong communication, shared values, credibility deposited in subsidiaries, and world standards in the search for global efficiency are elements that facilitate competence transfer. However, the lack of autonomy, together with standardization, requires that subsidiaries rely on competences developed at headquarters.

Subsidiaries may develop competences, but it is a development aligned and led by the parent company, which for some strategic reason is then developed in the subsidiary. This may be justified by lower development costs, adequate and cheaper external services, and tax-free research investments, among other reasons.

The third model is the *transnational* one, which is capable of adding the global and multidomestic models in a configuration that accommodates different types of subsidiaries with different types of relationships with the headquarters.

In the configuration of differentiated network, the relations between headquarters and subsidiaries are not uniform, which implies a more complex management style. The question of autonomy and integration, for example, is outlined differently: one subsidiary may present strong integration with the headquarters and little autonomy, whereas another may be highly autonomous and less integrated.

The question of competence development and transfer also becomes more complex. Competence distribution is fundamental to understanding the role and importance of subsidiaries. Depending on the resources and competences owned by a subsidiary, it may play different roles and be managed in different ways. This means that the internal organization of subsidiaries may vary considerably since, in differentiated networks, competences are located in different subsidiaries so that each may use their best abilities to contribute innovation to the headquarters. This scheme avoids the concentration or duplication of resources, minimizing costs, and maximizing efficiency.

Finally, the *metanational model* proposes to solve two points left untouched by the previous models: the insertion of companies in global business networks as a source of knowledge and competences and the governance relationship between parent companies and subsidiaries in competence development and transfer.

According to Doz *et al.* (2001), the greatest challenge faced by multinationals is developing global learning. In the metanational strategy, the multinational has the notion that the competitive advantage is not created only by headquarters or by major subsidiaries, but rather by each and every subsidiary, including those that were typically global or multidomestic subsidiaries only a while ago. This goes against approaches that advocate determined roles for subsidiaries and supports the evolutionary theory of competence development in any kind of subsidiary without previous acknowledgment or authorization.

A critical differential of the metanational strategic model is its focus on discovering and exploring hidden knowledge all around the world, as opposed to the transnational strategy model, which defends learning from a particular subsidiary as being of greater strategic importance. Hence, in the metanational model, entrepreneurial orientation is not exclusive to a particular subsidiary, but rather destined to all. As for autonomy and initiative, this approach presents itself as the best way for headquarters to induce strategic importance and for subsidiaries to seize it. Without autonomy and initiative, new organizational competences are unlikely to arise.

Thus, competences in the metanational model are developed both at headquarters and at subsidiaries of multinationals, including branches that have not yet received a strategic role of global importance but have developed their own initiatives for the creation of competences. The metanational model acknowledges the importance of actors external to the corporate network: subsidiary partners and the context in which they are operating. In other words, the places where subsidiaries and headquarters operate become equally important for corporate strategy. Hence, competences may be created by both headquarters and subsidiaries and valued equally regardless of origin.

A consequence of this process of strategic assignment arising from competences is the fact that the strategic role is emergent and transitory. The strategic role is emergent in as much as it depends on the development and ability of transferring competence instead of on a strategic assignment by the headquarters. The strategic role is transitory because once the competence has been created and transferred it has to be reinvented, or another competence has to be created to ensure corporate competitiveness, a process in which subsidiaries may win or lose their strategic roles according to their competence contribution to corporate strategy.

Three implications arise from the proposed configuration (Borini, 2008). First, each location of the network operation has to accept and appreciate the interdependency with the others; no unit alone has all competences necessary to develop an independent operation. Thus, competence transfer is essential; subsidiaries' initiatives together with a global entrepreneurial orientation should increment the creation of competences in different locations.

Second, in spite of the autonomy given to subsidiaries, each location should be receptive and flexible enough to adjust to innovation flows, ensuring efficient and scaled diffusion. Communication should be easy, frequent, and free. There should be no barriers to knowledge flows because the reason of existence for each one of the units is to help knowledge-building.

Third, because each location has its own values and contributes to the network, each subsidiary needs to constantly evaluate and renew its organizational competence. It requires continuous local learning to be able to reinvent competences.

Given this scenario, it is possible to understand the metanational mentality: "think locally and act globally." This means thinking locally about how to develop context-aligned and networking relevant competences that may contribute to the overall performance of the multinational.

As a last observation, it is important to highlight that each model implies its own concept of management style. The multidomestic model allows for a variety of styles, within a broader laissez-faire style: subsidiaries are autonomous to develop their own style according to the local operation context. In the global model, general principles are dictated by headquarters, but changes are permitted according to local conditions. In the transnational model, the parent company will take over the task of managing a diversity of management styles, seeking an optimal solution to the whole system. Finally, in the metanational solution, there is a question of sharing and cross-fertilization which, in fact, would be a management meta-style in the sense that it accommodates different forms of acting and increases the synergy between the parts.

5.3.4 Global production networks of competences

The result of focusing, outsourcing, offshoring, and partnering was the construction of global production networks. Global production networks can be defined as systems of operations with pivotal points in production processes, supply of inputs, production, and distribution across the whole spectrum of activities in the world economy. Each link is itself a network connected to other nodes, concerned with related activities. Such networks are increasingly important in the contemporary production of goods and services.

Global production networks have three main dimensions: (a) an input–output structure (i.e., a set of product and services linked together in a sequence of value-adding economic activities); (b) territoriality (i.e., spatial dispersion or concentration of production and marketing networks, comprised of enterprises of different sizes and types); and (c) a governance structure (i.e., authority and power relationships that determine how financial, material, and human resources are allocated and flow within a chain) (Gereffi, 1994).

Those networks are usually led by MNEs and their subsidiaries, which perform the central role and determine what will be produced, how and where. They decentralize and allocate the supply operations, production, and distribution by subcontracted companies in different countries, and control the activities generating higher value and performing a leading role in the productive chains.

It is important to observe that in addition to the traditional producer-driven production networks, buyer-driven production networks are now quite common. They are found in industries in which large retailers and brand-named marketers play a central role in the decentralized production networks located in several export countries, usually in the developing world. This industrial system controlled by commerce is often intensive in labor, at least in some of its phases, and typical of the consumer goods industries, such as apparel, shoes, and toys.

The positioning of each company in the global production network depends on their competence profile. Tables 5.6 and 5.7 were developed in a study about the positioning of Brazilian firms in global production networks in different industries: production-driven networks (automotive and electro-electronic) and in buyer-driven networks (apparel and shoes). What the tables show is the core competence

Table 5.6 *Core competences and strategic positioning in producer-driven networks*

Position	Production competences	Product development competences	Marketing competences
Leader	Strong (specifies, organizes, and controls)	Strong in product specification	Mass marketing for large markets
First tier	Strong	Strong in product design	Customer orientation
Second tier	Strong	Not required	Customer orientation

Source: Fleury and Fleury (2000).

Table 5.7 *Core competences and strategic positioning in buyer-driven networks*

Position	Production competences	Product development competences	Marketing competences
Leader	Supply chain management mainly	Product design and specification	Customer relationship
First tier	Strong (organizes and controls)	Not required	Customer orientation
Second tier	Strong	Not required	Customer orientation

Source: Fleury and Fleury (2000).

required for Brazilian enterprises, positioned in the first or second tiers of global production networks.

5.4 Multinationals from emerging countries appear on the horizon

Until the early 1990s, there was a widespread perception of developed countries as homes of MNEs and emerging countries as hosts of MNEs and "this was firmly rooted in empirical reality" (Dunning, 1993).

At that time, the literature characterized enterprises from emerging countries as: (a) mature and integrated enterprises which grew on protected or uncompetitive markets (Bartlett and Ghoshal, 2000); (b) based on natural resources and utilizing low-cost labor; (c) lacking technological capabilities (Dunning, 1993); (d) laggards in terms of managerial capabilities (Bartlett and Ghoshal, 2000); and (e) embedded in turbulent environments (Khanna and Palepu, 1999).

Without entering the merit of that outdated characterization, we observe that currently companies from emerging countries resort to internationalization under conditions radically distinct from the ones faced by those enterprises that pioneered internationalization, the so-called "early-movers." Among others, we highlight the following factors to explain the differences: (a) today there is excessive production capacity for goods and services, which creates fierce competition among global players and requires permanent orientation toward innovation; (b) established multinationals coming from developed countries are in the process of reviewing and redefining their organizational architectures, focusing on value-added activities, and trying to establish and lead global value networks (Gereffi *et al.*, 2005); (c) governments are interfering in the internationalization process, in order to meet their national development goals (Dunning, 1993) ; and (d) the economy is experiencing a stage in which institutional mechanisms that moderate the international trade are being consolidated at the global and regional level, strongly affecting developing countries (Messner, 2004).

In addition to questions related to the international context, firms coming from emerging economies such as Brazil, Russia, India, and China (the BRICs), usually face challenges related to the institutional context (Khanna and Palepu, 1999) in their domestic markets that are different from the ones faced by companies in developed countries. The local volatile and unpredictable context might be threatening, on the one hand, but also seems to qualify late-movers from major emerging economies to search for opportunities and deal with adversities differently from companies originated in developed countries. In a certain sense, the internationalization of firms from emerging countries might be a way to mitigate the turbulence faced in their domestic markets.

However, in today's global economy, the multinationals from emerging countries play more than a secondary role, as they lead several industries, such as mining (BHP-Billington, from Australia; Vale, from Brazil), steel (Arcelor-Mittal, from India), beverages (AB-Inbev, from Brazil and Belgium; SAB-Miller, from South Africa), oil and gas (Gazprom, from Russia), and cement (CEMEX, from Mexico), among others. In some cases, certain sectors in developed countries are controlled by multinationals from the emerging countries: Tenaris, from Argentina, and Gerdau, from Brazil, for instance, are the largest producers of drawn steel pipes for the US building industry.

This rapid growth of companies from emerging countries took policy-makers, researchers, and even managers of other multinational companies by surprise. Companies that were once considered laggards, performing in less developed contexts, suddenly started to challenge the global leaders.

Emerging country multinationals were then (re)defined as:

international companies that originated from emerging markets and are engaged in outward FDI [foreign direct investment], where they exercise effective control and undertake value-adding activities in one or more foreign countries. [Due to their origin and development] their "springboard" behaviors are often characterized by overcoming their latecomer disadvantage in the global stage via a series of aggressive, risk-taking measures by proactively acquiring or buying critical assets from mature MNEs to compensate for their competitive weaknesses. Luo and Tung (2007: 482)

This phenomenon generated new research questions: do multinationals from emerging countries have distinct characteristics from the classic multinationals? What factors justify their growing competitiveness in global markets? These questions generated new research approaches, capturing the common features of these new multinationals (Mathews, 2006; Cuervo-Cazurra, 2007, Guillen and Garcia-Canal, 2009).

To answer these questions, we will analyze the case of Brazilian multinationals in the coming sections. We examine the internationalization processes, based on a historical contextualization, and identify country-specific advantages and disadvantages. We will stress that the distinctive element in the internationalization of Brazilian companies – and what characterizes their own way of "walking" – is that their management model was self-developed, based on an original combination of organizational competences and management style.

We will show that emerging multinational companies, in order to compete at the same level of the major players in the global market, had to break the rules of the game, that is, they innovated in the development of niche markets or innovated radically in mature markets.

The concepts highlighted in the previous sections will be used in the study of Brazilian multinationals. We will organize the analysis by differentiating between three different stages in their trajectory: pre-internationalization, entry stage, and expansion.

PART II

Multinationals from Brazil and other emerging countries

6 The environment in which Brazilian firms grew

6.1 Brazil in the internationalization waves

This chapter aims at briefly describing Brazil's political, economic, and social development, in order to put the emergence of its multinational enterprises (MNEs) into context.

The presentation of Brazilian history is divided into periods aligned with the dynamics of internationalization waves. Brazil performed differently in each one of them. During the first wave, in the 1950s and 1960s, Brazil was essentially a receiver of foreign direct investment (FDI), playing host to new subsidiaries of foreign MNEs. During the second wave, in the late 1970s and early 1980s, isolated and unsuccessful attempts of native Brazilian firms to move into international markets took place. Finally, the third wave, in the 1990s and 2000s, is producing an effective internationalization movement.

More specifically, this chapter will focus on the evolution, as from the early twentieth century, of Brazilian firms and MNE subsidiaries, all of which had to operate within a complex institutional context whose main feature was uncertainty and discontinuity. It is within this context that Brazilian companies are born and evolve, i.e., in competition with foreign MNEs, to then grow into Brazilian MNEs. It is within this competitive system that local firms develop their competences and draft their internationalization strategies.

6.2 Brazil: from the colonial period to the second world war

6.2.1 Brazil's position in the international context

One can say that since its discovery in 1500, Brazil has always been involved in globalization-related issues.

In the fourteenth century, Portugal and Spain threw themselves into maritime navigation, in the urge to discover and incorporate into their territory the Indies, those countries with the spices that the

Europeans sought. They then pressured the Pope, Alexander VI, to split the world into two with the Treaty of Tordesillas: the eastern half would go to Portugal and the western half to Spain.

In 1500, the Portuguese navigator Pedro Alvares Cabral, in an attempt to sail to India, reached the coast of an unknown country whose natives lived in rather primitive conditions. He called these natives "Indians" and took possession of the lands to the east of Tordesillas for Portugal.

From 1500 to 1822, Brazil was a Portuguese colony based on the exploitation of natural resources. Whereas in North America the colonizers sought to build a new model of society, in Brazil, the land was parceled up into strips called *capitanias hereditárias* (hereditary captaincies), each of which was given by the King of Portugal to a noble family for its commercial exploitation.

The first type of riches exploited was Brazil wood, which lent its name to the country. Europeans valued this wood greatly for the highly appreciated red ink that it yielded. Besides the extraction of minerals, in particular gold, silver, and precious stones, agricultural commodities (first sugarcane, then coffee) also accounted for the generation of wealth. The exploitation system was based on large plantations and slave labor.

The country suffered through Dutch and French invasions, but the Portuguese managed to hold their Brazilian colony up until the early nineteenth century, when the heir to the Portuguese crown, D. Pedro I, proclaimed Brazil's independence. From 1822 to 1889, the country had a monarchic regime. The two emperors that reigned during this time were descendants of the Portuguese royal family. The republic was proclaimed in 1889, one year after the demise of slavery, Brazil having been one of the last countries to abolish it.

6.2.2 The political, social, and economic context

Although it became independent in 1822, Brazil's economy only began to develop truly as of the middle of the nineteenth century. Despite the efforts of the Barao de Maua, mentioned in the Introduction, and other not-so-known entrepreneurs, the agricultural and exporting sector was the only relevant one in economic terms until the end of the 1920s. Initially, the chief exports were rubber, sugar, cotton, tobacco, cocoa, mate tea, leather, and hides. As of the late nineteenth century, coffee became the most important and dynamic product, the engine driving Brazil's exporting economy.

The expansion of the exports of unprocessed products encouraged the diversification of the country's economic activities and modernized the economy. Income grew and with it the domestic market, the demand for wage goods, machines, and equipment. Investments in infrastructure and the monetization of the economy came as a consequence.

In the late nineteenth and early twentieth centuries, the trade of coffee involved a number of intermediaries. After being grown in single-culture plantations maintained with slave labor, coffee was carried by rail (the tracks often passed by the plantations themselves) to the ports of Santos or Rio de Janeiro. At the port, prior to being exported, it was warehoused in a commission house and only then was it sold to the exporters. The coffee brokers in general were Portuguese and Brazilian tradesmen, or major farmers who had diversified their activities by going into trading. The transportation and sale of Brazilian coffee to the European centers of consumption was conducted largely by foreign maritime carriers, especially by the English. For example, the E. Johnston & Sons coffee trading company started operating in Brazil in 1820 and by about 1870 had become one of the largest Brazilian coffee exporters (Jones, 2002).

In 1907, of the ten largest exporters, only one, Prado Chavez, was a Brazilian company. All the others belonged to foreigners, such as Theodor Wille (German), or Neumann & Gepp, E. Johnston & Sons, Knoules & Foster, and Wilson, Sons & Co (all four of them English). The last two specialized in trade between Brazil, Portugal, and England (Jones, 2002). Foreign sales generated huge profits for these trading firms, since the price of the coffee itself was often manipulated by the exporters.

Immigration incentive policies became stronger as of the second half of the nineteenth century. European immigration, in particular, was widely subsidized by the Brazilian government, which paid for the immigrant's passage and the initial costs incurred by the immigrant farm workers. The government even devised public projects to provide work for them. Those who came from Germany went mainly to the south of Brazil, where Spanish influence was stronger, whereas the Italian immigrants – in particular the anarchists – tended to go to the southeast. At the inception of the twentieth century, Japanese immigration began. Those immigrants, who went largely to the coffee plantations, helped improve the quality of agricultural production. When they migrated to the cities, they started engaging in industrial manufacturing activities and in commerce, thus also helping to make Brazil's economy more dynamic.

During Brazil's imperial period and after the republic was proclaimed, Brazilian government policies were important not only to support immigration but also to stabilize the price of coffee in the international markets. Coffee prices oscillated, however, as a result of international demand conditions and the world's economic cycles. It was incumbent upon the Brazilian government to establish policies to protect the production and commercialization of coffee in Brazil; in a way, these policies proved to be efficient until the 1929 crisis.

The 1929 crisis strongly affected coffee exporting and revealed the need for an industrial base capable of fulfilling the most pressing demands of the local society, thus substituting imports.

The post-1930 type of industrialization was qualitatively different from what had come before. Prior to 1930, industrial growth had been induced through the local income growth that had resulted from the export sector's expansion. According to Simonsen (1969), "Brazil adopted a policy of import substitution industrialization as of 1930. However, until the end of World War II, this was not associated with a long term development philosophy but consisted of a series of individual reactions to trade balance difficulties. Only after World War II did the notion that industrialization should drive the country's economy become firmly ingrained" (Simonsen, 1969).

In the industrialization of the early twentieth century, the technical and financial scale required for industrialization to progress exceeded the capabilities of the local capitalists by far; the only way to implement major industrial projects was through the state. This went hand-in-hand with the nationalistic proposals put forth by Getulio Vargas, when he was President of the republic.

Thus, in the 1940s, Companhia Siderúrgica Nacional, Companhia Vale do Rio Doce, and Petrobras, were created as state-owned companies in sectors regarded as strategic for the country (Table 6.1).

In 1952, the government created the Banco Nacional de Desenvolvimento Econômico (BNDE; the National Economic Development Bank), the aim of which was to provide support for enterprises in the industrial and infrastructure fields.

Table 6.1 *Main state-owned enterprises founded in the 1940s and 1950s*

State-owned enterprise	Foundation date	Industry
Companhia Siderúrgica Nacional (CSN)	1941	Steel
Companhia Vale do Rio Doce (CVRD)	1942	Mining and ore
Petrobras	1953	Oil

6.2.3 FDI and the action of MNE subsidiaries

From 1860 to 1889, licenses were granted for the opening of 137 foreign companies, of which 111 were English (Jones, 2005). Most of the firms were in the financial sector, such as banks and insurance companies (Lacerda *et al.*, 2006). The banks that set up operations in Brazil also operated in the main European financial centers of that time and justified FDI as support for commercial transactions.

Foreign investments in Brazil for the financing of infrastructure also increased. In practice, the creation of an infrastructure and of urban public services in the cities with the largest populations was conducted by foreign firms (energy, urban transport, rail, and the construction of ports). For instance, Brazilian Traction Light and Power, an American-Canadian firm, opened its São Paulo branch in 1899 and its Rio de Janeiro branch in 1905. Soon thereafter, it overtook American Foreign Power (Amforp), acquiring total control of the power industry in these two cities.

The flow of foreign investments became greater after the first world war. FDI from England reached £110 million, and from the US $193 million in 1929. "Generally speaking, the average yearly inflow of foreign capital into Brazil ranged from 65 to 75 million dollars, most of which went into industry" (Lacerda *et al.*, 2006). The arrival of the pioneering subsidiaries from MNEs in Brazil dates back to those times.

European MNEs preferred resource-seeking investments. In 1923, an English company, British-American Tobacco, started building Latin America's largest cigarette factory. Affiliates were established in Brazil by enterprises from the US, such as Armour (meat), and from Belgium, such as Belgo Mineira (metal works); in the electrical sector, Siemens and Philips established operations; in the chemical field, Rhone Poulenc; and in pharmaceuticals, Parke-Davis. In addition, the installed capacity of the affiliates of power companies was also increased.

The investments from North America were already centered on modern manufacturing concerns. In the automotive sector, the firms that first established themselves in Brazil were Ford (1919), General Motors (1925), and B. F. Goodrich (tires) and, in the agricultural machines sector, International Harvester.

One should stress Argentine investment, as far back as that time. In 1887, the German-Argentine firm Bunge y Born established the Moinho Fluminense flour mill in Rio de Janeiro. The first major footwear company, São Paulo Alpargatas, was created with Anglo-Argentine capital.

In the services sector, one must stress the 1913 inauguration of the first department store: a subsidiary of the Mappin Group, created in Sheffield in 1774. As the trade of the time was in the hands of small local tradesmen, Casa Anglo-Brasileira, or Mappin Department Stores, became a symbol of modernity, operating in down-town São Paulo until 1999.

When the first world war started, however, European FDI decreased. The 1929 crisis further enhanced the difficulties surrounding international transactions. During this time span, MNEs responded to the unencouraging foreign environment by becoming increasingly national. Thus, FDI coming into Brazil was insignificant in the 1930s and 1940s.

6.2.4 The birth of Brazilian companies

The Brazilian transformation industry was created by two groups of entrepreneurs: the coffee growers and the immigrants, in particular those of European origin. Warren Dean (2001) observed a direct relation between the growth of coffee exports and industrial development. He highlights that the so-called coffee barons invested in banks, railroads, immigration, and, to a lesser degree, the textile transformation industry. One of them began producing cement in 1897.

The coffee growers stood out as a new entrepreneurial class, as compared to the northeastern mill owners. They invested in infrastructure to the benefit of their businesses and had a greater commitment to economic policies and to promoting immigration (Furtado, 1999). The immigrants trod a different path. Many arrived in Brazil to work on farms and little by little managed to migrate to the cities. Others arrived in Brazil as importing and exporting tradesmen. All shared the hope of getting rich fast. In so far as their capital grew, they began organizing their own firms, often with the aid of an inflow of foreign capital, whether provided by companies or by banks. The companies Dell'Acqua (Italian) and Societé des Sucreries Brésiliennes (French), and the banks Banca Commerciale Italiana (Italian) and Brasilianische Bank fur Deutschland (German) were important players.

The Brazilian companies created at this time aimed at the local markets for essential goods, such as clothing, footwear, food, beverages, printing, furniture, and, in the metal-working industry, the manufacturing of parts for setting up sugar mills, cereal mills, and coffee processing plants.

Box 6.1 The Brazilian MNEs created during this time

Gerdau

Grupo Gerdau started in 1901, with Fábrica de Pregos Pontas de Paris (a nails plant), in the city of Porto Alegre, the capital of the state of Rio Grande do Sul. It was born out of the entrepreneurial vision of João Gerdau, a German immigrant who moved to Brazil in 1869. It was only four decades after it was founded that the decisive stage of its business expansion took place, when it acquired Siderúrgica Riograndense (metal works) and thus embarked upon its successful path toward becoming a steel production group. Thanks to this acquisition, Grupo Gerdau adopted the technology of mini-mills, characterized by employing electric arc furnaces, and using scrap metal as raw material.

Votorantim

In 1917, the Portuguese immigrants Pereira Inácio and Nicolau Scarpa took advantage of the bankruptcy of Banco União (a bank) to acquire in an auction the textile firm Votorantim, São Paulo's second largest company in this field. By that time, they had already gained control of eight of the fifteen cotton mills in the state of São

Paulo. In 1925, Pereira Inácio's son-in-law, J. Ermírio de Moraes, became the company's managing director and subsequently its sole owner. And, in 1939, still in the small town of Votorantim, a cement plant was founded that in the 1990s would be responsible for the group's internationalization.

Brahma

In 1888, Joseph Villiger, a Swiss immigrant, established Manufactura de Cerveja Brahma Villiger & Companhia (the Brahma Villeger and Company Brewery). In 1894, a new firm succeeded Joseph Villeger's pioneering initiative; the brewery Georg Maschke & Company. It then perfected the production of beer, imported equipment, and sponsored bars, restaurants, clubs, and artists, taking a strong foothold in the Rio de Janeiro market. Almost at the same time, in São Paulo, the Antarctica brewery was founded.

Antarctica

The Portuguese immigrant Joaquim Salles, along with other partners, established Antarctica in 1885, in the city of São Paulo. At first, the company was a hog slaughterhouse, but it also owned a small ice factory with spare capacity. This awakened the interest of the German brewer Louis Büchner, who had owned a small brewery in 1868. The two entrepreneurs formed a partnership and in 1891 they created Companhia Antarctica Paulista. This was set up as a corporation with sixty-one shareholders and it imported equipment from Germany in order to modernize beer production.

6.2.5 The inception of the national innovation system

Brazil's first university was created in the late nineteenth century, in Rio de Janeiro. Previously, there had been stand-alone schools of law, of mining, and of engineering. The Polytechnic School of the University of São Paulo was modeled on the Zurich Polytechnic, in 1894, and was geared toward civil engineering. The first research institute, Fundação Oswaldo Cruz, which targeted the study of so-called tropical diseases, was founded in 1913.

In the early 1930s, two institutes were set up in São Paulo: Instituto para o Desenvolvimento da Organização Racional do Trabalho (IDORT;

the Institute for the Development of Rational Labor Organization) and Instituto Roberto Simonsen (the Roberto Simonsen Institute), to disseminate the Taylor–Ford industrial organization model and to train management and labor. This project also had the political objective of countering the pressures of the union movement, which reflected anarchist influence brought by the Italians and had already shown its muscle in the country.

In 1942, Serviço Nacional de Aprendizagem Industrial (SENAI; the National Industrial Apprenticeship Service) was instituted through a decree of President Getúlio Vargas, obliging all industrial firms to make a financial contribution to the institute.

The 1930s saw the creation of the University of São Paulo and, in 1950, Instituto Tecnológico de Aeronáutica (ITA; the Technological Institute of Aeronautics) was created, with the Massachusetts Institute of Technology (MIT) as its role-model. Subsequently, in the 1950s, the government set up agencies to promote scientific research of a more academic nature, along the lines of the French model. In 1951, Conselho Nacional de Pesquisa (CNPq; the National Research Council) was created, with the mission of coordinating and encouraging scientific development. This was also when Coordenadoria de Ensino Superior (CAPES; the Higher Education Coordination Office) was set up, to ensure the training and qualification of university professors.

6.2.6 The transition to an industrial economy starts

Within the long time period that characterizes the beginnings of domestic industry the Brazilian companies operated basic technologies in traditional industries, and coexisted with a few MNE subsidiaries, both in manufacturing and in services.

In the value chains that were then established, there was already a clear predominance of foreign companies in the positions of governance: in the exporting and commercialization of coffee and other unprocessed products, in the importing of products with a higher added value, not produced in Brazil, and even in the local assembling of products designed in other countries.

The local firms focused on basic manufacturing, such as the textile, cement, and footwear industries, and on making basic inputs for industry and construction. Nonetheless, some of them would turn into Brazilian multinationals (BrMNEs) a century later.

On the institutional front, the government started playing an active role and embraced the cause of industrialization as a symbol of progress. Meanwhile, because of its populist character, it created labor regulations of a paternalistic nature. However, these clashed with the business thinking of the time, which espoused Taylorism–Fordism as a symbol of modernity and this conflict has underscored labor relations in Brazil ever since.

Studies of Brazilian industrial evolution during this time led to the development of what conventional wisdom has named the "theory of adverse clashes." This assumes that industrialization started as a response to the importing difficulties that arose out of the first world war, the great depression of the 1930s and the second world war.

This forms the basis of the theory of dependence, or Commission Economica Para America Latina (CEPAL) doctrine, the chief argument of which concerned the pattern of foreign trade relations among the "central" (industrialized) countries and the "peripheral" nations (i.e., Latin America). This supposedly generated an international division of labor that forced the peripheral countries to specialize in the production of primary goods to be exported to the central countries, which, in turn, supplied manufactured products to the peripheral ones. According to the terms of CEPAL's political economics, the "decision centers" of the economies of these peripheral countries lay abroad, thereby transforming them into "reflex and dependent" economies. The change to a new, "inward looking" pattern of growth would only become possible through industrialization, which would take place as the peripheral countries adjusted to the successive waves of foreign unbalance driven by the adverse clashes.

This theory influenced government operations during subsequent periods and led them to set up protectionist mechanisms.

6.3 Hosting the early-movers aiming toward industrial development (1950–70)

6.3.1 Brazil's position in the international context

From the end of the second world war until the 1970s, Brazil's international economic relations consisted of cautious and mostly defensive insertion in the global economic order (Almeida, 2007).

In regards to both goods and services, the first phase of the above-mentioned insertion was carried out with limited participation in the most dynamic commercial flows. The exports portfolio remained limited and was relevant only with regard to certain traditional commodities (coffee in particular). However, toward the end of this period, manufactured products started to creep into these exports.

On the other hand, inward FDI rocketed from an average of $64 million a year, from 1950 to 1955, to an average of $150 million a year, from 1956 to 1960. Brazil's dependence on foreign capital, know-how, and technology started to accelerate.

6.3.2 Political, social, and economic evolution

During this time, Brazil reached a new level of industrial progress, symbolized by an accelerated development project, by rising urbanization and by the strengthening of the imports substitution model. Thus, President Juscelino Kubitschek's administration (1956–61) was characterized by fast industrialization ("50 years in 5").

Between 1956 and 1961, the growth of the Brazilian economy achieved the most spectacular levels in 50 years. GDP expanded at the yearly rate of 7 percent. Industrial growth reached 11.1 percent a year, while the primary sector grew at the rate of 5.8 percent a year. The development formula adopted was industrialization at any cost, based on high import duties and tax incentives, as well as major public projects. Simonsen (1969: 42).

The price of fast industrialization was a strong FDI inflow (Figure 6.1).

In the 1960s, Brazil went through a period of turbulence that ended with the 1964 military coup. The country's macroeconomics had already changed: "As of 1962, growth rates became much less spectacular, leading some pessimistic analysts to propose a peculiar thesis, that of the structural stagnation of the Brazilian economy" (Simonsen, 1969: 43). However, industrial development resurged under a new philosophy, based on national sovereignty and security doctrines, five-year national development plans, and national science and technology development programs, all of which were put in place. The chief priority became the creation of infrastructure and the expansion of basic input industries, local companies having a larger

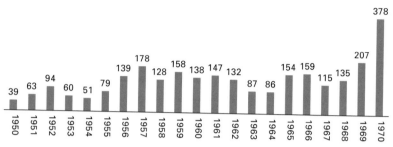

Figure 6.1 Inward FDI in Brazil, 1950–70 ($ million)
Source: Almeida (2007).

share of this. Nevertheless, MNE activities via their subsidiaries continued to increase substantially during this period.

The expansion of the late 1960s and early 1970s gave rise to the so-called "Brazilian Miracle" period, during which the country grew at annual rates of roughly 7 percent yet again.

Meanwhile, the urbanization process caused commerce to grow, as up-to-date forms of services organizations started to appear concurrently.

6.3.3 Subsidiaries and local companies play different roles in industrial development

The durable consumer goods industry (especially the automotive and white goods segments) was appointed the driver of Brazilian economic development. Its formation was supported by a large inflow of FDI: new MNE subsidiaries started to operate in the country and the MNEs already active in Brazil reorganized their operations.

The decision to rely on foreign MNEs to lead the industrialization process coincided with the aims and strategies of MNEs from the most advanced countries, which were expanding abroad at that time. From the Brazilian standpoint, it carried, implicitly, the idea that they would transfer the resources and competences that were needed to upgrade local industry. It was also convenient for Brazilian industrialists, who preferred to be involved as financial partners in the large investments required for the establishment of greenfield-type plants rather than being directly responsible for the creation or management of those enterprises. MNE investments in Brazil at the time came mainly from companies from the US (General Motors (GM), Ford, Whirpool, TRW, and Tecumseh) and from Germany (Volkswagen and Mercedes-Benz in 1953, and Bosch in 1954). Some Scandinavian firms, especially those of Swedish origin, were already established in Brazil: Ericsson (1924) and Electrolux (1926). In the automotive industry, Scania entered the country in 1957 and Volvo in 1979. The Japanese investment was of minor importance.

A number of Brazilian firms became important suppliers for the above mentioned subsidiaries: MetalLeve, Vargas, Cofap, and Sabo, in the automotive industry, and WEG and Embraco in the white goods industry. Nonetheless, the leading role remained in the hands of the subsidiaries of MNEs.

At the time of the military take-over, there was a general agreement that the supply of durable consumer goods was already settled. The concern was redirected to infrastructure and to the need to develop local firms. Three points merit attention.

First, in relation to infrastructural projects such as roads, airports, ports, and damns, Brazilian firms had preferential access. This influenced the growth of two types of local enterprises. In the capital goods industry, the existing Brazilian firms became large, diversified conglomerates that manufactured a broad range of complex products based on mechanical and electromechanical technologies. This was the case of the Villares Group and of enterprises such as Jaraguá and Confab. The second group comprised engineering services firms (such as Odebrecht, Camargo Correa, Andrade Gutierrez, and Promon), which were able build distinctive competences where project development and management were concerned. This last group was the first to go international while the first could not survive the turbulence of the 1980s and 1990s.

The 1960s also witnessed the establishment of the petrochemical industry based on a tripartite model: local private-sector capital and state capital joined foreign partners, who were chosen as technology suppliers (Evans, 1976; Fleury, 1989). Three petrochemical complexes were established around Petrobras' three main refineries. Again, it was assumed that the foreign partners would transfer technology, thus upgrading local enterprises in terms of their production and process competences. Several Brazilian groups joined the program, such as Odebrecht, Ultra, Mariani, and Suzano. Subsequently, when these associations were undone, the program's main drawback surfaced. The production chain had become segmented when it came to governance: Petrobras held the refining monopoly, Brazilian firms were responsible for the first transformation processes, and MNEs took care of the second transformation processes. This resulted in an absence of synergy between the different players in the transformation chain. Of the firms created at that time, two recently embarked upon an internationalization process: Braskem (Odebrecht Group) and Oxiteno (Ultra Group). Their international expansion, however, is heavily influenced and, to some extent, constrained, by their position in the petrochemical production chain.

The third point that deserves attention is the establishment of the Brazilian aerospace industry and, in particular, the creation of Embraer in 1969. The other two firms involved in the industry were Avibras (a producer of equipment for attacks by air, such as land-to-land missiles) and Engesa (a producer of ground military equipment). Unlike the latter, Embraer was a product of the nationalistic period that followed the second world war: in 1950, the government created the MIT-inspired Technological Institute of Aeronautics (ITA). The establishment of Embraer as a state-owned enterprise two decades later, in 1969, was due to the diligent work of entrepreneurs who had been educated within the institute's environment and to the interest of the military government, which envisaged Embraer as a supplier not only of regional civilian aircraft, capable of integrating the Brazilian territory, but also of military equipment.

At that time, Embraer was also seen as the pivot of an ambitious program to modernize Brazilian industry by creating demand for highly sophisticated and precise mechanical systems and components. This objective was not achieved, as local firms had grown accustomed to the automotive industry's high volume and low precision system and were unsuccessful in making the transition to the low volume, high precision standards of the aeronautical industry (Fleury, 1989).

For the military government at that time, two industries were expected to act as "technology-drivers": the aerospace and the nuclear industries. Neither achieved their objectives.

6.3.4 The institutionalization of the national innovation system

At the institutional level, the Industrial Development Council was implemented in 1969 to strengthen private enterprises, in particular domestic ones, whose competitiveness would have to be enhanced along with employment conditions. It was also meant to protect national technology and to absorb technology from abroad in a manner compatible with Brazil's production factors, besides planning the implementation of new production sectors and of more advanced technology, in so far as the dimensions of the domestic market might render them financially feasible.

Thus, on the financing side, Financiadora Nacional de Estudos e Projetos (FINEP; the Research and Projects Finance Agency) was set up in 1967, to manage the funds that were made available at that time.

On the academic side, the first two business schools and the first industrial engineering department were established in São Paulo in the late 1950s, thanks to the encouragement and resources of the Alliance for Progress program, and in the early 1970s, the first research and postgraduate programs in business administration came into being.

6.3.5 The emerging contradictions and ambiguities

During the 1965–80 period, Brazil's manufacturing sector reached an average growth rate of 9.5 percent a year. According to United Nations Industrial Development Organization (UNIDO) estimates, among the developing nations, this figure was only exceeded by South Korea, Singapore, and Indonesia. The industrial structure that resulted from this fast expansion period was not significantly different from that of most Organization for Economic Cooperation Development (OECD) countries. According to the same source, in 1980, the joint share of the chemical and metallurgical-mechanical sectors stood at 59% in Brazil, whereas for the most advanced economies – the US, Japan, and Germany – this figure was 64.4%, 64.5%, and 69.8%, respectively (Ferraz *et al.*, 1996: 55).

It is important to highlight that Brazil's manufacturing sector included Brazilian firms, both from the private sector and state-owned, as well as MNE subsidiaries. The latter remained uncontested in the most technology-intensive sectors.

However, at that moment, the reliance on subsidiaries of MNEs as drivers of Brazilian industrial development would have been questioned if the theories of international business, and particularly Vernon's product cycle theory, were taken into consideration. As explained in previous chapters, in that period of time, MNEs were internationalizing standardized, routine production processes. If the findings of the Nordic school were applied, the conclusions would be quite the same. Consequently, the idea that MNE subsidiaries in Brazil could drive local industrial development within an imports substitution system was somewhat misguided: given the dynamics of international competition, this could only occur on quite a limited scale. What was in fact delivered was explained by sociologists (Lopes, 1964; Rodrigues, 1970): MNEs' subsidiaries created labor-intensive industrial structures that enabled a large contingent of rural workers to migrate into industry. However, technological leadership lay beyond the scope of their roles and competences.

Thus, a contradictory situation was created in which policy-makers regarded MNEs as potential sources of technological innovation, whereas this was entirely outside the range of their intentions. The critiques that arose, however, brandished two banners: de-nationalization and technological dependence.

Concerning de-nationalization, the analyses indicated that foreign capital had expanded as of the mid-1960s. In other words, even with protectionist mechanisms and government support for the growth of home-grown enterprises, the MNE subsidiaries increased, as Table 6.2 shows.

On the other hand, the Brazilian firms also lacked the competences to lead this process. They were predominant in the so-called traditional sectors (timber, paper, furniture, textiles, food, beverages, publishing, and printing), whereas MNE subsidiaries were strong in the more modern sectors that relied on more sophisticated technology (mechanics, pharmaceutical products, and electrical material). As for the state-owned enterprises, they were limited to mining (Vale), oil, chemistry, and metallurgy.

Bielschowsky (1978: 124) voiced an interesting analysis of this situation. Though stressing that the Brazilian economy had little in common with the Japanese economy, he pointed out:

the huge contrast between the Japanese policy of actively creating and absorbing technology, while the Brazilian situation continues to be underscored by

Table 6.2 *The 300 largest companies in Brazil, 1966–72*

	1966	1972
Private-sector Brazilian companies	156	139
Foreign	134	147
State-owned	10	14

Source: Torta and Reis, 1978: 233

passiveness vis-à-vis this issue. This contrast results from the difference in the patterns of capitalistic development of the two countries. In Japan, this was about strengthening Japanese-owned, concentrated industrial capital ... whereas in Brazil, the pattern of capitalistic development is altogether different ... it is one chapter in the larger history of the most recent international capitalistic stage, that of the global expansion of the large multinational concerns.

The conclusion that Bielschowsky (1978: 100) reached is that:

the Brazilian economy continues to follow a path of accruing capital through progressive internationalization, which is further strengthened by the firm support of the dominant economic policy. Thus, one witnesses the peculiar coexistence of a national project aiming at achieving greater technological autonomy with an actual process that is going in the opposite direction.

The outcome of this contradiction was higher imports of production goods, reflecting the local industry's technological dependence and feebleness. Overall, inflationary pressures and the growth of trade deficits came into being. However, the chief problem that expansion generated was the growth of foreign debt. Consequently, the preceding subtle and implicit orientation toward industrial development vanished entirely: short-term economic policies prevailed over any long-term development decisions.

6.4 A poorly exploited opportunity: Brazil during the 1970s–80s world crisis

6.4.1 *Brazil's positioning within the international context*

The elements that typified this period were the changes that were becoming manifest globally as a result of the oil crisis, of the changes in international finances, of the global recession, and of the emergence of new microelectronics-based technologies. This created the internationalization wave that the Japanese companies embraced to their advantage.

From the Brazilian viewpoint, this context heightened the Brazilian debt crisis, which was a direct consequence of the country's process of international insertion, begun back during the days of the economic miracle. This generated a self-sustaining spiral that increased the cost of the country's own debt and led to the deterioration of the terms of exchange. Despite its magnitude and duration, it was essentially a foreign-exchange crisis with huge repercussions on the functioning and evolution of industry.

FDI fluctuated, reflecting the retraction of the early-movers that now embraced an inward-looking position, as they attempted to reposition themselves vis-a-vis the new competition. Thus, incoming FDI reached $3.1 billion in 1982, but dropped immediately thereafter to a meager $0.3 billion in 1986, the lowest figure since 1970 (Figure 6.2).

The novelty, however, was that outbound foreign direct investment (OFDI) started to appear. As we saw in Chapter 4, Brazil's OFDI grew during this period, as did that of other Latin American countries.

6.4.2 The political, social, and economic evolution

The new civilian government established in 1984 believed that as the industrial system was already complete and self-sufficient, long-term planning was no longer required. Therefore, ever since, the country ceased to engage in five-year planning or thematic planning (for science and technology, industry, etc.).

However, if in the previous period Brazil's manufacturing sector had reached an average yearly growth rate of 9.5 percent, the feebleness of the Brazilian domestic market emerged after the turn of the 1980s. The import substitution model had been exhausted, there was a deficient integration with the international markets, and a limited capacity of the domestic firms to develop new processes and products. Those became potential destabilizers of the Brazilian industrialization process.

During the 1980s, Brazil's economy suffered through a period of stagnation with high inflation rates. At first, from 1981 to 1983, the reduction in the pace of growth was ascribed to the adjustment efforts connected with the debt crisis. Then, a stage during which the trade balance was once again positive followed, as the result of a currency

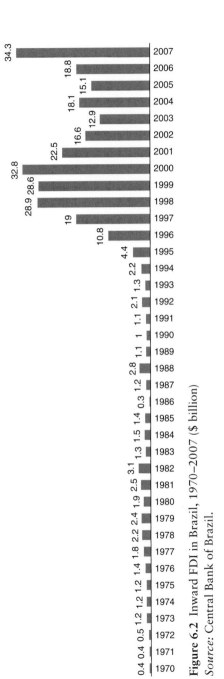

Figure 6.2 Inward FDI in Brazil, 1970–2007 ($ billion)
Source: Central Bank of Brazil.

devaluation. The country resumed growth, based on rising consumption. Toward the end of the decade, as successive inflation-fighting plans failed and as a result of the foreign debt moratorium, the crisis became serious. Inflation, which had already been scaling up since the middle of the preceding decade, increased further and reached critical levels of more than 1,000 percent a year. Companies ceased to be concerned with production issues: the most important thing now was to manage cash on a daily basis.

There was a general understanding that:

the mechanisms adopted to stimulate industrial development in Brazil since the early stages of the import substitution period were highly efficient in terms of production growth but had two negative effects. The first was the mismanagement of issues such as competitiveness (both internal and external) and efficiency, while the second was an anti-exporting culture that predominated at least until the mid 1980s. Bonelli (1997: 42)

Mytelka (1993: 636) argues that Brazil adopted a policy of import reproduction instead of import substitution: "Unlike the import substitution strategies pursued by more successful late-industrializers, the import reproduction strategies took 'product' as their point of departure, rather than 'purpose.' They thus ignored the extent to which products incorporated concepts of functionality, cost, quality, and aesthetics, that correspond to the producer's principal sales market."

In other words, the limited involvement of domestic manufacturers with technological issues, the restrictions to technology importation that ensued from policies and regulations, and the frail institutional support for industrial enterprises gave rise to a context that left Brazil increasingly far removed from the international frontier. The country continued to be dependent on MNE subsidiaries in the more dynamic industries while local firms were relatively accommodated in the remaining ones.

6.4.3 Foreign multinationals hesitate and buyer-driven value chains arrive

When productive globalization led to organizational restructuring at the headquarters in order to face Asian competition and to absorb the

Japanese model, that brought consequences over the operation of the early-movers' subsidiaries.

These had previously enjoyed periods of great autonomy, while their headquarters struggled with issues regarding internal reorganization and international operations.

Some MNEs thought about closing down their Brazilian operations. The emblematic example of this was Ford. The fact that its Brazilian operation was not very important for the corporation had been common knowledge for quite some time. In the early 1980s, when it launched its world car project, Ford decided to exit Brazil. It was only unable to do this entirely because of the contractual commitments it had to dealers and clients. So it established an alliance with Volkswagen, creating AutoLatina. Where the allocation of responsibilities was concerned, Volkswagen took over all the manufacturing, whereas Ford took over the management systems, in particular the financial one.

The story of AutoLatina is usually described as "water and oil": impossible to mix. In 1993 this association was undone, with Ford resuming normal operations in the country. During this time, Volkswagen's Brazilian subsidiary was able to deeply absorb Ford technology. When taking over the Ford truck assembly operations, Volkswagen engaged in reverse engineering. As a result, in just a few years, it launched the first Volkswagen brand truck in the world. Today, Brazil is the only country making Volkswagen trucks and, in the domestic market, it has become the light and medium-weight trucks segment leader.

Still, as we have already mentioned, the subsidiaries were allowed great autonomy, being required primarily to deliver financial results. However, some of them were requested to start experimenting with Japanese production techniques: Fiat, Philips, Johnson & Johnson, and Ericsson, among others.

In the case of the Japanese subsidiaries in Brazil, they were being forgotten, contrary to what was happening elsewhere. Despite the importance of the Japanese firms as bearers of new industrial organization models, a study by the Japanese Ministry of International Trade and Industry (MITI) showed a very different reality in the case of Japanese MNE subsidiaries in Brazil. The first finding was that although Japanese FDI in Brazil was the third largest, behind FDI from the US and from Germany only, the financial performance of the

Japanese subsidiaries was the worst of the nine developed countries
that maintained subsidiaries in Brazil:

The subsidiaries answered that out of their main competitors in the
Brazilian market (except for the other Japanese firms), 59% were foreign-
capital enterprises and 41% were native (Brazilian) companies. Taking into
account that native firms, generally speaking, have lower technological
standards as compared to foreign firms, we found that the Japanese companies are in a position of inferiority. The problem of the technological
level of the Japanese subsidiaries in Brazil is huge. Tanaka and Koike
(1995)

Investigating to what extent these subsidiaries would be disseminators of the Japanese Management Model, Carvalho *et al.* (1996)
found out that relationships between Japanese subsidiaries and local
suppliers hardly featured any features of trust and partnership. To
the contrary, the relationships were tense and conflicted, with the
Japanese subsidiaries behaving harshly, due to an alleged lack of
quality of Brazilian companies. However, the Brazilian suppliers
did not consider the quality of their products unsatisfactory and, as
evidence of this, they pointed out their strong relationship of trust
with other clients (non-Japanese subsidiaries), where quality was
concerned.

Considering the restructuring process that was taking place in
Brazilian industry, the authors conclude that, with the possible exception of Honda in Brazil, the Japanese subsidiaries were laggards
regarding the establishment of networks and the development of suppliers, and that they had virtually no influence on the dissemination
of Japanese management practices. In other words, "the Japanese
organization and management practices are not one of the Japanese
businesses in Brazil" (Carvalho *et al.*, 1996: 26).

Finally, a third, highly relevant point was that multinationals began
operating in Brazil as the leaders of buyer-driven global chains. The
typical case is the footwear industry, where global marketers began
subcontracting production in Brazil. American and European firms
sent information about design, quality standards, purchasing criteria, and production processes, and provided technological support
for Brazilian firms, who did the production activities. This type of
demand accounted for the growth of two major footwear clusters
in Brazil, in the south and in the southeast of the country. Other

Brazilian industries involved in buyer-driven production networks were textile-apparel and food stuffs.

The formation of producer-driven global production networks also had important impacts over the local industry. In industries such as automobile and electronics, both the headquarters and subsidiaries, following the new directions of focusing and subcontracting, changed the way in which they selected suppliers and managed the supply chain. Not all Brazilian firms were able to make the transition from a market type of relationship to a relational type of interaction with buyers.

Overall, the insertion of Brazilian firms in global production networks driven by foreign MNEs was not as strong as in other emerging countries, especially China. In the 1990s, those which were able to develop competences to become global suppliers started their internationalization processes, as we shall see later.

6.4.4 Brazilian enterprises find increasingly turbulent conditions

Large Brazilian firms also went through rough times. Because of the contingencies of that period, major firms and even corporate groups had to shrink or disappeared altogether. A striking example was the Villares Group. This conglomerate had specialized in the electromechanical industry and vied for leadership with the Votorantim Group. Villares produced a huge number of products under license and designed components and electromechanical systems to order, especially for the government's large projects. Its customized product line ranged from elevators (licensed by Westinghouse) to electrical locomotives (licensed by General Electric), also including traveling cranes and special types of steel. However, the company began having difficulties to focus when the international context became more competitive. Its licensers began restructuring their own operations and got involved in mergers and acquisitions or even shut down operations, all of which affected Villares and the continuance of its activities. An example of this was the sale of the Westinghouse elevators division to Mitsubishi, which took place concurrently with the cancellation of huge government projects in which Villares had already invested substantially. Villares then attempted to resume its original specialty, elevators and escalators, only to find itself unable to compete when the domestic market was opened to international competition. Its elevator business, a champion for many decades, was sold to Schindler, a German group; the last one that bore the Villares name, special steels business producer, became part of the Gerdau group in 2004.

On the other hand, some large Brazilian corporate groups managed to improve their positioning and progressed during this period, such as Votorantim, Odebrecht, Gerdau, and Ultra, among others.

The Programa Nacional do Alcool (Pro-Alcool; the national alcohol program) and Programa Nacional de Informática (the national information technology (IT) program), two large industrial modernization programs created at this time, led to the creation of companies with a different profile to the older ones.

Pro-Alcool was a program for wide-scale substitution of gasoline by alcohol. It was financed by the Brazilian government as from 1975, as a result of the 1973 oil crisis, and especially following the 1979 crisis. The program was born out of research carried out by the Aeronautics Technology Center (CTA), and resulted in 10 million fewer gasoline-powered automobiles in Brazil, thus diminishing the country's dependence on imported oil. The decision to produce ethanol through the fermentation of sugarcane was taken based on the price of sugar at the time, although alternatives were also tested as a source of raw material, such as cassava.

Brazil's alcohol production in 1975–6 was 600 million liters, before it grew to a peak of 12.3 billion liters. Copersucar, an enterprise formed along cooperative lines, went as far as to establish international operations through a trading company and became notorious for having developed a Formula 1 racing car.

The Pro-Alcool program started collapsing when the international price of oil began trending down, making fuel alcohol unadvantageous for both consumers and producers. The price of sugar then started rising in the international market, as the price of oil dropped, further enhancing the problem and making sugar a far more attractive product for the mill owners to produce than alcohol.

As a result, gas stations started running out of fuel alcohol on a regular basis, leaving the owners of alcohol-powered cars stranded. These successive supply crises, coupled with the higher rate of fuel consumption of alcohol-powered cars and the cheaper gasoline, caused the Pro-Alcool program to lose its credibility among consumers and automakers. Thereafter, the production of fuel alcohol and of alcohol-powered cars declined, until most automakers stopped offering new models of alcohol-powered cars.

The Brazilian IT program aimed at establishing a Brazilian industry in the area of IT. A government program was established in the mid-1970s to "pick winners." Five enterprises that made mini-computers were selected in a first round to compete and to become national leaders in this industry. However, the discontinuity caused by lobby pressures and changes in government institutions caused the program to fail dismally by the mid 1980s (Schmitz and Cassiolato, 1992). The firms created at that time were dismantled. The only group that survived and prospered consisted of the software producers for the financial sector. Consequently, the Brazilian software industry became specialized in niche type of software. The great majority are small producers, but some firms consolidated and became international players. In addition, some born-global firms are currently identified.

The formation of global production networks also changed the landscape. In the case of producer-driven value chains, what was seen was that the local subsidiaries of MNEs reorganized their supply chains based on the selection of preferred suppliers. The objective was to cut transaction costs by reducing the supplier base and thereby increasing supplier loyalty, along Japanese lines. In this selection process, some Brazilian companies climbed up the ladder, such as Sabo, Metagal, Nakata, MetalLeve, Cofap (auto parts industry), WEG and Embraco (white goods). Several of these are now MNEs of the global follower type.

The establishment of buyer-driven global chains involved mainly the consumer goods industries, as well as the footwear and clothing industries, as we saw in the preceding section. Differently from what occurred in other countries, the Brazilian enterprises were unable to take advantage of this opportunity. They did not develop the competences needed to vie for the position of commercial integrators, which is what the Korean firms (and later the Chinese ones) achieved, neither were they able to escalate the value chain so as to become market operators, such as some firms from Hong Kong.

The Brazilian companies that embarked upon the internationalization process, as we saw in Chapter 4, were also unable to benefit from this opportunity.

6.4.5 *The national innovation system seeks to upgrade the local industry*

The two major modernizing projects, the pro-alcohol and IT program, generated a large number of initiatives. Dedicated research centers were set up, such as Centro de Tecnologia de Informação (CTI; the IT Center), and a large volume of research and development projects were allocated to the universities and the research institutes that already existed.

On a different level, a set of institutions and programs was created to focus on industrial quality issues. This initiative was a reaction to the problems that had arisen in the early 1980s, when a government program to encourage exports resulted in international complaints against the poor quality of products delivered. This had huge negative repercussions for the image of all things "Made in Brazil."

One of these was the Program for the Development of Science and Technology, financed by the Word Bank, which was fundamental for the correct understanding and implementation of the concept of industrial quality in Brazil. Its results were the starting point for the establishment and implementation of the institutions that would come to govern the quality issues in the country.

Moreover, the Fundação Premio Nacional da Qualidade (the National Quality Award Foundation) was established along the lines of the Malcolm Bridge Award in the US, which, in turn, was modeled on the Deming Prize in Japan. Interestingly, the companies that won the award in the first three years were IBM, Xerox, and Citibank. However, soon after, Brazilian firms were able to catch up and compete head-to-head for the quality award.

6.5 Crisis, failures, and reaction

In sum, during this period Brazil entered a downturn. Hypothetically, the local industrial system was supposed to be complete. This is what was inferred from the comparative studies of the industrial structure of advanced countries. Brazil should, in theory, be able to manufacture everything locally, being allegedly self-sufficient. Thus, planning would no longer be required and the industrial system was supposed to "stand on its own two feet." At the government level, the areas of competence connected with formulating national development plans or national scientific and technological programs started being dismantled, as there was a belief that they were no longer required.

This government posture, along with the changes that materialized on the international front, led to a paradoxical situation. Brazilian companies lacked the momentum to lead because they were technologically dependent, while the local subsidiaries were uninterested in leading because this was not part of their headquarters' strategies. In reality, the Brazilian situation was so different from that of the countries of origin that the subsidiaries actually enjoyed enormous operating autonomy, being only required to achieve financial targets.

As a result, a number of flops occurred: the failure of the IT Program; the shutting down of the Pro-Alcool Program; the fiasco of the Export Program; and dependent insertion into the global production chains. All of these generated negative feedback and created a permanent crisis.

Nevertheless, it was within this complex and turbulent environment that the Brazilian companies developed distinctive competences that had not been foreseen.

As economic agents increasingly accumulated knowledge to behave under uncertain circumstances, their capacity to live with and to profit from such a context increased. In time, the preference for liquidity became anchored in very sophisticated indexation instruments ... Permanent price instability and institutional distortions created by the various ill-fated attempts to curb inflation affected demand negatively and shortened decision horizons: short-term investments were valued more than long-term ones; fast and secure returns prevailed over slower and more uncertain ones. Production investment plans were set aside and replaced by inflation-hedging behavior. In the firms' decision making process, financial management prevailed. Ferraz *et al.* (1999)

Moreover, the bases for the recovery of competences connected with the functions of production, design, and marketing started to be laid. The subsequent period, that of productive restructuring, was still traumatic, but it symbolized the resurgence of some Brazilian enterprises on the international scene.

7 | *The rise of Brazilian multinationals*

7.1 Brazil adheres to global productive restructuring

In the early 1990s, factors linked to the international and the domestic environments gave rise to a highly turbulent period in Brazil. On the political front, a series of scandals led to the impeachment of the elected president. On the economic front, inflation spiraled out of control, reaching more than 2,000 percent a year after a disastrous attempt to freeze it through the confiscation of savings. Furthermore, subsidies were slashed abruptly while tariff and non-tariff barriers were reduced, thus opening the domestic market to international competition. The presence of foreign subsidiaries increased significantly and importing became far easier.

Therefore, the period of productive restructuring in Brazil was particularly complex and exceptionally demanding for all corporations. Traditional industrial groups and leading firms disappeared. Important state-owned enterprises were fully privatized. Nevertheless, the competitive environment thus instated generated a selection process that revealed which Brazilian enterprises could develop the competences needed to survive and prosper and which could not. This was the setting in which the internationalization of Brazilian firms grew and became solid.

This chapter first describes the context of productive restructuring in the 1990–2008 period, to highlight how the selection process also laid the cornerstone of a sort of Brazilian management model. This is followed by a section on the resurgence of the movement of Brazilian firms toward foreign countries, starting with Mercosur. Then a panoramic view of Brazilian multinational enterprises (MNEs) is presented. The section closes with the results of a survey that reveals the main features of the internationalization process of Brazilian enterprises and how they manage their foreign subsidiaries, enabling us to sketch a Brazilian model of international management.

7.2 The transition from a closed to an open economy

During the 1980s, the pursuit of absolute self-sufficiency, which had been the aim of the imports substitution policy for decades, lost its importance as the chief objective and function of national development. Thus, Brazilian enterprises began looking in other directions for their decision processes. They began to save resources and to replace the local context by an international horizon in their strategies. On top of that, they had to manage the transition within an extremely turbulent political and economic context.

In 1991, Brazil's newly empowered president introduced major changes that redefined the country's structure and competitive system. His government began by freezing bank accounts, which had a brutal impact on demand, especially for unessential goods. Many industries had to rediscover their markets and establish new strategies. The automotive industry, for example, stood idle for more than three months.

Meanwhile, the government changed the competitive system by introducing a number of major policy initiatives: the industrial competitiveness program, the technological capability program, and trade reforms. The industrialization and foreign trade policy (IFTP) established a timetable for a progressive reduction of import duties, in order to expose Brazilian producers gradually to stronger foreign competition. "The aims were clear: to improve international competitiveness, deregulate trade and achieve marketing selectivity, a transparent industrial policy, and medium- and long-term improvements in competitiveness, by developing enhanced skills and product quality" (Fleury and Humphrey, 1993: 14). That set the stage for the process of productive restructuring in Brazil.

However, the objectives of stabilizing the economy and controlling rampant inflation were not achieved. On the contrary, inflation continued to rise to 1,783 percent a year immediately prior to the implementation of the Collor plan (1991) and then peaked at 2,781 percent a year shortly before the Real plan (1993).

The difficult circumstances that applied to working in Brazil, which ensued from a lack of macroeconomic control, plus the tensions connected with political and institutional events (among other facts, President Fernando Collor de Mello, elected in 1990, was impeached in 1992) put to the test the corporate competences of both Brazilian

Table 7.1 *Different responses of firms in the turbulent Brazilian environment of the early 1990s*

Managerial capabilities	Lower response capabilities	Higher response capabilities
Sector	Capital goods, traditional goods	Industrial commodities, durable goods
Size	Small, medium, and large	Very large
Ownership	State and private-sector domestic enterprises	Multinationals
Direction of sales	Only internal market and/or only external market	Intraindustry trade

Source: Based on Ferraz *et al.* (1999).

enterprises and MNE subsidiaries. A study by Ferraz *et al.* (1999) comparing MNE subsidiaries and Brazilian firms showed that the former performed better, thanks to their greater response capacity, as Table 7.1 indicates.

Table 7.1 summarizes the set of changes in Brazil's industrial structure, which signaled a new path for Brazilian enterprises, especially where internationalization is concerned. "The need to adapt to these changing, unstable and often abrasive circumstances caused Brazilian enterprises to develop a special capacity for survival" (Coutinho *et al.*, 2008: 74). The firms that survived this harsh selection process developed the competences required to compete internationally. They also reached the end of the decade well-capitalized, as we will see further on.

In late 1993, implementation of the Real plan began. This was an inflation-fighting plan designed by Fernando Henrique Cardoso, Brazil's finance minister at the time, who would later became president of the republic. Following a number of failed heterodox plans in previous years (the Cruzado, Bresser, Summer, Collor I, and Collor II plans), the Real plan finally managed to slash inflation and keep it under control to this day, notwithstanding the initial overvaluation of the Real, the financial international crises, the 1998/9 foreign exchange shake-up, and the subsequent devaluation of the Real. The exchange rate in 1994/5 went down to R$0.8/$, up to R$3.5/$ in 2002, then down again to R$1.8/$, and so on. Analyses show that the volatility of the Real is not only large if compared with advanced countries but also the greatest among Brazil, Russia, India, and China (the BRICs).

From 1994 to 2002, Brazil fully complied with the International Monetary Fund (IMF) and the Washington Consensus requirements, embracing a neo-liberal agenda, as did other developing countries. One of the outcomes of this was the deliberate abandonment of industrial policies, faithfully reflected in the utterance of the finance minister at that time: "the best industrial policy is no industrial policy."

From 1994 to 1997, trade liberalization, privatization of infrastructure, and deregulation made room for the foreign private sector. Among others, the following measures lowered entry barriers for foreign investors:

- extinction of entry restriction in the information technology (IT) industry in 1991;
- elimination of the limits to participation in privatization in 1993;
- elimination of the distinction between local and foreign capital, thus giving to the installed multinationals access to government loans and subsidies in 1994;
- income tax exemption for profit and dividend remittance in 1994;
- liberalization of restrictions to patenting in high-tech areas in 1995; and
- lifting of the prohibition of intra-firm remittance of royalties for trademarks and patents in 1997.

These changes, associated with the reorganization movements of the developed countries and of their MNEs, caused the flow of FDI into Brazil to recover gradually, as shown in Figure 7.1.

Consequently, "In 1998, Brazil held the eighth largest stock of FDI in the world: US$156.8 billion. Out of the 500 largest companies in the world, 405 had operations in Brazil, accounting for roughly 20 percent of GDP" (Matesco and Hasenclever, 2000: 161). This led some economists to identify a paradox: "Among the industrialized countries, Brazil probably has the lowest ratio of local to foreign capital ownership, a feature – and its implications – yet to be properly understood by analysts and policy-makers" (Ferraz *et al.*, 1999: 17).

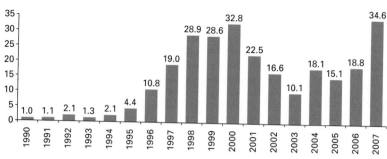

Figure 7.1 Inward FDI in Brazil, 1990–2007 ($ billion)
Source: UNCTAD (2008).

Therefore, three points are important to stress in relation to productive restructuring in Brazil: (1) the increasing proportion of MNE subsidiaries in the industrial sector and especially in the services sector; (2) the reduction of Brazilian firms' share of some strategic sectors, as a result of privatization policies; and (3) the emergence of internationally competitive Brazilian firms.

7.2.1 Share of subsidiaries in manufacturing and services increases

From the late 1950s until 1990, a co-existence of sorts between foreign and local enterprises was achieved, both groups operating within a highly protected environment. This balance was upset when foreign trade barriers were lowered drastically and Brazil entered the commercial globalization stage.

As shown in the previous chapter, in the early stages of MNE subsidiaries in Brazil, parent companies transferred technology (plants, products, and processes), along with management policies and procedures (including human resources management). This was followed by a period of a relative accommodation (1970–90). Subsidiaries were run along the lines of the multidomestic pattern, explained by the fact that their financial performance was satisfactory, sometimes even exceeding their headquarters' expectations. The transfer of technology, expertise, and information to subsidiaries was gradually reduced, so that they began operating with increasing autonomy. A byproduct of this was that they developed local competences, especially those related to the operation and management of production systems.

Then, once the economy was thrown open to productive globalization, the subsidiaries were reincorporated into the global strategies of their parent corporations. Two forces shaped the restructuring process: the new organizational directives issued by the headquarters of the MNEs, and the subsidiaries' operating conditions in the Brazilian market. Overall, two distinct phases of the restructuring process of foreign multinationals can be identified. In the first (1990–4), while the headquarters in the developed countries experimented with new ways of organizing business, the Brazilian market experienced enormous turbulence. Depending on the orientation of the headquarters and on the relative importance and autonomy of the Brazilian subsidiaries, the MNEs that were active in the country expanded in some cases but shrank in others. In other words, in the early 1990s, a clear transition in the modus operandi of the Brazilian subsidiaries was observed. Whereas previously they tended to be of the multidomestic kind, they now turned into a range of different types of companies: local implementers, specialized contributors or global mandate holders, according the Birkinshaw and Hood (1998) classification.

By the next phase (from 1994 to 2000, approximately), the international management model of developed country MNEs had matured somewhat. Concomitantly, Brazil's institutional, political, and macroeconomic circumstances had stabilized and a system to encourage the inflow of foreign capital had been set up. The action of foreign multinationals speeded up and the relative share of the Brazilian economy in the hands of MNE subsidiaries increased significantly, especially in the services sector.

For instance, in the automotive industry, virtually all the global manufacturers set up subsidiaries in Brazil. Those that had been long-established in the country, such as General Motors (GM), Ford, Volkswagon (VW) and Fiat, were joined by Toyota, Honda, Mitsubishi, Renault-Nissan, Peugeot-Citroen, Audi, Mercedes-Benz (cars), BMW (engines), and Chrysler. However, the last four shut down their Brazilian operations in the early 2000s. On the other hand, Hyundai arrived in the country in the 2000s. Mahindra, the Indian firm, started up its assembly operations in Brazil in 2008, while EFFA, a Chinese automaker, set up operations in Uruguay, from where it exports its products to Brazil. In the telecom sector, privatization brought international operators in its wake, especially from the Latin European countries. The grid of the large global firms

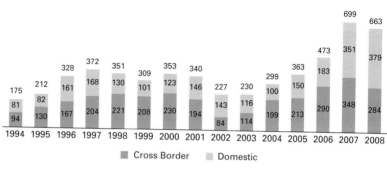

Figure 7.2 Number of mergers and acquisitions in Brazil
Source: KPMG.

became almost complete with the subsidiaries of Nortel, Huawei, Celestica, Flextronics, and Solectron, among others.

It is interesting to note that the new subsidiaries, from their very inception, were based on the new international management models, most of them following the Birkinshaw and Hood (1998) local implementer type.

However, this period's chief novelty was the arrival of MNE subsidiaries in the services industry. The global banks Santander and BBVA (Spanish), HSBC (English), and ABN-Amro (Dutch) began operating in Brazil. In the apparel retail sector, C&A (Dutch) and JCPenney (American) established shops and local supply chains. In the supermarket sector, Wal-Mart (American) and Casino (the French group that acquired control of the local Pão-de-Açúcar supermarket chain) started competing with Carrefour. In the building materials retail sector, St. Gobain (Telhanorte) and Leroy Merlin vied for business with the large local groups' retail chains. Along with the international brands that also stepped up their presence in Brazil, these firms became the drivers of local production chains.

This movement is clearly depicted in Figure 7.2, showing the figures for mergers and acquisitions (M&As) in Brazil. From 1994 to 2001, 60 percent of M&As were of the cross-border kind. In a study we carried out in the late 1990s with a sample of the 1,600 enterprises (local and subsidiaries), we found an unexpected and significant number of subsidiaries of small and medium-sized MNEs that had recently been set up in the country. However, that trend was reversed after 2001, when 52 percent of M&As involved enterprises already active in the country.

The share of the subsidiaries that produced goods and services in Brazil continued rising until 2005, when a new reverse trend came into play, as shown in Figure 7.2. One of the consequences of this was that Brazil's export performance has been driven by MNE subsidiaries. Of the total value exported by the 200 largest Brazilian exporters, 64 percent originated from MNE subsidiaries, 30 percent from state-owned enterprises, and only 6 percent from locally owned private enterprises (*America Economia*, August 16, 2006: 84).

7.2.2 Privatization redefines governance in strategic sectors

Starting in the 1990s, the Brazilian state-run production system went through deep restructuring and denationalization owing to the implementation of the Plano Nacional de Desestatização (PND; national privatisation plan) and of the opening of the domestic market to foreign firms. This process was implemented at the start of the decade (during the Fernando Collor de Mello administration) and became stronger in the 1996–8 years (of the Fernando Henrique Cardoso administration).

The first phase of the privatization process (1990–4) focused on certain sectors of the transformation industry, such as steel manufacturing and petrochemicals. As of 1995, the process turned mainly to the services and infrastructure sectors, such as telecommunication and energy (Laplane *et al.*, 2003).

The main feature of the 1990–4 privatizations period was the modest participation of foreign investors, in line with their introspective period to restructure in their home countries (Table 7.2). In this first phase, state enterprises were acquired mainly by large Brazilian private-sector groups, often with state aid in the form of loans, according to Banco Nacional para o Desenvolvimento Economica e Social, (BNDES, Brazil's national bank for economic and social development 2002). Certain sectors, however, such as electric energy, mining, and oil could not be sold to foreigners according to the 1988 constitution. Furthermore, "other issues favoured local investors at the first phase, such as difficulties working out the value of the assets of the several government enterprises, in the aftermath of years of high inflation, and the uncertainties regarding the positions of political groups regarding the privatizations" (Giambiagi and Vilela, 2005).

Table 7.2 *Sales result by type of investor, 1990–4 ($ million)*

Type of investor	Sales revenues	%
Domestic companies	3,116	36
Financial institutions	2,200	25
Individuals	1,701	20
Pension funds	1,193	14
Foreign investors	398	5
Total	8,608	100

Source: BNDES (2002).

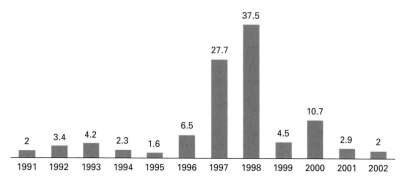

Figure 7.3 Revenues from the annual evolution of privatizations ($ billion)
Source: BNDES (2002).

As of 1995, the privatization and state reform processes were stepped up and utilities started to be transferred to the private sector. The initial objectives to resume investment in modernization of the Brazilian industrial complex were superseded by other aims. The privatizations became part of the economic policy, to keep the high government deficit of that time from pressuring public debt further. Thus, the privatizations were connected with the need to attract foreign capital as a means of financing part of the country's unbalanced current account (Figure 7.3). As of 1999, currency devaluation and fiscal adjustment corrected this issue and privatizations ceased to be a priority. The accrued revenues from the sale of government enterprises reached some $100 billion, with annual peaks of about $28 billion in 1997 and of $38 billion in 1998 (Giambiagi and Vilela, 2005).

The following sectors were included: electrical, financial, transportation, highways, sanitation, ports, and telecommunication. The

Table 7.3 *Sales result by type of investor, 1995–2002 ($ million)*

Type of investor	Sales revenues	%
Foreign investors	41,737	53
Domestic companies	20,777	26
Individuals	6,316	8
Domestic financial sector	5,158	7
Pension funds	4,626	6
Total	78,614	100

Source: BNDES (2002).

share of foreign capital was significant in the 1995–2002 period, during which it totalled 53 percent of the amount raised through all Brazilian privatization. The change in the rules pertaining to foreign capital called for an amendment to the constitution in order to make it possible for the mining and energy sectors to be exploited in part by international capital (Giambiagi and Vilela, 2005). Domestic enterprises accounted for 26 percent of the revenues, 7 percent being connected with organizations from the domestic financial sector, 8 percent with individuals, and 6 percent with the private pension plan funds, as shown in Table 7.3 (BNDES, 2002).

In general, the government's position was to give up its production activities entirely, delivering them into the hands of private sector firms, whether domestic or foreign, though it set up regulation processes based on regulating agencies to ensure the compliance of the services rendered with pre-defined performance criteria.

This had different consequences, depending on the sector. In the high-tech areas, the result was, essentially, a de-nationalization, state companies giving way to foreign enterprises. The telecom industry was the most visible case.

Box 7.1 The evolution of the telecommunication industry in Brazil

In the first part of the twentieth century, the telecommunication system consisted of a heterogeneous group of isolated regional telephone operators, each one serving a specific area, using imported equipment. In the late 1960s, a national telecom company, Telebras, was created as the main organization responsible for developing and running the telecoms. That decision combined the imperatives of the governing macroeconomic model of import substitution at that time with the interests of the military government, which regarded telecommunication as an area of strategic relevance for national security and technological development.

Telebras had an operating branch, Embratel, in charge of long distance services and of the organization and control of the twenty-three state network operators. The technological duties were assigned to the Center for Research and Development (CPqD), which, to some extent, played the role of a research laboratory. CPqD's chief concern was to create local capabilities in telecom technologies through its own research and to integrate the activities undertaken by universities, enterprises, and other research centers.

Until the 1980s, subsidiaries of foreign specialist equipment suppliers (NEC, Ericsson, etc.) were obliged to comply with the technological regime that Telebras and CPqD imposed upon them through specific operating standards, designs, and technologies. A very successful platform called Tropico was developed by CPqD for the specific conditions of Brazil.

The privatization process, however, meant that foreign enterprises, such as Portugal Telecom, Telefonica (Spanish), and MCI (US), among others, became the large network operators. The Brazilian firms only managed to establish themselves in a limited number of regions.

CPqD was then transformed into a private-sector foundation, putting an end to its role as the coordinating agency for the development of telecommunication technologies.

These changes led to improved telecom services but also to a strong reduction in the country's process of technological development, not only in this field, but also in the software area, one of the main telecom suppliers.

On the other hand, other state companies were kept under local control. Table 7.4 shows the dates of the Companhia Siderúrgica Nacional (CSN), Vale, and Embraer privatizations. As for Petrobras, even though the Brazilian government sold part of its shares, it is still the controlling stakeholder.

Table 7.4 *The privatization of Brazilian state-owned enterprises*

Enterprise	Year	Governance
CSN	1993	Brazilian Industrial Group, Bradesco Bank, Pension Funds
CVRD	1997	Brazilian Industrial Group, Opportunity Bank, Pension Funds
Embraer	1994	Brazilian Government, Brazilian Financial Group, Pension Funds
Telebras	1998	Telefônica (Spain), Portugal Telecom, and local financial groups

The privatization period also marks the entry of pension funds, mostly those of the former state-owned enterprises (Petrobras, Banco do Brasil, etc.). Certain financial groups, especially Garantia and Vicunha, became important players on the industrial scene.

7.2.3 Internationally competitive Brazilian enterprises stand out

For a large number of Brazilian firms, the early 1990s were an ongoing threat. The rising competitiveness in the domestic market due to imports, the increased participation of foreign MNEs' subsidiaries, and the possibility of them engaging in international procurement, made feasible by the newly established trade policies, resulted in what some authors called "the denationalization process." Several leading Brazilian firms, especially in the automotive and other technology-intensive industries, were sold to foreign MNEs. The most striking case was MetalLeve, previously one of Brazil's most advanced firms, a first-tier supplier with a research and development (R&D) laboratory in Detroit and distribution centers in other parts of the US, which was sold to German Mahle. Vargas (brake systems), Nakata (suspension systems) and Cofap (shock absorbers), among others, had a similar fate.

On the other hand, another group of Brazilian companies started to catch up by upgrading competences. The initial target was to reach the productivity and quality levels found in the international market. The Japanese management model became their chief source of inspiration, methods, and techniques.

The strong dissemination of Japanese management techniques was led by enterprises that were state-owned at the time, such as Petrobras and Vale, and that demanded better management from their suppliers. In parallel, the MNE subsidiaries, which were being restructured at that time, were also important in this regard.

The Programa Nacional de Qualidade e Produtividade (PBQP; national quality and productivity program) instituted by the federal government, was widely disseminated and influenced the access criteria to other financial support programs. The National Quality Prize (Premio Nacional da Qualidade), organized along the lines of the Deming prize in Japan and of the Malcolm Baldridge prize in the US, was also very important in this process. From 1991 to 2008, in the manufacturing area, the prize was awarded to MNE subsidiaries ten times and to Brazilian enterprises nine times. In the services sector, it was granted ten times to Brazilian enterprises and twice to MNE subsidiaries. Among the Brazilian MNEs, the prizewinners were WEG (1997), Gerdau (2002 and 2007), and Petrobras (2007).

After 1994, the course of action of Brazilian companies was modified, given the imperative of becoming effectively integrated with global production systems. Local firms began to see MNEs from a different perspective, as stronger competitors, potential partners and eventual suppliers. For example, Aulakh (2006) screened 357 cross-border alliances involving Brazilian firms. The author identified three different types: technology alliances (45 percent), marketing alliances (26 percent), and production alliances (29 percent).

Local leading enterprises dropped their defensive and isolated strategies and moved toward proactive integrative strategies. Strategic alliances became essential not only for transferring technology, but also to guarantee access to the international negotiation circuits. Priorities changed; from the individual pursuit of indicators of excellence, firms now aimed at institutional integration with international operations, by joining global production networks. The choice basically depended on the new structure of industry at the global level and the relative bargaining power of local companies vis-à-vis the MNEs operating in that industry.

Thus, a new profile of organizational competences was gradually consolidated within Brazilian enterprises. We will revisit this point in the next chapter.

7.3 Establishing the roots of international competitiveness

As a by-product of the restructuring process, Brazil and Brazilian firms began to identify the roots of their international competitiveness.

Evidently, the country's factors endowment (especially nature, climate, size of domestic market) was always seen as a country specific advantage. However, the other dimensions related to the local environment, namely the cultural dimension and the sociopolitical structure, were gradually unveiled and understood in terms of their potential contribution for the development of local enterprises.

In regards to the sociopolitical infrastructure, the difficulties and challenges of the 1980s and 1990s were tough lessons that spurred reparatory actions. In the 1990s significant changes were consolidated starting with the Fernando Henrique Cardoso administration, this process having continued in the Luiz Inacio Lula da Silva administration. However, effective supportive policies geared to internationalization were only established in 2004, when the tradeoffs associated with that decision became clear to the governmental agencies, especially BNDES.

Despite Brazil's new-found political and financial stability, some authors kept employing words such as disorder, uncertainty, attrition, and fluidity to describe the main features of the business environment, meaning a set of unique obstacles that make it harder to do business in Brazil than in other countries. Brazil still ranks badly in the competitiveness rankings: the World Economic Forum (WEF, 2009) classifies Brazil as 56th, behind China (29th), Chile (30th), India (49th) and Costa Rica (55th). On the other hand, there are more positive assessments of Brazilian overall competitiveness, based on different criteria. For example, in the ranking developed by the Institute for Large Scale Innovation, Brazil is ranked 12th among the twenty most innovative countries in the world.

In that context, it is not surprising that Sull and Escobari (2004) described Brazilian executives as "pilots racing on unknown tracks in the midst of a fog: as they can only see what lies ahead very vaguely, they must learn to react quickly to the changes that are typical of an environment in constant transformation."

At firm level, interestingly, the unveiling of the traces of Brazilian organizational culture started with the need to incorporate the Japanese approach to managerial processes. The exposure to new management models and techniques and the rupture with the until-then hegemonic "American way of organizing" led Brazilian enterprises to a reflection about their own style and competences.

Authors who have analyzed the characteristics of the Brazilian management style prior to that point in time (Barros and Prates, 1996; Tanure, 2005; Caldas, 2006), have associated it with national cultural traits allegedly rooted in the country's early history. Those traits would be the result of the colonization project of the Portuguese, who established rigid and hierarchical organizations, depleted the colony's natural riches, and exploited the land through a slavery-based regime, among other factors. The social elements that were introduced back then in the formation of Brazil's rural and agricultural society subsequently have influenced its urban and industrial society and the way in which Brazilian firms were managed as well.

These authors admit that, up to the 1980s, Brazilian management style had its roots in this heritage, thus summarized by Hickson and Pugh (1995):

- centralization of decisions at upper hierarchical levels, with clear incompatibility between responsibility and authority;
- immediatist views that target short-term results with an emphasis on solving crises;
- lack of strategic planning and/or a gap in planning between the tactical and the operating management levels;
- pursuit of reactive and adaptive (i.e., short-term) solutions, prizing "creative improvisation," known in Portuguese as the *jeitinho,* or "the Brazilian way around" things, as translated by Hickson and Pugh (1995: 85).

To all of the above, one can also add:

- openness to novelty; interest in and admiration for management practices imported from other countries (Caldas, 2006; Chu and Wood, 2008).

The "traditional Brazilian management style," prevalent up to the late 1980s, was compatible with a protected domestic market and dependent on the government actions. That helped to establish a "parochial" mentality in most industrial sectors, i.e., an inward-oriented entrepreneurial and managerial style that was devoid of a global overview. To survive, private firms developed competences mainly in the production area while state-owned enterprises invested more heavily in building technological and production competences. The negative experience of the first companies that embarked upon internationalization, the exposure to new management models, and the increasing competition for the domestic market, fueled a process of revision of local management models and furthered the development of a more global view of the world among managers and entrepreneurs. The new field of experimentation that Mercosur offered in the 1990s helped to trigger a global mindset among business people and prepared firms for a new style of competition.

It was under these circumstances that the Brazilian management model began to take shape. As in all other countries, the development of this model resulted from a complex process that involved cultural, social, and political factors, in addition to local endowments and the competitive dynamics of the business sectors. In Chapter 4, for instance, we described such a process for Japan in detail. In the case of Brazil, the cornerstone of its management model seems to have been a blend of the management model developed by the Brazilian private-sector enterprises that survived the tough 1990s and the management model of the former state-owned enterprises, which, once privatized, remained under domestic control. Among the private-sector enterprises, the ones that had truly developed the competences needed to survive and prosper in the competitive and turbulent domestic market, in which they had to fight MNE subsidiaries for every shred of business, stood out. In the case of the former state-owned enterprises, the privatization process injected new competences into them (especially in marketing and finance), complementing their strong production and technology competences, besides unveiling new horizons for their operations.

In that transition, Brazilian managers changed while maintaining their cultural background. For example, Tanure (2005: 98) observed that "the short-term pressure that inflation imposed for a long time on the Brazilian people was not internalized as a core cultural value, as is the case in the USA, where failure to meet quarterly targets may be fatal. There is a certain balance, in that the pressures and ruptures caused by the institutional context are moderated by the Brazilian cultural characteristics, which include a high degree of personal adaptability, the importance of status and the use of time to weave social relations."

Sull and Escobari (2004) identified the factors that led some firms in Brazil to be highly successful in the very turbulent local environment. To describe traces of the Brazilian way of managing, the authors created metaphors such as active waiting, golden opportunities, sudden death, and submarine fishing, among others. They found out that to strive in turbulent environments the important thing is:

taking action during comparative lulls in the storm. Huge business opportunities are relatively rare; they come along only once or twice in a decade. Moreover, for the most part, companies cannot manufacture those opportunities; changes in the external environment converge to make them happen. What managers can do is prepare for these golden opportunities by managing smartly during the comparative calm of business as usual. During these periods of active waiting, leaders must probe the future and remain alert to anomalies that signal potential threats or opportunities; exercise restraint to preserve their war chests; and maintain discipline to keep the troops battle ready. When a golden opportunity or "sudden death" threat emerges, managers must have the courage to declare the main effort and concentrate resources to seize the moment. Sull (2005a)

Sull's and Escobari's findings about Brazilian companies were based on previous analyses of entrepreneurial firms in highly dynamic industries, like the Internet business. In "Strategy as simple rules," Eisenhardt and Sull (2001) assert that:

managers of such companies know that the greatest opportunities for competitive advantage lie in market confusion, so they jump into chaotic markets, probe for opportunities, build on successful forays, and shift flexibly among opportunities as circumstances dictate. But they recognize the need for a few strategic processes and a few strategic rules to guide them.

Therefore, the management style developed by Brazilian leading firms may be regarded as peculiar, but not outdated. On the contrary, firms in very dynamic industries may be using similar styles.

Table 7.5 summarizes the competences of that new breed of Brazilian enterprises.

Evidently, the new set of organizational competences reflects a new management style where the challenges of a globalized economy and internationalized competition have been internalized.

Table 7.5 *Organizational competences in the traditional and new Brazilian management models*

Competences	Traditional	New
Organizing competence: to establish and implement management systems	Internally: centralization of decisions at upper hierarchical levels, with clear incompatibility between responsibility and authority. Externally: low propensity toward cooperation and partnerships	Organizational flexibility: capacity to adapt and change depending on external conditions: markets, macroeconomic conditions, etc. Externally: gradual understanding and acceptance of partnerships
Planning competence: to identify, develop, and implement business strategies	Immediatist views targeting short-term results with an emphasis on solving crises. Lack of strategic planning and/or a gap in planning between the tactical and the operating management levels	Active waiting: preparing for golden opportunities by managing smartly during the comparative calm of business as usual. Know-how to act in the political-institutional circuits
Production competence: to do things (goods and services) more quickly, flexibly, or reliably than competitors	Basic. Prefers high-scale and low-cost production systems. Cannot master process technologies. Buys equipment. Avoids investments in personnel development	World class. Strongly influenced by the Japanese approach to production management. Masters process technologies. Competes with MNEs' subsidiaries
Technological competence: to add value to products and processes	Basic engineering. Invests nothing or close to in R&D. Interactions with national innovation system is feeble	Strong in product and process development. Creativity in what concerns innovations. Some invest heavily in R&D

Table 7.5 (cont.)

Competences	Traditional	New
Commercial competence: to sell goods and services	Basic. Prefers to pursue the market that buys the product as it is, instead of upgrading the product according to the market's expectations. Low concern with brand and image	Developed to satisfy the complex characteristics of the Brazilian markets. Strong concerns with brand and image
Supply chain management competence: to manage purchasing and select suppliers	Accepted the impositions made to become members of supply chains. No efforts for upgrading	Learnt the rules for supply chain governance. Upgrading is part of the strategy
Customers relationship management competence: to bring a firm close to its customers	Non-existent	Learnt how to be customer oriented. Invested in the creation of B2B or B2C systems
Human resources management competence: to capture, develop, and compensate people	Traditional old-fashioned posture and conflicting attitude toward labor	The most advanced in the nation
Financial competence: search, allocation, and investment	Developed to survive in the turbulent domestic market; still dependent from the local governments and institutions	Developed to survive and learnt to operate in the financial markets; high concern with risk management

7.4 The evolution of Brazilian multinationals

7.4.1 Where it all began: the Mercosur experience

The internationalization of Brazilian enterprises from the early 1990s to the early 2000s concentrated on Mercosur (Mercado Común del Sur, a regional trade agreement between Argentina, Brazil, Paraguay, and Uruguay), which absorbed 36 percent of the country's outward foreign direct investment (OFDI) until 2002. The tax regime added to geographic proximity and smaller cultural distance to justify the trend.

The economic integration of South American countries takes us back to the 1960s. Under the tutelage of the UN Economic Commission for Latin America and the Caribbean (ECLAC)/Comision Economica para America Latina (CEPAL), an agreement was reached concerning the Latin American Free Trade Association. In practice, this agreement did not work, but it was used as a parameter for subsequent attempts at economic integration. In 1979, Argentina and Brazil signed a protocol of intent concerning trade, but little progress was made.

Mercosur was established in 1991, when Uruguay, Paraguay, Brazil, and Argentina signed the Treaty of Asunción. It is generally regarded as the result of the confluence of political projects that encouraged closer relations, coupled with the pressures of international economic circumstances. All of this was underscored by two conditioning factors: globalization and regionalization. According to this treaty, most of the goods and services produced in any of the signatory countries should circulate freely throughout the integrated region, free of duties or non-tariff encumbrances. In practice, Brazil and Argentina are the countries that make the most of the agreement. Uruguay and Paraguay, due to their small economies, play a less relevant role in the commercial flows.

Studies showed that Mercosur was the third most important reason for the establishment of subsidiaries abroad. The first was the local consumer market and the second was synergy with the production facilities in other Mercosur countries (BNDES, 1995).

Data on the foreign operations of Brazilian enterprises is not entirely reliable, but rough estimates indicate that some 300 subsidiaries originating from Brazil were set up in Argentina, profiting from the Mercosur tax breaks. This figure includes subsidiaries of Brazilian firms as well as affiliates of local MNE subsidiaries, especially of those in the electromechanical and automotive sectors. MNEs from developed economies invested in Mercosur, either directly or through a subsidiary in some other country, and especially by means of M&As. There is evidence that FDI through M&As in Mercosur countries went hand in hand with the opening of the economy and privatization cycles in this block's countries, in particular Brazil and Argentina. Bonelli (2000) concluded that developed country MNEs were in a better position than the firms from Mercosur itself, thanks to their technological and financial capacity and the possibility of applying the know-how and experience they had accrued in their subsidiaries to the streamlining and modernization of their local structures.

However, the aforementioned "de-nationalization of Brazilian industry" and Mercosur limitations caused the above figure to gradually shrink. Following the Argentine economic collapse in 2001, the number plummeted.

The operational regime of Mercosur is still an issue decided at the political and diplomatic levels, mainly. Unilateral decisions are still common and firms have to resort to lobbying to settle the grounds. The mobility of firms, especially between the Argentinean and the Brazilian borders, is still high. Depending on the exchange rates and the provisional state of affairs, a large number of MNEs is able to shift the workload from one country to another, profiting from modern production techniques.

7.4.2 The evolution of Brazilian outward foreign direct investment

As previously mentioned, from 1960 to 1982, Brazilian OFDI went through an outstanding initial phase as compared to the other developing countries. Official data put the OFDI figure at some $800 million, which, however, is generally considered underestimated. The main point is that these investments were concentrated in specific sectors: the oil industry, civil construction, and financial services. However, they were geographically dispersed.

From 1980 to 2003, OFDI more than doubled, reaching $2 billion. It became more focused on Latin America and more diversified in

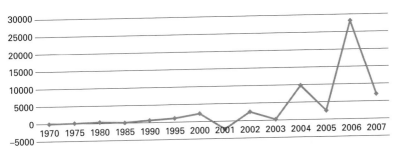

Figure 7.4 Brazilian outward FDI flows, 1970–2007 ($ million)
Source: UNCTAD (2008).

terms of sectors. Nevertheless, this growth was substantially lower than that of the Asian countries.

Beginning in 2003, OFDI started to rise significantly (Figure 7.4). This is mainly connected with the internationalization of Brazilian commodity producers, which encountered a fairly favorable international context; however, they were not the only parties to benefit from this.

It is important to stress that a large share, 58.2 percent of the firms, financed the internationalization of their activities with their own capital, while 27 percent got bank loans and raised funds through debt issues abroad (SOBEET, 2008). Only 6 percent of them resorted to loans from BNDES. The fact that Brazilian companies largely prefer to use their own capital to internationalize is due to their combined evaluation of cost, strategy, and capacity for debt. Still, one must stress that even before the world crisis, bank credit lines geared specifically to the activities of Brazilian firms abroad were scarce. BNDES only started providing funding for the expansion of Brazilian concerns abroad as of 2005. This was also the year in which Brazilian private-sector banks upped their support for the international operations of Brazilian enterprises.

Another important indicator is the M&As in which Brazilian firms were the buyers. Table 7.6 shows the geographic distribution of M&As involving Brazilian enterprises abroad, 1995/2004.

The pattern revealed by the above numbers reveals that:

• a third of foreign ventures is directed to developed countries while two-thirds targets developing countries; Argentina responds to a third of the total number of M&As;

Table 7.6 Geographic distribution of M&As involving Brazilian enterprises abroad, 1995/2004 (number of deals completed)

Country/region	1995	1996	1997	1998	1999	2000	2001	2002	2003	2004	1995–2004
World	14	6	4	13	11	10	8	6	8	10	90
Developed economies	3	2	1	5	3	3	5	0	4	3	29
US	0	0	0	2	1	1	2	0	1	1	8
Portugal	0	1	0	0	0	0	1	0	1	1	4
Spain	0	0	0	1	2	1	0	0	0	0	4
Canada	1	0	0	0	0	1	1	0	0	1	4
UK	0	1	0	2	0	0	0	0	0	0	3
Developing economies	11	4	3	8	8	7	3	6	4	7	61
Argentina	4	1	3	6	3	5	2	5	2	1	32
Colombia	1	0	0	1	0	0	0	0	0	2	4
Peru	2	0	0	0	0	0	0	0	0	2	4
Venezuela	1	2	0	1	0	0	0	0	0	0	4
Bolivia	1	0	0	0	1	1	0	0	0	0	3

Source: Almeida (2007: 75).

- the evolution in time reflects the expectations of Brazilian firms in regards to the positioning of the country in relation to the international environment; this was clearly the case for the drop in the figures in 2001–3 when the transition from the Fernando Henrique' term to the Lula's term created high levels of anxiety in regards to the directions of Brazilian economy.

Finally, it is interesting to introduce Fundacao Dom Cabal's Index of Regionalization. It shows that Latin America is losing relevance in the last years while North America, Asia, and Africa are becoming more important in regards to Brazilian OFDI (Table 7.7).

The investments in Africa are related to resources-seeking projects led by Petrobras and Vale, mainly, as well as to the participation of Brazilian engineering firms, like Odebrecht and Camargo Correa, in the development of large infrastructural projects mostly in the Portuguese-speaking African countries.

7.4.3 The Brazilian multinationals: a chronological view

The different definitions of what a multinational enterprise is and the deficient databases available mean that any attempt to picture an overall description of Brazilian MNEs (BrMNEs) is questionable and open to discussion. For example, according to United Nations Conference for Trade and Development (UNCTAD) data from 2004, more than 1,000 Brazilian enterprises invested abroad in some way starting in the early 1990s. However, that takes into account exports, joint ventures, and the various kinds of FDI. The number of new BrMNEs has been increasing since the 1970s, as shown by Figure 7.5.

For the purpose of this book, we assume that an MNEs is a company "... with some foreign sales and some foreign production, where the latter takes place in a wholly-owned subsidiary," according to Rugman and Li (2007), or a "... business that has productive activities in two or more countries," according to Hill (2008).

We have developed our own database which amounts to eighty companies (Table 7.8 on page 192). In the list we included all Brazilian firms that have had operations abroad at least once in their lifetime, including those which have already closed down.

In addition, it is revealing to look at the BrMNEs as they appear in the international and national rankings. These rely on a variety of

Table 7.7 *Brazilian multinationals – index of regionality*

Companies	Total countries	Latin America (%)	North America (%)	Europe (%)	Africa (%)	Asia (%)	Oceania (%)
CVRD	33	15	6	15	21	39	3
Petrobras	25	44	4	8	24	20	0
WEG	22	23	5	36	0	32	5
Camargo Corrêa	17	71	6	6	18	0	0
Odebrecht	16	38	6	13	31	13	0
Stefanini IT Solutions	14	50	14	29	0	7	0
Gerdau	13	69	15	8	0	8	0
Itautec	11	55	9	36	0	0	0
Andrade Gutierrez	11	9	9	45	18	18	0
Votorantim	10	50	20	10	0	10	10
Randon	10	30	10	0	40	20	0
Tigre	9	89	11	0	0	0	0
Marcopolo	9	33	0	11	22	33	0
Itaú Unibanco	8	50	13	25	0	13	0
Localiza	8	100	0	0	0	0	0
Marfrig	7	43	0	57	0	0	0
Natura	7	86	0	14	0	0	0

Sabó	6	17	17	50	0	17	0
Banco do Brasil	6	50	0	17	17	17	0
Metalfrio	5	40	20	20	0	20	0
Artecola	5	100	0	0	0	0	0
Ultrapar	5	60	20	20	0	0	0
Aracruz Celulose	4	0	25	50	0	25	0
Embraer	4	0	25	50	0	25	0
Totvs	4	75	0	25	0	0	0
Perdigão	4	25	0	75	0	0	0
Suzano	4	25	25	25	0	25	0
Lupatech	3	67	33	0	0	0	0
M. Dias Branco	3	67	33	0	0	0	0
Oi	3	67	33	0	0	0	0
DHB	2	0	50	0	0	50	0
Marisol	2	50	0	50	0	0	0
Sadia	2	0	0	50	0	50	0
América Latina Logística	1	100	0	0	0	0	0
Tam	1	100	0	0	0	0	0
Portobello	1	0	100	0	0	0	0
Cia Providencia	1	0	100	0	0	0	0
Porto Seguro	1	100	0	0	0	0	0
Cedro	1	0	0	100	0	0	0

Table 7.7 (*cont.*)

Companies	Total countries	Latin America (%)	North America (%)	Europe (%)	Africa (%)	Asia (%)	Oceania (%)
Arezzo	1	0	100	0	0	0	0
Cemig	1	100	0	0	0	0	0
Average index of regionality 2008		46.23	17.31	20.61	4.66	10.75	0.43
Average index of regionality 2007		40.38	14.72	20.00	8.3	16.6	—
Average index of regionality 2006		46.91	11.34	20.62	6.7	14.43	—

Source: FDC (2009).

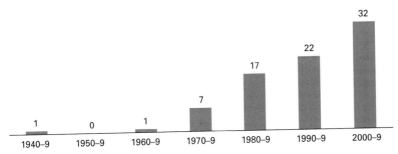

Figure 7.5 Brazilian multinationals – first operation abroad, 1940–2009

different inclusion criteria: financial and non-financial firms; firms with production facilities, commercial offices, or distribution centers abroad; manufacturing firms and service firms; and so on.

7.4.4 Brazilian multinationals in the international rankings

Four international rankings are relevant when it comes to measuring the size and value of firms' operations, regardless of whether they are in developed or developing countries: Fortune 500, Boston Consulting Group, Columbia Program for International Investment, and UNCTAD. Though they employ different metrics methodologies, some BrMNEs are repeatedly listed in these rankings.[1]

The Fortune 500 list includes Brazil's three largest banks: two private (Bradesco and Itaú) and one state-owned (Banco do Brasil). Three other enterprises: Petrobras (state-owned), Companhia Vale do Rio Doce (privatized), and Gerdau Steel are on this list. The World Investment Report (WIR) also includes the three of them among the

[1] Methodologies: *Fortune 500*: consolidated with subsidiaries and reported revenues from international operations. Main indicators: revenues, followed by profit. *BCG*: fourteen countries chosen based on gross domestic product (GDP) magnitude, value of exports, and amount of long-term FDI. Three-stage criteria: (1) selection only of firms with true FDI (excluding joint ventures); (2) firms with revenues greater than $1 billion; and (3) selection of the firms' internationalization criteria: presence of subsidiaries and control abroad, sales networks, production sites, R&D center, and the largest investments in internationalization over the last five years (including mergers and acquisitions), among others. *UNCTAD*: ranking by assets abroad and by transnationality index (consisting of the average: assets abroad/total assets, revenues abroad/total revenues, and employees abroad/total employees). *CPII*: criteria quite similar to UNCTAD's.

Table 7.8 Brazilian multinationals – main characteristics and internationalization data

	First operation abroad	Type of first operation abroad	First plant abroad	Company	Sector	Ownership
1	1941	Branch		Banco do Brasil	Bank	State-owned
2	1961	Plant	1961	Magnesita	Refractory producer	Private
3	1972	Acquisition (Colombia)	1972	Petrobras	Oil and gas	State-owned
4	1976	Commercial office	1995	WEG	Electric engines	Private
5	1976	Commercial office	—	Tupy	Metallurgy, steel	Private
6	1977	Plant	1977	Tigre	Construction materials	Private
7	1977	Services contract	2005	Camargo Corrêa	Engineering services	Private
8	1979	Services contract	1988	Odebrecht	Engineering services	Private
9	1979	Commercial office and after sales services	2004	Embraer	Aircraft	State-owned
10	1980	Plant	1980	Gerdau	Steel	Private
11	1980	Plant	1980	Caloi*	Consumer goods	Private
12	1980	Joint venture	1985	DHB	Autoparts	Private
13	1980	Plant	1990	Metal Leve*	Autoparts	Private
14	1980	Branch	—	Banco Itaú	Bank	Private
15	1980	Licensing	—	Staroup*	Apparel	Private
16	1981	Local representative	1992	Natura	Cosmetics	Private

#	Year	Entry mode	Company	Year	Sector	Ownership
17	1983	Strategic alliance	Arecola	2000	Mining	State-owned
18	1984	Plant	CVRD	1984	Capital goods	Private
19	1985	Plant	Romi	1985	Consumer goods	Private
20	1985	Licensing	Alpargatas	1989	Autoparts	Private
21	1985	Commercial office	Moura	1997	Consumer goods	Private
22	1985	Store	Boticário	—	Consumer goods	Private
23	1986	Commercial office	Tramontina	—	IT	Private
24	1988	Services contract	Itautec	2003	Vehicles/parts	Private
25	1988	Strategic alliance	Agrale	2008	Food	Private
26	1990	Joint venture	Perdigão	1990	Buses	Private
27	1991	Plant	Marcopolo	1991	Food	Private
28	1991	Plant	Sadia	1991	Food	Private
29	1991	Strategic alliance	IBOPE	1997	Specialized services	Private
30	1992	Plant	Sabó	1992	Auto parts	Private
31	1993	Plant	Ambev*	1993	Beverage	Private
32	1994	Plant	Randon	1994	Truck parts	Private
33	1994	Alliance/Born Global	Fugitec	2002	Software	Private
34	1995	Plant	Santista	1995	Textile	Private
35	1996	Plant	Klabin	1996	Pulp and paper	Private
36	1996	Plant/Born Global	Xseed	1996	Software	Private
37	1996	Plant	Metagal	1996	Autoparts	Private
38	1996	Commercial office	Stefanini	2000	Software	Private
39	1996	Office/Born Global	CI&T	2001	Business intelligence	Private
40	1996	Office	Facchini	-	Autoparts	Private
41	1997	Restaurant	Fogo-de-chao	1997	Food services	Private
42	1997	Office	Totvs	1997	IT	Private

Table 7.8 (*cont.*)

	First operation abroad	Type of first operation abroad	First plant abroad	Company	Sector	Ownership
43	1997	Office	2004	Coteminas	Textile	Private
44	1998	Office	1989	SMAR	Automation	Private
45	1998	Licensing	2007	Azaléia	Consumer goods	Private
46	1998	Commercial office	—	Romagnole	Mechanics	Private
47	1999	Joint venture	1999	Cipatex	Chemicals, petrochemicals	Private
48	1999	Plant	1999	Busscar	Vehicles and parts	Private
49	1999	Acquisition (railway)	1999	ALL América	Transportation, logistics	Private
50	2000	Services office	2001	Bematech	IT	Private
51	2000	Distribution center	2008	Maxxion	Auto parts	Private
52	2001	Plant	2001	CSN	Steel	Privatized
53	2001	Plant	2001	Votorantim	Cement	Private
54	2001	Services office	2001	Politec	Business intelligence	Private
55	2001	Strategic alliance	2007	Datasul	IT	Private
56	2001	Commercial office	—	Aracruz	Pulp and paper	Private
57	2002	Joint venture	2002	Lupatech	Mechanics	Private
58	2002	Joint venture	2002	Braskem	Chemicals	Private
59	2002	Plant	2002	Grupo Brasil	Vehicles and parts	Private
60	2002	Office/Born Global	2003	Ivia	Software	Private
61	2003	Logistics center	—	Inplac	Packaging	Private

No.	Year	Type	Year	Company	Sector	Ownership
62	2004	Plant	2004	Votorantim	Steel and metals	Private
63	2004	Services office	2004	CPM Braxis	IT and services	Private
64	2004	Office	—	Gol	Transportation, logistics	Private
65	2004	Services office	—	YKP	Business intelligence	Private
66	2004	Services office	—	Spring Wireless	IT and services	Private
67	2004	Services office	—	Atech	IT and services	Private
68	2005	Plant	2005	Camargo Corrêa	Cement	Private
69	2005	Plant	2005	Friboi	Food	Private
70	2005	Plant	2005	Metalfrio	Refrigeration systems	Private
71	2005	Restaurant	2005	Spoleto	Restaurant	Private
72	2005	Services office	2005	Griaule Biometrics	Software	Private
73	2005	Plant	2005	Marisol	Textile	Private
74	2005	Office	—	TAM	Transportation, logistics	Private
75	2006	Plant	2006	Marfrig	Food	Private
76	2006	Plant	2006	Suzano	Petrochemicals, pulp and paper	Private
77	2006	Commercial office	2006	FFS Filmes	Chemicals, petrochemicals	Private

Table 7.8 (*cont.*)

	First operation abroad	Type of first operation abroad	First plant abroad	Company	Sector	Ownership
78	2007	Store	—	Arezzo	Consumer goods	Private
79	2008	Store/strategic alliance	—	Bob's	Food chain	Private
80	2009	Store	—	Track & Field	Sportswear	Private
81	—	Branch	—	Bradesco	Finance	Private

Source: Firms' official websites; SOBEET (2008).
* Acquired by foreign capital.

fifty largest non-financial MNEs from developing nations, classified by assets abroad (UNCTAD, 2008). The Boston Consulting Group's report classifies fourteen Brazilian enterprises among the 100 global challengers from emerging countries, which are mainly from the BRICs (China has thirty-six companies in this ranking, India has twenty, Russia has six and Mexico has seven). Table 7.9 shows the position and recurrence of the main BrMNEs in these four international rankings.

7.4.5 Brazilian multinationals in the national rankings

Two rankings were developed by Brazilian institutions (Table 7.10): that of Sociedade Brasileira de Estudos de Empresas Transnacionais e da Globalização Econômica (SOBEET; the Brazilian society for the study of transnational companies and economic globalization) and that of *Fundação Dom Cabral* (FDC; the Dom Cabral foundation), partnered with Columbia University's Columbia Program on International Investment (CPII).

Based on data from Brazil's central bank, SOBEET estimated that there were 887 Brazilian firms with some form of activity abroad, meaning companies with more than 10 percent of their capital in foreign branches and OFDI greater than $10 million. As the central bank does not reveal names, SOBEET was only able to identify 211 of them, to which questionnaires were sent. Those criteria caused firms that normally would not be considered MNEs to be taken into account, such as two airlines that offer international services (Gol and Transportes Aeréos Manilia (TAM).

According to SOBEET's approach, Brazilian firms' foreign presence consists principally of sales offices (31.2%); however, 23.1% of the companies set up plants or service units abroad. A third group (18.9%) exports via licensing agreements with distributors, i.e., franchising. The number of BrMNEs that actually own companies abroad is twenty-three (11 percent).

The FDC index, in turn, presents the twenty main BrMNEs in terms of assets, employees, and foreign revenue, using the same methodology as UNCTAD. According to FDC, all the firms on its list belong to the private sector, other than Petrobras.

Their distribution by sector indicates a substantial concentration in natural resources, with two enterprises (Vale and Petrobras)

Table 7.9 *Brazilian multinationals – international rankings*

	Company	Industry	Fortune 500 (2009/2008)[a]	Forbes 2000 (2008/2007)[b]	WIR (2008)[c] Foreign assets	WIR (2008)[c] TNI[d]	BCG (2009)[e]
1	Petrobras	Oil and gas	34/63	29/88	12	94	X
2	Bradesco	Bank	148/204	85/208	—	—	—
3	CVRD	Mining	205/235	76/361	11	73	X
4	Itaúsa	Bank	149/273	175/477	—	—	—
5	Banco do Brasil	Bank	174/282	132/256	—	—	—
6	Gerdau	Steel	400/–	766/1,496	39	47	X
7	Braskem	Chemicals	—	1,091/1,170	—	—	X
8	Embraer	Aircraft	—	1,345/1,467	—	—	X
9	CSN	Metals	—	809/1,049	—	—	—
10	Unibanco	Bank	—	233/–	—	—	—
11	Sadia	Food	—	1,733–	—	—	X
12	Votorantim	Cement	—	1,487–	—	—	X
13	WEG	Electric engines	—	1,824/–	—	—	X
14	Aracruz	Pulp and paper	—	1,519/–	—	—	—

	Company	Industry	Fortune[a]	Forbes[b]	World Investment Report[c]	Transnationality Index[d]	BCG[e]
15	Suzano	Pulp and paper	—	1,971/-	—	—	—
16	Usiminas	Steel	—	736/-	—	—	X
17	Coteminas	Textile	—	—	—	—	X
18	JBS – Friboi	Food	—	—	—	—	X
19	Marcopolo	Buses	—	—	—	—	X
20	Natura	Cosmetics	—	—	—	—	X
21	Perdigão	Food	—	—	—	—	X
22	Camargo Corrêa	Engineering services	—	—	—	—	X

[a] *Fortune* (2008, 2009);
[b] *Forbes* (2007, 2008);
[c] *World Investment Report* (UNCTAD, 2008);
[d] Transnationality Index (UNCTAD, 2008);
[e] Boston Consulting Group (2009); X indicates inclusion in BCG's New Global Challengers List.

Table 7.10 *Brazilian multinationals – Brazilian rankings*

FDC ranking			SOBEET ranking			Company	Sector
2008	2007	2006	2008	2007	2006		
—	—	—	1	1	—	Friboi	Food
—	1	—	—	—	—	Camargo Corrêa Cimentos	Cement
6	2	—	2	2	1	Odebrecht	Engineering services
1	3	1	3	3	2	Gerdau	Steel
19	4	—	21	31	16	Votorantim Cimentos	Cement
—	—	—	5	4	—	Coteminas	Textile
—	—	—	6	5	3	IBOPE	Specialized services
—	—	—	10	8	5	Ambev	Beverage
4	5	2	11	6	6	CVRD	Mining
2	6	3	7	7	4	Sabó	Autoparts
5	7	14	4	9	14	Metalfrio	Refrigeration systems
15	8	9	19	13	9	Grupo Camargo Corrêa	Diversified
11	9	22	—	—	—	Lupatech	Mechanics
13	10	6	16	17	8	Embraer	Aircraft
7	11	23	37	28	23	Aracruz	Pulp and paper
9	12	12	12	10	15	Artecola	Chemicals
12	13	4	13	18	10	Marcopolo	Buses
8	14	8	—	—	—	Tigre	Construction materials
—	15	10	—	—	—	Duas Rodas	Food
20	16	18	28	25	20	Petrobras	Oil and gas

						Company	Industry
—	17	—	—	—	—	Camargo Corrêa	Engineering services
—	18	19	—	24	18	America Latina Logistica	Transportation, logistics
26	19	11	22	—	—	Andrade Gutierrez	Engineering services
21	20	17	29	33	26	Natura	Cosmetics
18	21	—	20	—	—	Stefanini	Software
38	22	—	—	—	—	Arezzo	Consumer goods
23	23	25	43	20	21	DHB	Autoparts
27	24	26	40	37	33	Totvs	IT
25	25	32	—	—	—	Ultrapar	Chemicals
28	26	—	—	—	—	Localiza Rent a Car	Transport
35	27	28	53	35	37	Sadia (merged Perdigao 2009)	Food
31	28	—	—	—	—	Randon	Truck parts
10	29	30	51	34	27	Suzano	Pulp and paper
33	30	27	50	45	46	Marisol	Textile
—	31	—	41	43	39	Bematech	IT
—	32	—	—	—	—	Politec	IT
32	33	20	—	—	—	Alpargatas	Consumer goods
3	34	—	32	26	19	Perdigão (merged Sadia 2009)	Food
—	—	—	9	11	29	Marfrig	Food
16	—	—	15	12	11	Gol	Transportation, logistics
14	—	—	14	14	7	WEG	Electric engines
—	—	—	18	15	13	Itautec	IT
—	—	—	—	16	12	Coimex Trading	Foreign trade
—	—	—	—	19	31	Metal Leve (linked to Mahle)	Autoparts
—	—	—	31	21	17	Grupo Brasil	Vehicles and parts

Table 7.10 (cont.)

FDC ranking			SOBEET ranking			Company	Sector
2008	2007	2006	2008	2007	2006		
—	—	—	23	22	22	Tupy	Metallurgy, steel
22	—	—	25	23	43	TAM	Transportation, logistics
—	—	—	33	27	28	Acumuladores Moura	Autoparts
—	—	—	39	29	25	Banco Itaú	Bank
—	—	—	30	30	—	CSN	Steel
—	—	—	35	32	24	Agrale	Vehicles and parts
—	—	—	—	36	35	FFS Filmes	Chemicals, petrochemicals
—	—	—	42	38	30	Braskem	Chemicals
—	—	—	—	39	40	Datasul	IT
—	—	—	55	40	32	Banco do Brasil	Finance
—	—	—	—	41	38	Cipatex	Chemicals, petrochemicals
—	—	—	—	42	34	Facchini	Autoparts
—	—	—	46	44	36	Inplac	Packaging
—	—	—	52	46	42	Klabin	Pulp and paper
—	—	—	—	47	45	CPM Braxis	IT
—	—	—	—	48	47	Cisa	Foreign trade
—	—	—	54	49	44	Romagnole	Mechanics

Company							Sector
CVC	—	—	—	—	50	41	Specialized services
Cia Providencia	29	—	—	—	—	—	Plastics
Oi	36	—	—	—	—	—	Telecommunications
Porto Seguro	34	—	—	—	—	—	
Cedro	37	—	—	—	—	—	Textile
Duratex	—	—	—	—	—	17	Specialized construction activities
CI&T	—	—	—	—	—	24	IT
Bertin (merged JBS Friboi 2009)	—	—	—	—	—	26	Meat
ALL América	17	—	—	—	—	27	Transportation, logistics
Romi	—	—	—	—	—	34	Capital goods
Alusa	—	—	—	—	—	36	Engineering services
Portobelo	24	—	—	—	—	38	Ceramic and tiles
Módulo Security Solutions	—	—	—	—	—	44	IT
Altus	—	—	—	—	—	45	Electrical equipment
Iochpe Maxxion	—	—	—	—	—	47	Autoparts
Minerva	—	—	—	—	—	48	Food
M. Dias Branco	—	—	—	—	—	49	Food
Telemar	—	—	—	—	—	56	Telecommunications
Cemig	39	—	—	—	—	57	Energy

Source: FDC (2006; 2007; 2008); SOBEET (2006; 2007; 2008).

accounting for more than two-thirds of the foreign assets of the twenty most internationalized firms. A second group, comprising firms that provide inputs for other industries, accounts for more than 19%. The BrMNEs that make end products and the service companies account for some 6%, respectively. This leaves less than 1% for Natura, the only consumer goods concern in the FDC's ranking. As for the percentage of the firms' total assets, the foreign assets of the top twenty range from 1% to 46%; only two hold foreign assets in excess of $10 billion. Concerning the group as a whole, their foreign assets, in 2006, accounted for 20% of their total assets, versus 12% in 2005.

7.5 Strategies and competences for internationalization: the Brazilian experience

7.5.1 The research design

Aiming to advance in the analysis of "strategies and competences of Brazilian MNEs," we conducted a survey in 2007. The concepts and structure of organizational competences presented in Chapter 2 and refined in Chapter 5 formed the theoretical framework for this survey.

The preceding section, in which we presented the several rankings and data sources, illustrated the great diversity of BrMNEs. The criteria for defining this survey's universe was to classify as MNEs firms with at least one actively managed production operation abroad. In late 2006, this led to a list of forty-seven BrMNEs, including companies with foreign manufacturing operations, as well as technology-based professional services enterprises (in the engineering and IT industries) with project offices abroad. Some born global firms were identified in the latter category. The survey did not take into account pure service companies, such as banks and restaurants, or firms that were only exporters.

Out of the forty-seven firms contacted, thirty (63%) agreed to answer a questionnaire. Of these, twenty-two were from the industrial sector (73%) and eight were from the technical and professional services sector (28%). The senior managers in charge of international operations at the headquarters of these BrMNEs were the respondents. Only two of the seventeen missing firms were truly important for the survey's purposes. They were unable to take part in this study because

Table 7.11 *Percentages of the different industries in the sample*

Industry	Number BrMNEs	Sample/total	%
Based on natural resources	4	3/4	75
Basic inputs	14	7/14	50
Producers of consumer goods	7	2/7	29
Parts and components suppliers	8	6/8	75
Systems assemblers	4	4/6	66
Technical and professional services	8	8/8	100

they were on the brink of major acquisitions and thus prohibited from disclosing information to the public. The other firms declined, either because their international operations were small, or because they were unsure whether to expand in the international arena or withdraw from it. The head offices that agreed to take part authorized us to contact their foreign subsidiaries. These totaled ninety-three, sixty-eight of which responded. The questionnaire was based on tested and published research tools, especially from Birkinshaw *et al.* (1998). It was then pre-tested in two BrMNEs. Table 7.11 shows the relative participation of the different industrial sectors in the sample.

The sample of subsidiaries included 64 percent of the total subsidiaries of 63 percent of all BrMNEs. This seems to be a very representative sample, thus reinforcing the results obtained in regards to the role of subsidiaries of Brazilian multinationals.

7.5.2 *Internationalization drivers*

According to 96 percent of the surveyed firms, internationalization was on their strategic agendas a long time before the decision to internationalize. In other words, Brazilian firms were prepared to take the plunge into foreign waters.

The firms that started going international prior to 2000 put less effort into planning this, perhaps because the investment was lower and targeted regions that were psychically and physically closer. The research data reveal, however, that the planning for internationalization became increasingly careful as time went by. Planning became more elaborate to minimize consolidation and expansion problems, "the day after" effect.

Table 7.12 *Factors influencing internationalization decision*

Firm strategy related factors	- Exploit intangible assets (36%) - Meet need for hard currency revenues (63%)	Resources
	- Create new markets due to domestic market saturation (64%)	Markets
	- React to international competitors (56%) - React to local competitors (18%)	Competition
	- Meet international clients' demand (68%) - Outsourcing in other country (7%)	Global production networks
Environment related factors	- Exploit comparative advantages (79%)	Country endowments
	- Overcome technical barriers (23%) - Overcome commercial barriers (42%)	International institutional aspects
	- Exploit tariff advantages (31%) - Gain access to other financial markets (59%)	Site advantages

The factors that influenced the internationalization decision were classified into two categories: those that concerned the firm's strategy and those that concerned the environment, as listed in Table 7.12.

The first point to be highlighted concerns the first line of environment-related factors: four out of five Brazilian multinationals considered comparative advantages as an important factor for internationalization. These advantages should be interpreted broadly, being related to the firms' operating circumstances in the country. Here, we are essentially referring to country-specific advantages, which encompass elements such as natural resources, market size and particular features, development stage relative to other countries, and specific operational challenges in a turbulent environment.

Two types of competences and resources were highlighted by the answers: financial resources and intangible assets. As for financial resources, a significant percentage of BrMNEs declared that their decision to internationalize was influenced by their need for foreign currency revenues (63 percent) and to gain access to other financial markets in order to obtain financing under more equitable terms relative to their international competitors (59 percent). These high percentages reveal the difficulties and limitations of operating within the Brazilian institutional context, given the exchange rate volatility relative to that of other countries. The data corroborate the argument that the importance of these factors was enhanced when it came to deciding to become international, due to the series of economic crises that the country suffered in the late 1990s and early 2000s.

On the other hand, more than one-third of the firms indicate that they internationalized because of the specific ownership advantages associated with intangible assets. This ratio struck us as significant in that it is not in line with the more traditional international business approach. It signals that there may be new ways for late-movers to develop intangible assets that will lend them strong positions in the international competition arena.

Two questions put competition in the position of being an influencing factor in the decision to internationalize. Actually, 56 percent of the firms indicated that, indeed, their decision had been influenced by the movements of other global competitors. In other words, when international competitors move about in the international arena, Brazilian firms become international to gain and safeguard positions. Ambev, Embraer, and Vale are examples of this. In the second case, when developed country multinationals expand in the domestic market, Brazilian firms react, looking for new positions in the international market. This is the case, for instance, of Votorantim, in the cement industry, and of the IT firms.

The variable "markets" also stands out. Nevertheless, responses mainly emphasize domestic market limitations, rather than foreign market potential: 64 percent of the firms felt that the domestic market was small or saturated, this being one of the factors that had induced them to internationalize. Here, Gerdau (steel mills) is an interesting example. It supplies components for the building industry, a major market in Brazil. However, Brazilian construction has not evolved in its use of metallic structures and only a meager 3 percent of construction projects might come to use Gerdau components. This was therefore a determinant for its speedy internationalization. Indeed, the firm recently set up a plant in an inner-Brazilian state that works entirely in inches, targeting only the export market. The standard in Brazil is metric.

There is still a group of firms whose internationalization decision was tied to global production networks, driven by international clients. These are the cases of supplier followers. The most typical cases concern the automotive chain (Sabó, Metagal, etc.), the white goods chain (Embraco, WEG) and the IT firms specializing in solutions. A still modest number of firms (just 7 percent) have set up a base for outsourcing in other countries.

The institutional factors that influence internationalization decisions are mentioned by a significant number of the cases studied: 42 percent of the BrMNEs feel that trade barriers or the lack of trade agreements influenced their decision to set up operations abroad. For instance, the failure of the Free Trade Agreement of the Americas (FTAA) negotiations has led Brazilian firms to set up subsidiaries in Mexico in order to gain access to the US market. As several studies have pointed out (Chang, 2002; Messner, 2004), technical barriers may be raised for political purposes and interests. In the case of Brazil, this has had a greater impact on the food and agricultural industries.

7.5.3 *Competences for competing in the domestic markets*

In the beginning of this chapter, we described Brazil's productive restructuring in the 1990s, the bankruptcy of traditional corporate groups or their sale to foreign firms, the privatization of state enterprises, and the entry of new international competitors.

In this turbulent context, Brazilian firms were not only able to gain strength to compete in the domestic market but also to brave international markets. What we investigated was whether the competences that were important to survive and prosper in the domestic market are the same that supported the internationalization process.

The firms were required to rate the importance of nine competences (Table 5.3) for competing in the domestic market. Overall, the organizational competences hierarchy is shown in Table 7.13.

The technological, production, customer relationship management (CRM), organizing, and financial competences emerged as the most strategic ones for competing in the domestic market. They reveal the profile of a firm already strongly influenced by the international context and innovative in products and services. They are concerned about cost effectiveness and prioritize the development of management

Table 7.13 *Organizational competences hierarchy for domestic competition*

(1) Technological
(2) Production
(3) Customers relationship management (CRM)
(4) Organizing
(5) Financial
(6) Supply chain management (SCM)
(7) Planning
(8) Commercial
(9) Human resources management (HRM)

models in order to survive and prosper within a complex institutional environment. In respect to the financial competence, it has always been highly relevant for their survival in the turbulent local institutional environment, as earlier commented. Therefore, the profiles of the organizational competences developed to compete in the domestic market were shaped by the competitive regime of the respective industry, by the national environment and also by the firm's own features.

An interesting example for that prioritization of competences is Brazil's textile apparel enterprises. Up to the mid-1990s, they were vertically integrated concerns that covered the gamut of their sector's activities, from fiber production to end-product manufacturing. Their core competence was production. However, owing to competitive context changes, the textile firms that survived and prospered were those that changed their position in the value chain, by creating CRM competences centered on the management of brands, distribution channels, and retailing, in order to serve their customers better. Meanwhile, they also rationalized their production processes, outsourcing those activities that added less value. All of this altered their competitive positioning, better equipping them to face the marketing chains that were set up at the time (like C&A and JC Penney) and the competition of imports, while increasing awareness of customers' tastes and preferences.

Technological competence is ranked as the most important competence, indicating the degree of concern of successful Brazilian firms in their catching-up efforts. This trend is reinforced when we notice that production is ranked as the second most important competence

Table 7.14 *Influence of the business environment on competence development (%)*

Foreign consumers' requirements	78
Relation with corporate customers abroad	77
Global competitors' strategies	73
Financial market rules and regulations	63
Relations with corporate customers in the country	63
Relations with foreign suppliers	59

and the one that ensures cost effectiveness. The cases that will be presented in the next chapter will clarify how this strategic positioning came about.

Table 7.14 shows that the international environment factors were those that most influenced the development of competences for domestic market competition. In other words, there has been an internalization of the conditions prevailing in the international markets within the domestic markets: local firms were already exposed to the demands of international clients and consumers, as well as to global competition. Perhaps that is why 96 percent of the firms answered that internationalization has already been on their strategic agendas for quite some time.

These findings are further supported by the firms' assessment of the influence of the several government policies on the development of their competences and their international competitiveness. The vast majority of the firms felt that the policies that govern the local competitive regime were those that most heavily influenced such decisions.

On the other hand, the industrial, science, and technology policies were considered relatively unimportant. Table 7.15 is particular telling when we compare the Brazilian case with China, India, and Korea.

7.5.4 Competences for the entry phase

The relative importance of organizational competences changes when one takes into account the international entry phase (Table 7.16).

This stage is particularly relevant because "the period when a company is going through the [internationalization] process is essentially a highly unstable phase between two more stable phases: the domestic

Table 7.15 *Perception of the influence of policies on the development of competences (%)*

Foreign trade policies	63
Economic policies	57
Science and technology policies	41
Labor and union relations policies	38
Infrastructure policies	30
Industrial policies	30
Education policies	23

Table 7.16 *Organizational competences hierarchy for internationalization – entry phase*

Competing domestically	Entering international markets
(1) Technological	(1) Production
(2) Production	(2) Organizing
(3) CRM	(3) HRM
(4) Organizing	(4) Planning
(5) Financial	(5) Technological
(6) SCM	(6) Commercial
(7) Planning	(7) CRM
(8) Commercial	(8) Financial
(9) HRM	(9) SCM

state and the state of having become a global company" (Ghoshal, cited in Korine and Gómez, 2002: xi).

Compared to the previous profile of competences for competing in the domestic market, there seems to be a profound reorganization of the key competences. To make the international undertaking operational and feasible, production is the first competence to be mobilized, which turns it into the most important one, followed by organizing and human resources management (the least important prior to internationalization). This new profile reveals the challenges of intervening quickly in the reality of foreign investments (plant/factory/office), to render the operation efficient, transfer the management model in order to integrate the international unit, and expatriate employees.

It is interesting to note that human resources management (HRM) was not previously considered important for competing in the domestic market, as firms were able to draw, develop, and retain the necessary personnel; however, during this second period, new and different requirements arose that transformed HRM into a highly relevant competence.

The change in the profile of competences reflects a Brazilian firm's entry mode through acquisitions and organic growth as well. In both cases, they have to incorporate a large volume of input from the foreign location, abruptly. Production has to redevelop the competences that, through the mutual interaction between firm-specific resources and environment-specific resources, enable the subsidiary to attain international productivity standards as fast as possible. The transfer of personnel (coordinated by HRM) and of the organizational model aims at putting the newly acquired subsidiary in place in its new orbit.

It is interesting to compare this with the Japanese case. As the Japanese firms already had a consolidated management model that lent them a competitive edge, the challenge was to create the conditions needed to transfer the model to the host country. In the case of Brazilian firms, however, we observe an intervention process designed to help the headquarters to figure out how to take effective action over the incorporated subsidiary, thereby establishing a specific, though perhaps transitory, organizational model.

7.5.5 Competences for international expansion

In the subsequent phase, international expansion, a new and significant change arises in the prioritization of organizational competences. The commercial and CRM competences now became the most important, followed by technological and production competences (Table 7.17).

One possible interpretation is that, after the new subsidiary's internalization, the head offices try to consolidate a new product and market configuration. At the same time, they need feedback on the subsidiary's efficacy and input to assess new investment possibilities. The fact that the technological and production competences follow each other on the list of priorities seems to indicate that these

Table 7.17 *Organizational competences hierarchy for internationalization – expansion phase*

Domestic market competition	Entry into international market	International expansion
(1) Technological	(1) Production	(1) Commercial
(2) Production	(2) Organizing	(2) CRM
(3) CRM	(3) HRM	(3) Technological
(4) Organizing	(4) Planning	(4) Production
(5) Financial	(5) Technological	(5) SCM
(6) SCM	(6) Commercial	(6) Financial
(7) Planning	(7) CRM	(7) Organizing
(8) Commercial	(8) Financial	(8) HRM
(9) HRM	(9) SCM	(9) Planning

functions are involved in this consolidation and expansion, guaranteeing the delivery and development of new products and services. In other words, the technological competences continue to be very important even after internationalization: although many BrMNEs develop distinctive competences in order to be competitive in the domestic market, these competences are relevant in the expansion phase. However, the presence of the CRM competence in this block seems to indicate that the issue here is the development of a new competence that will enable the firm to work efficiently within the new MNE configuration, complying with the orientation of a customer-oriented strategy, as seen in Chapter 2. It is as if, in the pursuit of a new international management model, the development of technological competences becomes a function of international customers' demands.

HRM competence, however, after braving the challenges of the entry phase, is better consolidated and drops down a few notches on the scale of priorities.

Figure 7.6 depicts the most important changes observed in the architecture of competences of Brazilian multinationals in the three stages of the internationalization process. However, it is necessary to consider that since the entry stage, subsidiaries will start to play a role in the development of competences of the Brazilian firm.

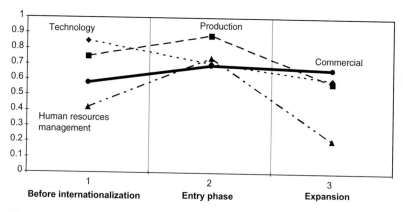

Figure 7.6 The hierarchy of competences changes during the internationalization process

7.6 Brazilian multinationals as networks of competences

7.6.1 The Brazilian subsidiaries in the survey

The configuration of the subsidiaries that responded to the survey reflects Brazilian firms' internationalization pattern: an initial movement into South American countries, for Mercosur-related economic and financial reasons, along with geographic and cultural proximity, followed by their advance into other regions.

The subsidiaries' sample involved Latin America (35%) mainly. The country with the largest number of subsidiaries is Argentina (14%), followed by Mexico (8%). China was present with four subsidiaries. Overall, 43% of those subsidiaries were the result of acquisitions, 42% were greenfield investments, and 15% were joint ventures. Greenfield investments were the chief form of entry abroad up to 2000, after which Brazilian firms started preferring acquisitions strategies.

The initial preference for greenfield investments can be explained by the fact that Brazilian firms' original expansion targeted Mercosur countries, where the opportunities for the purchase of attractive firms in terms of their resources were limited (Table 7.18). Such acquisitions, in so far as they did occur, took place in Argentina, which had strong companies in the consumer goods and natural resources sectors. In these cases, the investments were primarily market-seeking and efficiency-seeking, rather than resource-seeking. The change in the entry strategy, which turned to acquisitions in developed countries,

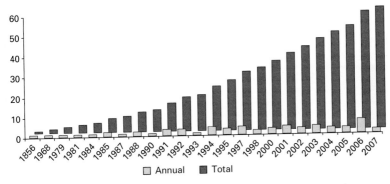

□ Annual ■ Total

Figure 7.7 Evolution of the number of Brazilian multinationals and their subsidiaries

Table 7.18 *How Brazilian firms entered foreign countries (%)*

	Acquisitions	Greenfield investments	Joint ventures
Before 2000	15	28	7
After 2000	29	13	8

is related with Mercosur's decline and the consolidation of globalization, as we saw in previous chapters.

The age of the subsidiaries also varies a lot. The sample's oldest one was set up back in 1968, whereas two were newly acquired at the time of the survey. Half of the subsidiaries are less than ten years old, which illustrates how early is the stage of Brazilian firms' internationalization (Figure 7.7).

Of these subsidiaries, 40% sell only to their host country. The others (60%) serve international markets. The Latin American subsidiaries sell 70% of their output to Latin America itself, 10% to North America, and 20% to Europe. The North American affiliates sent 10% of their production to Latin America and 29% to Europe. The main foreign market of the European subsidiaries is Eastern Europe, followed by Asia. The Asian subsidiaries are more globally oriented, exporting primarily to Europe but also to North and South America. The Eastern European subsidiaries export little, and only to Europe. As for Africa, it does not appear on the graph, because its subsidiaries serve only their local markets (Figure 7.8).

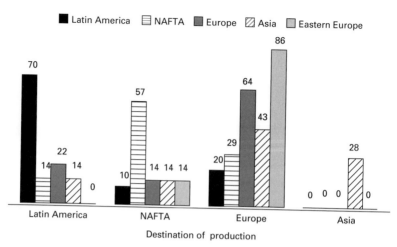

Figure 7.8 Destination of subsidiaries' production according to their location

The subsidiaries' size was measured by the number of staff. Some 30% of the subsidiaries have fewer than 50 employees and 20% have 50 to 200 employees (these are engineering and IT services offices mainly). In other words, half of them have at most 200 employees. Another 25% have a staff of 200 to 1,000 and the last 25% have more than 1,000 employees.

When it comes to the subsidiaries' annual sales, the first 25% of them sell $1 million to $16 million, while another 25% sell $20 million to $125 million; in other words, half of the subsidiaries invoice less than $125 million; 35% of them sell $125 million to $0.5 billion, and another 8%, $0.5 billion to $1 billion. Only 7% of the subsidiaries sell more than $1 billion a year.

Thus, a characterization of the "average" BrMNE subsidiary indicates that:

- the first foreign entry is in a Latin American country;
- the subsidiary is medium-sized; and
- it mainly serves the host market, although 60% serve regional markets.

7.6.2 The headquarters–subsidiaries relationship

Hypothetically, Brazilian MNEs, as late-movers, should need to make the most from the competences and resources of their

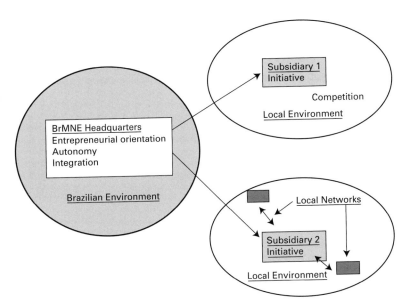

Figure 7.9 Headquarters–subsidiaries relationships: analytical framework

subsidiaries, in order to catch-up and compete with mature and well-established MNEs. In other words, the development and operation of a headquarters–subsidiary management model should be much more critical for emerging MNEs from less developed countries than for traditional MNEs.

To answer the question "what are the relationship patterns that BrMNEs are establishing vis-à-vis their subsidiaries?" we investigated the research data, aiming to extract an explanatory model.

We departed from the international management models presented in Chapter 5: multidomestic, global, transnational, and metanational. We also considered that the development of competences within a firm may lead to local, non-local, and specific competences. We were primarily interested in the development of non-local competences, those that are transferable between headquarters and subsidiaries. Otherwise said, we have tried to assess whether the subsidiaries are contributing to the BrMNEs' corporate performance through the development of non-local competences.

Figure 7.9 shows the analytical framework for analyzing the relations between headquarters and subsidiaries.

7.6.3 *The management of Brazilian subsidiaries*

When the six dimensions that define headquarters–subsidiaries are considered, the outcomes from the survey data are shown in Table 7.19. Thus, we can conclude that:

- In the headquarters–subsidiaries relationship, the latter see themselves as more autonomous and enterprising than the headquarters believe they are allowing; subsidiaries make decisions on products, processes, and markets, bearing the risks inherent to such decisions. According to the views of their headquarters, however, the subsidiaries lack the autonomy for this.
- The subsidiaries report that they are in a competitive environment but that they operate weakly in corporate networks; and
- A significant percentage of the subsidiaries define themselves as possessing initiative and being decision-makers: one in three admits to being responsible for the creation of new business; one in four is charged with the acquisition of new firms; and one in two for their own R&D budgets.

To conclude, headquarters' views of their subsidiaries' role seems to be divorced from the subsidiaries' actual operations. The characteristics highlighted above seem to configure what is sometimes considered as "rebel subsidiaries."

7.6.4 *Competences profiles: the differences between headquarters and subsidiaries*

Table 7.20 shows subsidiaries' perceptions of what might be the areas in which their competences exceed those of their headquarters. Most subsidiaries feel that their competences in the commercial, financial, and HRM areas are superior. At first sight, all these competences have strong local content, i.e., they are specific competences. At the same time, 27 percent of the subsidiaries feel that they are more competent than their headquarters in technology, and 25 percent, in CRM. This may indicate that the BrMNEs have a significant number of subsidiaries that might actually be able to contribute to their upgrading.

Table 7.21 conveys the idea of the transfer of competences between headquarters and subsidiaries. Three out of every four subsidiaries report receiving technological competences from their headquarters,

Table 7.19 *Dimensions which define headquarters–subsidiaries relationships for Brazilian multinationals*

Autonomy	Autonomy was evaluated in connection with decisions about products, processes, markets, upstream and downstream relations, and budgeting; regarding all of these, a far larger number of subsidiaries reported high autonomy than the number of headquarters that admitted to delegating high autonomy.
Integration	An ambiguous relation: the subsidiaries indicated that headquarters resort heavily to communication and socialization mechanisms; nevertheless, for half of the subsidiaries studied, the headquarters fail to understand their affiliates' activities and role.
Entrepreneurship	A high percentage of the subsidiaries admit that they have a strong entrepreneurial orientation, even with regard to decisions that involve risk. However, the number of head offices that admit to encouraging this is far lower.
Initiative	One-third of the subsidiaries reported operations that show initiative; the areas in which this dimension becomes most obvious are the adaptation of products and services, in order to meet local market requirements, and technology-related investments.
(Local) business networks	The subsidiaries report far stronger downstream relations than upstream relations, i.e., they explain themselves as having been attracted by global clients rather than as organizers of international supply chains; the local characteristics concerning the science and technology context indicate low intensity.
(Local) competitive environment	The vast majority of the subsidiaries admitted to being in a highly competitive environment with demanding markets and rivalry among firms.

Table 7.20 *Competences regarding which subsidiaries believe that they are better than headquarters (self-evaluation) (%)*

Technological competence	27
Production competence	42
Commercial competence	63
CRM competence (marketing)	25
SCM competence (logistics)	45
HRM competence	48
Financial competence	53

Responses on planning and organizing competences were not requested.

and half from production. However, the most revealing element here is that those that believe that their technology and production competences are superior (81 and 71 percent, respectively) indicate that they are transferring competences to their headquarters.

Based on Table 7.21, we surmise that headquarters make use of subsidiaries' competences mainly in the CRM and supply chain management (SCM) areas. In other words, BrMNES, through their subsidiaries, seek to establish new positions in global production networks. This is, apparently, what headquarters most value. On the other hand, among the subsidiaries that believe that they have superior competences, it is the HRM competence that is least valued by their headquarters.

7.7 Toward a Brazilian model of international management?

The general characteristics of the Brazilian firms' internationalization process are:

- The majority of Brazilian firms took a long time to become international, as in general this occurred decades after they were established. In the 1980s, they gave birth to a modest internationalization movement, which, however, only became significant as of the late 1990s, following a series of events that changed the firms' operating context.
- Brazilian firms internationalized autonomously, in accordance with their own decisions and strategies; there was no cooperation either

Table 7.21 *Perceptions of subsidiaries in regards to organizational competences (%)*

	Gets from headquarters (1)	Transfers to headquarters (2)	Is more competent than headquarters (3)	Is more competent than and transfers to headquarters (3/2)
Technological competence	73	22	27	81
Production competence	51	30	42	71
Commercial competence	25	31	63	49
CRM competence	57	23	25	92
SCM competence	32	39	45	87
HRM competence	46	21	48	43
Financial competence	59	24	53	45

Responses on planning and organizing competences were not requested.

among industrial firms or between the latter and financial institutions and there was no government support.

- The privatized firms were among the largest Brazilian MNEs of the 1990s.
- A large number of Brazilian multinationals are part of family groups.
- At first, the internationalization strategies favored Latin American countries, as their geographical distance was shorter and their cultural and institutional differences smaller. Recently, a shift toward more developed markets was observed.

A noticeable specificity of the BrMNEs is their management model. The preceding discussion helps one to understand this model's roots, which was hegemonic up to the 1980s and 1990s (although they can still be found in many firms). Some Brazilian firms broke away from their cultural legacy, by facing challenges and taking advantage of opportunities, thus developing a distinctive profile of organizational competences, articulated through a novel management style. These allowed them to capture, as well as to create, opportunities in the international arena and claim a visible position among multinationals. In certain cases, internationalization was also "induced by the transformation of the operating conditions in the home country that followed the process of economic reform" (Cuervo-Cazurra, 2007).

In general, internationalization was a strategy that took a long time to mature in Brazilian firms. Initially they preferred adopting uncertainty and risk avoidance mechanisms (for example: preferring exports to FDI), tending to choose outwardly similar markets and adopting individual, non-cooperative decisions to internationalize.

Their internationalization is not always fast. Although their strategy is based on fast responses, as foreseen by Sull (2005a), that does not mean that their pace of internationalization is rapid. There is a consensus among Brazilian firms that, due to their relative resources, mistakes can have dramatic repercussions. Therefore, Brazilian MNEs tend to embrace a cautious posture.

At first, the internationalization strategies favored greenfield investments in Latin American countries. Over time, BrMNEs started resorting to several types of entry (greenfield investments, alliances, partnerships) and undertook a mix of activities, with a view to making their need for horizontal expansion compatible with the imperative of a vertical upgrade, as foreseen by Guillén and Garcia-Canal (2009).

In general, the corporate competence that constitutes the cornerstone of their internationalization strategy is production; in the early stages, that is where their competitive differential resides. However, during the expansion phase, other competences are called to play more strategic roles. Still, for historical and institutional reasons, the most critical but evidently weak competence is HRM.

Table 7.22 synthesizes the evolution of the architecture of competences in Brazilian firms.

Certain competences can be considered peculiarities of emerging country companies in general and can be a source of competitiveness in their international forays. As emphasized by Guillén and Garcia-Canal (2009), these firms show excellent performance in institutionally complex and turbulent environments due to their political experience and ability to manage acquisitions. The authors highlight that those

Table 7.22 *The evolution of the architecture of competences in Brazilian firms*

Competences	Traditional	New	BrMNEs
Organizing	Hierarchic; centralized	Flexible; invested and learnt to create partnerships	Competent in managing acquisitions; developing international management model
Planning	Immediatist; "intuitive"	Active waiting; proactive in regards to the sociopolitical infrastructure	Developing new competences to strive under uncertainty and turbulence
Production	Primary: high volume and low quality to get low cost	World class; masters process technology	World leader; innovates in process engineering
Technological	The minimum investment necessary	"Creative innovation." Some invest in R&D	Moderate investments and reliance on partnerships
Commercial	Seeks the markets that buy its products; low concerns with brand and image	Learnt from the diversity and complexity of domestic market. Concerned with image and brand	Upgrading through experiential learning
Supply chain Management	A passive supplier; no efforts to upgrade	Learnt the rationale of global protection networks (GPNs) and seek strategic positioning.	Some are leaders of GPNs

Table 7.22 (*cont.*)

Competences	Traditional	New	BrMNEs
Customers relationships management	Non-existent	Learnt the strategic value of CRM and invested	Upgrading through experiential learning
Human resources management	Conservative	Local leaders	The most difficult front for international expansion
Financial	Had to learn but is dependent on government	Strong competence; concerned with risk management	Learnt to operate in international financial markets
Corporate social responsibility			Critical to overcome liability of foreignness

companies "absorb technology, combine resources, and innovate from an organizational point of view in ways that reduce costs and enhance learning" (Guillén and Garcia-Canal: 31). Moreover, some of the cases reflect the importance of their participation in global production networks, to leverage the competences differentials.

The relationship between the local environment and competence development at firm level is mediated by the firm's management style, promoting the unique characteristics in different contexts. The "Brazilian management style" contributes to competence development at firm level. A typical feature is related to seeking creative and adaptive solutions, which contributes to organizational flexibility and adaptation to new operational contexts.

The very process of internationalization is imposing profound changes in organizational competences, especially in what concerns the direct relationships in foreign countries, which creates new demands for the commercial and CRM competences.

However, the internationalization process of Brazilian enterprises revealed that there is a new competence to be nurtured and grown that is related to corporate social responsibility. This finding seems to be related to the new demands faced by Brazilian enterprises in their insertion within the foreign local communities. It is a new version of how foreign firms must cope with the liability of foreignness. This point will be further elaborated in the next chapter.

The Brazilian model of international management is still under construction but its foundations are already visible. The consolidation will depend on the speed of the leaders and the demonstration effect, thus attracting new contenders in the international markets.

8 | *Cases of outstanding Brazilian multinationals*

8.1 Picking up cases of outstanding performers

In this chapter, we elaborate upon the most important cases of Brazilian multinationals. The cases were selected according to:

- the degree of importance on the international scene, i.e., the main global players;
- the different sectors of the manufacturing and services industries;
- the possibility of drawing comparisons with multinationals from other emerging countries.

We tried to organize each case within the same format, following the analytical framework that is guiding our analysis. However, the nature of each case and the information available does not allow a perfect fit. There is however a degree of heterogeneity in terms of breadth and depth with which each case is presented.

Table 8.1 summarizes the cases that were chosen in each segment of economic activity and the reasons that led us to prioritize them in relation to others. Some of them are already widely known, but the approach that we developed places them under a new light. Other cases are original and reveal new facets of the process of internationalization of Brazilian companies.

To enrich the cases we prepared an introductory short text explaining the most relevant environmental features that influenced the process of internationalization of each Brazilian firm. The texts emphasize more the international scene or the local context, depending on the characteristics of each case.

Table 8.1 *Cases of outstanding Brazilian multinationals*

Classification	Case(s)	Most relevant features
State-owned multinational	Petrobras	"The Brazilian state-owned enterprise," oil and gas, global player, Fortune 500s
Privatized multinationals	Vale	World's second largest in the mining industry, Fortune 500s
	Embraer	World's third largest in the aircraft industry
Agro-business	JBS-Friboi	World's largest in the beef industry, meteoric ascent
Natural resources	Votorantim	Traditional family conglomerate, fourth largest in Brazil
Steel	Gerdau	Pioneer and one of the most internationalized, Fortune 500s
Petrochemicals	Braskem	Most relevant in the industry, part of the Odebrecht group
Consumer goods	Ambev	AB Inbev's driver, a distinctive case of entrepreneurship
Construction inputs	Tigre	An example of regional internationalization
Components and subsystems	WEG	A successful case of expanding horizontally (second in the world) while moving up the value chain
Systems assemblers	Marcopolo	A local optimizer operating in every emerging country
Capital goods	Romi	The only Brazilian capital goods producer remaining
Engineering	Odebrecht	World top twenty, developer of organizational competences
IT	Stefanini	Rare case of internationalization of a software producer
	Bematech	Rare case of internationalization of a hardware producer
Services	IBOPE	Developing services for the Latin Americans
Born globals	CI&T	Born global in the software industry
	Griaule	Born global in the biometrics field

8.2 Petrobras: the state-owned multinational

Box 8.1 An introductory note on multinationals in the oil industry

The largest multinationals developed in oil sector activities. Exploration began in the US in 1859, but production intensified with the use of oil to produce motor fuels. The pioneering, dominant company in the business was the Standard Oil Company, and it became America's and the world's largest company in oil exploration. In 1907, Standard Oil controlled fifty-five companies outside the US. In 1911, the company was ruled a monopoly that violated American anti-trust law, and it was broken up into three companies. There were new American entries into multinational oil production, such as the Texas Company (Texaco), which initiated its activities abroad in 1905.

In Europe the pattern of growth for the oil industry was different. Until the discovery of the North Sea reserves, there was practically no exploration on the continent. Thus, European companies in the sector emerged in oil commerce and distribution and in researching new reserves in foreign countries. European banks became the grand source of financing for foreign investment in oil. The two largest European oil multinationals were also founded before 1914. In 1907 a merger between a Dutch group and a British group created the Shell Group, and in 1908 British Petroleum (BP) was founded.

The Seven Sisters consisted of three companies formed by the US government's break-up of Standard Oil, along with four other major oil companies: Standard Oil of New Jersey (Esso), Standard Oil of New York (then Socony, now Mobil), Standard Oil of California (Socal), Royal Dutch Shell, Anglo-Persian Oil (now BP), Gulf, and Texaco. Well-organized and able to negotiate as a cartel, the Seven Sisters were able to have their way with most third world oil producers. It was only when the Arab states began to gain control over oil prices and production, mainly through the formation of the Organization of the Petroleum Exporting Countries (OPEC), beginning in 1960 and really gaining power by the 1970s that the Seven Sisters' influence declined. (Based on Jones, 2005.)

Selected case

Petrobras was created in 1953. It is ranked sixty-third in *Fortune 500* (2008), eighty-eighth in *Forbes 2000* (2008), twelth largest emerging country multinational enterprise (MNE) when ranked by foreign assets, and ninety-fourth when measured by the transnationality index (TNI), according to UNCTAD's World Investment Report (WIR) (2006), and one of the Boston Consulting Group's (BCG's) global challengers (2008).

8.2.1 Petrobras: origin

Petrobras (PB) was founded in 1953, within a strongly nationalistic atmosphere, as a result of pressure from a broad coalition of forces that included everyone, from the communists to the student movement to the military.

Oil exploration and production, as well as other activities linked to the oil, natural gas, and derivatives sectors (other than wholesale distribution and retail sales by gas stations) were a PB monopoly from 1954 to 1997.

8.2.2 Developing production and process competences

When it was founded, PB's mission was to refine oil as efficiently as possible in refineries that were built on a turn-key basis by large foreign engineering firms. It was essentially a time of learning by doing.

In 1955, just a couple of years after PB was established, the Center for the Development of Personnel (CENAP; Centro de Aperfeiçoamento de Pessoal) was set up. In 1966 this center became responsible for research and development, was relocated to a site adjacent to the Federal University of Rio de Janeiro, and renamed CENPES (Centro de Pesquisas Leopoldo Americo Miguez de Mello).

Thereafter, CENPES acquired a fundamental role in lending support to PB's strategies. As mentioned, the first petrochemical complex was set up in the 1950s using a turn-key contract. In the 1960s, CENPES became involved with the design and implementation of the second complex, as a technology receiver. For the third center, built in the 1970s, PB decided to negotiate a contract that involved the open transfer of technology. Although the global engineering firms declined bidding for this, PB found a French company that had just completed a similar project and that was willing to accept PB's terms. Together with CENPES, it developed and implemented the third petrochemical complex in the south of Brazil.

To comply with the goal of nationalizing its equipment, PB ordered as much as possible from Brazilian capital goods manufacturers, thus enabling them to develop technologically and to build further competences.

Moreover, the oil crisis of the 1970s and the ensuing supply shortage in Brazil gave rise to a critical situation, which spurred the creation of the alcohol program, to replace fossil fuels. Thus, the Brazilian energy matrix was substantially modified. PB succeeded in changing its cracking composition and in operating as efficiently as possible, processing raw material of uncertain origins and fluctuating characteristics. This forced PB to develop operating competences that allowed it to engage in a systematic reconfiguration of its production processes. As a result, PB was able to maintain its operating efficiency throughout the many oil crises and energy matrix changes that have occurred in Brazil and elsewhere. And, when the time came, CENPES had acquired the competences needed to design refinery projects for implementation in less developed countries.

8.2.3 Learning to internationalize – the quest for resources

The first oil crisis was decisive in changing PB's aims. The company embraced a strategy of "producing Brazilian oil abroad," to minimize Brazil's vulnerability vis-à-vis foreign supply sources. Meanwhile, on the domestic front, PB adopted a strategy of exploring and exploiting oil in the high seas, while also expanding its refining capabilities and pipelines.

Starting in 1972 and for some thirty years thereafter, PB's activities abroad were conducted by Braspetro (Petrobras Internacional SA). Braspetro's activities centered on the upstream segments (exploring and producing, while also rendering engineering and well-drilling services) and, to a lesser extent, on the downstream segments (refining, marketing, transport, and logistics). The first country that Braspetro entered was Colombia, in 1972, when it acquired Tennecol. In 1976, it made a major discovery in Iraq: the giant field of Majnoon, with reserves estimated at 7 billion barrels of oil. In 1978, it discovered another field in Iraq, Nhrumr. Together, they formed the world's greatest oil discovery of the 1970s and comprised a reserve of roughly 30 billion barrels of oil. In 1979, PB signed an agreement with the Iraqi government and returned the fields in exchange for payment of $1.402 billion, thereafter becoming merely a provider of technical services in that country.

By 1979, Braspetro was surveying for oil in Angola. In China, which PB entered in the late 1970s, it signed five exploration contracts in 1983. However, it stopped operating in this country as of 1986, because its discoveries were not economically feasible. In 1987, the firm expanded its activities to North America, by acquiring a share of eight blocks in the Gulf of Mexico.

8.2.4 *Petrobras moves up the value chain – the Petroquisa years*

When it had its second petrochemical complex built in the 1960s, using a tripartite system, PB advanced along the value chain and became a producer of fertilizers and petrochemical products, through Petroquisa and Petrofértil.

With these investments, PB followed a competences creation strategy similar to what it had done in regard to refining, so as to ensure the development of local knowledge and to minimize dependence on foreign firms and institutions. In these cases, CENPES was once again instrumental in the creation of organizational competences. These PB subsidiaries were privatized during the 1990s.

8.2.5 *Acquiring competences in services – Petrobras as a supplier of services*

In 1971, PB moved into services when it created Petrobras Distribuidora, a distributor and marketer of oil products, alcohol, and other fuels. This subsidiary is active in several industries, such as the automotive, maritime, rail, and aviation sectors. It runs some 6,000 gas stations in Brazil and is currently the country's largest retail company, with revenues that are twice as great as those of the second and third ranked firms (Ipiranga and Shell).

Internationally, PB is also a distributor in Argentina, Bolivia, and Chile. In Argentina, it has roughly 800 gas stations, or 15 percent of the market. To work in the Argentine market, the company had to change the way it provided service, by setting up convenience stores adapted to local habits. Marketing investments were also required, in order to get the Argentine consumers to accept the Petrobras brand. At present, among other investments, PB sponsors the Racing football team from Buenos Aires.

8.2.6 *Learning to innovate – offshore operations*

In the 1980s, oil reserves were discovered in the deep waters of the Campos Basin. At first, tried and tested technologies were used to pump oil to a water depth of as much as 120 meters. From this point on, PB began developing its own technology, exceeding depths of 500 meters in around 1990, when it won the Offshore Technology Conference Prize. By 1999, it had reached a depth of 1,853 meters, still in the Campos Basin.

PB's technological developments resulted in its taking out 817 patents and brought internationalization advantages in their wake. Currently, one of PB's strengths in operations outside the Southern Cone, in places such as Africa, the Middle East, and the Gulf of Mexico, consists of taking advantage of its proprietary competence and technologies as a competitive differential.

8.2.7 *Learning the trade: expanding internationally while competing in its own backyard*

The early 1990s were an unstable time for PB: some of its subsidiaries were privatized and the industrial policy of the Fernando Collor de Mellor administration and the Fernando Henrique Cardoso administration were not clearly defined with regard to PB's sector. The chief objective of the company's internationalization, at that time, was to expand its business in such a way as to enhance the aggressive strategy it had embraced in the preceding decade.

In 1997, the Oil Law put an end to PB's monopoly, by opening the oil industry in Brazil to private initiative. Consequently, multinationals such as Shell, Exxon Mobil, Texaco, and BP started moving into various oil-related and oil product sectors, obliging Petrobras to implement several transformations. One of these consisted of restructuring itself and stepping up its globalization process, so as to make it more competitive in foreign markets.

The company expanded the scope of its field of action from oil to energy, aiming to operate in the production and distribution of gas and biofuels. When its upstream subsidiaries were privatized, PB went back to being a concern essentially centered on the oil chain (exploration, production, refining, and distribution), as it distanced itself from the strategy typical of the major international players in the oil industry in general and in particular of the super-majors, such as Exxol-Mobil, Shell, BP-Amoco-Arco, Elf-Total-Fina, and Chevron-Texaco. The latter, besides maintaining very vertically integrated structures, also have a diversified portfolio, as they pursue innovations and products with higher added value, such as those resulting from fine chemistry or the fourth generation of petrochemicals.

In addition, PB's corporate governance changed. The Brazilian government continues to be the main stakeholder, with 56 percent of PB's voting shares and 32 percent of its total shares, but the company is now traded on stock exchanges, the PB pension fund holding a substantial chunk of its stock. Moreover, in 1999, the PB corporate bylaws were amended, to ensure standards of corporate governance in compliance with the US Securities and Exchange Commission (SEC) regulations, thus enabling trading of PB shares on the New York Stock Exchange (NYSE), which started in 2000. Finally, the company adopted a management model that allows it to seek financing and contracts abroad.

8.2.8 Petrobras international operations after privatization

The main objectives of PB's international operations changed over time. In the 1970s, its strategy was to guarantee oil for the domestic market, whereas in the 1980s, in addition to guaranteeing supply, it also aimed at exporting oil.

Following privatization, a more structured action plan was developed. Its key element was to make the most of Southern Cone synergies, particularly of those involving Argentina and Bolivia.

However, PB also expanded its activities in Africa and North America. Its new organizational structure created the International Business Unit in 2000, which took over the management of assets and activities abroad. It encompasses five departments: corporate strategy, technical support, business development, Southern Cone operations, and rest of world operations.

Two PB shifts pointed to a more effective Southern Cone expansion strategy, especially in the Argentine market. The first took place in July 1997, when the firm Companhia Mega SA was formed by PB (34 percent), Repsol Yacimientos Petroliferos Fiscales (YPF) (38 percent) and Dow Chemical (28 percent). The second was an asset swap with Repsol YPF, a Spanish concern, which gave PB an initial share of 12 percent of the Argentine market, along with 700 gas stations of the EG3 brand plus the Bahia Blanca refinery.

In 1997, construction of the Brazil–Bolivia gas pipeline (Gasbol) was begun. This was considered the chief integration project between the Andean countries and Mercosur. Two year later, in 1999, PB formed an association with Perez Companc to acquire two refineries in Bolivia, one in Cochabamba and the other in Santa Cruz de la Sierra, thus creating Empresa Boliviana Refinación (EBR). In 2002, as a result of acquiring Perez Companc outright, PB also acquired full control of EBR.

The first years of the 2000's were underscored by a series of acquisitions, especially from Argentina. As a result, PB's activities abroad became even more diversified, encompassing oil exploration and production, refining and marketing, distribution, and gas and energy.

In 2002, when PB acquired the Argentine group Perez Companc, its downstream assets abroad increased considerably, as did its proven reserves. Then, as a result of the acquisition of Pecom, PB also became active in Ecuador, Peru, and Venezuela. Yet another major acquisition in 2002 was the Santa Fé oil company, the Argentine branch of Devon Energy Corporation in 2002.

The acquisition of 50 percent of the Pasadena refinery in Texas (Houston) followed and marked PB's entry into the US refining sector. Regarding the company's operations in the US, its objectives are to export its surplus heavy oil production from the Campos Basin to process it in Houston.

In 2004, PB stepped up its efforts in Asia, when it opened a representation office in China, to enter a strategic cooperation agreement with Sinopec, the Chinese state-owned concern. Then, in 2007, it acquired the Okinawa refinery in Japan.

By 2008, PB was active in twenty-seven countries, from which it drew about 12 percent of its total revenues, and had more than 7,000 employees engaged in a broad range of activities abroad.

However, its discovery of huge oil fields in the pre-salt layer within Brazilian territory may result in more selective investments abroad.

8.2.9 Learning to innovate II – deep water offshoring and renewable energy

PB's latest discoveries in the last few years are all in ultra-deep waters, more than 5,000 meters below sea level, and under a 2,000-meter layer of salt. This so-called "pre-salt" layer contains light oil of which the recoverable volume is estimated at some 5 billion to 8 billion barrels. Its exploitation poses technological challenges that are unprecedented in the oil industry. Therefore, the production start-up in May 2009 was a milestone in PB's history. The company is still developing a new business model specifically geared to this, a model based on its competences and proprietary technologies for pumping oil from Brazil's reserves under ultra-deep waters. Drawing oil from the pre-salt layer is also giving rise to a major national project that may leverage the development of several industrial and service sectors in Brazil.

Another area of PB involvement is biofuel, as evidenced by the establishment, in July 2008, of Petrobras Biocombustivel, a PB subsidiary in charge of developing projects for the production and management of ethanol and biodiesel.

In the ethanol segment, the company created a business model based on a policy of partnering with international firms that have access to markets, for export purposes, and with Brazilian ethanol producers already active in this sector. For instance, through its acquisition of the Okinawa refinery in Japan, in 2007, PB started to supply the Asian market with ethanol. This initiative is part of the effort to comply with environmental pollution reduction targets.

The biofuel and renewable energy area stands out in PB's 2020 strategic plan and in its 2008–12 business plan, which estimate investments of approximately $1.3 billion in renewable energy.

8.2.10 Petrobras: a company with a portfolio of unique competences

Thanks to its development history, PB now has a very special portfolio of competences in all activities of the oil-based energy business.

At present, it operates in twenty-seven countries and is active in the entire operating chain of the oil and gas industries. Additionally, it recently entered the electricity sector in the Southern Cone, also expanding its share of enterprises in North America, Africa, and Asia. In associations with seventy-one oil companies, where exploring and producing oil are concerned, PB is the operator for 17 blocks of the 357 in which it holds a share.

According to its 2006–10 business plan, PB has aggressive growth targets, as established in its 2015 strategic plan. Its planning foresees total investments of $56.4 billion, or an average of $11.3 billion a year. The estimated investment abroad for the 2006–10 period amounts to $7.1 billion, or 13 percent of the total. This means doubling the size of the international areas within the PB system during this period.

8.3 Vale: privatized and competing for global leadership

> **Box 8.2 An introductory note on multinationals in the mining industry**
>
> The massive growth in foreign direct investment (FDI) in mining in around 1870 began in England, and that country became the industrial center for international mining. A large number of the companies were small, private capital, such as the Rio Tinto Company. The main investments in this period were in mines in Spain and the US. Around 1914 the major British investments were in extraction of gold and diamonds in South Africa.
>
> Three German companies also became large-scale corporations in metal mining: Aron Hirsch, Beer Sondheimer, and Metallgesellschaft, the largest of the three. These companies had explorations in the US, Mexico, the Congo, and other European countries.
>
> At the end of the nineteenth century, North American companies began to internationalize to explore mines in Canada, Mexico, and Central America. After the first world war, North American mining companies started to invest in mining in South America.
>
> A British venture in the Brazilian mining industry was started in 1909. In 1942, it became a state-owned enterprise named Companhia Vale do Rio Doce (Vale). Vale currently competes with BHP-Billinton and Rio Tinto for the leadership of the industry worldwide.

Selected case

Vale is currently ranked as 235th in the 2008 *Fortune 500* (2008), 361st in *Forbes 2000* (2008), eleventh largest emerging country MNE when ranked by foreign assets and seventy-third when measured by the TNI, according to UNCTAD's *WIR* (2006), and one of the BCG's global challengers (2008).

8.3.1 Vale: origin

In 1909, a British consortium called Brazilian Hematite Syndicate was set up to exploit iron ore in the Vale do Rio Doce region of the state of Minas Gerais. Soon after, in 1911, it acquired Companhia Estrada de Ferro Vitória a Minas (CEFVM), a railroad that was being built to link Minas Gerais to the port city of Vitória. At this time, the firm changed its name to Itabira Iron Ore Company.

The difficulties surrounding the company's relations with the federal and the state governments led it to appoint as its president the American entrepreneur Percival Farquhar. He had previously been vice-president of the Atlantic Coast Electric Railway Company and of the Staten Island Electric Railway Company (which controlled the New York streetcars service), as well as a partner and a director of the Power Company of Cuba and of the Guatemala Railway. Farquhar was regarded as the largest private investor in Brazil from 1905 to 1918 and his business empire was comparable to those of the greatest entrepreneurs in Brazilian history up to that time.

In 1941, Farquhar formed an association with Brazilian entrepreneurs to transform Itabira Iron Ore into two domestic companies: Companhia Brasileira de Mineração e Siderurgia (mining and steel milling) and Companhia Itabira de Mineração (mining).

In June 1, 1942, as a result of the Washington Agreement, Brazil's president, Getúlio Vargas, signed a law nationalizing all of Farquhar's companies as well as the Vitória-Minas railroad. The said agreement involved Brazil, the US, and Great Britain. Its aim was mutual cooperation in the second world war effort and the exploitation of Brazil's natural resources, to be achieved by taking over and improving the railroad and having a Brazilian enterprise exploit the Itabira mines. All of this was to be financed by the Export-Import Bank of Washington and the iron ore production was to be sold to the British government and to the Metals Reserve Company, a US government concern.

The company that ensued, a corporation in which the Brazilian government also had a substantial stake, was named Companhia Vale do Rio Doce, now known merely as Vale.

8.3.2 Learning how to internationalize: an integrated company focused on exporting

One of the objectives of setting up Vale during the second world war was to guarantee the supply of iron ore for steel mills in other countries. Vale had extremely high quality reserves plus a railroad linking these to the sea port of Vitória, where it built a dock for minerals. This was completed in 1945, forming the company's first integrated infrastructure.

In 1949, Vale was already responsible for 80 percent of Brazilian iron ore exports and, by 1974, it had become the world's largest iron ore exporter, with a 16 percent share of the overseas iron ore market.

By 1954, Vale had changed its foreign trade practices, having established direct contact with the steel mills, with no intermediation of traders. At first, its chief clients were steel mills in the US. However, in 1961, the German steel mills became the company's main foreign clients. But in 1969, the Japanese took over the position of largest clients and economic partners. They were to become very important for Vale, not only as trading partners but also as providers of a management model, and have remained so to this day: there are still stories in the air about how the firm outdid itself and performed heroic feats to fulfill the needs of its Japanese clients, in line with whatever had been agreed. Vale followed the development of the Japanese production model very closely right from the start. Japanese quality methods, for instance, guided the project and implementation of entire production units, such as the pelletization one.

In 1962, Vale set up another subsidiary, Vale do Rio Doce Navegação SA (Docenave), a navigation company, thus integrating its logistical network. Today, Vale runs the largest logistics operation in Brazil and the second largest in Latin America.

The same mine→railroad→port structure was put in place to exploit the Carajás region, the world's richest in terms of minerals. Its investment in this amounted to some $4.3 billion.

Vale's strategy hinges on operating excellence. It pursues differentiation not only where quality is concerned, but also in its support services: it guarantees reliable delivery of its high-performance product at a price comparable to that of competitors. To achieve this, it has developed distinctive competences in the running of two integrated mine/railroad/port production systems (Itabira and Carajás), several pelletization mills and shipping company, management of raw materials and transformation resources (mainly power), and environmental stewardship.

The concepts drawn from the Japanese management methods have been guiding Vale's management processes for roughly fifty years. Since 1992, Vale has practiced total quality control (TQC) in an all-encompassing manner. Its certifications were obtained as of 1990 in response to pressure from the automotive industry's supply chain. However, Vale was the first mining company ever to implement the ISO 14000 environmental certification, back in 1997.

The Vale strategy has born fruit. For example, because it was the supplier of choice of Japanese mills, when the Japanese started developing steel projects for other countries (China, for example), they used input specifications provided by Vale, thus providing this Brazilian firm with special access to these new countries.

8.3.3 Developing mineral prospecting competences

In 1965, Vale established a development and technology department. A little later, in the early 1970s, Vale established Docegeo, a subsidiary that focused on non-ferrous minerals, to take advantage of the government's concern with the trade deficit of the mineral sector and of the fact that the non-metals sector had become an industrial policy priority, reflected in the government's first national development plan. This was the kickoff for Vale's diversification, so that today the company deals with nickel (Vale's major acquisition, International Nickel Company (INCO), in Canada, is a nickel mine), coal, aluminum, potassium, copper, manganese, ferroalloys, china clay, and steel milling.

Vale also has a mineral projects development department whose mission is to generate new projects and businesses. It is responsible for identifying new mineral exploration areas and has undertakings in twenty-one countries in six regions: North America, Andean America, Africa, Eurasia, Australasia, and Brazil. Vale's prospecting takes into account mineral fertility, the maturity of mineral production, and the manageability of risks in connection with copper, manganese ore, iron ore, nickel, bauxite, phosphate, potassium, coal, uranium, diamonds, and metals from the platinum group.

To this end, it brings together competences in geological research, mineral processing, engineering, and mineral economics. These competences are managed in such a way as to keep costs low, accelerate the cycle of discoveries, and guarantee the quality of projects up to their pre-viability stage.

The company's location and its state-owned nature have made it easier to get the support of federal and state universities (in particular of the Federal University of Ouro Preto) and of technical schools in the training of its employees and in the development of technological services.

8.3.4 Vale's international operations after privatization

Even before privatization, Vale was an unconventional state-owned concern:

Its development strategy is closely linked to the expansion of the Brazilian economy, particularly the State production sector ... [However], as a result of the characteristics of its production activities and its involvement with international markets, the company has managed to define its growth strategies with a certain degree of autonomy vis-à-vis government policy. Its autonomous entrepreneurial character is highly valued internally. Fleury (1986)

By 1989, Vale's strategic plan was already focusing on internationalization, for corporate reasons related to its capital structure, to help minimize risk and, above all, because of the company's past trajectory (path dependence). There were also structural factors at play, such as the industry's competitive dynamics, economies of scale, new technologies, and oligopolistic interdependence. Previously, the company had invested solely in Brazil and its internationalization consisted mainly of exports, the only minor exception to this being its investment in a US company, California Steel, in 1984.

In 1994, Vale launched an American Depositary Receipts (ADR) program, tradable in the US in the over-the-counter market.

As of 1997, thanks to its privatization, the company gradually gained agility. The winners of the Vale privatization auction were a consortium led by Companhia Siderurgica Nacional (CSN; steel mills), which has Vale as a supplier and a competitor in other industries. The full unwinding of the crossed shareholdings involving Vale and CSN was only completed in 2001.

Vale's stock, at present, is held by Valepar (owned by Previ, Bradesco, Mitsui, BNDES, and Opportunity), which accounts for 33.3 percent of its equity; the free float shares account for another 61.3 percent (of which 39.2 percent is in the hands of Brazilian investors and 60.8 percent in the hands of foreign investors); and the final 5.4 percent belongs to other parties.

8.3.5 The internationalization of exploration and research

Vale's strategy was two-pronged. One centered on the issue of how to continue to grow in the face of the consolidation and strengthening of its clients (the steel industry) and of its direct competitors, namely, BHP-Billiton and Rio Tinto. Since 2003, Vale's share of the world market has stood at some 16 percent, five points higher than the share of its closest competitor, Rio Tinto (11 percent). The world's three largest mining companies (Vale, Rio Tinto, and BHP Billiton) jointly account for 35 percent of the entire global production of iron ore.

Given this context, besides making some acquisitions in the recent past, Vale also implemented a number of actions to better serve its clients, largely by establishing alliances and networks aimed at deepening its relations with its clients and strengthening its commercial relations.

The second front concerned Vale's medium- and long-term outlook, and implied in uprating its mineral prospecting program. At present, the company has enterprises in twenty-one countries, comprising 154 projects at different stages of development and in different sites. In Africa, Vale's investments center on deposits that are close to the surface, which can therefore be extracted more easily and consequently pose less risk. In mature countries, such as Australia, Canada, and Chile, Vale employs cutting-edge technology to discover deeper deposits, besides pursuing partnerships with the firms that hold local mining rights.

At present, Vale has 13 joint ventures abroad, of which 3 concern mining and 10 concern prospecting. Besides these joint ventures, Vale has another 9 alliances in Brazil, all of them with foreign investors. Thus, one should highlight that 62% of Vale's alliances are international, i.e., they involve foreign investors located abroad. Oliveira and de Paula (2006)

In other words, Vale has been focusing on greenfield projects, rating mineral prospecting as a top corporate need. This means that the company's significant investments in mineral prospecting set the direction of the internationalization of future production, via organic growth. This also means that Vale's mineral prospecting is more "internationalized" at present than its actual mining.

As for mineral production itself, it is important to highlight that the company produces them in the US (steel), Bahrain (pellets), France (ferroalloys), Belgium (manganese), and Norway (ferroalloys and manganese). It also has a global mining prospecting program in three continents and eight countries (Chile, Peru, Venezuela, China, Mongolia, South Africa, Mozambique, and Angola), in addition to commercial offices in New York (US), Brussels (Belgium), Tokyo (Japan), and Shanghai (China).

Vale recently purchased Inco, a Canadian company, the largest acquisition abroad ever made by a Latin American enterprise. As a result, Vale became the second largest mining company in the world, after BHP Billiton. However, if one were to disregard BHP's oil and gas businesses, then Vale would rank as the world's largest mining company.

8.3.6 *Vale: escalating the learning curve*

The quality and quantity of the natural resources to which Vale has access cannot be used as the unique or even as the major factor to explain its successful performance. It is important to stress that the very challenge of efficiently exploiting resources led Vale to develop the strategies and competences that were enablers to climb to their prominent current positions in the global market. Today, Vale is competing in markets in which the scale of operations and volume are increasingly rising. This calls for the development of innovative management strategies and models. The technological competences developed by Vale have become the asset determining its internation-alization path and dictating its strategic alliances with practically all other world renowned enterprises in its field.

However, in Vale's self assessment, what it must improve most concerns corporate social responsibility (CSR). The last straw for them to reach that conclusion came from the difficulties that Vale is currently facing with INCO, in Canada. Those are far greater than Vale had predicted before the acquisition and, in reviewing their previous experiences, Vale came to the conclusion that upgrading their CSR competences is crucial to overcome the liability of foreignness, especially because it is a multinational from an emerging country moving to the developed world.

8.4 Embraer: innovating in the aircraft industry

Box 8.3: An introductory note on the aircraft industry's market niches

In the aeronautics industry, the production of very large aircraft has been under the control of a duopoly, Boeing and European Aeronautic Defence and Space Company (EADS)–Airbus, for quite some time. However, the segment of regional aircraft presented a fierce competition until the early 2000s. Although some of those companies were already in decline, the sudden death threats and the golden opportunities were in the aftermath of the September 11, 2001 attack to the World Trade Center in New York. The competences shown by those firms to react to the turmoil that followed were decisive. Embraer came out stronger while Fairchild Dornier and Fokker closed definitely.

The global aircraft industry is composed of a relatively small number of enterprises which network according to different configurations, depending on the type of product under development and the company who is leading the global production network.

Embraer penetrated that network not only as a manufacturer of regional aircraft but also as a supplier of parts for other producers. In its early years, Embraer supplied McDonnell Douglas mainly.

Currently, Embraer competes with companies from Japan, Russia, China, India, and Mexico as a parts supplier.

In the regional transportation market, Bombardier from Canada is the main competitor while ATR, an Italian manufacturer, leads on turbo-propelled regional transporters. However, the Russian Suckoi 100, quite similar to Embraer's 175, has already made its debut and it is expected that the Chinese will develop their regional transporter very soon. In the different segments of executive jets (heavy jets, super mid-size jets, mid-size jets, and light jets) Embraer competes with Bombardier, Dassault, Gulfstream, Cessna, Hawker Beechcraft, Grob, Honda, and Piper, among others. Embraer also competes in the markets related to defence.

Selected case

In regards to rankings, Embraer is number 1,467 in the *Forbes 2000* (2007), mentioned in the BCG's global challenger list (2008), seventeenth in the SOBEET ranking (2007) and tenth in the Fundacao Dom Cabral's (FDC) ranking (2007).

8.4.1 Embraer: Origin

The history of Embraer dates back to 1941, when the Ministry of Aeronautics was created, and to 1950, when Brazil's Technological Aeronautics Institute (ITA), was established.

The first class of aeronautical engineers graduated in 1954. Most went to work for the newly created Research and Development Institute (IPD). This group was to have considerable influence on the creation of Embraer sixteen years later.

In 1962, an IPD study showed that the number of Brazilian towns served by air carriers was dropping noticeably and that no aircraft then produced met the technical and financial requirements for efficient operation under Brazilian conditions at that time. The group prepared a report for the Ministry of Aeronautics requesting aid for the development of a new product to fulfill that need. Thus, Embraer was founded in 1969 as a state-owned enterprise, linked to the Brazilian Aeronautics Ministry. Nevertheless, it was an international firm from its very inception, as aircraft are a global product.

8.4.2 *Developing technological competences: the Embraer take-off*

Embraer's first product, the Bandeirante regional aircraft, was a non-pressurized, twin-engine turboprop developed for the domestic market. However, it met with success in the US market, so that by 1982 it had gained a 32 percent market share in the segment of ten- to twenty-seat planes. The Bandeirante's successor was the Brasilia, a thirty-seater launched in 1985, of which Embraer sold 352 units worldwide. Just one US regional airline, SkyWest, bought 74.

Up to 1974–5, Embraer was "learning by doing," especially in terms of production technology. International acknowledgement of Embraer's competences in this field came in the form of its certification by the French and British authorities (1977) and by the US Federal Aviation Agency (1978).

Nevertheless, to keep abreast of aeronautical production technology, the company tried to absorb technology. For example, in the early 1970s, a number of techniques were being developed for bonding rather than riveting the structural parts of the aircraft. Embraer managed to have a clause inserted in a contract between the Aeronautics Ministry and Northrop for the purchase of F-5 fighters, according to which its engineers would be trained on their premises, in order to assimilate modern aeronautical technologies. From then on, a technological learning strategy started to be developed, at first through licensing agreements and later through ventures involving the execution of specific projects. Where this strategy was concerned, Embraer relied on the discreet but effective collaboration of the Aeronautics Ministry.

8.4.3 *Partnering to acquire international competences for servicing: the Piper case*

Around the time when Embraer was founded, Brazil's general aviation market started growing exceptionally fast. The number of lightweight planes imported in 1974 was 726, worth a total of $600 million. Of these, 400 were manufactured by Cessna, which therefore captured roughly 60 percent of the market.

That same year, however, the federal government intensified its drive to achieve equilibrium in the country's balance of payments, shaken by the oil crisis. The drastic scheme of import duties put in place to curb the deficit included lightweight aircraft. Following this, a number of contacts involving the Planning Bureau, the Aeronautics Ministry, and Embraer took place, to discuss the feasibility of having lightweight aircraft manufactured locally under license. As a result, a mission was sent to visit the major American aircraft manufacturers to discuss proposals for a licensing agreement to make American planes in Brazil.

Cessna declined the invitation, but Piper agreed. Cessna then organized another arrangement, to assemble its own planes in Brazil through other partners. But the Aeronautics Ministry refused permission. This led Cessna, in reaction, to lobby the US government and demand retaliation, in the form of a blocking of Brazilian imports, to cover not only Embraer products but other goods as well, such as footwear. The dispute was only settled when Embraer pointed out that, in fact, only the fuselage of its planes was Brazilian-made, the propulsion and avionics being almost entirely American.

In regards to contractual arrangements, Embraer negotiated to have Piper transfering know-how not only about production techniques but also about organizational aspects, maintenance, and after-sales management of the aircraft in international markets. This became one of the cornerstones of Embraer's international expansion.

8.4.4 The rigidity of technology as a core competence: the 1990s crisis

In 1985, Embraer started producing a subsonic bomber in partnership with Italian firms, thereby assimilating new technologies.

Meanwhile, it also began developing the nineteen-seat, twin engine, turboprop Vector in partnership with a state-owned concern from Argentina, Fábrica Militar de Aviones (FAMA). The Vector was an extremely sophisticated, high performance commuter aircraft with radical design architecture. However, no demand for the aircraft materialized because of its high cost, driving Embraer to abandon the project. The firm then spiraled downward into a crisis resulting from a lack of products and almost went bankrupt. This is illustrated by the number of its employees, which plummeted from 12,000 to 2,500.

Nevertheless, its technological learning would turn out to be crucial for the development of the ERJ-145 project, which went on to become a major international sales success.

8.4.5 The acquisition of marketing, finance, and planning competences through privatization

In its pre-privatization years, Embraer was a firm driven by a technology push. Once it was privatized and its new administration took over, however, there was a radical shift in the way it did business, thanks to an injection of financial and market orientation, so that market pull became its driver. Mauricio Botelho, its new chief executive officer (CEO), came from Bozzano-Simonsen, one of the financial groups that controlled Embraer.

The new orientation was to absolutely prioritize the project of a new regional jet, the ERJ-145. Since Bombardier already had a product in this range, Embraer started building up its client relations, while transforming its business model and its organizational culture from a technology-oriented organization into one oriented to clients and services. "A large banner with the phrase 'back to basics' was hung on a wall in the engineering department. A team of engineers visited 15 British and 11 American aerospace companies with the declared aim of benchmarking their product development practices. The team was somewhat surprised by the openness of many of the companies visited" (Yu and Tromboni, 2002). Meanwhile, Embraer also opened offices in Australia (1997), China (2000), and Singapore (2000), to improve its relations with oriental clients, besides establishing a new service center for its US clients in Dallas.

8.4.6 The creation of an innovative business model

A new business model was put in place: for the launch of a new product, a forty-five-seat regional jet, risk partnerships were established with four foreign suppliers from Chile, Spain, Belgium, and the US. This model was innovative not only because it was based on a global supply network, but because of its cooperative character and its association with partnering and risk sharing.

One year after the first ERJ-145 delivery, Embraer engineers were already working on designs for the next generation of Embraer jets, the Embraer 170 (Figure 8.1). After extensive consultation with regional airline companies all over the world, the firm came up with a new jetliner family. Embraer increased the number of risk partners to eleven, including large traditional MNEs, such as Kawasaki

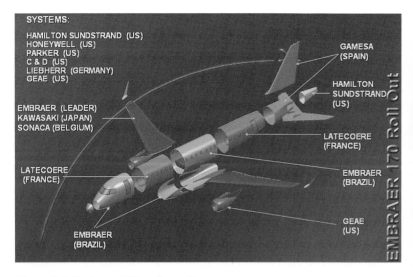

SYSTEMS:

HAMILTON SUNDSTRAND (US)
HONEYWELL (US)
PARKER (US)
C & D (US)
LIEBHERR (GERMANY)
GEAE (US)

EMBRAER (LEADER)
KAWASAKI (JAPAN)
SONACA (BELGIUM)

LATECOERE
(FRANCE)

EMBRAER
(BRAZIL)

GAMESA
(SPAIN)

HAMILTON
SUNDSTRAND
(US)

LATECOERE
(FRANCE)

EMBRAER
(BRAZIL)

GEAE
(US)

EMBRAER 170 Roll Out

Figure 8.1 Embraer 170 and suppliers

(Japan) and Latecoere (France). Unlike the preceding case, the partnering firms took responsibility for the technical specifications and detailing of sub-projects, while Embraer remained in charge of detailing clients' needs, the general project specifications, the structure sub-projects, the integration of all the systems, and the final assembling.

In the aeronautical industry, the product cycle begins with marketing and sales. Thus, Embraer undertook to deliver the product to its first buyer thirty-eight months after the order was placed, when the norm was some sixty months. To achieve this target, Embraer developed and implemented an innovative project management model that integrated 400 engineers from sixteen firms in several countries with 600 engineers in Brazil. This organizational model was unprecedented anywhere in the world. It consisted of three matrices of three axes linked to managerial cells and it benefited from competitive advantages versus the competition. Therefore, Embraer developed distinctive competences related to an innovative business model combined with a breakthrough-type of management system for product development and globally dispersed manufacturing. As a result, it was able to attract partners and lead a network, because it had technological and project competences acknowledged by the market.

8.4.7 *Embraer as a systems integrator of global production networks*

Thanks to the aforementioned actions, Embraer consolidated a strong position as a prime contractor in the global aeronautical chain of production.

In this chain, the **integrators**, or prime contractors, are enterprises with competences in the integration of aeronautical systems. These firms include Boeing, Airbus, Embraer, and Bombardier, among others.

They serve the **operators**, the organizations that interact with the end markets and consumers. In the case of the civil aviation industry, these are the air carriers, the courier firms, and the companies that purchase executive aircraft, among others.

The prime contractors develop, produce, and deliver products making use of subsystems ordered from **developers**, companies whose competences lie in the research and development field. In the case of the aeronautical industry, they develop the so-called systems and modules that are part of the aircraft, which is the end product. Firms such as GE, Rolls Royce, Allison, Honeywell, and Parker Hannifin, among others, are developers.

The developers order the manufactured parts and components from the **producers**, enterprises with special competences in industrial process engineering and in production process management (manufacturing and logistics). In the aeronautical industry, these firms range from large enterprises, such as GKN-Aerospace, to small companies that make specific products to order on a small scale.

Thus, Embraer built up distinctive competences in developing projects, implementing and coordinating globally decentralized production systems, and managing complex projects.

Once Embraer had consolidated this position, it opened new niches, trying to reduce its dependence on commercial aviation. It expanded its product line to defense and branched into the market of executive aircraft. On the financial front, it sold 20 percent of its common stock to a consortium of French firms (Dassault Aviation, Thales, Aerospatiale-Matra, and Snecma), thereby diversifying its sources of revenue.

In 2002, it opened Embraer Aircraft Maintenance Services (EAMS), a maintenance unit in Nashville, US. That same year, it entered a joint venture with AVICII, a Chinese company, to produce the ERJ-145 aircraft. Embraer kept 51 percent of the stock while its Chinese partner held 49 percent.

In 2004, Embraer, in partnership with EADS, acquired a 65 percent stake in Oficinas Gerais de Manutenção Aeronautica de Portugal (OGMA), the former Portuguese state-owned concern in the field of civil and military aircraft maintenance and repairs, manufacturing of structural components, and support for engineering. Embraer has a 70 percent stake in the business while EADS holds the other 30 percent.

In 2006, Embraer undertook a corporate restructuring and became the first sizeable Brazilian enterprise with stock held by a large number of shareholders, thus becoming free from any controlling group or major stakeholders. This laid the cornerstone for its sustained growth via free access to the global capital markets and it increased the firm's capacity to fund the development of its expansion programs.

Today, Embraer has seven units abroad: Nashville and Fort Lauderdale (US), Villepinte and Le Bourget (France), Alverca (Portugal), Harbin (China), and Singapore. Except for Harbin, which also assembles planes, the other units focus on customer service. The company has announced the construction of two new plants in Portugal in the town of Evora; its investment plans for the next six years indicates it plans to invest roughly $100 million in a metal structures plant and another $48 million in a composite materials unit.

8.4.8 The Embraer subsidiary in China

Embraer's plant in Harbin, China, was a prerequisite for delivering jets to Chinese airlines, as part of an industrial offset agreement. Offset agreements within the aircraft industry have become increasingly complex, so that by now major producers such as Boeing and Airbus operate with globally decentralized supply networks that are not shaped by cost, quality, or logistic factors. These subcontracting relationships have been configured in response to the industrial development priorities of foreign governments that control the purchasing decisions of their domestic airlines. The Chinese operation is a joint-venture with a local manufacturer and relies on a completely knocked down (CKO) assembling system.

8.4.9 *Embraer: striving in a complex global industry*

The way in which Embraer developed its competences had some striking features. Before its privatization, the company worked in a low-pressure environment, within a context of relative protection and government subsidies. Under these circumstances, it developed fairly advanced technical and production competences locally, which nevertheless were insufficient to avoid the 1990s crisis.

Its turnaround implied in developing a new culture and new organizational competences, which drove it to become an enterprise both client-oriented and competent in the handling of financial issues.

Its innovative business model was its solution for rising above a crisis. It embraced and competently developed this model, turning it into a competitive advantage that the market gradually acknowledged. At first, Embraer sold products that did not carry its brand name to peripheral markets; these were named regional transporters or regional jets. Still, Embraer captured a golden opportunity (Sull, 2005a) when the regional transport markets boomed. This was when it became a trademark.

Embraer can be regarded as a successful case of internationalization despite having no plants abroad. The firm leads a complex international supply chain, coordinated by three international offices and logistics centers. Its involvement in international assembling, in the form of its joint venture in China, was essentially driven by political constraints.

It is important to add that Embraer's financial operations benefit from strong government aid via Brazil's National Economic and Social Development Bank (BNDES), which set up a specific program and an administrative office to provide support for the financing of Embraer's products.

8.5 JBS-Friboi: from butcher's shop to world's largest producer in fifty years

> **Box 8.4 An introductory note on the meat industry in Brazil and worldwide**
>
> Throughout the 1980s and 1990s a complete restructuring of the beef industry took place in Brazil: the traditional Brazilian producers went out of business, the traditional multinationals, such as Swift, closed their subsidiaries, and a new group of companies

emerged. At the same time, the Brazilian herd had become the world's largest at the turn of the century and the country assumed the world's leadership of beef exports in 2001.

This is an industry where operational excellence prevails, because the processes are known and spread worldwide: the technological standard is homogeneous. To the extent that the most important technological innovations are developed outside the slaughtering and meat preparation industry (pesticides, animal genetics, food additives, machinery and equipment, packaging, etc.) and are available on the market, the most important from the standpoint of competitiveness is related to how the company absorbs and applies these technologies.

However, in Brazil, the sector's growth came to depend on problems of coordination and management of the production chain, especially with regard to overcoming sanitary barriers. That depends on a wide movement of the meat industry and other regulatory and supervisory institutions in Brazil articulated into the international circuits that regulate trade.

The movement toward the internationalization of Brazilian meat produces is, at least partly, motivated by the need to access markets which are resistant to Brazilian products, such as the US, Japan, and the European Union (EU). These markets demand more and more products which comply to the most stringent norms and standards of quality and ethics. These entail international trade barriers that are subject to political pressures. Producing locally in these countries they are able to supply local markets and export to other countries without depending on restrictions imposed on the industry in Brazil.

In recent years, Brazilian meat-producing companies acquired subsidiaries in fifteen countries. The Brazilian currency's appreciation against the dollar facilitated the purchase of units in other countries, which often cost less than local firms. Some of these companies had government support through BNDES.

However, the key question becomes: how do those companies manage their international operations? We will answer the question through the analysis of the case JBS-Friboi that is currently the world's largest protein producer, a global challenger according to BCG, and ranked as number one on the 2008 SOBEET's ranking.

> **Other Brazilian multinationals in the industry**
> Marfrig and Brazilian Foods (a merger between Perdigão and Sadia).

8.5.1 JBS-Friboi

In September 2009, when JBS-Friboi acquired 64 percent of Pilgrim's Pride, one of the icons of American capitalist agriculture, based in Texas, it became the largest company in the world of animal protein. On the same day the company announced a merger with Bertin, previously the second largest meat producer in Brazil, which resulted in a 22 percent increase in meat production, enlargement of the customer base in 110 countries, and expansion of the product line. JBS-Friboi is now the largest beef producer in the world with production capacity in the four major producing countries: Brazil, US, Australia, and Argentina. However, among the cases of Brazilian multinationals, it is perhaps the most paradoxical, the one that has less evidence to be analyzed, due to the speed and the conditions surrounding its internationalization strategy.

8.5.2 Origin

The company's story begins with José Batista Sobrinho, who in Annapolis, Goiás State, Brazil, bought cattle to resell to stores. In 1953, he opened a butcher shop and, in 1957, when the construction of Brasilia took off, expanded the business, establishing one of the first slaughterhouses in that region.

In 1969, José made a downstream movement by establishing a cold storage plant and changed the company name to Friboi. To strengthen the visual identity, the logo was created by a Catalan painter in 1970. He than organized the family to take care of business: his six children were trained to occupy positions in the structure of business.

In the 1980s and 1990s, major decisions were the acquisitions of Mouran, formerly the largest meat producer in Brazil, SB Holdings, an American distributor of meat, and an abattoir in Buenos Aires. Simultaneously, the company invested in expanding the local facilities.

8.5.3 Internationalization

Exports of fresh beef begin in 1997. In 2005, the group acquired Swift Argentina, becoming the first Brazilian multinational in the meat sector. In 2006, the company name changed to JBS, the initials of the founder, and Friboi became one of the brands. In March 2007, JBS became the first company in the industry to go public on the stock exchange in Sao Paulo. In July 2007 it acquired 100 percent of American Foods Swift and Company (with units in the US and Australia), becoming the largest firm in the beef industry with a slaughter capacity of 47,100 heads per day. With the acquisition of 50 percent of Inalca, one of the largest producers of beef in Europe, in December 2008, JBS incorporated ten plants in Italy. In March 2008, Friboi announced the purchase of National Beef, Smithfield Beef, and Tasman, but these were blocked by the US government. However, with the purchase of Pilgrim's Pride, JBS-Friboi became the largest company in the world of animal protein.

In addition to the need to overcome technical barriers, the internationalization of JBS-Friboi seems related to an internal competition with Brazilian competitors, based on the assumption that the industry will concentrate. Despite its large size and global leadership, JBS' market share is no more than 7.6 percent of the total cattle slaughtered in Brazil. In the US, the concentration process is underway and the fifty largest companies account for 90 percent of slaughter, revealing the tendency of the formation of megaplayers in a production chain that does not yet have a governance structure established; it is very fragmented. For example, in the case of JBS-Friboi, there are more than 6,000 clients, the largest accounting for no more than 1.4 percent of gross operating revenue. The same holds for exports, where concentration is less than 4.5 percent.

8.5.4 Competences for competition

At first, we can assume that the main competence developed by JBS-Friboi is the management of the production and distribution chain, operating under the criteria of operational excellence. Two examples are revealing. In the area of supplier development, the group was the first to implement a tool for quality management on farms supplying animals. It is called Quality Friboi Farms and aims to prepare farmers for the Global Partnership for Good Agricultural Practice (EurepGAP), thus enabling its products to enter the European market. The second comes from the area of logistics, in which Friboi developed a transportation system that increases production and preserves the quality and characteristics of the product.

The speed of JBS-Friboi's movement did not leave enough time for in-depth analyses; information is anecdotal. In recent interviews, Friboi's CEO described the management system as "FROG" (FROm Goias, Goias being the Brazilian state where JBS was first located). Perhaps the most detailed report on JBS-Friboi is the one produced by Bell and Ross (2008) describing the intervention of JBS-Friboi on the newly acquired Swift & Co. For these authors "the company's culture prioritizes simplicity, directness, and the absence of internal politics and egos, in operations, prizes efficiency, economies of scale, a lean cost structure, quality and operating as close to full capacity as possible" (p. 5). The intervention under the new US subsidiary, led by one of the sons of the founder, was described by authors as back to basics: management restructuring, getting incentives right, cost-reductions and cost-consciousness, operational improvements and increased productivity.

JBS ended 2008 with 64.6% of its employees, 59.2% of its assets and 81% of its revenue abroad. With these numbers, firstly, the company has benefited from the global crisis due to the appreciation of the dollar against the Real, as the company owned more than 80% of its cash flow in US dollars and most of its debt in Real. Thus, its debt has declined since the global crisis started. But its profitability fell significantly when compared to other Brazilian competitors.

8.6 The Votorantim Group: a multinational based on natural resources

---

Box 8.5 An introductory note on the cement industry worldwide

In this commodity-type of industry, the manufacturing process uses natural resources inputs. Moreover, markets are regional, because cement cannot be transported over long distances. Most cement plants restrict their service to a few hundred miles away, limited by production capacity and logistical costs of distribution. This makes internationalization necessary for business growth. The largest cement manufacturers are already globalized and the world market is being dominated by seven multinational corporations, five European (Holderbank, Lafarge, Heidelberger, Italcementi, and Blue Circle), Japan's Taiheiyo and Ube-Mitsubishi, and Mexico's Cemex. Votorantim is eighth in the ranking. The percentage of assets under control of this selected group is higher than the ones observed in other industries, thus making cement a truly global industry.

Selected case

Votorantim Cement is considered a global challenger by the BCG, is ranked fourth in the FDC ranking and thirty-first in SOBEET's.

Other Brazilian multinationals in resource-based industries

CSN, Magnesita, Aracruz, Camargo Correa, Suzano, and Klabin.

8.6.1 Votorantim

The Votorantim Group is the fourth largest conglomerate in Brazil after Petrobras, Vale and, recently, JBS-Friboi. Its companies are leaders or have outstanding shares in all markets in which they operate, such as in cement production, pulp and paper, aluminum, zinc, nickel and long steel products, speciality chemicals, and orange juice. It also has important participation in the financial sector through Banco Votorantim. The search for new businesses capable of generating long-term value is adding new activities, such as biotechnology and information technology (IT), to Votorantim's portfolio.

8.6.2 Origin

In 1917, the Portuguese immigrants Ignacio Pereira and Nicholas Scarpa acquired at auction the textile company Votorantim, the second largest branch in Sao Paulo. In 1925, José de Moraes, son of

Ignacio Pereira, who had worked at St. John Del Rey Mining Co., became managing director of the company and, later, its sole owner. Rapidly, Votorantim Textiles became one of the largest producers of cotton and synthetic fibers in Brazil.

In 1936, when the foreign monopoly in cement was broken, Votorantim opened its first cement plant. In 1937, Votorantim invested in chemicals (producing rayon), in 1938 in basic chemicals, in 1948 pulp and paper, and in 1955 Votorantim settled the Companhia Brasileira de Aluminio (CBA).

Votorantim became an exporter when a severe frost destroyed orange plantations in Florida, in 1962. It rapidly mobilized competences and resources for that new resource-based business, and started exports a year later. Rayon was the second product to be exported, starting in 1970. In 1991, the Votorantim Bank and in 1992 Votorantim International were established. Finally, in 1997, a holding company was established and the internal restructuring process began. It was only in the late 1990s that the company set out the strategic guidelines that would influence the decision to internationalize: (a) maintain a strong leadership in the domestic market; (b) reinforce operational excellence and market leadership to ensure advantages in terms of cost and premium prices in the global market; (c) promote the external perception of being a highly efficient and unbeatable player; (d) pursue international acquisitions, diversifying the generation of cash flows.

Therefore, in general terms, Votorantim strategy developed in the extractive industries and primary processing. It can be considered a late-mover even among Brazilian companies. This delay should be credited, however, to the long process of restructuring in order to adapt the family structure to the demands of the globalized economy. In 2005, Votorantim was elected by the International Institute for Management Development (IMD) Business School as the best family company in the world.

8.6.3 *Internationalization – cement*

The first step in the internationalization of Votorantim was in the business in which it has uncontested leadership: cement. However, that was done after a gradual yet aggressive movement of the global leaders (the French Lafarge, the British Blue Circle, and the Swiss Holcim) into the Latin American and Brazilian markets.

The internationalization of Votorantim Cement began in 2001 with the acquisition of St. Marys, a Canadian company which had two cement plants, two crushing plants, nine distribution terminals in the US Great Lakes, and thirty-nine concrete plants located in the state of Canadian Ontario. The next step was made in Brazil when Votorantim acquired Engemix, a cement transporter. This provided support for subsequent investments abroad.

In early 2003, Votorantim made a joint venture with Anderson Columbia, a civil engineering firm that designed and built the Suwannee American Cement Company, located in Florida. In 2004 it acquired S & W Materials Inc., one of the largest concrete producers in Florida, and in 2005 it acquired from CEMEX the plants Cherlevoix and Dixon-Marquette at the Great Lakes.

Then, Votorantim Cement decided to internationalize the business related to distribution and delivery, partly seeking to emulate the successful strategy adopted by CEMEX. The acquisition of Prairie, in 2007, represented a step similar to the one realized through the acquisition of Engemix, years before.

8.6.4 Competences for internationalization

From the beginning, the idea of assuming total control of the foreign plants was discarded. Knowing that their strength relied on process engineering and operations management, Votorantim decided that they would transfer know-how through best practices. With the support of an international consultancy firm, a task force was established and, in a short period of time, the first version of the Votorantim Cement Best Practices (VCBP) was consolidated. Simultaneously, exchange programs involving Canadian and American managers were implemented. Visits to the local plants to learn about the local way of managing made the implementation of the VCBP easier at the Canadian plants. In organisational terms, Votorantim decided that its subsidiaries would operate with greater autonomy following the operational procedures established by VCBP.

The international experience of Votorantim reveals that the most demanding aspect of their learning processes was associated with the management of cultural differences, human resources, and labour relations.

8.7 Gerdau: a pioneer and one of the most internationalized Brazilian multinationals

---

Box 8.6 An introductory note on the steel industry world-wide and in Brazil

In the period after the second world war, Brazil followed the world-wide trend and the government invested in a steel producing park devoted to the domestic and export markets. CSN, the national steel company, began operations in 1946 as a government-owned company and was part of the import substitution model, like the other steel mills installed during this period.

Brazilian steel companies were kept under government guardianship until the early 1990s. Beginning in 1993, the privatization process for the Brazilian steel industry was accelerated under the national privatization program, leading to a significant reduction in the number of companies. Currently, nine companies are responsible for 96 percent of Brazilian production, and these are organized into five main groups: CSN, Usiminas/Cosipa, Arcelor-Mittal/Acesita/CST, Belgo Mineira/Mendes Júnior, and Gerdau/Açominas.

In 2005, China was the largest steel producer in the world with 349.4 million tons, almost a third of world production. It was followed by Japan with 112.5 million tons, and the US with 93.3 million tons. Brazil produced 31.6 million tons, ranking ninth among producers worldwide. Despite its position Brazil has no company among the world's twenty largest, and Arcelor-Mittal, the largest producer, has a greater capacity than the total Brazilian production.

The industrial park for steel production in Brazil is technologically up to date and its competitive advantages extend throughout the production chain. These are mining of high quality iron (an input which has significant weight in the cost of raw steel), dedicated logistics (mine–rail–port), the excellence of its production standards and the level of productivity achieved. The cost of producing plates in the country remains the lowest in the world, over 10 percent less than in the countries of the former Soviet Union, where production costs are second lowest.

Selected case

The Gerdau Group is the thirteenth largest steel producer in the world, according to the Iron and Steel International Institute. It is also the long steel segment leader in the Americas, and is ranked as the most international of Brazilian firms, as measured by the TNI, according to UNCTAD (2006).

Other Brazilian multinationals in the steel industry
Companhia Siderurgica Nacional (CSN).

8.7.1 Gerdau: Origin

In 1884, the immigrant João Gerdau opened a small business in the city of Porto Alegre in the south of Brazil. In 1901, he and his son Hugo acquired Fábrica de Pregos Pontas de Paris, which made nails, and began supplying the building industry. By 1962, Gerdau had become the world's largest producer of nails.

In 1946, German-born Curt Johannpeter, who had had a career at Deutsche Bank and was Hugo Gerdau's son-in-law, took over the company and put in place a new strategy. By 1947, it was trading on the Porto Alegre stock exchange. Then, in 1948, the firm acquired Siderúrgica Riograndense, a steel mill, thus entering the steel sector and increased its product offerings for the building industry.

Thereafter, Gerdau expanded its business throughout Brazil by means of acquisitions and organic growth. 1971 stood out in the firm's history for the creation of Comercial Gerdau (a commercial operation) and for a joint venture with Thyssen.

The year of its first international acquisition, in Uruguay, was 1980. However, Gerdau does not regard this as the beginning of its internationalization because of the geographic and cultural proximity of the acquisition.

Also in 1980, Gerdau entered into an international technical service agreement with two Japanese enterprises, Funabashi Steel and Nippon Steel, and adopted the Japanese production method as the basis of its organizational process.

Gerdau grew abroad primarily through acquisitions at first, and subsequently by expanding the businesses it acquired. Joint ventures have also played a major role in its development. In 2007 and 2008, the firm invested some $7.7 billion in acquisitions and joint ventures outside of its home country.

By the end of 2008, 56.3 percent of Gerdau's installed capacity was abroad. Overall, the company owns forty-eight steel mills outright, of which thirty-three are abroad, and ten in which it is a partner. Additionally, it is a party to joint ventures in six countries. Thus, it operates in fourteen countries and 57.7 percent of its invoicing comes from its foreign operations and its exports from Brazil.

8.7.2 Developing production competences

Gerdau's business model was developed from two basic options. First, it resorted to electricity-powered mini-mills that used scrap metal as their main raw material. The optimal operating scale of these mills was small, meaning that they could be efficient while merely supplying local or regional markets. This technological option resulted from the acquisition of the Siderúrgica Riograndense mill back in 1948. Gerdau's expansion remained true to this model, so much so that 90 percent of its current production still comes from its mini-mills, which process more than 10 million tons of scrap a year. This also means Gerdau has become one of the main recyclers in the Americas. A technical service agreement with Badische Stahlwerke Gmbh provides support for the process engineering.

The second strong element was that Gerdau fully embraced the Japanese production model. As of 1980, it invested systematically in this, becoming one of the main leaders of the dissemination of Japanese industrial practices in Brazil. In 1991, it was one of the enterprises that instituted the Premio Nacional de Qualidade (national quality award). Then, in 1993, it launched the country's first branded, quality-guaranteed product in its field, winning the national quality award in 2002.

8.7.3 Developing the local business model

In 1993, Gerdau acquired Aços Finos Piratini, a steel mill, in a privatization auction. As a result, it became a producer of special steels and started to serve new market segments, such as the automotive industry.

In 1994, it opened the Banco Gerdau bank to provide financing for its clients, suppliers, and service providers. This was followed by a corporate restructuring in 1995, which transformed the group into two companies: Gerdau SA and Metalúrgica Gerdau SA, a holding company. Gerdau was consolidated as a vertically integrated steel company, whose activities ranged from procuring raw materials to marketing. It was also horizontally integrated, thanks to its financial enterprise.

In 1999, Gerdau equity started trading on (NYSE) and the enterprise stepped-up its internationalization process.

8.7.4 Gerdau's internationalization

Because it supplies metal products to the building industry, the domestic market became too small for Gerdau, given that Brazil's building industry is yet to resort strongly to metal-based construction techniques. This is also true of the rest of Latin America.

Therefore, Gerdau's investments in Latin America meant simply that it was expanding its capacity. However, its investments in North America, where building is essentially metal-based, led to an upgrading of the firm's competences. Gerdau was especially interested in the American market and, in its internationalization process, it preferred to purchase companies outright rather than set up joint ventures.

Between 1989 and 1992, Gerdau acquired four steel producers: Courtice Steel (Canada), Indac and Aza (Chile), and Inlasa (Uruguay). All of them were small steel mills apart from the Canadian company, which was of medium size.

However, in 1999, Gerdau acquired its first large mill: AmeriSteel, the US' second largest producer of steel rods and third largest producer of steel bars and profiles. This firm also owned four other mills in the US. AmeriSteel's installed capacity was 70 percent greater than that of the eight companies Gerdau had acquired abroad up to then.

In 2005, Gerdau acquired mills in Argentina and Colombia and in 2006 took its first step toward producing steel outside the Americas and outside the civil construction market, by acquiring 40 percent of the corporate capital of Corporación Sidenor SA, the largest producer of special steels and one of the largest manufacturers of stamp-forged products in Spain. In doing so, Gerdau became part of the automotive global value chain. Part of the Sidenor "package" that Gerdau acquired was Aços Villares, which had been one of Brazil's "crown jewels" during the country's industrialization period.

In 2006, Gerdau expanded in the US market by acquiring Callaway Building Products (Tennessee), Fargo Iron and Metal Company (North Dakota), and Sheffield Steel Corporation (Oklahoma). However, the company's largest acquisition took place in 2007, when it bought the Chaparral Steel Company, North America's second largest manufacturer of structural steel.

8.7.5 Developing an international business model

Gerdau's business model implies in regional, vertically integrated operations, whose activities range from collecting and processing scrap metal to the distribution of product, generally manufactured in accordance with end clients' customized projects.

Gerdau was able to select this model because the building industry lacks strong governance standards. Relations within the production chain must adapt to the characteristics of the local and regional firms and institutions. In other words, only the technical standards are really global.

The similarities of the structure of its activities by region allow the company to apply the Gerdau business system widely. This is similar in nature to the Toyota production system. It conveys the firm's mission and values, in addition to formalizing its best administrative and operating practices. It covers sixteen macro-processes, ranging from marketing and sales to social responsibility, and each macro-process has a global manager.

The investment strategy and the integration of operations are the responsibility of the strategy committee and of the excellence committee respectively. The latter is charged with encouraging the interchange of knowledge between the units. As a result of this modus operandi, the company can acquire low-productivity enterprises, take over their operations, and quickly implement the adjustments required to run these acquisitions in accordance with Gerdau's standards of excellence.

Gerdau's international personality seems to stretch all the way back to its founders and their descendants, who carried on developing the company. On the other hand, it gradually built competences linked to a business model that was expanded and consolidated little by little.

8.8 Braskem: producing petrochemicals in Latin America

Box 8.7 An introductory note on the petrochemical industry

In Brazil, the petrochemical industry developed under the tripartite model. Petrobras was called the mother company of Brazilian petrochemicals and, in addition to providing the main raw materials for the sector, it played a strategic role in strengthening the production chain overall and in defining policies and projects for the sector. However, in the second half of the 1980s, the tripartite model began to show signs of exhaustion. The privatization

---

of part of Petroquisa at the beginning of the 1990s caused both great discomfort and a sense of lack of definition to the Brazilian petrochemical sector. Petrobras began to concentrate its resources in the area of oil exploration and production, against the current of the major international oil players who maintained investments in petrochemicals due to the greater value added of the products. After the breakup of the oil monopoly, Petrobas restructured and resumed activities in the petrochemical industry. However, it no longer exerts a leadership role. For example, the control of the third petrochemical pole, in the south of Brazil, was acquired by the Odebrecht and Ipiranga groups who managed to maintain harmonic relationships directed toward expanding infrastructure and updating technology.

Selected case

Braskem, the largest petrochemical company in Latin America, and forty-second in SOBEET's ranking.

Other Brazilian multinationals in the petrochemicals industry

Oxiteno, Artecola, FFS Filmes, Implac, and Cipatex.

8.8.1 *Braskem: origin*

The Odebrecht Group (also discussed in this section within the engineering services industry) was established in 1944 in Salvador, Bahia. Since its early years, it was a service provider for the petrochemical industry that was set up in that region. Odebrecht grew to become one of the four biggest heavy engineering and construction services providers, its internationalization dating from 1980. In the diversification of its business portfolio, Odebrecht moved into petrochemicals in the 2000s.

The opportunity to do so came when the Economico Bank (also based in Salvador) went bankrupt due to the economic crises of the late 1990s. In July 2001, Odebrecht and the Mariani groups bought the bank's participation in Conepar, a controller of Companhia Petroquimica de Nordeste (COPENE) – the center for raw materials in the petrochemical pole of the northeast. Braskem was created in the following year, when the groups decided to integrate their second-generation industry assets with the first-generation operations of COPENE. On a second stage, five other companies were merged with Braskem, which became the leader of thermoplastic resins in Latin America. Other shareholders were Petroquisa (the petrochemical arm of Petrobras) and the pension funds Petros (of Petrobras) and Previ (of the Banco do Brazil). Braskem shares are traded on the stock exchanges of São Paulo (BOVESPA), New York, and Madrid.

The current challenge for Braskem is to become one of the ten largest petrochemical companies in terms of market value. In pursuing that target, Braskem shares the partnership of Odebrecht Engineering, which has developed a remarkable management model and has worldwide reputation and relationships.

8.8.2 *Developing a business model*

In its role as a catalyst in the consolidation of the Brazilian petrochemicals industry, Braskem's legacy (in terms of production infrastructure and human resources coming from different sources) demanded an integrative management model and the creation of a new business proposition. As to the management model, Braskem inherited the Odebrecht entrepreneurial technology (OET), which must be adapted to a different type of business. In the engineering services, due to the nature of the tasks, the OET seeks to develop the sense of entrepreneurship and anticipation; efficiency, in its strict sense, is not as functional as those two requirements. However, that is not the case in an industry such as petrochemicals. Therefore, Braskem has to adapt the OET and develop a derivative type of management approach to integrate different organizational cultures and operating systems from six companies and thirteen plants in different regions of Brazil. Concurrently, to achieve the operational targets, Braskem is adopting operational excellence programs and benchmarking the best performer in the industry worldwide.

As to the new business proposition, that is related to shifting from a strictly "bulk-type of approach" to a customer-oriented strategy, where customer relationships and technology competences play a key role, to produce higher added value products.

8.8.3 Technological strategy and fitting the international competitive context

Braskem's positioning as a fast-follower of technologies and innovations of the major petrochemical competitors worldwide has already shown results in the research and development (R&D) of differentiated technologies such as nanotechnologies and polymers of renewable raw materials.

Braskem has an average annual investment in R&D between 1.5 and 2 percent of its revenue. Its fast-follower strategy directs around 55 percent of that sum for product development projects, 24 percent for innovative product development projects and 7 percent of these projects are related to entry into new markets (Garcez and Vasconcellos, 2008). That reflects the competitive strategy whereby customer orientation overcomes pure innovative research. Notwithstanding, Braskem has already 200 patents applied for with the Instituto Nacional de Propriedade Industrial (INPI; national institute of industrial property) and an average of four patents applied for per year in the international circuit. One of the most important developments is the high-density green polyethylene derived from sugar cane ethanol. Of the revenue obtained from the sales of resins, 18 percent came from innovations that arrived on the market in the last three years.

8.8.4 Internationalization process: from export to more complex activities

Braskem continued to increase its activities in export right after its creation and, in terms of scope, by 2003, the company was exporting to over thirty countries. In 2007, export totaled $2.3 billion, and this amount represented 24 percent of liquid revenue for the year. The main export destinations were: North America 36 percent; South America 33 percent and Europe 26 percent. Due to increased exports, the companies invested in sales offices and distribution systems in Europe, the US, and Argentina.

Projects in Venezuela, with the government-owned petrochemical Pequiven, are currently the main platform for Braskem's internationalization. They provide access to competitive raw materials for producing polyethylene and polypropylene, since that country has high availability of natural gas and oil. The projects are in the development phase and production startup is forecast for the end of 2011 for Propilsur and 2013 for Polimérica.

Negotiations with Peru's government-owned oil company, PetroPeru, for future investments in polyethylene production based on natural gas are under way. Braskem's international projects have different market rationales. The undertakings in Venezuela focus on the Brazilian and North American markets, while the Peru project is destined for the Pacific coast, specifically Chile, Ecuador, and Peru, as well as Asia.

8.9 AmBev: at the world's largest brewery driver's seat

Box 8.8 An introductory note on the wage goods industry in Brazil and the challenges of internationalization

In Brazil, the "wage goods" industry includes six sectors of the transformation industry: textiles and clothing; leather and footwear; furniture and lumber; plastic products; personal hygiene, perfume, and cosmetics; and food and beverages.

The dynamics of those markets is strongly marked by the organization of global chains of production, commercialization, and distribution of products, in which the main coordinators along the chains are the large international buyers, who retain the brands or distribution channels and are capable of commanding a complex, globalized network of producers. This international dynamic directly influences the local strategy of producers, since few Brazilian companies in these sectors are capable of internalizing capacities to permit a manner of insertion less dependent on the strategies of these large international buyers.

AmBev is a counter-example to that trend. In recent years, the beer market has been characterized by a tendency to international consolidation. As a result of several mega-mergers, such as the merger of South African Brewery (SAB) with Miller of the US and Belgium's Interbrew with Brazil's AmBev and then with the American Annheuser Busch, the ranking of the leading brewers has been changing a lot. To the extent that some markets, especially in western Europe and North America, are approaching saturation point, new opportunities for expansion are concentrated in emerging markets, especially China that, in 2003, had already surpassed the US and had become the largest beer market in the world. The global beer market is still fragmented because the top ten producers account for less than 45 percent of total sales. In comparison, in the market for soft drinks, the five largest firms have more than 50 percent of global sales.

Selected case

The case of AmBev is unconventional. AmBev is part of the group that controls the world's largest beverage company. It does not control the company in the strict sense of the term but it drives its strategy. Therefore, it is a very insightful case.

Other Brazilian multinationals in the consumer goods industries

Coteminas, Natura, Boticário, Azaléia, Havaianas, Santista, Marisol, Arezzo.

8.9.1 *AmBev–InBev–AB InBev: origin*

The AmBev case has two different origins. The obvious one is Brahma, a brewery founded by a Swiss immigrant in 1888, that merged with Antarctica, the other Brazilian large producer during the 1990s.

The second, and most important, is the Garantia Group, founded by the three "Brazilian Musketeers": Paulo Jorge Lemann, Carlos Alberto Sicupira, and Marcel Telles. In the 1980s, they created the Garantia Bank, operating aggressively in the international financial markets under a management model that was classified as "hypercompetitive." The bank had problems in the early 1990s and closed down. But the Garantia Group, the brand and the management model remained and, even if controversies exist, the three musketeers are icons for the Brazilian business community.

8.9.2 *The making of AmBev*

During the crises of the 1980s in Brazil, Brahma, which was run very loosely, got into financial problems. Its capital stock was acquired by the Garantia Bank and went through a profound reengineering process, adopting the high performance management model, inspired by the bank. Meanwhile, Antarctica maintained its conservative strategy and management style which helped the company to survive the crisis.

Brahma's first experience of internationalization was in Venezuela in 1994. Antarctica stayed still. However, as the industry was concentrating, in 1999 Brahma and Antarctica merged to create the American Beverage Company (AmBev). In this merger the aggressive style of Brahma prevailed over Antarctica's conservative one. In the merge, Antarctica contributed to AmBev's competences in production, logistics, and distribution, mainly. Therefore, AmBev was born with a strong competences profile, a market share of 60 percent plus in beer and 17 percent in soft drinks in the Brazilian market.

8.9.3 The internationalization of AmBev

In 2003 AmBev intensified its internationalization process by taking an initial shareholding of 40.5 percent in Quilmes Industrial (Quimsa), thereby establishing a leading presence in the beer markets in Argentina, Bolivia, Paraguay, and Uruguay. Also in 2003 and 2004, AmBev expanded its operations to the north of Latin America through a series of acquisitions in Central America, Peru, Ecuador, and the Dominican Republic.

On August 27, 2004, AmBev and Interbrew SA/NV from Belgium merged to create International Beverage (InBev). In that merger, Interbrew became the majority shareholder. AmBev became responsible for the Americas' operations, where it took control of Labatt, one of the leading breweries of Canada, formerly part of Interbrew.

Interbrew's roots can be traced back to 1366 in Den Horen in Leuven when the Artois brewery was founded. Starting as early as the 1960s, the Artois brewery acquired several local breweries and hence consolidated its position in Belgium, until finally in 1987 Artois, and the Walloon-based brewer Piedboeuf, came together to form Interbrew. By 1991, a second phase of targeted external growth began outside of Belgium's borders. The first transaction in this phase took place in Hungary, followed in 1995 by the acquisition of Labatt, in Canada. In 2000, Interbrew acquired Bass and Whitbread in the UK, and in 2001 the company established itself in Germany, with the acquisition of Diebels. This was followed by the acquisition of Beck's & Co., the Gilde Group, and Spaten. Interbrew operated as a family-owned business until December 2000. At this point it organized an initial public offering (IPO), becoming a publicly owned company trading on the Euronext stock exchange (Brussels, Belgium). In 2002, Interbrew strengthened its position in China, by acquiring stakes in the KK Brewery and the Zhujiang Brewery.

The association of AmBev and Interbrew merited special attention in Brazil due to the fact that the company remained in a minority position even though it had a strategy that was previously recognized as being aggressive. On the other hand, on analyzing the reasons that might have led to the association, it is interesting to observe that the financial performance of the two companies was very different, despite both being of a similar size: AmBev's profitability was more than double that of Interbrew's. One of the possible explanations lay in the management model, which has a direct influence on the production and distribution operations.

8.9.4 The Garantia's business model prevails

After the merger AmBev's executives started to occupy positions of prominence in InBev's management and to introduce the "AmBev/Brahma/high performance model" which aims for operational excellence. Despite strong resistances the model was implemented worldwide and two years later revenues increased by 20 percent and profit doubled. Moreover, AmBev's operational know-how is considered as the key factor for expansion of InBev worldwide because that concerns operating in emerging economies, the only ones where demand is expected to grow.

In 2006, InBev acquired the Fujian Sedrin brewery in China, making InBev the third biggest brewer in China – the world's largest beer market. And in 2008, Inbev merged with Annheuser Busch to create the largest brewery in the world. That was a bold move having strong repercussions not only at the political level but in the American self-image as well. Anheuser-Busch InBev manages a portfolio of nearly 300 brands that includes global brands such as Budweiser, Stella Artois, and Beck's, smaller multi-country brands like Leffe and Hoegaarden, and regional brands. The company employs 120,000 in over thirty countries. On a pro-forma basis for 2008, the combined company would have generated revenues of €26.5 billion.

As a final remark, the Garantia Group controls a large portfolio in Brazil, including one of the largest department stores, the pioneering website for on-line purchasing and the largest logistics operator in Brazil: All-America Logistics.

8.10 Tigre: an example of regional internationalization

Box 8.9 An introductory note on the construction materials industry in Latin America

Every country or geographical region is endowed with certain types of natural resources and the civil construction sector is particularly influenced by that. In Brazil, as in Latin America, soil and climate conditions, combined with the purchasing power of the population, have dictated the types of construction and the materials used. Therefore, product development and commercialization competences have played an important role for success in the local markets, which are characterized by enormous fragmentation. In this particular context, two Brazilian companies have become international: Tigre is a producer of PVC tubes and materials, and Duratex manufactures materials for hydraulic installations and bathrooms.

For Tigre, the transportation of plastic tubes over long distances is uneconomic, which makes imports/exports of little interest. Therefore, the product/market conditions recommends decentralized small operations to supply regional/local markets. On the other hand, Duratex operates in a market where products have greater value added, design counts and, since products are compact, transportation is not problematic; exports are a competitive option. Therefore, Duratex has had an operation in Argentina since 1994, the time of the Mercosur, and seems reluctant to expand to other countries.

Selected case

Tigre is ranked as twenty-first in Fundacao Dom Cabral's 2008 ranking.

Other Brazilian multinational in the materials for construction industry

Duratex.

8.10.1 Tigre

The company started in 1941 as a producer of combs. At the end of the 1950s, when the company had already made considerable progress, with an extensive range of extruded and injected plastic products, it invested in a project that was innovative for its time: PVC tubes and connections for hydraulic installations. Tigre, therefore, assumed a comfortable leadership position in the local market.

Tigre developed a business model that was appropriate to the reality of the local market, which was extremely fragmented: sales occur in small quantities at more than 100,000 outlets spread throughout a territory where access is difficult. Tigre innovated in marketing their products to mass markets and excelled in production and logistics.

In 1977, Tigre made its first move toward internationalization, when it formed an association with Paraguayan businessmen and set up a greenfield plant in Paraguay. Since then Tubopar has had an 80 percent market share in this country.

In Brazil the outlook changed with the arrival of the Swiss company, Amanco (today controlled by the Mexican group, Mexichem) which, in 1991, took over Fortilit and in 1999, Akros, which was Tigre's biggest competitor. Amanco already had operations in other countries in Latin America. Therefore, global competition was set up in a very small city, Joinville, in the south of Brazil.

In 1997, Tigre started to intensify its internationalization efforts. Four companies were acquired in Chile, where Tigre has a market share of 42 percent. In 1998, the target was Argentina, where, via acquisitions, it took 27 percent of the local market. In Bolivia the acquisitions were made in 2000 and took the company to a market share of 80 percent.

Subsequently, Tigre invested in increasing exports by opening up fronts in Dubai, in the Middle East. In the US, Tigre recently built a greenfield plant to produce and sell for both the construction and the infrastructure markets.

In 2006, Tigre inaugurated a greenfield plant in Chile, and in 2007 opened its first plant in the US.

8.11 WEG: expanding horizontally and moving up the value chain

---

Box 8.10 An introductory note on the electro-metal-mechanics industry in Brazil

Brazil holds a significant position in the world market for machinery and equipment. It is tenth in the ranking of the main manufacturers, behind the US, Japan, Germany, the UK, Italy, China, France, South Korea, and Switzerland.

However, machinery and equipment producers are, normally, suppliers to global networks that produce different products and services, and compete in different markets. At the time when global production networks began to be structured as a consequence of productive restructuring, in the 1990s, a few Brazilian enterprises had the competences and resources to become global suppliers.

Selected case

WEG: World's second larger producer of electrical motors, and fourteenth in SOBEET's list.

Other Brazilian multinationals in the machinery and equipment industry

Embraco, Sabo, DHB, Metagal, Grupo Brasil, Maxxion.

8.11.1 The WEG Group: origin

The WEG Group, established in 1961 by a business manager, an electrician, and a mechanic, the name WEG corresponding to the initials of their surnames, is the leader in the electric motors segment in Brazil and in Latin America, and the second in the world. In addition it manufactures equipment for industrial automation, transformers, components, electric starters, and industrial paints and varnishes.

Right from the outset the company introduced a participative management model and profit sharing. Investment in R&D is around 2.4 percent of net operating revenues. It has technological interchange with the research labs of Brazilian universities, especially the

Federal University of Santa Catarina, and with international ones like Hannover and Aachen in Germany, and Wisconsin in the US.

8.11.2 Internationalization

WEG's internationalization strategy underwent three phases. In the first, from the 1970s to the 1990s, the expansion to Latin America, South Africa, and Canada was based on the commissioning of local representatives and distributors. For WEG's executives that was the alternative that reduced investments and risks while bringing in expertise about the foreign markets. They recognized, later, that the conflicts in regards to the distribution of margins was insurmountable.

In the second phase, WEG opened sales subsidiaries in Fort Lauderdale (US), Brussels (Belgium), and Australia to develop the regional markets. The European subsidiary was a failure and closed. The best results came from the Australian subsidiary.

In the third phase, WEG established production facilities abroad. It started in Mexico through the acquisition of a plant from Asea Brown Boveri (ABB). Investments were then made in Portugal (acquisition), Argentina (acquisition), China (acquisition of a state-owned company), India (new plant), and then in Mexico again (two plants acquired from the same owner in 2005 and 2008) to supply the US market.

At the same time, WEG has been trying to move up the value chain, becoming a supplier of technological solutions, or an integrating firm. To be successful in this strategy WEG is preparing to compete with worldly known firms like Rockwell Automation and Emerson Electric, among others.

8.12 Marcopolo: a local optimizer operating in every emerging country

---

Box 8.11 An introductory note on systems assemblers

In contrast with the parts and components suppliers that were highlighted in the previous section, systems assemblers, or integrators, are the companies in charge of assembling the final product and delivering it to the client. Therefore, their profile of competences is quite different from the former.

In the global value chains, integrators are in a more powerful position in general. In the automotive and white goods value chains, mentioned previously, the integrators are the traditional multinationals, like VW, Ford, FIAT, Whirlpool, and so on.

In Brazil, a few companies were able to escalate the value chain to the position of integrator. Embraer is the most knowledgeable of them all, but the Marcopdo case is also very insightful.

Selected case

Marcopolo: thirteenth in SOBEET's list and in the FDC list as well.

Other Brazilian multinationals operating as systems assemblers

Metalfrio, Busscar, Agrale, Randon, Aeromot, and Embraer.

Marcopolo is a manufacturer of buses that sells in more than a 100 countries. Its share in the world market is 8 percent and 40 percent of their $1.3 billion annual revenues are generated abroad, in nine factories in all continents.

8.12.1 Marcopolo: origin

Marcopolo was founded in 1949 in the south of Brazil. Along with other regional companies it competed with Mercedes Benz that was the major supplier of buses in Brazil. As from the mid-1990s Mercedes product line became too sophisticated and expensive for the Brazilian market and local production was discontinued. At the same time Brazilian companies started their consolidation process. Marcopolo stood out from the others and at one point it had more than 50 percent of the Brazilian market. Its global competitors are Irizar (Spanish, which already has a not very successful subsidiary in Brazil), Vanhool (Belgian), Bova (Dutch), and Orlandi (Italian), in addition to the chassis/engine producers themselves (Mercedes Benz, Scania, Volvo, Iveco (which is setting up in Brazil), and Toyota.

8.12.2 Internationalization

The internationalization process started in 1991, thirty years after it had made its first export, in 1961, to Paraguay. Marcopolo currently has plants in eight foreign countries: Argentina, Colombia, India (joint venture with Tata Motors), Mexico, Portugal, South Africa, Russia, and Egypt.

Marcopolo has developed products that are best suited to the emerging markets and has a globalization strategy that is guided by a very interesting business model. As a producer of bodywork, Marcopolo depends on the manufacturer of the chassis/engine. Its international operations are always carried out jointly with one of the three chassis/engine suppliers: Daimler, Scania, or Volvo. In the Argentinean operation, the relationship involved Scania and Volvo; in Mexico the joint venture is with Mercedes Benz, and in South Africa with Scania. The operation in China started with Iveco (FIAT) but the contract ended in 2007 and Marcopolo is deciding how to move forward. The operation in India is a joint venture with Tata Motors and in Russia with Ruspromauto.

Marcopolo considers that its internationalization process underwent two stages. In the first, which lasted until 2003, the company relied on a modular approach for the production and assembly of buses. It then "bundled" the modules according to four types of package, depending on the features of the subsidiary. That followed a customer-oriented strategy: each subsidiary is apt to develop and deliver products that meet the specific demands of each country or locality.

In the second and current stage, Marcopolo is focusing on knowledge management and technology transfer through the design and support for other firms to produce the buses, and the development of their supply chains as well.

That is also true of the plants in India and Russia. Marcopolo, as a minority shareholder is, in practice, providing guidance in the development of the plant and product designs, as well as production and operations management. In the case of Colombia, Marcopolo was invited not only because of its competence in producing bus bodywork, but also because of the knowledge it brought to the project for restructuring the transport system in Bogota, the Millennium Project. Marcopolo started to develop competences in this area when it took part in the urban transport system project in Curitiba, Brazil.

8.13 Romi: the only Brazilian capital goods producer remaining

---

Box 8.12 An introductory note on the machine-tool industry in Brazil

The machine-tool industry is generally made up of enterprises of relatively small size, and is not an important generator of income, or jobs. Its importance stems from its role as a catalyst for new technologies and innovations diffuser for all industrial sectors.

In Brazil, the machine-tool industry was born during the second world war. Since there was no possibility of importing machines, some local companies began to make copies of imported machinery. The demand created by the implementation of Brazilian state-owned enterprises in the resources-based industries created conditions for the most competent companies to find niches and preferential relations.

The structure of the local machine-tool industry was radically changed when the automotive industry was established, in the 1950s. To the extent that foreign multinationals arrived with "carte blanche," they brought together the subsidiaries of their preferential machine-tool suppliers, especially of German origin. Thereafter, two clusters operated in that industry: the foreign manufacturers of high added value special machines, and the local manufacturers producing conventional and larger scale standard machinery.

The Brazilian machine-tool industry grew until the 1970s, when the crises began to manifest. They were caused by technological changes arising from the application of microelectronics and the demands of higher quality, combined with precision and reliability. Most Brazilian companies had not developed technological competences to meet that demand and the import regime adopted by the government did not create safeguards for them. The industry collapsed, and few companies survived. With the opening of the market in early 1990, the fortunes of the Brazilian machine-tool industry were finally sealed, leaving a handful of small producers of standard machines for small industrial and medium-sized

---

concerns, and one only medium-sized company when compared to global standards: Romi, which internationalized in 2008.

In a sense, that description is applicable to the Brazilian industry of capital goods in general.

Selected case

Romi.

Other Brazilian multinationals in the capital goods industry

None.

8.13.1 Romi: origin

Romi was founded by a son of Italian immigrants in 1930, as a repair shop for automobiles. In 1934, it began the production of agricultural implements, to replace imported products. In 1941, the company entered the business of manufacturing of machine-tools, making copies of German products.

The company climbed the value chain to enter the automotive segment, in 1948, with the launch of the first tractor in Brazil. In 1956 Romi boldly decided to produce cars when the program for the automotive industry was implemented. Romi released the first car produced by a Brazilian company, the Romi-Isetta, after the transfer of the whole machinery of the Italian ISO Automoveicoli-Spa, an Italian manufacturer of small motorcycles and tricycles, which developed the Isetta project. The car had unique characteristics such as being very small, front door, and a reasonable performance for that time (maximum speed of 70 km per hour). Curiously, the resemblances to the Tata's Nano, launched with global roar, fifty years later, are striking. However, in the Brazil of the 1950s, those vehicles had a very short life: no more than 3,000 units were produced (Figure 8.2).

One of the main problems for the production ramp-up was a decree of the Brazilian government, in 1959, granting incentives for the manufacturing of vehicles, provided they met some standards. One of these ruled that a car should have at least two banks and two doors. All vehicles manufactured by subsidiaries of multinationals complied to the rule but the Romi-Isetta could no longer be considered as a car. Romi lost access to the incentive program and discontinued production in 1961. Since then it focused exclusively on machinery, where it now

Figure 8.2 The Romi-Isetta

stands as the largest producer of machine-tools and plastic injection machines in Brazil. It delivers to companies in various industries such as automobiles (to the tooling shops), energy, and infrastructure.

8.13.2 Learning through all types of technology transfer mechanisms

After the second world war Romi signed several contracts for technical assistance and renewed its machinery park through the purchase of surplus machines in the US. In the 1950s, engineers from Italy, Germany, and the US were hired to establish the product development department. To consolidate its pioneering style and innovative competences, manifested beforehand through the products previously mentioned, Romi was responsible for the production of the first numeric control lathe in 1973 and the first computer-controlled milling machine in 1987.

Romi established strong relationships and partnerships with foreign companies. The most relevant were with the Japanese Yamazaki Mazak, whose products Romi produced under the brand Romi-Mazak, and the American Bridgeport. The contract with the latter implied that Romi produced the mechanical part of the Bridgeport machines; the computerized control systems were incorporated into the machine in the US for international distribution. This line of lathes came to account for 20 percent of Bridgeport's sales. The partnership ended when Bridgeport was acquired by another American company.

In 1974, Romi signed a cooperation agreement with the Italian company Sandretto, for the production of plastic injection machines. This is a common tactic among machine-tool companies because demand for machine-tools is often very volatile: it is the first to feel effects of any downturn in economic activity and the last to recover. In a country like Brazil that makes companies subject to these cycles even more complicated to manage. As plastic injection machines are countercyclical and share similar technical specifications, it is not unusual that machine-tool producers increase their product portfolio this way.

Romi currently invests about 5 percent of its net sales in R&D, has sixty-one patented inventions and over twenty-five patents filed in North America, Europe, and Asia. Among the 202 engineers, 141 work in the development of products.

8.13.3 Internationalization

Romi started exports in 1944 to Argentina. But it was only in the 1970s, within the context of crises, that Romi intensified exports, to South America and the US, mainly. In 1985 Romi Machine Tools, the US subsidiary of Romi, was established to facilitate the distribution of and provide support for Romi's products in the US market. The movement was repeated in 2002 when Romi Europa GmbH, based in Germany, was established.

The partnership with Bridgeport scored the most important activity in terms of internationalization in the lathes market. However, it was on plastic injection machines that the internationalization really took shape.

In 2008, Romi completed the acquisition of the assets of Sandretto Industrie, its partner for more than thirty years. The complex business of Sandretto comprises two units in the Italian cities of Grugliasco and Pont Canavese, in the Turin area, plus four commercial subsidiaries in Europe and several service centers, sales offices, and commercial representations in several countries. The strategic objectives regarding this acquisition are: to expand the distribution base, take advantage of the broad Sandretto commercial network, develop a technology center in an area with recognized expertise in the machinery sector, and expand its role as a global supplier. Romi is currently negotiating a majority state to acquire Hardinge in the US.

8.14 Odebrecht Engineering: among the world's top twenty

Box 8.13 An introductory note on the heavy construction industry

The construction industry is sometimes treated as an industry and sometimes as a service. This ambiguity is connected with the very characteristics of construction as well as with the difficulties in characterizing what a service is. Depending on the type of work and contractual relationship, a broad spectrum of the product/service mix might be encompassed. Big-sized construction projects are much riskier and unpredictable than industry in general. Within the international context, differences in the interpretation of legislations, stakeholders' interests, and cultural rules resembles a "Babel Tower": it is very hard to find out what the rules of the game are and, even so, "during the match," they might change.

The international market for large construction projects is in the hands of only a few companies: the turnover of the thirty biggest companies in the period 1985 to 2005 corresponds to circa 73% of the total international amount of business done. European companies have been dominating the market (57%), followed by the American (17%), from Brazil, Russia, India, and China (the BRICs; 9%), and the Japanese (8%).

In Brazil there are four large construction engineering firms: Odebrecht, Camargo Correa, Andrade Gutierrez, and Mendes Junior, which have developed projects abroad since the 1960s. They were catapulted during the period of the military government, when the conditions for their fast development were created. The case of the Rio–Niteroi bridge, the second longest in the world, is revealing. The project financing was under the responsibility of M. Rothschild and Sons and construction started in late 1960s. However, two years after the start, the contract was reelaborated

---

and three Brazilian engineering firms (Camargo Correa, Mendes Junior, and Rabelo) took charge of the completion of the project.

Early exposure to international finance, international partnering, and international management led Brazilian engineering firms to develop distinctive competences in the management of large infrastructural projects. In addition, the need to comply with international certification standards played an important role in the maturing of their management models. Working according to the international standards became ingrained within the Brazilian engineering firms since that early stage.

Mendes Junior was the first to move abroad, to Bolivia in 1969, Mauritania in 1975, and Iraq in 1984. Odebrecht's first international project was in Peru in 1980. However, from the four, Odebrecht is the one that most persevered in the international markets; it is currently one of the top international engineering firms, while the other three adopted home-oriented strategies. Further, Odebrecht diversified into petrochemicals with Braskem while Camargo Correa diversified into cement and consumer goods (Alpargatas and Tevex-Santista). We will analyse the Odebrecht case.

Selected case

Odebrecht Engineering: the world's twentieth largest engineering firm, the most internationalized Brazilian firm according to the FDC, and second according to SOBEET.

Other Brazilian multinationals in the heavy construction industry
Camargo Correa, Andrade Gutierrez, Mendes Junior.

8.14.1 Odebrecht: origin

The first Odebrecht arrived in Brazil in 1856, a time when German immigration was peaking. He was an engineer who had graduated at the Greifswald University in Prussia. Following a sequence of successful and unsuccessful family ventures, Odebrecht Engineering was founded in 1944.

8.14.2 Building the management model

The company founder inherited from his father a construction company that was in debt, almost bankrupt. The well-qualified master builders were the only patrimony it had. It was from this human patrimony, with a focus on the creation of a captive client base and with a decentralized organizational structure, with people participating in the results, that he was able to recover the company and build the foundations of its company culture. From its very inception, the company developed strong values centered on trust, cooperation, innovation, simplicity, and a service mindset. The power structure has been directed to those that serve the client. Thereby the person responsible for a client/contract is empowered with the decision-making and resources to innovate in their relationships with clients, establishing it as the "business owner." For the client it means agility and flexibility in rendering the services.

In addition to the dissemination of the core values mentioned, which provides the elements of "desirability," the company's culture supplies marks to guide its behavior in business such as, confidence and cooperation, knowing how to influence and how to be influenced, respecting other people's ideas but provoking thought causing other forms of thinking, harmonizing interests, and leading through the service spirit. This is what made possible building up relationships inside the organization and, most importantly, with its clients and the stakeholders.

8.14.3 Internationalization path

Odebrecht's first international project was in Peru, in 1980. It then moved to other Latin American countries and Europe. In the 1990s, Odebrecht entered the North American market focusing in the southern states: Florida and Louisianna. Africa was also targeted, especially the Portuguese-speaking countries. In the 2000s, Odebrecht began operations in the Middle East, with an office located in Abu-Dhabi, and in North Africa, Libya.

8.14.4 Creating competences to enter "the big league"

The mutual reinforcement of two innovative dimensions, customers relationship management with stakeholders and services clients, was applied not only in turbulent environments but also to chase opportunities in more stable environments. That was the case of the construction of the biggest bridge in Europe at that time, the Vasco da Gama Bridge in Lisbon. In that case, Odebrecht approached the client aiming to better understand its needs. It then developed a project to make feasible the construction of the bridge and related infrastructure through concession contracts. Later, it participated in the bidding process, competing with the biggest European and engineering firms, won. This led Odebrecht to enter the global team for the first time.

8.14.5 Learning as the key organizational process

In the 1990s Odebrecht's expansion abroad allowed it to learn very important lessons. It learned with its strategic mistakes upon establishing its business in Germany to take advantage of the potential for construction works following reunification. It tried to emulate the strategies of traditional MNEs, that is, it tried to "win the market" instead of specific clients. The company amalgamated three German companies and began participating in public bidding processes, where it failed to differentiate itself from others before the clients. The results were very negative, forcing the company to leave that market.

8.14.6 Developing competences to operate in turbulent environments

As the company adopts a decentralized management system, it has competitive advantages to do business in countries which are considered to have turbulent environments, such as Angola, during almost the entire thirty-year period of the war; in Peru during the years of activity of the "Senderos Luminosos" guerillas; in FARC-dominated regions of Colombia; in Venezuela at the time of social unrest resulting from the ascent of president Chavez; and in Iraq after the deposition of Saddam Hussein. In all cases, the network relationships which were built from its intangible asset were the main sources of information and support for contracting.

During the 2000s new lessons were learnt. It was understood that it was not enough for the company to stand out before its clients just by developing enterprises with differentiated service rendering. Its focus could no longer be the enterprise, even if it had aggregated services. What it really should do was to meet a wider requirement of the client, even though it meant more than developing engineering works. In respect to the governments of the emerging or underdeveloped countries, their requirement was to build sustained development. Therefore, Odebrecht developed competences to propose projects that were economic and socio-environmentally sustainable.

In respect to its private clients, Odebrecht began to offer its competences and resources to turn into reality their projects by handling the whole and complex institutional network before the external stakeholders. This new business orientation was made easier because of the experiences conducted by the private trust created by the company's founder, which had already been developing self-sustainable socio-environmental projects, based on the creation of production and marketing chains in some regions of the Brazilian northeast that were very poor.

This new orientation has been disseminated throughout several countries. In South America, Odebrecht has been working with several governments to turn into reality the South American Regional Infrastructure Integration (IIRSA), with the collaboration of many international development agencies. Its role in this case has been to create a self-sustainable business architecture, both in economic and in socio-environmental terms, taking advantage of its capability to create relationships with the local agencies and communities. In some other Central American and African countries, it has been a partner of the governmental agencies also in the creation of enterprises that leverage their development.

That strategic learning process, which was based on a process of continuous assessment about the experiences that were lived, demanded another qualitative jump in the early 2000s: the formation of competences should be based as the outcome of a permanent learning process both in relation to the specificity of every client as well as in relation to environmental uncertainties. As Odebrecht is a decentralized organization, it is much more agile, adapting to environmental conditions and profiting from windows of opportunities. However, the experiences were isolated and "dos and don'ts" were not analysed in a joint manner. It also became evident, from the German experience, that the growth of the firm depended on having people really integrated in its entrepreneurial culture, its main asset.

Thereby, since the beginning of the decade, it has been active on two fronts: the registration of its success and failure cases by means of knowledge communities and the creation of qualification programs for all hierarchical levels and countries, aiming at transferring the knowledge and experience accumulated by the leaders of the three generations of the company. A vision of sustainability also became part of its strategic concerns.

The whole process is showing to be extremely profitable: in 2006, Odebrecht had already reached the target set for 2010.

8.15 Stefanini: a case of internationalization of a software producer

---

Box 8.14 An introductory note on the IT industry in Brazil

IT services represent a movement of $491 billion worldwide and the growth rate is a little over 5 percent. Brazil contributed with a modest 1.7 percent.

The main Brazilian groups active in IT services are: Totvs, Stefanini, CPM Braxis, Atech, Bematech, Itautec, YKP, and Politec. These companies compete on the domestic and international markets in specialized services and in certain market niches not taken by the large multinationals of the sector. Large multinational groups such as IBM, Microsoft, Accenture, Hewlett Packard (HP), and others are also active in Brazil.

Moreover, Brazil has attracted a number of new multinational suppliers of IT services. Several Indian, European, and American companies initiated or intensified their presence in Brazil in the 2000s. The market continues to be fragmented despite strong mergers and acquisitions. The ten largest IT services companies represent less than 40 percent of sales in the country. The entry of new multinationals, the fact that companies from other sectors have begun to explore services, and the rise of small companies, have restrained concentration in the Brazilian market.

Profit margins in IT service activities in Brazil have declined in recent years. Company costs have increased year by year, whether due to inflationary readjustments to the payroll, or the "formalization" of the companies. On the other hand, given heightened competition, it is increasingly difficult to pass on these cost increases to customers. Thus, the service companies are reinventing themselves, looking for labor in smaller cities, creating new partnerships, and improving employee productivity, among other measures.

Selected cases

Stefanini is twenty-first in FDC's TNI ranking and twentieth in SOBEET's list.

Bematech is thirty-first in FDC's ranking and forty-first in SOBEET's list.

Other Brazilian multinationals in the IT industry

Totvs, CPM Braxis, Atech, Itautec, YKP, and Politec.

8.15.1 Stefanini: origin

Stefanini IT Solutions was founded in 1987. Marcos Stefanini, the founder, is a geologist from the University of São Paulo, who began a career in information sciences as a trainee at Bradesco bank. In 1987 he founded Stefanini at his home. Today the company is considered one of the most important IT consulting companies in Brazil in providing software development and maintenance services.

The company strategy is based on customer orientation and customized services. It has 350 clients in Brazil and another 120 in the other sixteen countries where it operates. Presently Stefanini's international operations represent 22 percent of the company's total business. After the US and UK, South America is the region with the highest expansion rate over the last five years.

8.15.2 National growth concomitant with international expansion

Stefanini adopted a strategy of organic growth since its early years. The industrial restructuring and outsourcing established by various large Brazilian companies in the 1990s brought opportunities for Stefanini's domestic growth. In 1995, the company opened offices in large Brazilian cities. Still in the 1990s, it began to expand beyond the large Brazilian centers, following the clients.

The process of internationalization began in 1996 with the opening of an office in Argentina. Meanwhile, international expansion consolidated beginning in the 2000s. Thus, in 2000 it entered the Chilean and Mexican markets, and in 2001 it opened offices in Peru, Colombia, and the US. Operations in Europe started in 2003 with the opening of offices in Spain, Portugal, and Italy.

8.15.3 Internationalization strategy

Stefanini's first international venture was in Argentina, in 1996, as an experiment: it was an attractive market where risks were low. The real decision to internationalize was taken in 2001, with the firm following a strategy defined as "client supported international anchor contracts." In other words, risks were mitigated by contracts with larger contracting firms which pulled Stefanini to operate in Chile, Mexico, Peru, and Colombia. Soon after, Stefanini adopted a parallel strategy based on setting up international offices without anchor contracts. That was done in the US and Europe.

In 2008, the company consolidated two software factories in Latin America, one in Peru and one in Mexico. The Mexico factory is its first large development center outside Brazil. In addition to local actions, the office serves customers located in the US, Europe, and Latin America.

Also in 2008, Stefanini opened its fourth office in Mexico and established its first affiliate in Canada. The North American Free Trade Agreement (NAFTA) became essential to the success of the internationalization process. The company opened its fourth US affiliate in 2009.

8.15.4 Developing competences for internationalization

Stefanini's competitive advantages derive from technological competences, ethics, trust, and client relationships because its main operations are performed "inside the client's house." Since the client is anywhere in the world, and "each mountain is different," to use their analogy, Stefanini adopts a decentralized management model where the 400-plus consultants share great autonomy. Actually, Stefanini inspired its management principles on Odebrecht's model.

Stefanini's clients include Dell, IBM, and other global players. That was a driver for Stefanini to establish a subsidiary in Bangalore, India. To manage that operation, Stefanini hired the son of an Indian immigrant who grew up in Brazil, where the Indian community is very small, with a background in computers. There are plans to make that subsidiary an international reference with 1,000 employees. Stefanini currently has 8,000 employees in total, 1,000 of whom work abroad. Following its management principles, locals are preferred for the foreign offices.

In the technological front, Stefanini is investing in developing competences with the cloud computing model. The company formatted a long-term strategy to offer solutions while the model matures in the Brazilian market. The process began in 2008 and resources are directed at preparing the development team, strategic alliances with providers of software as a service (SaaS), and preparing to offer infrastructure technology for data centers.

As of the beginning of 2009, thirty R&D professionals from Stefanini had been trained to work with the cloud computing technology model. The effort aligned itself to the new realities of software factories in a concept of applications hosted "in the cloud," reducing the distance among development and operational environments.

In early 2009, Stefanini closed a deal to acquire the Brazilian start-up Callere, manufacturer of the eForm solution and which has strong features of innovation, research, and development. According to the company, the acquisition adds expertise in automatic reading and documentation processes to its operations. With the incorporation, Stefanini will create its document solutions unit, and offer solutions directed especially to the financial sector.

8.16 Bematech: a case of internationalization of a hardware producer

8.16.1 Bematech: origin

Bematech was created in 1990 in a company incubator in the city of Curitiba in the state of Paraná, to be active in the matrix printer market. The idea was derived from two MSc dissertations leading the two entrepreneurs to focus on telex machines as the first market niche. In 1991, after several unsuccessful attempts to raise funds from national agencies that stimulate technological development, Bematech secured financial resources from private sources, admitting six new partners. Thus, Bematch was transformed into Bematech Indústria e Comércio de Equipamentos Eletrônicos SA.

Bematech was the first Brazilian company to manufacture miniprinters on a large scale and the first to provide integrated block printers for automatic teller machine (ATM) terminals and thermal printing technology. However, Bematech's mission is defined as "making retail more efficient" through the delivery of integrated solutions.

8.16.2 National growth concomitant followed by international expansion

In 1995, the company opened an affiliate in São Paulo to service its main customers and the second half of the 1990s was decisive for the growth of the company in the Brazilian market. In 1999 and 2000, there was an explosion of sales of physical printers in Brazil, due to a law which mandated having financial receipts for transactions. In this period, the company reached the apex of its revenues to date, being responsible for 50 percent of installed printers.

Bematech was essentially domestic for ten years before beginning activities abroad. The company began its internationalization process in 2000 with an order by an American company for kiosk printers to be installed in game machines. The contract required the opening of the first affiliate in Atlanta, Georgia in 2001, creating Bematech International Corp. Contact with its first international customer was established during a technology fair in Germany where Bematech was showing its products.

Between 2002 and 2004, the company experienced its largest expansion, in the domestic as well as the international market. The company's main growth strategy was a blend of horizontal acquisitions in Brazil with greenfield investments abroad.

In Brazil, Bematech acquired a company that manufacture printers with the Yanco brand, a rival company and market leader in the cash register segment, expanding its product line for commercial automation. It also consolidated acquisitions of competing Brazilian companies such as Gemco, GSR7, Rentech, Bios Blak, and Mister Chef. With the acquisitions and new plants, the company improved its manufacturing competences.

In 2003, it created Bematech University and centralized management of its training activities and knowledge management, which had been taking place in a dispersed manner in several Brazilian cities. Bematech University is a center to integrate and disseminate knowledge for the company's business network, both national and international, by means of training employees and partners, and distributing knowledge and practices.

There were changes in the commercialization channel during this period. Due to the growth of operations, the company developed sales competencies and began to work with a hybrid commercialization model of which distributors, resellers, and representatives were part.

International expansion took place in parallel with domestic expansion. The company entered the Asian market and opened a sales office in Taiwan in 2003. To operate in Asia it was necessary to develop supply chain management competencies to be able to manage the network of product suppliers and product assemblers. The company strategy for Asia was to design the solutions in Brazil and buy supplies and assemble products in the Asian market in partnership with Chinese assemblers.

To structure its operations in Latin America, formerly intended solely for export, it opened a subsidiary in Argentina in 2003. In 2007, Bematech Europe GmbH opened with headquarters in Berlin, aiming to extend commercial channels in Europe which was already receiving exports from the company. The European unit also began to do business in India and Pakistan.

In 2007, the company opened its capital on the stock market. The latest international acquisition was Logics Controls, a $22 million deal made by Bematech International Corp., an American subsidiary, in 2008.

8.17 IBOPE: developing specialized services for the Latin Americans

---

Box 8.15 An introductory note on the services sector in Brazil

In Brazil, the tertiary (services) sector generates more than 60 percent of national income, industry between 30 and 35 percent, and agriculture about 10 percent. It is characterized by great heterogeneity, in relation to company size, capital intensity, and technological level. The range of segments that are part of the sector ranges from household services to data transmission over the Internet. The Brazilian Institute for Geography and Statistics (IBGE) classifies as services sub-sectors: trade, hotels, food (bars and restaurants), transport, telecommunications, financial intermediation, insurance and retirement plans, real estate activities, computer services, public administration, research and development, education, health and social services, and personal and household services.

There is a very strong presence of subsidiaries of multinationals in the Brazilian services sector. On the other hand, the internationalization of Brazilian firms is very discreet, with exceptions in the engineering sector and in the IT industry. An incipient movement is being witnessed in the food industry and banks.

Selected case

IPOBE is the fifth most internationalized company in Brazil in the SOBEET (2008) ranking. It also appears as the seventh largest company in terms of revenue and assets in Brazil ($250 million in 2007, 39 percent of company revenue) and the second ranked company with the highest number of employees abroad (3,900).

Other Brazilian multinationals in the sector

Itaú/Unibanco, Bradesco, Banco do Brasil, Fogo de Chão, Spoleto, Bob's.

8.17.1 IBOPE: origin

IBOPE was created in 1942 and was a pioneer in opinion research in Brazil. IBOPE's founder, Auricélio Penteado, owned a radio station in São Paulo in the 1940s and to get to know his radio audience he went to the US to study at the American Institute of Public Opinion, created in 1935 by George Gallup, to learn their research techniques. Upon returning to Brazil, he began to measure the audience for radio stations in São Paulo and dedicated himself exclusively to research activities.

Still in the 1940s, IBOPE incorporated the Cipex company, which specialized in surveys about publication of advertisements in the daily newspapers of São Paulo, Santos, and Campinas.

8.17.2 Innovating in the service sector

In the 1970s, IBOPE undertook its first election day exit polls in Brazil. In the 1980s, it created the company Painel and launched the national consumer panel. On the technological side, IBOPE developed "people meter" devices with its own competences and resources making it feasible to collect, process, and deliver audience data in real time.

8.17.3 The internationalization throughout Latin America

The internationalization of IBOPE gained importance at the beginning of the 1990s when the company associated with local companies in Peru and Ecuador. At first, expansion to Latin America took place via alliances with companies already established in those countries. Soon, partnerships were signed with potential international competitors interested in the region.

IBOPE took the technological competence developed by the company in Brazil to Latin American countries where it began to operate. In the countries of operation, for example, it replaced the old research notebooks with the people meter, a device installed in homes which register the channel the household is watching and transmits data automatically. Thus, the technology and experience accumulated by IBOPE in Brazil, in addition to the cultural affinity among the countries of Latin America, were important differentials for entry into the Latin countries. Currently, the company has a presence in twelve Latin American countries (Argentina, Chile, Colombia, Costa Rica, Ecuador, Guatemala, Mexico, Panama, Paraguay, Peru, Uruguay, and Venezuela).

The company has 100 percent control over affiliates in Argentina and Uruguay. It is the majority holder of Grupo Time (Chilean), in Chile, Peru, Guatemala, Costa Rica, and Panama. It has a partnership with AGB Nielsen Media Research for their Mexican and Ecuadorian operations. In Paraguay and Colombia it is associated with small local business people as the majority shareholder. It is minority shareholder only in Venezuela in association with AGB Nielsen Media Research.

8.17.4 Taking advantage of knowledge to enter the North American market

The North American office was initially created in New York in 1997, to meet the demands of American clients for information on cable TV audiences in the major Latin American markets. The office was transferred to Miami in 2000, centralizing responses to international requests for data on various associated companies. The Miami sales office is responsible for selling the surveys taken in Latin America to American cable channels that send their signal to the region.

The company is betting that US advertisers push the growth of IBOPE in the coming years. The company considers that the Spanish-speaking public represents around 14 percent of the US population, and that demand for services is growing. The company uses the knowledge and technology it has to offer research on demand to the North American market.

8.17.5 Strategic alliances

Presently, the Grupo IBOPE is composed of two big businesses: Ibope Media and Ibope Intelligência, as well as some strategic partnerships. Ibope Media is responsible for research on the media, advertising investments, and consumption habits for communications media, public relations agencies, and advertisers.

Ibope Inteligência does studies on the market, behavior, brands, public opinion, and the Internet. The data collected aids organizations in developing strategies, decision-making, and innovation processes.

In addition to these businesses, IBOPE also has an important equity share in two companies: Ibope Nielsen Online and Millward Brown do Brasil. Ibope Nielsen Online is a joint venture between Ibope Media and Nielsen, a North American company active in the areas of information and media, which details behavior in the use of digital media. Millward Brown do Brasil is a partnership of IBOPE with British companies Millward Brown, Inc. and the Grupo WPP, world leaders in advertising, brand names, and marketing. Millward Brown do Brasil is a company that does research on demand, dedicated to creating and maintaining strong brands.

It was with funds provided by the entry of WPP into the media measurement business in recent years that IBOPE managed to intensify its expansion in Latin America. The strategy was to ally itself with its competitor to grow and assure its own space.

8.18 CI&T and Griaule: born globals in creative industries

Box 8.16 Born globals in Brazil

In the last decade, several studies have shown that small and medium companies (SMEs) have been successful in their international ventures. The so-called "born global" phenomenon is not restricted to high technology companies, but is more frequently found in sectors where accelerated innovation is a key feature.

Because they internationalize soon after their foundation, born globals are expected to have a distinct set of competences. Moreover, the specific characteristics of the entrepreneur(s) involved play a decisive role in the international path of the firm.

In Brazil, despite the relatively large number of SMEs, the number of born global firms seems to be small. Evidently, there are no reliable figures at aggregate levels about this category of firms and it is quite difficult to find sound evidence. However, it is hypothesized that, currently, the local environment is seldom supportive for the internationalization effort.

In this section, two cases of Brazilian born global firms will be presented, one in the software industry and the other in the new biometrics industry.

Selected cases

CI&T: born global in the software industry.
Griaule: born global in the biometrics field.

Other Brazilian born-globals

Xseed, Fujitec, Ivia, Tritec.

8.18.1 *CI&T Software SA: origin*

CI&T was created in 1995 for business software development. According to one of its founders, the idea occurred right after finishing a master's in computer sciences, for the main purpose of making money to pay the cost of a doctorate program in the US.

8.18.2 *Moving to the international market*

This company is a classic example of a born global, with its internationalization beginning two years after its founding, when the partners took on service delivery for IBM, with projects in the US and France. The company began small and its services were based essentially in the scientific and technological knowledge of its founders. The distinctive technological competences were enhanced through the cooperation agreement with the University, encompassing laboratories and research infrastructure.

Currently CI&T has 730 employees and competes with companies such as Tata, which has 130,000. Its strategy is to have a portfolio of large customers and to work in market niches, acting globally for few customers. In 2007, the company was certified for the highest rank of the Capability Maturity Model Integration (CMMI) and was judged a rising star by *Fortune* magazine, and was the only Brazilian company on the Global Outsourcing 100 list.

8.18.3 *Learning to (re)act in the Brazilian market*

Two years after its foundation, and until 2001, CI&T focused on the Brazilian market. That was motivated by the entrepreneurs' realization that the country had competences in software development which were compatible with developed countries. To keep up-to-date, not just technologically, but especially in terms of market knowledge, in 2001 the company began to attend fairs in the US.

However, contrary to that of India, the Brazilian software industry is not focused to the external markets. One of the explanations pointed out by CI&T is the size of the domestic market. However, there is great unused potential, since this is an industry which is by nature free of prejudice – customers are much more concerned with competence and costs than the country of origin of the service provider. With the entry of the Indian business process outsourcing (BPO) companies in Brazil, internationalization has became a necessity, under threat of losing competitiveness even in the Brazilian market.

The company obtained support from the government for its effective internationalization, in 2001, from the BNDES, for its first large contract in the US. In 2005, CI&T opened a subsidiary in Philadelphia, in a joint venture operation with BNDES, which owns 30 percent of the company. Financing provided funds for infrastructure investment, training, R&D, marketing for opening the new software factory and the new trade office in the US.

8.18.4 *Learning to do international marketing*

According to the CI&T, one of the major barriers to becoming active in other countries is the local language. Even though negotiations anywhere in the world take place in English, product marketing and services must always be put into operation by people who speak the local language. Issues of international marketing in the local language are becoming even more essential in the company's third phase of internationalization, the opening of an office in China (CI&T Pacific), already inscribed in the owners' plans and which will be the local base for serving the Asian market.

To resolve the question of marketing and making services operational, the company provides training in English in Brazil for professionals from foreign countries in which it is active. These professionals are responsible for dissemination of the product and spreading information on services in their countries. In this way, the company has the competence to train foreign partners and has specific processes and technology to attract customers in the external market.

The internationalization of CI&T was not undertaken according to a deliberate strategy, but was the result of the global nature of the industry. Its management competences and innovative products serve international customers, including those from countries more technologically advanced than Brazil.

8.18.5 *Griaule Biometrics: origin*

Griaule Biometrics was created in a University's incubator in 2002. It provides solutions in biometrics, especially through the development of software for fingerprint recognition, network logon, identification of point of sale, and for civil and criminal case identifications for security applications.

The initial idea was developed in the early 1990s, but the project became a reality only in the incubation program, ten years later. The University of Campinas provided the entrepreneurs with the physical structure the company needed, as well as business consultants. These consultants aided in the process of changing the company focus from hardware to software, by which it would be possible to obtain greater competitive advantages.

8.18.6 *International orientation and formulation of competences in e-business*

The company was not created with the intention of becoming international, rather internationalization was something that came naturally due to the sector of activity and the technology it uses, which are global. Three years after its founding, the company got its first international customer in the US; the deal resulted in the opening of a sales office in Silicon Valley, California in 2006. That subsidiary develops joint research with the University of San Jose, which is being considered as a leveraging factor to increase sales in the American market.

The company developed a number of commercial competences to begin sales on the Internet, especially in e-business. In addition to the Internet sales tools, the company site appears in five languages: Portuguese, English, Spanish, German, and Chinese. The role of the intermediary reseller is essential to product distribution.

Currently, the company sells its products to over eighty countries, using the Internet as its basic channel. The main markets are the US, followed by Europe, and there are also plans to enter the Asian market. Presently, sales abroad represent 80 percent of total company revenues. Customers are generally integrators, companies that integrate the Griaule component into its product. It manages to be competitive internationally by supplying large corporations and global institutions, despite being a small company with only twenty-two employees in Brazil.

The company's business model is not to sell software to the final customer, since this would involve creating a much stronger, better integrated sales strategy and establishing post-sales services. The competence focus of the company is R&D of technology in biometrics. In this way, Griaule only needs to find integrators and sell the technology via the Internet. The integrators are those who serve the final customer to install the systems and resolve the clients' problems.

Griaule had government support in specific R&D projects through the regular circuits established by the Brazilian research agencies. Opening and supporting the office in the US was accomplished entirely with its own financing.

8.19 Closing remarks

This chapter showed how Brazilian companies have broken with the cultural heritage to meet the challenges and opportunities opened by internationalization. These firms overcame the traditions that settled for strongly hierarchical structures and low levels of participation, interpersonal relations prevailing over organizational procedures, reactive strategies, low propensity to innovate, emphasis on the exploitation of natural resources, focus on short-term defensive mechanisms, dependence on government and political networks, and dependence on protected markets, among other things. The cases illustrate how Brazilian firms developed a distinctive architecture of organizational competences that were integrated by proper management styles to become internationally competitive.

Overall, the cases confirm that internationalization was a decision that matured for a long time in Brazilian companies and was somehow induced by the transformation of the conditions of operation in the domestic markets. However, the relationship between the local environment and competence development at firm level was mediated by the firm's management style, which led to distinct internationalization choices and paths.

Initially, Brazilian firms excelled in operations (like CSN, Vale, JBS-Friboi) and had a good standing in regards to technology (WEG, Romi, Gerdau, Braskem). Other distinctive competences that were leveraged by local conditions were related to commercialization (AmBev, Tigre) and customer relationship management (Odebrecht, IBOPE) due to conditions prevailing in local markets.

The entry modes of Brazilian multinationals are multiple, combining a mix of activities that occur simultaneously and encompass asset seeking and efficiency seeking strategies. The learning process triggered by the internationalization challenge led to the enhancement of organizational competences. From the cases shown, the following must be highlighted:

- organizing (Embraer, Odebrecht, Vale, Votorantim);
- commercial (Embraer, Petrobras, Votorantim, WEG);
- customer relationship management (Gerdau, Odebrecht, WEG);
- supply chain management (Embraer, Petrobras, Tigre);
- corporate social responsibility (which was not considered in the analytical framework) (Vale, Petrobras, Gerdau).

Therefore, competences which are considered peculiarities of emerging country firms can be a source of competitiveness in their international forays. As emphasized by Guillen and Garcia-Canal (2009), these firms show excellent performance even in institutionally complex and turbulent environments due to their political experience and their ability to manage acquisitions. They "absorb technology, combine resources, and innovate from an organizational point of view in ways that reduce costs and enhance learning" (Guillen and Garcia-

Canal, 2009: 31). Moreover, some of the cases reflect the importance of their participation in global production networks, to leverage their competences differentials.

In summary, the cases reveal the rationales and strategies that lead firms from a given emerging country to outperform in the global economy. Next, we will focus on emerging country multinationals from other origins – Latin America, China, India, Russia, and South Africa – seeking for common and differentiating characteristics in relation to the Brazilian case. Comparative analysis always brings valuable insights.

9 | *Multilatinas*

9.1 The multinationals from Latin America

Brazilian multinationals are often analyzed as part of the group of "multilatinas" the multinationals that originate in Latin America. Nonetheless there are authors such as Santiso (2007), that include the Iberian multinationals in this group.

The first multilatinas were Argentinean firms that, in the nineteenth century, sought internationalization and aimed at Uruguay, considered the "Switzerland of the South," on the other side of the River Plate, and Brazil, which was essentially agrarian at the time. In the 1970s, a new internationalization movement materialized, with Brazilian and Argentinean firms venturing abroad. The outcomes, however, were modest.

Now, Latin American countries are in the third wave of internationalization. Existing analyses of multilatinas (Brazilian multinational enterprises (BrMNEs) included) can be classified into two currents. The first of these highlights the relative timidity of these companies' internationalization processes, and, based on a comparative analysis of what occurred in the developed countries and what is happening today in the Asian countries, questions whether the firms and countries meet the basic requirements needed to become truly international (Grosse and Mesquita, 2007; Haar and Price, 2008). The second approach focuses on multilatinas and, recognizing the limits of their activities, seeks to understand their strategies, trajectories, and the factors that justify the process of internationalization. Along these lines, we highlight the work of Álvaro Cuervo-Cazurra (2007) and Santiso (2007).

In this chapter we will deal with the following issues:

- are the Brazilian multinationals similar to the multinationals originating in other Latin American countries? Are there differences?

- taken as a group, are the multilatinas different? What insights do they bring to the study of internationalization processes?

9.2 What Latin America is: diversity nurtured from common roots

Despite its common denomination, what has been called "Latin America" is, in fact, a region of great heterogeneity and low integration, beginning with its geographic features. The southernmost point of Latin America is Patagonia, at a latitude of 53 degrees south, and its northernmost point is Tijuana, Mexico, a neighbor of San Diego, at 32 degrees of latitude. The distance between these two points is 10,600 kilometers, approximately that same distance between Lisbon, Portugal and Tokyo, Japan.

The topography is rich and varied with the Andean mountains, the Amazon, and Central America itself, with rough terrain that makes movement and transportation difficult. Central America and the Caribbean are comprised of twenty countries and sixteen territories, the largest of which is Nicaragua, with a size the equivalent of Greece.

Despite the fact that its religious and linguistic roots (Catholic and Latin) contribute to defining the concept of Latin America, we need to pay attention to nuances that make up the cultural portrait of the region, reflected in its corporations.

One classic study, for example, identifies greater cultural similarity between countries such as Argentina and Brazil with the Latin European countries (which include Belgium, France, Italy, Spain, and Portugal), than with other Latin American countries (which include Chile, Colombia, Mexico, Peru, and Venezuela), defining specific cultural clusters (Hefstede, 1980). Ronen and Shenkar (1985) locate Brazil in an independent cultural cluster (along with Japan, India, and Israel) of countries which, given their diverse specificities, are not included in the other groups encountered. In this analysis, the Latin American cluster comprises Argentina, Chile, Colombia, Mexico, Peru, and Venezuela. The grouping is associated to three interconnected dimensions: language, religion, and geographic region; they are also related to technological development, since these influence the attitudes of the managers (Ronen and Shenkar, 1985).

Even though their economic history has many points in common, their political and economic options are today very different. On the economic plane, Mexico and the countries of Central America and the Caribbean are under the sphere of influence of the US and Canada, articulated through the North American Free Trade Agreement (NAFTA) and the Central American Free Trade Agreement (CAFTA). The northern countries of South America, those that face the Pacific Ocean, establish commercial relations via the Andean Pact and also maintain bilateral agreements with Asian countries, especially Korea and China. The southern Latin American countries, including Brazil, established the Mercosur. An attempt to establish a Free Trade Agreement of the Americas (FTAA) failed, and today the European Community is making a strong effort to establish trade agreements with the Mercosur countries, seeking to counterbalance North American influence. Some authors use the metaphor of sitting ducks and flying geese to compare the behavior of the governments of the Latin American countries to those of Asia respectively (Mortimore, 1993; Jank, 2005). In contrast to their Asian colleagues, Latin American countries are friendly and meet frequently, but rarely arrive at practical agreements.

9.3 The economic development of Latin America

At the beginning of the twentieth century, Argentina and Uruguay were considered the most developed countries in Latin America. Uruguay was considered "the Switzerland of the South" and Argentina was the first Latin American country to experience growth. After 1875, through the export of livestock and grain commodities, as well as through British and French investment, Argentina went through a significant era of economic expansion. During its most vigorous period, from 1880 to 1905, this expansion resulted in a 7.5-fold growth in gross domestic product (GDP), averaging about 8 percent annually. GDP per capita rose from 35 percent of the US average to about 80 percent during that period. Growth then slowed considerably, although throughout the period from 1890 to 1939 the country's per capita income was similar to that of France, Germany, and Canada.

Although Argentina led the way, the histories of the different Latin American countries have many points in common. The most predominant is the fact that they are agro-exporting economies, thanks to these countries' soil and climate (hence the development of the production of meat in Argentina, wine in Chile, and coffee in Colombia, Costa Rica, and Brazil), as well as their minerals (copper in Chile and Bolivia), among others.

The Latin American economies, despite their "peripheral status" among the main economic regions of the world (Rojas, 2004), have undergone successive internal transformations as a consequence of external economic shocks and international political changes (Cardenas *et al.*, 2001). Some of these shocks had similar effects in various Latin American countries, such as the first world war and the post-war boom and crash, the great depression of the 1930s. Other international events had specific impacts on countries, such as the collapse of coffee prices at the end of the nineteenth century, the rise of Nazism in Europe and the advance of the cold war.

In the context of the end of the nineteenth century and the beginning of the twentieth, the exporting sectors usually represented the most dynamic element in the Latin American economies and constituted a channel by which these countries were connected to the international economy. With rare exceptions, the exporting sectors were intimately related to the natural resource base or specific agricultural products that had international demand (Cardenas *et al.*, 2001).

Foreign interests, especially European countries and groups, were involved principally in the trade and transport of these commodities and their production. In the great majority of cases, these remained in the hands of the local aristocracy, which benefited enormously from international commerce and also from foreign investment in some local activities.

The growth of the modern international monetary system contributed to the expansion of trade and to some foreign direct investment (FDI) in the region. International migration received by Latin American countries was intense at the beginning of the twentieth century and constituted another link with the outside world. The immigrants, mainly Europeans, became the most active segment of the economy and of the formation of industrial society in Latin America.

The crisis of 1929, which in the advanced capitalist countries manifested with the closing of markets and reinforced protectionism, in Latin America took the route of a process of economic modernization and industrialization. What would be called the import substitution model began during this period and intensified over the following decades (Cardenas *et al.*, 2001).

In the period between the world wars, the hegemony Europe had exercised over Latin America for four centuries was replaced with a new hegemony, in the form of the US. The reach and impact of this change in economic and political hegemony and the change in the role of "foreign presences" was profound in the face of the internal process of reorganization and the first social modernization of Latin America, accompanied by the move to replace the ruling agrarian elites in several countries (Rojas, 2004).

The industrial development of Latin America after the second world war can be broken down into two different stages. The first began in the late 1940s and persisted into the early 1970s. This was the time of industrialization through import substitution.

After the second world war, the Latin American countries had substantial repressed demand for consumer durables and capital goods, impossible to import during the war. The government policies of that time, which introduced tariff barriers, encouraged technology licensing, subsidized financing for "industries of national interest," created state-owned enterprises and attracted MNEs in order to induce local production of these goods. Investments were directed toward the production of basic inputs such as petrochemicals, iron and steel, pulp and paper, aluminum, vegetable oil, and mineral products, mainly. This movement was particularly important for Brazil, Chile, and Argentina.

The most dynamic local industries of this period were those manufacturing textiles, wage consumer goods, agricultural equipment, and technologically unsophisticated capital goods. Nevertheless, the incipient industrial base led many firms to vertical integration and to producing parts, components, and services that were provided by specialized producers in more industrially advanced societies. To a certain extent, this caused firms to diversify their activities and generated a lack of focus on their core products.

The durable consumer goods segment, the economy's most dynamic one, was handed over to MNE subsidiaries. In some cases, for a certain time, they set up partnerships with local firms. For instance, in 1913, Ford entered the Argentine market: it was the first Latin American branch and the second in the world after the UK. General Motors

(GM) started up its operations in 1925. The two enterprises closed their plants during the second world war because it was impossible to get parts for making vehicles. In 1958, Ford resumed its Argentine operations, inaugurating a new plant. However, both Ford and GM also set up subsidiaries in Chile, Ecuador, Mexico, Colombia, and Venezuela. Renault entered Argentina via licensing in 1960 and, in 1975, it took over the operation, establishing a fully owned subsidiary. In the appliances sector, Philco had established itself in Argentina at the start of the century, expanding into Brazil in 1950. Thus, during this period, the result was a restrained, strongly local orientation that was devoid of integration with the rest of the world.

In the early 1970s, the limitations of the import substitution model started surfacing. During this period the East Asia economies were already embracing a more open strategic orientation.

In the 1980s, there was a reduction in FDI and in the presence of foreign MNEs in the manufacturing sector. That made room for local enterprises. Industry became strongly concentrated, with a small number of domestic family conglomerates that in general maintained strong relationships with governmental instances. Guillen (2001) considers that to be a competitive advantage for their internationalization.

The overall assessment for the import substitution period is positive:

On one hand, it is evident that import substitution industrialization (ISI) efforts triggered a dynamic mechanism of technological learning and modernization which significantly improved domestic technical capabilities, total factor productivity and international competitiveness. Thus, despite the isolation experienced during the period of import substitution, there is evidence that the development of domestic technological competences has been strongly enhanced through learning mechanisms and that many individual firms and industries managed to modernize and upgrade themselves substantially, expanding both their productivity and their competitiveness in world markets. Katz (1994: 161)

9.4 Productive restructuring and opening up to international markets

Toward the end of the 1980s and in the early 1990s, the structure and behavior of industrial sectors were affected by the opening and

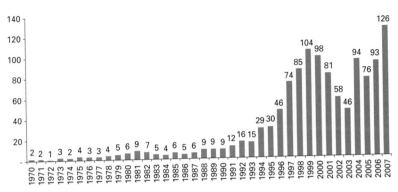

Figure 9.1 Inward FDI in Latin America and the Caribbean, 1970–2007 ($ billion)

deregulation of the economy and by the privatization of government-owned enterprises. The region's countries embraced these measures with an industrial policy that differed from the "direct" interventions of previous decades. This process led to deep structural changes in microeconomic terms. These measures led to a significant increase in inward FDI as shown in Figure 9.1.

Concurrently, foreign investment by Latin American firms increased. According to the available statistics, outward FDI from Latin America and the Caribbean leaped from an annual average of some $52 million between 1970 and 1974 to $1.7 billion in 1985–9, and then to $24.5 billion between 2000 and 2004. Excluding the main financial centers (Bermuda, the British Virgin Islands, and the Cayman Islands), the annual average was $9.2 billion in the last period. By contrast, outward FDI from developing Asia increased from an annual average of $3 million in 1970–4 to $7.4 billion between 1985 and 1989, and then to $51.1 billion in 2000–4.

Most of the Latin American FDI in the last fifteen years came from four countries, Argentina, Brazil, Chile, and Mexico, with Colombia and Venezuela having become involved more recently (Tavares and Ferraz, 2007).

Figure 9.2 shows the evolution of total outward FDI from emerging economies. It also highlights the share of the different country blocks: Latin America and the Caribbean, South-east Europe and the Commonwealth of Independent States (CIS) transition economies (the former Soviet Republics), Asia and Oceania, and Africa. In the 1970s

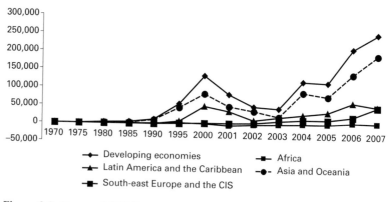

Figure 9.2 Outward FDI flows, 1970–2007 ($ million)

and 1980s, the difference between the investment of Latin America and of the Caribbean vs. the Asian countries, greater for the former, is imperceptible. The subsequent growth of the Asian economies is evident.

In the 1970s and 1980s, the leading Latin American countries in terms of outward FDI were Argentina, Brazil, Colombia, and Mexico. Most of this investment targeted other developing countries, in particular their neighbors, and the main sectors involved were natural resource extraction, engineering, and construction services, as well as manufacturing operations set up to avoid trade restrictions in the recipient countries. Partnerships were often formed with local companies, and investments focused mainly on supplying the markets of the recipient country, other than in the case of investments in seeking natural resources, where the purpose was to supply markets in the home country (Chudnovsky and López, 1999a). Argentine and Brazilian companies were the leaders and their direct investments abroad were largely market-seeking, the intention being to exploit competitive advantages (product design or adaptation capabilities, and commercial and productive management) in less sophisticated markets (Chudnovsky and López, 1999b).

Still, intraregional FDI in Latin America has grown significantly since the early 1990s, for the following reasons, among others:

- the creation of Mercosur, which led to greater integration and tariff exemptions among Argentina, Brazil, Uruguay, and Paraguay;
- an increase in the region's companies' access to oil and gas reserves (Petrobras in Argentina, Bolivia, and Venezuela); and

- the consolidation of the state's regional energy integration policies (Petroleos de Venesuela in Argentina, Brazil, Cuba etc.).

As to the future, the most problematic issue seems to reside on the sociopolitical infrastructure dimension. As Price and Haar (2008: 3) put it, "Over the long term Latin América will enjoy favorable economic prospects thanks to its enviable supplier position in many commodity markets. However, the region's ability to compete will remain hampered until it takes on the politically sensitive battles of reforming its policies and codes."

9.5 Multilatinas: patterns and features

In this text, we have adopted the term multilatinas, although alternatives such as translatinas are also used. The ranking provided by *América Economia* magazine shows how different each country's development is when it comes to large companies. Brazil, Mexico, Chile, and Argentina head the ranking and have been expanding their share in the last few years (Table 9.1).

When we compare Latin American firms with the global standard, we find that their positions are relatively modest, as Table 9.2 shows. There are only ten multilatinas among the *Fortune 500* (including three Brazilian banks), fifteen among the world's 2,000 largest firms according to *Forbes*, eight in the list of the fifty largest MNEs from emerging countries (financial enterprises excluded) and twenty-four in the "100 Global Challengers" list of the Boston Consulting Group (BCG).

One of multilatinas' striking features is that a large proportion is part of family-run corporate groups (Table 9.3).

Guillen (2000: 362) recognizes that "Business groups are becoming major players in the world economy and that little effort has been devoted to understanding the rise of business groups in emerging economies in terms of resources and capabilities." Grosse (2007: 370) explains that these close-knit groups of stakeholders (e.g., families or groups of families) have held tight ownership control of corporations by vertically integrating and forming larger capital and labor pools. "That confers on them an edge over the domestic and foreign competitors in this Latin American environment, which is characterized by failing markets for these very resources."

Table 9.1 500 largest Latin American companies

Rank 2007	Country	Number of firms						Share % 2007
		2002	2003	2004	2005	2006	2007	
1	Brazil	137	195	203	204	207	211	42.2
2	Mexico	241	170	154	138	111	134	33
3	Chile	45	48	48	54	63	55	8.1
4	Argentina	24	25	32	36	41	36	5.5
5	Colombia	25	18	28	30	35	31	3
6	Peru	7	8	11	12	18	15	1.5
7	Venezuela	10	9	11	11	12	7	5.6
8	Costa Rica	3	5	6	4	3	3	0.3
9	Ecuador	2	3	2	5	3	3	0.5
—	Guatemala	—	1	2	1	2	—	—
10	Panama	1	2	1	2	2	2	0.1
11	Uruguay	3	2	1	2	2	2	0.1
12	El Salvador	1	2	1	1	1	1	0.1
	Total	500	500	500	500	500	500	100

Source: América Economía.

Table 9.2 The presence of multilatinas in international rankings

	Company	Industry	Fortune 500 (2009/2008)[a]	Forbes 2000 (2008/2007)[b]	WIR (2008)[c] Foreign assets	WIR (2008)[c] TNI[d]	BCG (2009)[e]	Home economy
1	Petróleos de Venezuela	Petroleum	27/–	–	15	89	–	Venezuela
2	Pemex	Petroleum	31/42	–	–	–	–	Mexico
3	Petrobras	Petroleum	34/63	29/88	12	94	X	Brazil
4	Bradesco	Banking	148/204	85/208	–	–	–	Brazil
5	CVRD	Mining and quarrying	205/235	76/361	11	73	X	Brazil
6	Itaúsa – Investimentos	Banking	149/273	175/477	–	–	–	Brazil
7	Banco do Brasil	Banking	174/282	132/256	–	–	–	Brazil
8	América Móvil	Telecommunications	273/283	453	14	54	X	Mexico
9	CEMEX	Cement	421/389	249/361	4	21	X	Mexico
10	CFE	Utilities	370/408	–	–	–	–	Mexico
11	Carso Global Telecom	Telecommunications	464/–	346/1,171	–	–	–	Mexico
12	Gerdau	Metals	400/–	766/1,496	39	47	X	Brazil
13	Falabella	Retailing	–	1,238/1,777	–	–	X	Chile
14	Femsa	Food and beverages	–	582/809	47	84	X	Mexico
15	Braskem	Chemicals	–	1,091/1,170	–	–	X	Brazil

Table 9.2 (*cont.*)

	Company	Industry	Fortune 500 (2009/2008)[a]	Forbes 2000 (2008/2007)[b]	WIR (2008)[c] Foreign assets	WIR (2008)[c] TNI[d]	BCG (2009)[e]	Home economy
16	Embraer	Aerospace and defense	—	1,345/1,467	—	—	X	Brazil
17	Grupo Bimbo	Food and beverages	—	1,312/1,881	91	76	X	Mexico
18	Grupo Alfa	Conglomerates	—	1,255/989	—	—	X	Mexico
19	CSN	Metals	—	809/1,049	—	—	—	Brazil
20	Mercantil Servicios	Diversified Financials	—	1,467/1,333	—	—	—	Venezuela
21	Teléfonos de Venezuela	Telecommunications	—	1,960/1,727	—	—	—	Venezuela
22	Unibanco	Banking	—	233	—	—	—	Brazil
23	Grupo EleKtra		—	1,278	—	—	—	Mexico
24	Sadia	Food	—	1,733	—	—	X	Brazil
25	Votorantim Group	Diversified	—	1,487	—	—	X	Brazil
26	WEG	Electric engines	—	1,824	—	—	X	Brazil
27	Aracruz Celulose	Pulp and paper	—	1,519	—	—	—	Brazil
28	Suzano	Pulp and paper		1,971	—	—	—	Brazil
29	Usiminas	Steel		736	—	—	—	Brazil

			a	b	c	d	e	
30	Gruma	Food and beverages	—	—	81	38	X	Mexico
31	Coteminas	Textile	—	—	—	—	X	Brazil
32	JBS-Friboi	Food	—	—	—	—	X	Brazil
33	Marcopolo	Vehicles and parts	—	—	—	—	X	Brazil
34	Natura	Cosmetics	—	—	—	—	X	Brazil
35	Perdigão	Food	—	—	—	—	X	Brazil
36	Camargo Corrêa AS	Diversified	—	—	—	—	X	Brazil
37	CSAV	Diversified	—	—	—	—	X	Chile
38	Tenaris	Metals	—	—	—	—	X	Argentina
39	Grupo Modelo	Diversified	—	—	—	—	X	Mexico

[a] *Fortune* (2008, 2009); [b] *Forbes* (2007, 2008); [c] *World Investment Report* (UNCTAD, 2008); [d] *Transnationality Index* (UNCTAD, 2008); [e] Boston Consultancy Group (2009); X indicates inclusion in BCG's New Global Challengers List.

Table 9.3 *Latin American family groups*

Country	Family (group)	Industry	Financial institution	Multilatina	Regions
Mexico	Slim	Telecommunications, metals, financial services, and agribusiness	Yes	American Móvil, Telmex	NAFTA, LA
Mexico	Zambrano	Cement		CEMEX	Global
Mexico	Femsa	Beverage		Femsa	LA
Mexico	Bimbo	Food		Bimbo	NAFTA, EU, Asia
Mexico	Salinas	Media, financial services, and retail	Yes	Elektra	LA
Mexico	Bal	Mining, steel, chemical, and financial services	Yes		US, Japan, Finland
Mexico	Grupo México	Mining, logistics, and transportation			LA
Mexico	Grupo Alfa	Metals and food		Nemak	LA, NAFTA, EU, China
Mexico	Gruma	Food		Gruma	EU
Brazil	Moraes (Votorantim)	Pulp and paper, cement, metallurgy, steel, financial services, and agribusiness	Yes	Votorantim Cement, Metals, Siderurgy	NAFTA, LA
Brazil	Steinbruch (Vicunha)	Steel and metallurgy		CSN	US, Portugal

Country	Group	Industry		Company	Region
Brazil	Gerdau	Steel and financial services	Yes	Gerdau Steel	US, EU, LA
Brazil	Batista	Agribusiness	Yes	JBS-Friboi	US
Brazil	Camargo Corrêa	Construction, metallurgy, cement, energy, and agribusiness	Yes	Loma Negra	US, LA, Espanha, Africa
Brazil	Fontana e Furlan	Agribusiness and food		Sadia	EU
Brazil	Odebrecht	Construction, chemical, and petrochemical		Odebrecht	Global
Argentina	Rocca (Techint)	Metallurgy, steel, oil, and gas		Tenaris	Global
Argentina	Pagani (Arcor)	Food		Arcor	US, LA

Source: América Economia.

The research on the largest multilatinas shows that they take a long time, after their establishment, to internationalize. "There is a relatively large gap between the time when the firms were created and when they first engaged in FDI. The average gap is over 49 years. Most of the multilatinas became MNEs in the 1980s and 1990s, but all of them were created before 1980, and most of them much earlier, some going back over a hundred years" (Cuervo-Cazzurra, 2007). For this author, "The exceptions to this rule include Techint, created in Argentina in 1945, which one year later was operating in Uruguay; Televisa, created in Mexico in 1954, which seven years later had established a joint venture in the US; and Embraer, created in Brazil in 1968, which 11 years later set up an aircraft servicing facility in the US. However, most Multilatinas became MNEs only after being in business for 20 years at least."

Analyzing twenty leading multilatinas (Brazil included) in regards to their choices of country for the first entry, Cuervo-Cazurra (2008) identified two dominant patterns (called dominant because of the higher number of firms following them). They are:

(a) to start in countries that are proximate in both culture and development (Latin America itself); these firms often sell products dependent on government relationships and institutional/developmental conditions;

(b) to start in countries that are distant in both culture and development (like North America and Anglo-Saxon Europe); these firms search for opportunities in larger markets, often selling products that are culturally bound.

The secondary patterns, called secondary because of the limited number of firms using them, are:

(c) to start in countries that are proximate in culture but distant in development (like Latin Europe); firms that sell products that are not culturally or development bound, or firms that are in search of assets and capabilities to complement their resource pools;

(d) to start multinationalization in countries that are distant in culture but proximate in development (like Asia and Africa); these firms sell products adapted to the needs of consumers in developing countries, but that are not culturally bound.

Cuervo-Cazurra's findings are not intuitive because it is common thought that there is a trend for multilatinas to concentrate investments in other Latin American countries, especially in what concerns items (b) and (c). The implications will be discussed in the next sections.

9.6 Sources of international competitiveness: are there common patterns?

Grosse (2007) admits that North and South American writers and analysts have not been able to identify particular capabilities of firms from Latin America that enable them to compete successfully in the increasingly open markets around the world. He notes that "It seems that Latin American firms are viewed as less-efficient outgrows of the US company model, tend to be smaller than their US counterparts, while their competitive advantages and strategies tend to mimic those of the US firms" (Grosse, 2007: 1).

In Chapter 7, we showed that in the case of Brazil, this stereotype was justified up to the end of the 1980s, when a series of factors led to a rupture. There followed the development of a new management model and the creation of a sociopolitical infrastructure that favored the growth and the internationalization of local companies.

Of all the Latin American countries, only Brazil, Mexico, Argentina, and Chile have companies that are classified as multinationals. This group includes companies that range from those at the start of the internationalization process to those recognized as global players, such as CEMEX and Techint, not to mention a bunch of Brazilian multinationals. There are cases that are still not well configured as a multinational, such as Café de Colômbia, a cooperative comprising 500,000 small producers, with its own stores on 42nd street in New York, competing with Starbucks.

In the identification of country specific factors, Brazil, Chile, Mexico, and Argentina have very distinct sets of advantages and disadvantages. Perhaps the only common advantage is natural resources, but it is necessary to stress that there is a significant percentage of multilatinas that are not natural resource based industries. If we consider the disadvantages, then the political-institutional turbulence is a common factor, with lesser importance to the case of Chile. On the financial level, Edmunds (2007) argues that the weaknesses in the financial institutional environment (e.g., financial markets are small, often non-liquid, and too focused on financing the expansion of traditional commodity production and exports, as opposed to financing innovation and new technologies) have often held Latin American firms back from becoming internationally competitive. Thus, we return to the argument that, in each country, there is a specific interaction between country specific advantages and firm specific advantages that sustained the internationalization of their companies.

In sum, economic and industrial development had very different results in each of the Latin American countries due to different endowment factors, to distinct political-institutional contexts and different national cultures. Consequently, the Latin American countries have unequal histories with respect to the phenomenon of internationalization.

9.7 Argentinean multinationals

9.7.1 The institutional and economic context

Argentina was the first Latin American country to have MNEs; then they expanded during the second internationalization wave. However, only a few survived the crises that struck that country in the 1980s and 1990s. Macroeconomic problems were the most important factors for this outcome.

In the early twentieth century, Argentina was the most economically advanced country in Latin America and the Caribbean. Despite its exceptional wealth of natural resources, the severe macroeconomic crises in which it floundered, often accompanied by radical transformations of the dominant economic model, resulted in long periods of low growth. The local companies, particularly in recent times, had to operate in a turbulent and uncertain business environment.

From the 1960s to the early 1990s, Argentina pursued an ambitious program of nuclear energy and technological development. This worked as a technology pull for some of the most important Argentinean firms like Perez Companc and Techint. The program was discontinued due to the nation's macroeconomic crises.

The opening of the economy to external competition in the 1990s put substantial pressure on Argentina's firms, mainly because these transformations were very fast and far reaching. Deregulation and privatization of the energy sector were very important in this respect. The Argentine government did not promote outward FDI and the regulations that were in effect during the crises tended to discourage it.

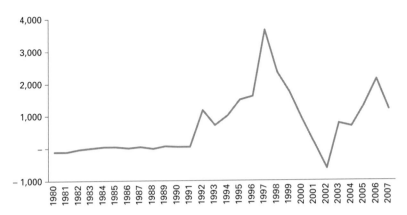

Figure 9.3 Stock and flows of outward FDI in Argentina, 1980–2004 ($ million)
Source: UNCTAD (2008).

9.7.2 *Argentine's investments abroad*

As already mentioned, Argentine companies were the first in Latin America to go international. Among the first to invest abroad were: Alpargatas, a textile firm that set up a branch in Uruguay in 1890 and then another in Brazil; SIAM di Tella, an engineering firm; and Bunge & Born, a diversified agribusiness conglomerate that established plants in the neighboring countries in the first half of the twentieth century.

The firm's investments abroad, encouraged at first by export-oriented agriculture, were reduced during the import substitution period, but resumed growth in the early 1980s. At first, the commercial and financial liberalization, deregulation, privatization, and stabilization programs generated a growth outlook. Some of the largest Argentine groups made direct investments in the neighboring countries. The chief fields of activity were natural resources and industries derived from natural resources. In the 1990s, foreign FDI centered mainly on energy (oil and gas), iron, steel and the food sector (Figure 9.3).

However, this situation soon came to an end. The stabilization plan based on a fixed exchange rate (the parity between the Argentine peso and the US dollar was written into the constitution) and too much in the way of foreign loans eventually undermined macroeconomic performance, unleashing the global-reaching Argentina crisis in 2001. One of the key indicators was that the subsidiaries of MNEs that had been set up in Argentina retreated. Of the Brazilian enterprises that had developed Argentine operations, taking advantage of the Mercosur rules, virtually all shut down their plants. Sabó, a Brazilian auto parts producer, one of the few that did not repatriate its investments, was actually decorated by the Argentine government for that.

Consequently, as of 1998, Argentina's outward FDI declined constantly, with only a small recovery in 2003. From a peak of $3.7 billion in 1998, external investments became negative in 2002. These figures show that businesses that had prospered experienced a severe retraction during the downturn, which forced them to give up many of their activities, both local and foreign. Although the stock of FDI had reached $21.8 billion in 2004 (only exceeded in the region by Brazil), these data conceal a very different reality.

9.7.3 The Argentinean multinationals

The first icons of Argentinean internationalization: Alpargatas, SIAM di Tella, and Bunge & Born, followed unique paths. Alpargatas became a minority shareholder of its main operations in Brazil, controlled by the Camargo Correa Group, SIAM di Tella was nationalized following a period of major losses, and Bunge & Born moved its headquarters abroad. This was also the case of Argentine enterprises that invested abroad more recently, such as Yacimientos Petrolíferos Fiscales (YPF) and Pérez Companc, both of which were acquired by foreign companies (Repsol, from Spain, and Petrobras, from Brazil, respectively). Thus, even though Argentina pioneered the multilatinas, many of its MNEs passed into the hands of other enterprises over the course of time. There are no Argentine firms in the list of the top fifty non-financial transnational corporations (TNCs) from developing nations (UNCTAD, 2008).

The most impressive feature of Table 9.4 is the disparity that exists between Techint and all the other Argentine multinationals.

The drivers that led Argentine MNEs to engage in FDI include their high domestic market share and the country's chronic macroeconomic instability. Many firms chose to internationalize their competitive advantages and to capitalize on the international experience and image that they built as exporters (i.e., Arcor) and to expand the minimum scale of operations required to maintain existing capacity (i.e., Impsa).

Table 9.4 *Argentinean multinationals in the international rankings*

	Company	Industry	CPII (2009)	BCG (2009)
1	Techint Group[a]	Conglomerate	17,406	X
2	Arcor SAIC	Food products	491	—
3	IMPSA[b]	Machinery and equipment	300	—
4	Bagó Group[c]	Pharmaceuticals	192	—
5	Molinos Rio de la Plata SA	Food products	190	—
6	Los Grobo Group	Crop and animal production	175	—
7	Cresud	Crop and animal production	68	—
8	Roemmers	Pharmaceuticals	58	—
9	TECNA	Specialized construction activities	50	—
10	Iecsa SA	Civil engineering	50	—
11	SA San Miguel AGICI	Food products	23	—
12	BGH	Computer and electronic products	15	—
13	CLISA[d]	Waste collection and disposal activities	8	—
14	Petroquímica Rio Tercero SA	Chemicals	8	—
15	Assa Group	IT Services	7	—
16	Plastar Group	Rubber and plastics products	5	—
17	Sancor Coop. Unidas Ltda.	Food products	3	—

Table 9.4 (cont.)

	Company	Industry	CPII (2009)	BCG (2009)
18	Havanna[e]	Food and beverage service activities	2	—
19	Bio Sidus	Scientific research and development	1	—

Source: Columbia Program for International Investment (CPII, 2009); Boston Consulting Group (BCG, 2009).

[a] For the purpose of this ranking, the Techint Group is comprised of four companies: Tenaris, Ternium, Techint Compañía Técnica Internacional, and Tecpetrol.

[b] Belonging to the Pescarmona Group.

[c] Includes information on Biogénesis Bagó, a leading pharmaceutical firm specialized in animal health with foreign affiliates in six countries and $11 million in foreign assets in 2008.

[d] The company is also active in civil engineering and land transport services.

[e] While Havanna is a food producer, its internationalization process is based on the food and beverage service business. (Food production is still located in Argentina.)

Some firms tried to enhance their competitiveness through internationalization advantages, such as access to new markets and the incorporation of highly trained human resources. Some expanded these special advantages through a communication network and by inheriting the understanding of the industry from the enterprise's founders, generally European immigrants.

The international expansion of Argentine firms was limited to Latin America and, on a far more modest scale, to North America and Europe. From 1990 to 1996, some 84 percent of total Argentine FDI was directed to Latin American countries, especially Brazil (31 percent) and Venezuela (28 percent) (Kosacoff, 1999). This geographic expansion model remains in effect to this day.

Nevertheless, the most striking feature of this group of multilatinas in the present decade is how easily they are sold, in whole or in part, to their chief competitors (Kosacoff, 1999). Besides YPF and Pérez Companc, the acquisition of the Quilmes brewery by AmBev (now InBev) was symbolic. Other firms, such as Mastellone and Grupo Macri, remained under Argentine control, but sold many of their businesses abroad, including some of their most valuable assets. To date, only three multilatinas, namely Techint, Arcor, and to a lesser degree, Impsa, are still operating under the Argentine flag.

9.7.4 Techint: fast internationalization and takeover of Brazilian rival

Compagnia Tecnica Internazionale, now known as Techint, was founded as an international corporation in 1945. The founder was Agostino Rocca, an innovative engineer, manager, and entrepreneur, and a key force behind the development of the Italian steel industry in the 1930s. To create Techint, Rocca had "seed capital provided by a handful of wealthy Milanese families" (Goldstein and Toulan, 2007: 275). Its core business consisted of pipeline systems for major infrastructure projects.

A little earlier, in 1943 in Brazil, Confab, a company with the same activity profile, was established as part of the Grupo Vidigal. Interestingly, the company that the Baron of Maua created in Brazil, a century before, had a similar business proposition. However, Techint and Confab were both created to take advantage of the historical moment of the installation of basic industries in their respective countries, and the demand created by the transition from an agrarian to an industrial economy.

Techint's internationalization was very rapid: one year after it was set up it already had operations in Uruguay. Additionally, it started building a large-diameter pipeline system linking Argentina and Brazil. "The firm's rise to international prominence, however, did not occur until the end of the 1970s and the 1980s when heavy capital investments were undertaken, including the backward integration of the firm into primary steel production" (Goldstein and Toulan, 2007: 275).

The company set up operations in new regions, such as Saudi Arabia and Australia, and became one of the world's chief pipeline builders, as well as a supplier of turnkey petrochemical plants and infrastructure (bridges, tunnels, ports, and airports). In the 1980s, it also diversified its line of business, as it entered the field of nuclear facilities and offshore oil platforms.

Its international expansion continued throughout the 1990s in Ecuador, Chile, Colombia, Venezuela, Bolivia, Brazil, Mexico, Nigeria, Uruguay, and Trinidad and Tobago.

Techint is now a corporate conglomerate with more than 100 subsidiaries and 51,600 employees worldwide. It is the global leader in a niche segment (tubes) and a major regional player in the larger flat products market.

It is organized around customer segments, including:

- Tenaris, which produces steel tubes and provides services for the oil and gas industry and for specialized automotive and industrial applications in several countries;
- Ternium, the Latin American supply leader for flat or long steel, made at three globally integrated mills in Argentina, Venezuela, and Mexico;
- Tenova, a supplier of technology, products, and services for the metallurgical and mining industries;
- Tecpetrol, which explores and produces oil and gas; it promotes and runs natural gas distribution and transmission lines in Latin America; and
- Humanitas, a network of high complexity healthcare institutions in Italy.

For Goldstein and Toulan (2007: 269):

Techint is among the South American firms that arguably best epitomize world-class manufacturing based not only on the intensive use of natural resources, but also on technology and human capital. [Moreover] the firm's extensive experience with governments and highly regulated industries has given it an advantage when entering newly liberalized markets compared to firms from the OECD countries.

As for Confab, in 1993 it was capitalized by Techint, which took full control through its affiliate Siderca, in 1999. During the 1990s, the Vidigal family, an important name in the Brazilian business world, with banks and companies in different industrial sectors, and even a Coca-Cola bottling plant, went broke. Today, Tenaris-Confab is the largest producer of tubes in Brazil, exporting 70 percent of its production. The Venezuela operation, Siderurgica del Orinoco (SIDOR), acquired in 1998 during the privatization process, was returned to the state sector by the Chavez government in 2008.

9.8 Chilean multinationals

9.8.1 Economic and institutional context

Chile can be regarded as a small island in the midst of Latin America. It is isolated from its neighbors by the Andes to the east and by the Atacama Desert to the north. The country's south is characterized by glaciers, while the country's west consists of thousands of miles of Pacific coast.

Chile was the Latin American pioneer where economic reform projects are concerned. In the early 1970s, its military government changed the course of its economic model, opening the economy to external competition, deregulation, and privatization, while also shrinking the size and functions of the state and putting in place a predominantly market economy.

These reforms were the inspiration for the measures later implemented in most of the region's nations. After an initially chaotic period of high inflation, an excess of loans from abroad, and economic recession, Chile became the country with the best economic performance in Latin America.

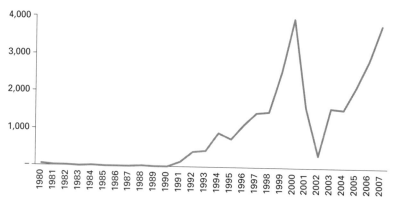

Figure 9.4 Stock and flows of outward FDI in Chile, 1980–2004 ($ million)
Source: UNCTAD (2008).

In addition to macroeconomic stability and growth, the country quickly joined the international market by signing several free trade and bilateral investment agreements with countries from Latin America, North America, Europe, and especially Asia and Oceania. Thus, it became a major host for inbound FDI and expanded its trade relations.

The Chilean economic reforms, put in place before those of its Latin American neighbors, conferred upon it a competitive advantage relative to the latter. Some Chilean firms internationalized to provide the same type of service in other Latin American countries.

9.8.2 Chile's investments abroad

Because of its demographic and economic features, the level of concentration in the main sectors has increased. The largest enterprises began investing abroad due to the growth of external competition and the saturation of the domestic market (Figure 9.4). From 1985 to 2004, the Chilean stock of FDI rose from $100 million to $14.5 billion (ECLAC, 2008).

The main Chilean investment focused on utilities (power generation and distribution), manufacturing (pulp and paper), and natural resources (oil and gas, and forestry), mainly. The earliest investments targeted neighboring nations, Argentina in particular, and consisted of acquiring firms that were being privatized. Many of these investments occurred in the energy sector: Enersis, Empresa Nacional de

Electricidad (ENDESA), and Chilgener (later Gener and now AES Gener).

In the case of the industrial sector, internationalization was stronger among the business groups that enjoyed natural comparative advantages, such as food, soft drinks and beer, pulp and paper, and minerals. The main targets of these investments were first Peru, and later, Colombia and Brazil.

An original internationalization case, typical of Chile, concerns the pension fund managers (PFMs). In the early 1980s, the Chilean authorities reformed the pension system. The country's PFMs acquired a wealth of experience in the local market. This was then used to internationalize their operations to other Latin American countries. As major synergism could be established between the management of pension funds and other financial activities, the major international financial organizations became interested in the Chilean PFMs. In 1982, a Spanish concern, Santander Central Hispano (SCH), acquired the PFM Summan, and one year later Banco Bilbao Viscaya Argentaria (BBVA), also a Spanish bank, took over the management of Provida, Chile's leading pension fund. Thus, the international presence of the Chilean PFMs slipped while the two Spanish banks, along with the American firm Citicorp, began dominating the regional pension funds market. In this case, as in the case of electric energy, the regional communication network created proved to be a valuable asset for international operators that wanted to establish a solid presence in Latin America quickly (ECLAC, 2008).

In the late 1990s, some of the largest Chilean MNEs were acquired by other foreign MNEs. The deterioration of the economies that played host to these investments (Argentina, Brazil, and Peru) and the global economic crisis, led the Chilean firms to build up their positions in the local market and to postpone their plans to invest abroad. In Peru and especially in Argentina, contingency plans were implemented and in some instances a radical restructuring of production and finances was put in place to deal with the huge losses.

However, favorable economic circumstances in Chile and its neighbors rendered new investments easy. Except for the power sector and the pension funds, Chilean multilatinas' investments continued to focus on a small number of natural resources sectors, services, and natural resource-based manufacturing. For some of these firms, in particular the retailers, the competitive advantages acquired at home provided them with great potential for regional expansion, that is the case of Ripley and Falabela.

The drivers of the Chilean MNEs' internationalization fall into four categories. First, there is the natural limitation of the local business environment, i.e., a small and saturated market. Second, certain firms (telecom, power, retail, pension funds) show built assets as competitive advantages while others rely on natural resources (pulp, paper, minerals) enabling the companies to internationalize early. A third derives from the need to open new markets for exports and consolidate the old ones, in order to increase sales and get international financing. Finally, the fourth group of drivers includes the early adoption of restructuring policies, which lent the Chilean MNEs considerable advantage over their neighbors and over MNEs with little Latin American experience.

However, with few exceptions, the international expansion of the Chilean MNEs was limited to Latin America. The level of internationalization, again with a few exceptions, is below 25 percent of total sales. Therefore, the Chilean multilatinas appear to have gone international warily. Many had difficulties along this path, while others were acquired by other MNEs when they grew a great deal or created regional contact networks that turned them into highly attractive targets.

In sum, the internationalization of Chilean companies centered on Latin America. After a period of stagnation, Chilean investments abroad are again on the rise, reinforcing their historical levels.

There are no Chilean multinationals listed in the international rankings. Masisa, one of the most important Chilean multinationals, was chosen to exemplify the strategies of Chilean firms in regards to internationalization.

9.8.3 Masisa: firm foothold in Brazil to expand abroad

Masisa is Latin America's leading company in the production and marketing of wood boards for furniture making and interior design, selling its products in nine countries in the Americas. It was established in 1960, in the south of Chile, the initiative of enterprising families from the city of Valdivia. An open capital company which trades on the Santiago Stock Exchange and American depositary receipts (ADRs) traded in New York, Masisa is a company of the GrupoNueva. Its entry strategy combines greenfield investments and the acquisition of forestry reserves. At present, Masisa's largest market is Latin America, which accounts for 77 percent of its total sales. The firm has production facilities not only in Chile, but in another four countries in the region: Brazil, Argentina, Venezuela, and Mexico. It also has commercial offices in six countries and a franchised distribution chain covering twelve. The chief Latin American markets, in order of sales, are Chile, Brazil, Argentina, and Mexico. The US has grown over the last few years in terms of importance, reaching 17 percent of Masisa's sales. Besides its operations in Latin America, the company began exporting to Europe, Asia, and Africa in 2003, as a reaction to the Argentine economic crisis. It now serves forty-seven countries.

The firm's internationalization process began in 1992, thanks to a greenfield investment in Argentina. Masisa moved to Brazil in 1995, noticing that the domestic market was supplied by a few large producers, but there was also a technological gap to be filled (particle board such as medium-density fibre (MDF) and similar products, with higher density). Its major competitor is Duratex, a firm from the Itau Group that produces materials for construction. The Duratex internationalization strategy is quite timid; its only subsidiary is a small plant in Argentina that produces hydraulic components, acquired in 1995.

Brazil became one of Masisa's main markets. In terms of consolidated sales, Chile was always the chief market but, in 2003, Masisa sales in Brazil (26 percent) were almost equal to sales in Chile (27 percent). Currently, the firm's sales in Brazil account for some 20 percent of the total. Its main Chilean competitor, Madeco, entered Brazil in the early 2000s, drawn by growth prospects.

In 2000, the firm started up in Mexico, where it set up a subsidiary: Maderas y Sintéticos de México SA de CV. There was also the acquisition of the particle board facilities of MacMillan Guadiana SA de CV in Durango.

Because of the Argentine economic crises of 2001, which affected many Latin American countries, Masisa also implemented an aggressive plan for winning new markets, such as Europe and the US.

Finally, to improve customer relationships, Masisa has a network of 280 "Placacentros," stores specialized in products and services for carpenters in ten Latin American countries, with forty-two in Brazil.

This is one of the components of a business model that has proven effective in this type of product market.

9.9 Mexican multinationals

9.9.1 The institutional and economic context

The Mexican economic model, like that of other Latin American countries, changed several times during the course of the twentieth century. In the late 1980s, a radical reform was put in place that opened the economy to trade and foreign investment, also cutting the size and functions of the state. Policies were created to make the economy more liberal; several services were deregulated, state property privatized, and local subsidies slashed. The new model also involved measures to increase the attraction of export zones (the maquilas).

In 1994, Mexico entered NAFTA with the US and Canada. Then Mexico negotiated similar agreements with several Latin American countries, as well as with the European Union (1999) and Japan (2004). These economic policy changes were also acknowledged by the developed nations when they admitted Mexico to the General Agreement on Tariffs and Trade (GATT), in 1986, and to the Organization for Economic Cooperation and Development (OECD), in 1994. The country's involvement with NAFTA enhanced the exposure of its enterprises, generating pros and cons.

The changes in the macroeconomic circumstances and the new standards of competition with MNE subsidiaries in the domestic market pushed Mexican firms into reviewing their strategies. The sense of urgency increased with the 1994 Mexican financial crisis. Given this context, Mexican enterprises started investing abroad, gradually increasing their FDI in other nations. The destination of these investments was largely the US and Central America, extending, in some cases, to South America. A few investments were directed to areas such as Europe and Asia.

9.9.2 Mexico's investments abroad

Figure 9.5 depicts the evolution of Mexico's outward FDI. The statistics may not reflect the scale and trend of Mexican investments, because the Mexican accounting systems did not keep track of FDI.

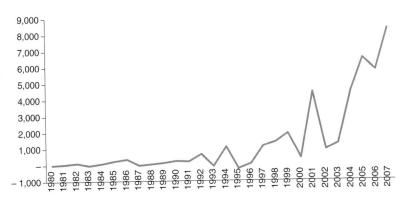

Figure 9.5 Stock and flows of outward FDI in Mexico, 1980–2004 ($ million)
Source: UNCTAD (2008).

Nevertheless, it is estimated that Mexico has a significant FDI stock (some $16 billion in 2004) and that this figure increased in the first few years of the twenty-first century.

9.9.3 The Mexican multinationals

Table 9.5 shows the Mexican multilatinas, according to the international rankings. These firms' level of internationalization can be classified into four groups. The first consists of Cementos Mexicanos (CEMEX), the only enterprise headquartered in Mexico that can be regarded as a major global MNE, given the percentage of its sales generated abroad and the extent of its geographical coverage. The second comprises companies with an advanced level of internationalization, such as América Móvil, Gruma, San Luís Rassini, and Grupo Alfa. The third consists of firms with a moderate level of internationalization, such as Coca-Cola FEMSA, Grupo IMSA, Grupo Bimbo, TELMEX, and Mabe. Finally, there are firms with limited internationalization, a category that includes another nine enterprises. Notwithstanding, Grosse (2007: 255) asserts that "The leading Mexican groups have not been particularly successful in their overseas expansion with the exception of Cemex, Femsa and Carso."

Most Mexican multilatinas concentrate their international operations in Latin America and North America. Eight have operations in the European Union. Only one, CEMEX, operates in Asia, although Gruma is about to start operations there as well. Almost half of

Table 9.5 *Mexican multinationals in the international rankings*

	Company	Industry	Fortune 500 (2009)[a]	Forbes 2000 (2009)[b]	WIR (2008)[c]		BCG (2009)[e]
					TNI[d]	Foreign assets	
1	Pemex	Oil and gas	31	—			
2	América Móvil	Telecom	273	163	52	17	X
3	CFE	Utilities	370	—			
4	CEMEX	Construction	421	249	21	2	X
5	Carso Global Telecom	Telecom	—	346			
6	Femsa	Food, drink, and tobacco	—	582	86	52	X
7	Grupo Mexico	Materials	—	602	—	—	—
8	Grupo Carso	Conglomerates	—	744	—	—	—
9	Grupo Modelo	Food, drink, and tobacco	—	764	—	—	—
10	GFNorte	Banking	—	782	—	—	—
11	Grupo Televisa	Media	—	960	—	—	—
12	Inbursa Financiero	Banking	—	1,175	—	—	—

No.	Company	Industry	[a]	[b]	[c]	[d]	[e]
13	ALFA	Conglomerates	—	1,255	—	—	X
14	Grupo Elektra	Retailing	—	1,278	—	—	
15	Grupo Bimbo	Food, drink, and tobacco	—	1,312	—	—	X
16	Industrias Peñoles	Materials	—	1,347	—	—	—
17	El Puerto de Liverpool	Retailing	—	1,455	—	—	—
18	Soriana	Retailing	—	1,586	35	—	—
19	Gruma	Food, beverages, and tobacco	—	—	—	94	X
20	Telefonos De Mexico	Telecom	—	—	89	56	—
21	Mexichem	Chemical	—	—	—	—	X

[a] *Fortune* (2009); [b] *Forbes* (2009); [c] *World Investment Report* (UNCTAD, 2008); [d] Transnationlity Index: average of foreign assets to total assets, foreign sales, to total sales, and foreign employment to total employment; [e] Boston Consulting Group (2009); X indicates inclusion in BCG's New Global Challengers List.

these enterprises make basic products, such as cement, glass, food-stuffs, beverages, petrochemicals, etc. However, two other activities are important: autoparts and electro-communication. In many of these fields, international expansion has been driven basically by the quest for new markets. The autoparts case is slightly different, since Mexican suppliers work in a highly competitive local environment where this sector is concerned. This is forcing autoparts makers to improve their efficiency and to set up new plants close to the main automakers' plants in the US and Europe. Generally speaking, these multilatinas expanded internationally by buying existing assets, rather than through greenfield investments.

The drivers for the internationalization of the Mexican corporations are similar to cases already mentioned: limited long-term opportunities in the domestic business environment, volatile domestic demand, exploration of firm-specific advantages, and competences to open new markets and improve the position in the value chain. Evidently, government policies also had an influence, as the decision to open the Mexican economy to foreign competition, including privatization and the deregulation of utilities, obliged these firms to embrace more aggressive strategies. Mexican enterprises took advantage of several free trade agreements to gain preferred access to these markets.

The Mexican MNEs enjoyed location advantages regarding the host countries. They focused mainly on the US and on Latin America, showing that geographic proximity and ethnic contacts (language/culture) or country nationals (Mexicans living abroad) carried substantial weight in the context of renewed growth opportunities in these markets. Alliances with MNEs were very important for companies such as América Móvil, Gruma, San Luis Rassini, Coca-Cola, FEMSA, and Mabe.

In sum, the economic reforms and the rising integration with the American market led to substantial changes in the corporate strategies of the large Mexican enterprises. Thus, the growth of domestic competition and easy access to other markets encouraged Mexican businesses to abandon their passive defense strategies and to actively embrace more aggressive strategies vis-à-vis the new opportunities abroad. At first, the firms focused on the US and Central America, but later they ventured into South America and other regions. For example, Grupo Azteca developed a retail business model specifically for low income markets, which it then transferred to the northeast of Brazil, where the large Brazilian retail chains, like Casas Bahia, the largest Brazilian retail store, were yet to establish themselves.

Still, many of these firms experienced difficulties before and during their internationalization. Apparently they were successful in learning from their mistakes (Gross and Thomas, 2007). Very quickly, several Mexican enterprises achieved a good position in the ranking of the largest emerging country multinationals. The case that stands out is that of Cemex.

9.9.4 The case of CEMEX: *the most internationalized multilatina*

In twenty-five years, from 1982 to 2007, CEMEX evolved from a small, privately owned, cement-focused Mexican company of 6,500 employees with $275 million in revenue, to a publicly traded global leader, with 67,000 employees, a presence in fifty countries, and $21.7 billion in annual revenue in 2007.

CEMEX was founded in 1906 in Mexico, when Cimentos Hidalgo was established near the city of Monterrey in the north of the country. In 1920, the company controlled by the Zambrano family constructed Cimentos Portland Monterrey. In 1931, the two enterprises merged, giving rise to Cimentos Mexicanos (CEMEX).

The company operated as a small regional player for most of its history. In the 1960s and 1970s, its share of the domestic market increased thanks to the acquisition of other small firms. In the 1970s, it also tried to diversify by entering a number of other fields of business, such as petrochemicals and hotels. In the 1980s the company divested these assets, focusing solely on cement and pursuing internationalization.

Cement is a commodity that cannot be transported for long distances, which lends specific connotations to the internationalization process. The internationalization of the developed country cement producers, like the French Lafarge and the Swiss Holcim, through mergers and acquisitions, was already in course when CEMEX decided to internationalize. For Zambrano, Cemex's chief executive officer (CEO), the company either had to grow fast or be acquired by global competitors. The CEMEX internationalization strategy was stepped up in the 1990s.

However:

Well before its first significant step toward international expansion, in 1992, Cemex had developed a set of core competences that would shape its later trajectory, including strong operational capabilities based on engineering and IT, and a culture of transparency. It also had mastered the art of acquisition and integration within Mexico, having grown through acquisitions over the years. Lessard and Lucea (2009: 290)

The beginning of its international expansion was underscored by the acquisition of two large Spanish cement concerns, Valenciana and Sanson, in 1992. As of 1994, a number of acquisitions were made in several Latin American countries. In 1997, the firm entered the Asian market by acquiring Rizal Cement in the Philippines.

The strategy that guided its internationalization, in particular its acquisitions abroad, was based on the market's economic attractiveness and the country's cultural proximity. CEMEX prioritized countries where the political and institutional environment was turbulent, there was little market information and poor infrastructure, as is the case in many Latin American nations. This could look like a disadvantage, but in fact it was an advantage for CEMEX, as it had experience working in chaotic environments, coming, as it did, from Mexico. This factor, derived directly from CEMEX's origins, set it apart from the European cement concerns, which regarded the chaos of non-developed countries as a barrier to the expansion and growth of their operations.

The distinctive CEMEX competences for working in chaotic environments were logistics and its information system, both of which underwent changes as the firm's internationalization expanded. In the early 1990s, CEMEX delivered cement one day after getting the order. This indicated poor optimization of the use of its trucks rather than customer satisfaction. Today, the company has a system whereby delivery is made two hours after the order is placed, with a maximum delay of no more than twenty minutes. The distinctive competence is its logistical system. This has to do with how its concrete mixers drive through cities. "Cemex uses algorithms based on greed (or voracity, i.e., 'delivering as much cement as possible, as fast as possible, to the largest number of customers') and repulsion (or aversion: 'renouncing the duplication of efforts and keeping each truck far away from the others.')" (De Marchi, 2005). This allows it to deliver concrete without its drying up inside the mixers, besides improving truck productivity by 35 percent, while also ensuring customer satisfaction.

Though logistics and information technology (IT) were the main weapons upholding CEMEX's competitive advantage in its field, there was still the dilemma of how best to transfer these competences to plants outside Mexico. To achieve this, after every acquisition, a CEMEX team was dispatched to the new subsidiary to transfer administrative capabilities, improve the IT infrastructure, standardize the business processes, and train the employees.

In IT and knowledge management terms, a global database was developed containing information on production, buying, sales, and benchmarking. This was accessible to the several managerial and operational levels, reducing skepticism as to the enterprise's internationalization, and also contributing to new initiatives and organizational learning, by sharing best practices through the firm's information system.

Thanks to its core competences in the area of information management and technology, CEMEX opened paths to other businesses, such as IT systems implementation consultancy, given its vast experience in this field, acquired because every new company CEMEX acquired abroad had to have the same IT system implemented and adapted for the local people. Furthermore, it also moved into web-based business, such as customer and supplier relations portals, given that its large and speedy database made it possible for the value chain to become better organized through a web-based system of purchases and sales. This generated not only cost savings and improved productivity, but also enhanced the relationship with the other members of the value chain.

The Brazilian counterexample is Votorantim, which was analyzed in the last chapter. Votorantim's internationalization started ten years after CEMEX and its pace is slower. We might say that its core competences and competitive strengths were not as mature and structured as CEMEX's were to cope with the demands of internationalization.

9.10 Can Latin America compete?

Despite the common roots and the timing of development since the arrival of the Iberians to the present day, the study of Latin American countries reveals surprises.

The main insights are:

- the subsidiaries of multinationals from advanced countries have played an important role in the industrialization of the large majority of Latin American countries;
- only four countries (Argentina, Chile, Mexico, and Brazil) have their own multinationals which, in general, delayed the decision to go international;
- most multilatinas are solely-owned or part of large family groups;
- the expansion of multilatinas from countries other than Brazil involve service activities directed to other Spanish-speaking countries, as a priority; this suggests that they developed business models appropriate to the Latin culture;
- the entry of multilatinas into Brazil prioritized the manufacturing sectors with the exception of Mexican multinationals, that entered the services sector (telecommunications, distribution, retail);
- the expansion of Brazilian multinationals to Latin America prioritized manufacturing and small and medium firms that supply multinationals from developed countries that have subsidiaries in Brazil and in other Latin American countries; only recently has the expansion of large service companies, such as banks (Itaú/ Unibanco) and food chains started;
- the movements of multilatinas in Latin America seem to be little influenced by global production networks; on the contrary, they seem to be linked to the establishment of regional production networks; the Techint/Confab case is revealing of how Techint got out in front, created international business competences and established governance over Confab;
- the poor management of public policies can profoundly affect the performance of local firms in international markets, as was the case of Argentina.

The movements of the multilatinas are based on differentiated competences that sustain their processes of internationalization. For example: competences in production and operations (Bimbo, Arcor, Ambev, Gerdau, CEMEX), competences in product development (Natura, Embraer), commercial and marketing competences (Ambev, Bimbo), the capacity to manage mergers and acquisitions (CEMEX, Bimbo, JBS-Friboi), and to act in highly complex environments, from the political and institutional point of view (all of them), not to mention the firms that are based in the exploitation of natural resources (all the oil companies, and those in mining and agro-industry).

Can Latin American firms compete? We agree with the qualified "yes" of Grosse and Mesquita (2007: 364) as well as the "yes, but moderately" of Wood Jr. and Caldas (2007: 246). But we understand that the logic of internationalization in Latin America takes place within a specific context, not allowing an easy comparison with what occurs in other regions of the world.

10 | *Multinationals from Russia, India, China, and South Africa (RICS)*

10.1 The new global players

In 1421, some eighty years before the Portuguese sea voyages took place, a vast Chinese armada set sail to explore the world. The armada was intended to map unknown lands, rather than to conquer them.

> The last surviving ships returned to China in the summer and autumn of 1423. The maps showed they had not merely rounded the Cape of Good Hope and traversed the Atlantic to chart [the Caribbean] islands, they had then gone on to explore Antarctica and the Arctic, North and South America, and had crossed the Pacific to Australia. They had solved the problems of calculating latitude and longitude and had mapped the earth and the heavens with equal accuracy. Menzies (2002: 36)

However, when they returned, China had changed. The Emperor was dying and the mandarins were dismantling the worldwide empire apparatus he had nearly created. China was entering a long night of isolation from the rest of the world. Though most of the maps were burned, a few survived and were traded with European countries. The Portuguese and the Spanish probably had some of them when they ventured into sea voyages toward the end of the fifteenth century.

In the late sixteenth century, China accounted for some 30 percent of global gross domestic product (GDP), while Western Europe represented about 20 percent and Japan less than 5 percent; at that time, North America was still a wild country. During the eighteenth and nineteenth centuries, Western Europe in general (and the UK in particular) came to dominate the world economy, their roles having been supplanted as of the late nineteenth century by the US. Portugal and Spain were important powers in the transition phase, which comprised the sixteenth and seventeenth centuries.

The Asian revival began in the 1960s with Japan, followed by the Asian Tigers (Hong Kong, Singapore, South Korea, and Taiwan). At the dawn of the new millennium, the momentum of Asia was strengthened further by the fast growth of two large economies, China and India, along with Russia. The latter, generally seen as European, is near China geographically and maintains strong bonds with it. Together with Brazil, these countries became known as BRIC (i.e., Brazil, Russia, India, China). Sometimes South Africa is included in this group, which is then called BRICS.

The second part of this book began with a description and analysis of the internationalization of Brazilian and Latin American firms. This chapter will focus on the other BRICS: Russia, India, China, and South Africa.

China has strong trade relations with Brazil, as we shall see. As for India, "despite significant political initiatives, which have included several head of state level bi-lateral visits and collaboration in multiple multi-lateral funds, Indo-Brazilian trade and investment remains small" (The Jai Group, 2007: 1). India, South Africa, and Brazil entered into a cooperation treaty with a view to increasing South–South relations, but the practical outcome of this is yet to materialize. Finally, when it comes to Russia, relations with Brazil are weak.

We will open this chapter with a brief characterization of these countries, particularly where their international business roles are concerned. Then we will study each country, beginning with China. Our approach will first emphasize the historical and factors endowment aspects. Then we will address their main decisions about their internationalization. Some cases of outstanding multinational enterprises (MNEs) will be discussed in detail, to illustrate the rationale underlying the internationalization process of each country. We will also highlight any special aspects of the relations of each of the other BRICS (i.e., the RICS) with Brazil.

10.2 Snapshots of recent economic development in Asia

Asia, the world's largest continent, accounts for 30 percent of the Earth's land mass and is home to some 60 percent of the world's population, with almost 3.8 billion people. China and India alone harbor 20 percent and 16 percent of the world population, respectively. Because Asia comprises countries with a wide range of ethnicities and religions, not to mention the major socio-economic, religious, and cultural differences among them, it is generally subdivided into major areas, based on geographical and cultural similarities:

- Middle East: seventeen Asian countries in the area that lies between the Mediterranean to the west and the Red Sea and the Indian Ocean to the south.
- South Asia: Pakistan, India, Sri Lanka, the Maldives, Nepal, Bhutan, and Bangladesh.
- East Asia: the Chinese territories (the People's Republic of China plus Macau, Hong Kong, and Taiwan), North and South Korea, Japan, and Mongolia.
- Southeast Asia: mainland Indochina plus a large number of islands; these countries have formed the Association of South East Asian Nations (ASEAN) – Indonesia, Malaysia, the Philippines, Singapore, Thailand, Brunei, Vietnam, Myanmar, Laos, and Cambodia.
- Russia: considered a European country, although it borders on Asia.

In economic terms, Asia has the third largest nominal GDP of all continents, trailing behind the US and Europe, but the largest GDP in purchasing power parity (PPP) terms. In 2007, China had the largest GDP in Asia, followed by Japan, India, South Korea, and Indonesia (OECD, 2009). The region remained the largest recipient of foreign direct investment (FDI) of all the developing regions and transition economies, accounting for two fifths of such flows. India is now among the top investors in the UK. China is rapidly becoming a leading investor in many developing countries, including African ones. Enterprises from some ASEAN countries and the Republic of Korea have also been actively investing abroad.

When one takes into account traditional macroeconomic indicators, such as the GDP growth rate, the growth of income per capita, and PPP, one finds that Brazil, Russia, India, and China (the BRICs) are the major emerging powers. However, these countries have very different institutional contexts (Khanna and Huang 2003).

India is a democracy that leans heavily toward socialism, though it does not aim to eliminate private property. In China, on the other hand, the Communist Party ascended to power in 1949 with the intent of eradicating private property and did so quickly. In the last few decades, the country has become more open and has embraced a market reform policy, but there are still controversies about the unfolding

Table 10.1 *Percentage growth rates*

	2005	2006	2007	2008
World output	4.9	5.4	5.2	4.8
US	3.1	2.9	1.9	1.9
Euro zone	1.5	2.8	2.5	2.1
Japan	1.9	2.2	2.0	1.7
China	10.4	11.1	11.5	10.0
India	9.0	9.7	8.9	8.4
Brazil	2.9	3.7	4.0	4.2
Mexico	2.8	4.8	2.9	3.0
Russia	6.4	6.7	7.0	6.5

Source: IMF: *World Economic Outlook* (October, 2007).

and the results of this process (Khanna and Huang, 2003). As we have seen, Brazil and Latin America followed different paths. South Africa emerged from the apartheid regime little more than a decade ago and has a political and cultural context that is entirely different from that of the preceding cases.

The growth rates of China and India in the last few years have been impressive. Despite the 2008 recession, future estimates remain highly positive for the BRICs in general and for these two countries in particular (Table 10.1).

Table 10.2 of economic and social indicators also reveals the evolution of the BRICs on the economic, human development, poverty reduction, and environmental responsibility fronts. The only figures that are not entirely positive refer to the concentration of wealth in India and China, an expected outcome in countries that are moving into market regimes.

The international orientation of these countries has no clearly defined leadership. Panibratov and Kalotay (2009) state that Russia now has the largest stock of direct investment abroad among the BRICS ($203 billion), followed by Brazil ($162 billion) and China ($142 billion). Those figures are contested by Lacerda (2009), who estimated Brazilian FDI stock at $288 billion, China's at $378 billion, Russia's at $213 billion, and India's at $123 billion. This would make Brazil the largest investor abroad in terms of outward FDI stock as a percentage of GDP. On the other hand, it is an acknowledged fact that

Table 10.2 *Economic and social indicators, BRIC countries*

Country	GDP based on PPP per capita 2006 ($)	GDP based on PPP per capita 1990 ($)	HDI 2006	HDI 1990	GINI 2005	GINI 1990	HPI*-1 2007	HPI*-1 1997	% population below the poverty line 2007	% population below the poverty line 1990	ESI 2005
Brazil	8.949	3.092	0.800[a]	0.708	0.52[a]	0.61	9.1	15.8	18.3	21.2	10.3
Russia	13.205	3.485	0.806	0.717	0.39	0.46[b]	7.6	—	2.0	12.1	—
India	2.489	373	0.609	0.494	0.37	0.34	28.5	35.9	75.6	80.4	31.3
China	4.682	3.105	0.762	0.607	0.47	0.25	7.9	12.3	36.3	34.9	12.3
US	43.968	29.605	0.950	0.920	0.40	—	—	—	—	—	—

Source: IMF; World Bank: World Development Indicators database; IBGE; CIA World Factbook; UNDP: Human Development Report.
[a] 2007, [b] 1996
* Human Poverty Index

it is difficult to calculate China's outward FDI due to its umbilical relationship with Hong Kong: "The domestic capital flowing back to China via 'round tripping' represents a substantial amount of so-called 'foreign direct investment'" (Yin and Choi, 2005: 118). Thus, while one is witnessing the emergence of the BRICS and of their firms, new conceptual and methodological challenges are being identified. Let us now move on to the RICS.

China is a country of continental dimensions, with an area greater than 9 million square kilometers. The fourth largest country in the world, behind Russia, Canada and the US, it is home to some 1.3 billion inhabitants. For almost four thousand years it was governed by successive dynasties of emperors, until it became a republic in 1912.

At the end of the second world war and following the last Chinese civil war between the communists and the anti-left nationalists, two political entities emerged in 1949, both referring to themselves as China: the People's Republic of China (Communist China or, simply, China), which controls the mainland, and the Republic of China, Nationalist China, or Taiwan, which controls the islands of Taiwan, Pescadores, Kinmen, and Matsu.

Mainland China became an autocratic regime led by Mao Zedong. The government took over the control of the economy and, in terms of industrialization, followed the soviet strategy, centered on heavy industry.

The first five-year economic plan (1953–7) promoted a policy of rapid industrial development, known as the "Big Leap Forward." In the industrial sector, the priority was coal, electric energy, iron, steel, building materials, basic chemical products, and heavy engineering. Following the soviet model and with the technical aid of the Russians, the economic plan succeeded in building technologically sophisticated plants.

Soon after the introduction of soviet-style plans in the 1950s, Mao Zedong realized that the soviet methods were unsuitable for the Chinese peasantry (Story, 2004). Thus, the priority became agriculture, which employed some 80 percent of the workforce; people's communes were established and private ownership of land was eliminated. However, the Chinese peasants were ill-prepared for a communal system. As a result, production plummeted, which gave rise to famines. Therefore, in the 1960s, private ownership of land was reinstated and more state resources were channeled into agriculture (Story, 2004).

The Chinese cultural revolution, which extended from 1966 to 1976, contrary to the policy underlying the "Great Leap Forward," bore no direct relation to economic plans. However, its legacies were problematic where the economy is concerned. For instance, in industry, wages were frozen. Along with the policy of employing more workers than needed, to absorb the unemployed, incentives to professional growth were eliminated.

Until the 1960s, China was closed to foreign influences, except for exchanges with other communist bloc countries. However, the China–Soviet Union relations crisis intensified as of the 1960s and, in the 1970s, China started to show some signs of opening. Since 1972, when President Nixon and Mao Zedong signed the Shanghai Communiqué, the target of most of China's foreign relations became the US. After 1978, under Deng Xiaoping's leadership, economic reform began, aiming at the implementation of market-oriented economic development. This was maintained in the administrations of Jiang Zemin (1992 to 2003) and Hu Jintao (2003 to date).

In the 1980s, economic planning tapered off. Private ownership of agricultural properties was once again permitted, and private ownership of production assets was legalized, even though most factories continued to be state-owned. The government also encouraged activities unrelated to agriculture, such as the establishment of small businesses in rural areas, besides fostering greater autonomy among state-owned enterprises.

The Soviet Union's collapse in 1992 deprived the Chinese communist leadership of its fraternal rival, sharpening the drive to create a "socialist market economy" under the dominance of a single party (Story, 2004). Thus, the Chinese economy gained momentum during the 1990s.

In 1993, production and prices rose and Chinese economic expansion was enhanced thanks to the creation of more than two thousand special economic zones. From 1995 to 1996, the inflow of FDI accounted for more than 25% of domestic investment, 13% of industrial production, 31% of exports, 11% of tax collection, and 16 million jobs (Story, 2004). This put China, along with the US and the UK, among the three main recipients of FDI, turning it into the main recipient of FDI among the developing countries, by far.

In the 1990s, the Chinese government approved a series of long-term economic reforms and vowed to give market institutions even

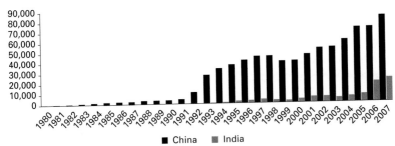

Figure 10.1 Inward FDI in China and India, 1979–2007 ($ million)

more power. The reforms, however, further increased state control of the financial system, while state-owned enterprises continued dominating many industrial sectors. China's economy grew some 10 percent a year from 1990 to 2005, the strongest economic growth in the world.

Compared with India, China has been bolder in its attempts to attract foreign investments since the 1980s and has been drawing a strong flow of FDI, as shown in Figure 10.1.

The phenomenal growth of Chinese exports is largely due to its having attracted FDI. From 1978 to the 2000s, Chinese trade grew four and a half times faster than global trade, which is unprecedented in the history of any other country. Foreign businesses played an important role: from 1985 to 2000, the share of exports of the subsidiaries expanded from 1 percent to 45 percent.

India's ability to attract FDI is far weaker than China's. This disparity reflects, to some extent, international investors' confidence in the Chinese market reform prospects, but skepticism when it comes to India's commitment to reform, not to speak of the policy differences concerning attracting foreign MNEs.

India and China's different ways of drawing FDI had a significant impact on domestic entrepreneurship and on the incorporation of these countries' firms into the international market (Khanna and Huang, 2003). For the last twenty years, the Chinese economy has drawn large FDI flows. This trend worked as a surrogate system for domestic entrepreneurship, given that domestic and foreign enterprises are accorded different treatment (Khanna and Huang, 2003). In general, the legal and regulatory treatment of FDI-based enterprises is tougher than that of domestic firms, especially in the private sector. The dualistic nature of China's legal regime aims at insulating the economy from the full effects of FDI and protecting socialism (Huang, 2003).

The Chinese government closely monitored the establishment of Western MNEs in China. Coca-Cola and McDonald's, both of which are symbols of Western culture, were allowed to set up operations in the country in 1980 and 1990, respectively. It is a well-documented fact that there is heavy involvement of foreign enterprises in China's economic development.

The first MNEs to establish themselves in China had to enter into partnerships with Chinese firms via a system of equity joint ventures. The basic rationale underlying such investments was the potential of the Chinese market; their strategy consisted of establishing plants, so as to take advantage of the low cost of labor, in offshore type operations. Over time, the operating strategy in China changed, as the partnership system evolved into contractual joint ventures. Today, most of the MNEs have wholly owned subsidiaries.

Concurrently, the MNEs changed the profile of their operations in China, gradually transferring their research and development (R&D) activities to their Chinese subsidiaries. Three drivers propelled this trend: (1) China is a large developing country with substantial differences in consumer tastes relative to developed economies, therefore, market penetration dictates substantial product localization R&D efforts; (2) the level of scientific research in China's universities has been improving thanks to the government's strong policy of fostering the development of science, technology, and anything high-tech; and (3) China is an attractive country when it comes to low-cost, high quality human resources. The number of engineering and science students is now greater than in Japan and second only to the US. The supply of trained labor enables MNEs to hire well-educated Chinese students at very reasonable wages.

There are three major regions that host substantial amounts of FDI: Beijing, Shanghai, and Guangdong. Beijing is the city of the scientific sector and home to major universities and a substantial number of public research institutes. Zhongguancun in the Haiden district is China's "silicon valley," as it harbors a cluster of scientific institutes and a tremendous number of high-tech start-up enterprises. Shanghai is a large industrial base with manufacturing firms, where science and technology activities are mainly conducted by the private sector.

Finally, the Guangdong province is a world center for electronic components firms. Although there are only a few universities and research institutions there, a substantial number of MNEs have set up plants in the "IT [information technology] factory of the world." Evidently, the international R&D drivers differ substantially according to these specific regional factors.

Since 1989, China has been accruing a considerable portfolio of international activities. Nevertheless, the international growth and impact of Chinese enterprises is still a novel and, to some extent, limited phenomenon (Khanna and Huang, 2003). Most of this expansion reflects the demise of the commercial monopoly of the central government and the great expansion of the number of commercial concerns established by provincial and municipal governments (Story, 2004).

The outward FDI of Chinese firms has several distinctive features. To explain why Chinese investments grew so fast despite the lack of ownership advantages, are concentrated in a few developed countries, and involve governmental institutions, Child and Rodrigues (2005) argue that "the dominant motive among non-primary producing companies for undertaking foreign acquisitions has been to accrue market strength by gaining access to technology, securing R&D skills and acquiring international brands." In other words, Chinese outward investment is asset seeking. The case of the Shanghai Auto Industry Corporation (SAIC), which acquired Britain's Rover, exemplifies this argument.

Box 10.1 The world's big carmakers have unwittingly created a new Chinese rival

The new Roewe 750 saloon, which goes on sale in China this month, would appear to be a textbook example of why the world's big carmakers have nothing to fear so far from their Chinese rivals. Like many Chinese-built cars, it is based on a Western design – in this case the Rover 75, the last model to be introduced by Britain's now defunct MG Rover. That hardly inspires confidence. And given the poor reputation of Chinese cars, which tend to be cheap rather than reliable, it is not surprising that the new car has failed to cause much of a stir within the industry.

But the Roewe, launched by the Shanghai Auto Industry Corporation (SAIC – a state-owned carmaker that has joint ventures with General Motors and Volkswagen to make Chinese versions of their cars) is not the cheap knock-off its name implies. Unlike other Chinese firms, SAIC has not "borrowed" technology, components, or designs for its new car. It has bought them or developed them in-house.

The original Rover 75 design has been substantially improved by engineers and designers in Britain and Italy and at Ssangyong, SAIC's South Korean subsidiary. And MG Rover's ultimate collapse notwithstanding, the 75 was actually a good car. Developed by BMW, which owned MG Rover for a while, and with an excellent engine designed by Honda, the 75 has a fine pedigree. SAIC has spent two years changing the styling, upgrading the chassis, and designing a new interior.

To manage its independent production division, SAIC hired Phil Murtaugh, who previously ran GM's Chinese operation. He has been able to call upon the 5,000 engineering staff who work for subsidiary suppliers to the GM and VW joint ventures. The joint ventures also mean that SAIC already has a strong relationship with car dealers throughout China.

The Economist, February 22, 2007, p. 75.

That is the route that a rising number of Chinese firms prefer. The Lenovo, TCL, Huawei, and Machine-Tool Nr 1 cases, among others, have similar features. This entry mode enables a rapid advance toward securing international differentiation and brand advantage, though it is unclear how these firms can handle post-acquisition integration and manage their network of subsidiaries efficiently.

Studies on emerging market MNEs suggest that these firms' characteristics, the nature of their ownership, their motivation for internationalizing, and the advantages to be gained in the international market, are fundamentally distinct from those of developed country MNEs, besides being different depending on the emerging home country. The section that follows discusses the particularities of the different internationalization strategies of the Chinese MNEs.

10.3 The internationalization of Chinese firms

10.3.1 *China's investments abroad*

Discrepancies in the figures notwithstanding, of all the emerging countries, China is the one with the greatest outward FDI, as we mentioned at the beginning of this chapter (see Figure 10.2).

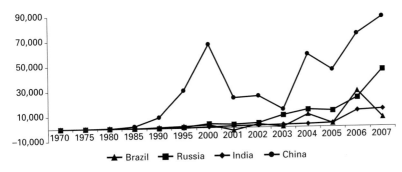

Figure 10.2 Outward FDI flows in the BRICs, 1970–2007 ($ million)

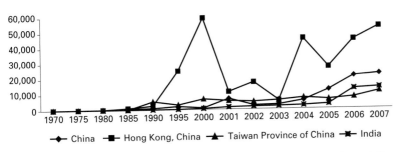

Figure 10.3 Outward FDI in China, Hong Kong, Taiwan, and India, 1970–2007 ($ million)

Hong Kong maintains a leading position when one breaks down the investments abroad by region, as shown in Figure 10.3.

10.3.2 *Chinese multinationals*

The list of Chinese MNEs shown in Table 10.3 was produced according to the following criteria: the enterprise should be listed either in the ranking of the largest MNEs from emerging countries in UNCTAD's World Investment Report (WIR), or should be included in the Boston Consulting Group's 100 Global Challengers list. The firm's position in the *Fortune* and *Forbes* rankings is merely an added piece of information in regards to their relative size.

As far back as early 2004, Chinese enterprises had 7,470 subsidiaries spread across more than 160 countries (Chung, 2001).

The ownership structure of Chinese MNEs is quite varied. Based on the MOFCOM 2006 Statistical Bulletin of China's outward FDI,

Table 10.3 *Chinese multinationals in the international rankings*

	Company	Industry	Fortune 500 (2009)[a]	Forbes 2000 (2009)[b]	WIR (2008)[c]		BCG (2009)[e]
					TNI[d]	Foreign assets	
1	China Petroleum & Chemical (Sinopec)	Oil and gas	9	94	—	—	X
2	PetroChina (CNPC)	Oil and gas	13	57	100	21	X
3	Jardine Matheson	Diversified	29	—	28	9	—
4	Citic Group	Diversified	30	—	92	7	—
5	China Mobile (HK)	Telecom	99	128	—	—	X
6	Hon Hai Precision Ind	Technology hardware	109	525	45	18	X
7	Noble Group	Trading	145	—	48	69	
8	Baosteel Group	Metals	155	—	—	—	X
9	Hutchison Whampoa	Specialty retailers	220	150	18	1	—
10	China State Construction Engineering	Engineering, building	252	—	80	19	—
11	Quanta Computer	Technology hardware	327	879	68	30	—
12	Sinochem	Oil and fertilizers	170	—	55	26	—
13	Lenovo	Computers and related businesses	—	1,114	58	49	X
14	Taiwan Semiconductor	Semiconductors	—	383	66	29	

	Company	Sector					
15	Cnooc	Oil and gas	—	491	—	—	X
16	CLP Holdings	Utilities	—	629	77	23	X
17	Huawei	Telecom	—	—	—	—	—
18	United Microelectronics	Semiconductors	—	801	71	36	—
19	China Netcom Group	Telecom	—	823	—	—	—
20	Formosa Plastics	Chemicals	—	945	65	8	—
21	Acer	Technology hardware	—	1436	27	48	X
22	Haier	Technology hardware	—	—	—	—	—
23	Tianjin Development	Diversified	—	—	1	77	—
24	Lee & Man Paper Manufacturing	Paper	—	—	2	93	—
25	First Pacific Company	Electrical and electronic	—	—	4	55	—
26	TCL Multimedia Technology	Electronics	—	—	5	78	—
27	Road King Infrastructure	Transport	—	—	6	88	—
28	Guangdong Investment Limited	Diversified	—	—	8	42	—
29	Aluminum Corporation of China (Chalco)	Metals	499	—	—	—	X
30	Chery Automobile	Automotive	—	1,973	—	—	X
31	BYD Group	Automotive	—	—	—	—	X

Table 10.3 (*cont.*)

	Company	Industry	Fortune 500 (2009)[a]	Forbes 2000 (2009)[b]	WIR (2008)[c]		BCG (2009)[e]
					TNI[d]	Foreign assets	
32	Dalian Machine Tool Group (DMTG)	Capital goods	—	—	—	—	X
33	Faw Group	Automotive	385	—	—	—	X
34	Galanz Group	Electronics	—	—	—	—	X
35	Gree Electric Appliances	Electrical and electronic	—	—	—	—	X
36	Hisense Group	Electrical and electronic	—	—	—	—	X
37	Johnson Electric	Electronics	—	—	—	—	X
38	Li & Fung Group	Diversified	—	—	12	—	X
39	Midea Group	Electronics	—	—	—	51	X
40	Shanghai Automotive Industry Corporation (SAIC)	Automotive	—	—	—	—	X
41	Sinosteel	Metals	372	—	—	—	X
42	Suntech Power	Solar technology	—	—	—	—	X
43	Techtronic industries	Electrical and electronic	—	—	—	—	X
44	Vtech Holding	Diversified	—	—	—	—	X
45	ZTE	Telecom	—	1,527	71	95	X

Rank	Company	Industry	Fortune[a]	Forbes[b]	WIR[c]	TNI[d]	BCG[e]
46	Wanxiang Group	Autoparts	—	—	—	—	X
47	China Shipbuilding Industry Corporation (CSIC)	Shipbuilding	—	—	—	—	X
48	China Communications Construction Company (CCCC)	Infrastructure and engineering	333	—	—	—	X
49	China International Marine Containers Group (CIMC)	Shipping and logistics	—	—	—	—	X
50	China Minmetals	Metals	331	—	95	97	X
51	China National Chemical Corporation (ChemChina)	Chemicals	—	—	—	—	X
52	COFCO	Food	335	—	—	—	X
53	Sinomach	Diversified	—	—	—	—	X
54	Cosco Group	Shipping and logistics	—	—	—	—	X

[a] Fortune (2009); [b] Forbes (2009); [c] *World Investment Report* (UNCTAD, 2008); [d] Transnationality Index: average of foreign assets to total assets, foreign sales to total sales, and foreign employment to total employment; [e] Boston Consulting Group (2009); X indicates inclusion in BCG's New Global Challengers list.

Wang (2009: 5) calculated their relative share as follows: state-owned enterprises, 28%; collective companies, 2%; joint-stock companies, 9%; affiliated companies, 1%; limited liability companies, 33%; limited stock companies, 11%; privately owned enterprises, 12%; Hong Kong, Taiwan, and Macau companies, 2%; and foreign companies, 4%.

In Table 10.3, besides Lenovo, Haier, Huawei, Acer (Taiwan), and TCL, all of which are well-known, we see a large number of oil and gas firms, as well as building companies. These enterprises are part of the "new Chinese armada," which has been deployed around the world and which is in charge of guaranteeing the supply of basic inputs for Chinese growth, prioritizing Africa.

For the purposes of this book, we focused on the cases of two enterprises that developed outstanding and distinctive organizational competences, in order to illustrate our analytical approach. This allowed us to draw comparisons between China and Brazil and their MNEs. The first case is that of Huawei, of which we made a comparative analysis relative to what occurred in Brazil, to grasp the potentially strategic role of the telecom industry. The second is Lenovo, which, through the boldness of its internationalization strategy, reveals the difficulties of emerging country MNEs during the post-acquisition stage and in the development of their international management model.

10.3.3 The Huawei case: how the Chinese develop competences in technology intensive industries

The Huawei case is representative of other Chinese enterprises in the telecommunication equipment industry, such as Julong, Datang, and Zhongxing (ZTE). "The telecom equipment industry has miraculously become the number one in China and Huawei has become the most dynamic and ambitious company in the country" (He, 2007: 37).

The Chinese telecom equipment market was originally controlled by foreign companies, but the vast majority of consumers could not afford to buy high quality but expensive imported products. Huawei Technologies was established as a private company in Shenzen, in 1988, by a group of seven investors who invested the equivalent of $2,400, as a telecom equipment vendor. Huawei's strategy focused on developing cheaper products to meet demand. Its first switching product, developed through imitation and innovation, was sold at less than half the price of the competitors. Huawei grew based on that strategy in its early years. Three phases then emerged:

Phase 1 (1996–9): from continuous failure to zero breakdown. This was the period when foreign MNEs stepped up their operations in China. The increasing competition in the domestic market led Huawei to internationalize as a means of survival. The first step outside China consisted of a contract to supply Hutchinson Telecom in Hong Kong, which at the time was still under British rule. Hutchinson's high quality requirements propelled Huawei to standards of an almost international level.

Huawei then began focusing more strongly and taking part in international bids for telecom systems, which it first won in Russia, Cuba, and Yugoslavia. In addition to persistent efforts to persuade potential clients that Chinese products could meet their specifications, the diplomatic relations between the countries seem to have played a role in the outcome.

Phase 2 (1999–2001): getting Huawei to be identified by clients. Huawei focused on countries with a large population. To improve its image, the firm invested in a program that took potential customers to China and created visual aids to demonstrate the quality of its products:

Huawei executives arrived in Brazil in 1999 and for two years gave frequent presentations and insisted that the executives of Telemar [one of Brazil's largest telecom firms] visit Huawei's headquarters in China. By 2001, Telemar had become sufficiently impressed to try Huawei, awarding it a contract to provide Internet equipment for home use. Today, Huawei provides 60% of such equipment for the Brazilian firm, a business that used to be handled solely by Alcatel. He (2007: 59).

Phase 3 (2002 to date): move into developed countries and compete with two lines. Huawei started to explore developed markets in 2001. By the end of 2004, its products were used in fourteen developed countries in Europe and North America. Globally renowned operators such as British Telecom, France Telecom, and Telefonica, among others, are now Huawei clients.

Currently, 75 percent of Huawei's contract sales come from the international market, where the corporation has set up more than 100 subsidiaries; it has also established fourteen R&D centers in places such as Silicon Valley and Dallas in the US, Stockholm in Sweden, and Moscow in Russia. Huawei's operation in Brazil comprises three commercial offices and one training center.

A point that has always been unclear is the relationship between Huawei and the Chinese government. This issue has caused developed country equipment producers, such as Nortel, to protest. Recently, the Indian government asked the Chinese government for information, when Huawei decided to bid for the assets of Indian Telecom Industries, a state-owned telecommunication system. "The Indian government has already been apprised of the situation. Huawei is a private company. Though owned by the [Chinese] government, it is entirely managed and run by private-sector entrepreneurs," was the response of the China Council for International Trade. Nevertheless, the Indian government decided to ban Huawei and other Chinese companies from bidding for Indian Telecom Industries, citing security concerns.

10.3.4 The Lenovo case: moving up the value chain through acquisitions

Lenovo belongs to the Legend group, developing, producing, and marketing technology products and services worldwide. The firm has research centers in Beijing, Shanghai, and Shenzhen in China, Yamato in Japan, and North Carolina in the US. It maintains operating centers in Beijing, Paris, North Carolina, and Singapore. The firm's geographic segmentation encompasses the Americas; Europe, the Middle East, and Africa (EMEA); and the Asia-Pacific countries, including China.

The acquisition of IBM's PC division by Lenovo for $1.75 billion, announced in December 2004, entitled the firm to use the IBM brand for five years and gave it control of the trademark "IThink" for popular laptops of the IBM ThinkPad line. This business agreement not only enabled Lenovo to use the IBM brand, but also resulted in its acquiring IBM's laptop factories, the supply chain, and the distribution networks. Lenovo's president indicated that because of all this, his company should be able to challenge Dell and HP in global markets: "We are unhappy to be just the number three" (Financial Times, 2004), he stated.

This particular acquisition illustrates several important issues for the analysis of the internationalization of Chinese enterprises and of the MNEs from emerging countries in general. In the Lenovo case, we observed the rising pressure of local and foreign competitors in its home market. Although it led the Chinese PC segment, Lenovo was attacked by its competition, in particular by Dell, and its share price dropped 23 percent in 2004.

The aforementioned acquisition provided Lenovo with a dramatic increase in the scale of its operations, as a result of which its yearly sales increased fourfold. However, certain challenges did ensue, such as how to retain clients and talent, or how to manage the Lenovo business network abroad. In a recent article, Lenovo's chief executive officer (CEO), (Liu, 2007: 576) said that two initiatives had been especially important to retain IBM talent:

First, we widely publicized to management our vision that the new Lenovo would provide more career opportunities for progression to top management, which were more limited under the former IBM PCD. We emphasized that we were not a traditional Chinese company, with a rigid and closed mindset; rather, the culture of the new Lenovo is fully open and global ... Second, we announced that there would be no changes to the compensation of former IBM employees.

Lenovo also had to manage the strong resistance of IBM's distributor and technical service networks, which felt that the IBM-Lenovo arrangements had caused them to lose status. In other words, the Lenovo international management model was obliged to adjust to major cultural and management style differences and to blend the IBM tradition with the millenary Chinese culture.

The third challenge concerns the capability of a Chinese enterprise to build a global reputation quickly in order to retain brand loyalty in the international market and maintain the value of a brand that was already strong previously. To date, Lenovo has been very successful, even though it did face certain obstacles.

On the other hand, a brand name per se is not always very important in the acquisition process. For instance, when TCL acquired the French firm Thomson, it got a slipping business and a worn-out brand (RCA). In the aforementioned case of SAIC, the Rover brand was already "defunct," as *The Economist* observed. Indeed, the Chinese buyers launched a new car under the name Roewe 75 rather than Rover. Obviously, therefore, the acquisition of the brand was not at the heart of the transaction in this case.

10.3.5 Is there a Chinese model of international management?

When China opened itself to the world, it was fully aware of the extent to which it lagged behind other countries, Brazil included. It is a well-known fact that China monitored Brazil's development with interest, to learn from it and to avoid making the same mistakes. Its opening was structured in such a way as to make catching up feasible. The local partner requirement for all MNEs that might wish to set up subsidiaries over there was the most evident manifestation of this aim.

Box 10.2 How a Japanese saw the Chinese industry at the end of the twentieth century

In 1996, I had an opportunity to visit nineteen major machinery factories in Beijing, Tianjin, and the northeastern part of China, as head of a study team sent by the Ministry of International Trade and Industry (MITI) in connection with the Japanese government's technical co-operation programme. Chinese government officials told us that most existing factories were obsolete and that foreign firms' collaboration was indispensable for their modernization. What foreign collaboration was secured had been largely confined to township enterprises in coastal regions. Among the companies we visited, only Beijing No.1 Machine Tool Factory, Changchun FAW Auto, Shenyang Jin Bei Auto, and Shenyang No.2 Machine Tool Factory had at least the partial appearance of a modern factory. Even at these companies, those plants where no foreign collaboration had been secured were extremely old and poorly maintained, and production floors were in a great mess.

The Chinese automobile industry produced mainly trucks until the 1980s. "One auto factory for each province" became a rule during the Great Cultural Revolution period, and many small factories were created by upgrading repair shops. In the mid-1990s, there were some 3,000 auto and autoparts companies, including over 130 truck factories, 164 bus factories, 125 special-purpose

---

vehicle factories, and 6 passenger car factories. Their scale of production was small and productivity, quality, and technical standards were low. Only Dongfeng Motor Co. produced more than 100,000 units (trucks) in 1991. This total, however, was assembled in 9 provinces and autonomous areas, using chassis from the main factory in Hubei Province and parts from about 300 factories scattered over 28 provinces, autonomous areas and municipalities.

For the automobile industry, the Chinese Government announced a special policy programme in 1994, with a view to promoting it as a "pillar" of the national economy. Tax and financial incentives were to be provided for officially designated companies and company groups, which met certain conditions. They were to raise the local content of their products and strengthen their product development abilities, so that three or four internationally competitive firm-groups could be formed out of about 120 existing auto-producers by 2010. This was to be achieved through joint ventures with foreign companies, which were to have their own product patents and trademark rights, original product-developing and manufacturing technology, independent international marketing channels, and sufficient financial capacity. The joint-venture firms were to establish an in-house R&D institute, and their products were to be technologically up to the international standards of the 1990s. Insofar as auto-assembly is concerned, therefore, 100 percent foreign ownership is not permitted and investment in R&D facilities is compulsory. Even parts and component manufacturers are often required to go into a joint venture.

Extracted from Watanabe, 2007.

Besides the plants' precariousness, the other Chinese characteristic that drew the attention of researchers and managers was "guanxi." Guanxi literally means "relationships," standing for any type of relationship. In the Chinese environment, it is understood as the network of relationships among various parties that cooperate with and support each another. For the international business community, the interpretation was that getting the right *guanxi* was fundamental for corporate success in China.

The point is that the Chinese prefer to deal with people they know and trust. At first sight, this does not seem very different from doing business in the West, but in reality, the heavy reliance on relationships means that Western companies have to make themselves known to the Chinese before any business can take place. Furthermore, this relationship is not simply between firms but also between individuals on a personal level.

The experience of the subsidiaries of the Brazilian corporations that set up operations in China ratifies the points above. For instance, Embraco entered the Chinese market through a joint venture with Snowflake. The first visit to the plant, acquired in 1994, revealed a thick layer of dirt on the ground. Major rebuilding had to be undertaken. Now, however, Embraco/Snowflake operates within a world-class plant and makes products developed in China specifically for the Chinese market.

During this time, one of the major challenges was developing a local organizational culture compatible both with guanxi and with the corporate culture from Brazil, which applied to all the other subsidiaries.

The Snowflake example complements the case of outstanding MNEs, such as Lenovo and Huawei. It shows that although the circumstances of such enterprises may be precarious when they first turn toward expansion, they advance fast. The competences that are most highly valued are production and logistics, as they lead to low-cost manufacturing. Nonetheless, the awareness of these other competences is gradually growing.

Resuming the discussion of outstanding MNEs, one should mention the study conducted by Donald Sull (2005b) on the Chinese management style. In this study, he used the same framework as in his analysis of Brazilian firms. Working with a sample of eight leading enterprises (Legend Group/Lenovo, Sina Corporation, Haier, Galanz, UTS, AsiaInfo, Hangzhou Wahaha, and Tsin Hsin), Sull found certain features that were similar to those of the Brazilian case (though others were quite different), such as:

- active waiting, supported by mechanisms similar to those found in Brazil;
- operational and financial discipline;
- strong partners;
- ownership and governance structure that allows for long-term action; and
- managers willing to take the plunge.

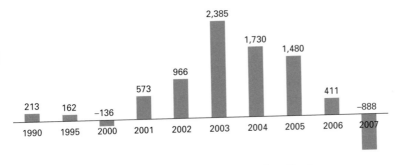

Figure 10.4 Brazil–China bilateral trade balance ($ million)

10.3.6 *The relationship between China and Brazil during global productive restructuring*

Bilateral trade between Brazil and China increased substantially in the last decade. In 2008, China was the third largest destination of Brazilian exports (after the US and Argentina) and the sixth supplier of imports. However, the bilateral trade balance was reversed in 2007, as shown in Figure 10.4.

It is not only the growth rate of the bilateral trade that is asymmetric, but also its composition. Brazil exports basic commodities and natural resource-intensive products, such as coal, grain (soy), steel and associated products, and meat (poultry and swine). Manufactured and semi-manufactured products accounted for only 5.5 percent of Brazil's exports to China. By contrast, Brazil largely imports manufactured goods from China: electronics components, telecom products (especially mobile phone handsets and liquid crystal displays), textiles, footwear, toys, tyres, and components for motorcycles and bikes.

"The accelerated development process of the large Asian countries and their incorporation into global value chains has both direct and indirect effects upon Brazilian industry" (Fleury and Fleury, 2005). The direct effects are associated with direct trade relations and a mutual influence on the countries' industrial structures through cooperation and competition. The indirect effects involve third parties – MNEs and their strategies with respect to their global sourcing and location decisions.

The relocation of production is the most visible feature of China's entry into the global market and reflects the generalized adoption of offshoring strategies. Mexico has been more deeply affected by this than Brazil, as some 600,000 jobs were transferred from the Mexican maquiladoras (operations that involve manufacturing in countries other than the clients') to Chinese suppliers. No such figures are available for Brazil, but it is a well-known fact that many individual MNEs moved their production from Brazil to China. The auto industry is a case in point. After significant investments in Brazil in the second half of the 1990s to modernize existing plants and to set up new plants (many designed around radically new concepts), there is clear evidence that the industry turned almost completely toward the Asian markets in the new millennium.

The entry of new Asian enterprises into the high-scale, low-priced, basic products market forced many MNEs to abandon commodity segments and to specialize in more complex products. This posed challenges for their operations in developing countries such as Brazil, where many of their subsidiaries produced commodity products. In the early 1990s, new, large, integrated Chinese producers of commodity fibers forced MNEs such as BASF, Dow, and Rhone Poulenc to embrace new niches. Gradually these MNEs changed the profile of their Brazilian subsidiaries, moving toward special, highly value-added products, largely abandoning their commodity fiber plants. Some of the latter were sold very cheaply to local groups but, overall, the quantity and variety of local supply diminished and consequently imports grew strongly.

The third indirect effect can be called "Asian sourcing." It concerns the possibilities of Brazilian subsidiaries of MNEs to source their products from China, whether directly or indirectly, thus changing the structure of the local supply chains. Unilever is a case in point: inputs purchased in Brazil are now imported from Asia, especially China, in larger quantities. In the telecom industry, large global manufacturing and services providers, the so-called manufacturing contractors, were established during the 1990s (Sturgeon, 1997). When subsidiaries of manufacturing contractors were established in Brazil, the subsidiaries of specialized equipment suppliers, such as Ericsson, NEC, and Motorola, among others, began subcontracting from them. However, these manufacturing contractors operate globally and now source parts and components from Asia. In both cases, the configurations of the local supply chains were substantially altered and local suppliers were urged to redefine their strategies.

Concerning the process of internationalization of their own enterprises, Brazil and China pursued different tracks. In Brazil, public institutions only recently became supportive, following a period during which ambivalence and suspicion prevailed. By contrast, the Chinese orientation to international institutions and markets is quite different. First, there is a strong inclination toward trying to influence the way in which international trade is governed; China's strong involvement with the institutions that set international standards (Deloitte, 2004) illustrates the extent of their concern with all the aspects that might influence the future of their enterprises. Second and foremost, the way in which China is approaching the issue of competence formation for international competitiveness is truly innovative. Rather than waiting for the development or speeding up the creation of local competences to then go international, China is internationalizing fast to internalize rapidly those competences that are seen as strategic in the long term. This is different from what Japan was allowed to do in the second half of the twentieth century. Given the characteristics of world markets at that time, Japanese enterprises had plenty of time to learn with foreign firms, internalize competences, and improve on them to become competitive, only then venturing into the international arena. Toyota is a good example: it had the opportunity to emulate the Ford production model in the early 1950s to become a global player in the late 1980s. However, as we have already mentioned, world markets now have distinct features and the timing must be different.

10.3.7 *The international competitiveness of Chinese enterprises*

Westerners still find it hard to interpret the China phenomenon; deciphering the rationale underlying Chinese MNEs' actions continues to be a major challenge.

Huang (2003) stated that China could be understood as "a macroeconomic miracle and a microeconomic failure." The assessment of Rugman and Li (2007) follows the same line of thought, arguing that "Chinese MNEs are building scale economies based on China's country-specific advantages. Unlike Western MNEs, which transfer knowledge and technology through their firm specific advantages, China's MNEs will lack such firm specific advantages (FSAs) for some years to come. Thus, China MNEs will have difficulty in sustaining their initial forays abroad."

Nonetheless, according to Zeng and Williamson (2007), "the sources of Chinese competitive advantage rely on their competences to apply high technology rapidly to mainstream markets, deliver variety at a low cost penalty and re-engineer niche products for the mass market, thus disrupting incumbents' business models."

Summing up all of the above, we can say that Chinese firms are competitive as a result of the following factors, at country level:

• economies of scale, which benefited from a large domestic economy and market;
• a highly internationalized domestic market; and
• institutional advantages.

These led to the development of organizational competences in:

• operational excellence, leading to advantages in production, labor, and overhead costs;
• innovative products for niche markets;
• effective marketing and services; and
• appropriate management systems.

"What precisely characterizes the emerging generation of Chinese internationalizing firms is their willingness to become path-creators, in the sense of moving away from crystallized social practice, regulations or institutions by combining innovative, proactive and risk seeking behavior" (Child and Rodrigues, 2005).

10.4 The internationalization of Indian firms

10.4.1 Productive restructuring in India

India, home to the world's second largest population of over one billion inhabitants, is the seventh largest country in the world. Though 80 percent of its population is Hindu, it also has the second largest Moslem group in the world, which accounts for 13.4 percent of its population. Most of the population lives in rural areas and their chief economic activity is agriculture.

India's civilization is one of the world's oldest. It is an area crossed by historical trade routes and it has held vast empires. After being gradually taken over by the British East India Company from the early eighteenth century and actively colonized by the UK from the mid-nineteenth century, the country rid itself of British rule only in 1947, following an independence effort underscored by a campaign of non-violent resistance led by Mahatma Gandhi.

After independence, India embraced a socialist, centralized planning strategy that pursued self-sufficiency. However, the Indian socialist experience, or "Fabian Socialism," was not based on the Marxist–Leninist revolutionary premises (Khanna and Huang, 2003) and did not aim at the elimination of private property. Thus, the 1950s stood out for their import substitution policy; foreign investments and imports were limited, in order to protect local industry. Under a nationalist administration, the state participated heavily in the country's early industrialization process. At the time, India invested primarily in heavy industry, the arms industry, and infrastructure.

In a way, protectionist policies lasted until the late 1980s. During this decade, foreign loans fostered economic growth and put pressure on the balance of payments. Furthermore, India's share of international trade dropped from 2.5% at the time of its independence to less than 0.5%; its growth rates stood at some 3.5% a year and its population grew at the rate of 3.1% a year.

In the wake of the 1991 Gulf War, India faced a serious shortage of foreign exchange and accepted the Structural Adjustment Program led by the International Monetary Fund (IMF) and the World Bank in order to secure loans from these institutions. Consequently, the government had to instate a new industrial policy, liberalizing investment in most industries. The importation of capital goods, industrial location, capital and technological collaboration with foreign firms and the like were also liberalized. Moreover, this period saw the demise of the raj license, a licensing system that had been in place since independence and that placed the state in the position of omnipresent intervener in all economic activities. As a result, foreign capital began to flow into the country almost immediately, but the subsequent rate of foreign investment appears to have been far slower than in China.

In the post-financial liberation era, India experienced a huge influx of MNEs. It is a well-documented fact that US enterprises account for roughly 37 percent of the turnover of the top twenty firms in operation in India. The situation, however, has changed in recent years, since more and more European Union enterprises (from the UK,

Italy, France, Germany, the Netherlands, Finland, Belgium, etc.) have established subsidiaries in India. Nokia, the Finnish mobile handset manufacturing giant, has its second largest base in India. British Petroleum and Vodafone represent the British. A host of automakers, such as Fiat, Ford Motors, and Renault, has established operations in India along with an R&D section. The major heavy engineering firm Alstom and the major pharmaceutical company Sanofi Aventis, the earliest French entrants, are expanding very fast. Oil companies and infrastructure builders from the Middle East are also flocking to India to catch the boom. South Korean electronics giants Samsung and LG Electronics, and small and mid-segment automaker Hyundai Motors, are doing excellent business and using India as a hub for global delivery. Japan was among the first foreign countries to establish itself in India, especially in electronics and automobiles.

A second phase in the flow of foreign investment to India relates to the establishment of R&D centers by Western multinationals, similar to what happened in China. Bruche (2009) estimates that the number of MNE R&D centers has grown from 100 in each country in 2001, to around 1,100 in China (representing 920 MNEs) and 780 in India (representing 670 MNEs).

On the other hand, the government began encouraging Indian enterprises to undertake FDI, whether in greenfield operations or loan-based acquisitions, gradually repositioning itself from regulator to facilitator, even though bureaucratic issues continued to be a problem. The "caged tiger" metaphor is often linked to the Indian case.

10.4.2 The Indian multinationals

Sanjaya Lall (1983: 31), in his book *Third World Multinationals*, observed that in the early 1980s:

> there were over 100 Indian enterprises or business groups engaged in foreign operations. Some are relatively small enterprises which have drifted into overseas investment by dint of historical accident or due to the peculiar temperament of the entrepreneur concerned. Some are medium-to-large specialized firms which have gone international to exploit their accumulated knowledge of a given activity. And some are parts of enormous

conglomerate business houses which have gone abroad as a conscious strategy of group diversification and growth.

Indian investments abroad at that time were quite concentrated in three groups: the Birla Group ("a metals powerhouse"), the Thapar Group (various lines of business; textile-led internationalization), and the Tata Group. These three accounted for 40 percent of total investment abroad.

The affiliates were located in neighboring countries; more than 60 percent of them were very small-scale operations. Lall identified thirteen ventures that were sizeable as compared to the affiliates of the "real" MNEs in the small host countries frequented by Indian firms.

Following a study of the Indian Investment Centre, Lall (1983: 36) gives five explanations for the poor performance of Indian subsidiaries: (a) lack of experience; (b) smallness; (c) lack of proper assessment of foreign conditions and inability to cope with tougher competition than previously imagined due to technological lags, poor marketing know-how, inadequate managerial techniques, and so on; (d) wrong choice of local partners; and (e) the inadequate policies of the Indian government.

The current wave of outward FDI from countries such as India is a scaled-up version of what happened in the 1980s: the same business groups are prominent in the new wave of internationalization. For Khanna and Palepu (1997), the prominence of those Indian "business houses," similar to the Korean "chaebols" and the Latin American "grupos," are a way of coping with institutional voids in developing countries, derived from information problems, misguided regulations, and ineffective judicial systems. However, several new Indian firms became multinationals.

Ramamurti and Singh (2009: 113) observe that the new wave of internationalization is different from the former in the following sense:

- the choice of country: in the previous wave, 80% of all outward FDI went to other developing countries, whereas in the new wave almost 70% flowed into developed countries, in particular European ones;

- the mode of entry: in the previous wave, more than 80% of all outward FDI was in manufacturing, whereas in the current wave only 36% is in manufacturing, while services accounts for 62% and software for nearly 30%; in the new wave, acquisitions are more frequent than greenfield investments; majority-owned or wholly owned subsidiaries are more common than joint-ventures; outward FDI takes the form of cash or stock instead of investments in kind (technology or know-how);
- state-owned enterprises (SOEs) played a peripheral role in internationalization, with the exception of the oil and gas sector; however, they have important domestic roles in regard to technology development and dissemination.

The Indian MNEs are listed in Table 10.4. The list covers all Indian MNEs that were either considered a Global Challenger by the Boston Consulting Group (2009) or mentioned in UNCTAD's *World Investment Report* (2008). Their rankings in the *Fortune* 500 and *Forbes* 2000 listings are added information that helps to characterize the corporations' relative size.

We can see that the Indian MNEs operate predominantly in five economic sectors:

- oil and gas;
- natural resource-based manufacturing;
- engineered goods;
- pharmaceuticals;
- IT services.

A large number of Indian MNEs have become renowned, major global players. For instance, Ramamrti and Singh (2009) chose Mahindra and Mahindra (automotive), Infosys and Wipro (IT), Hindalco (steel), and Suzlon (wind-power) as Indian examples of generic internationalization strategies. Other authors, such as Goldstein (2009), conducted a vertical study of the Tata Group or business house, or focused on the pharmaceutical companies.

For our purposes, the idea is to focus on cases of firms that developed outstanding and distinctive organizational competences, in order to illustrate our analytical approach and to compare India and Brazil and their respective MNEs. Therefore, we will discuss the cases of Tata (steel and automotive) and Wipro (IT).

Table 10.4 *Indian multinationals in the international rankings*

	Companies	Industry	Fortune 500 (2009)[a]	Forbes 2000 (2009)[b]	WIR (2008)[c] TNI[d]	WIR (2008)[c] Foreign assets	BCG (2009)[e]
1	Indian Oil	Oil and gas	105	279	—	—	X
2	Tata Steel	Metals	258	1,302	—	—	X
3	Reliance Industries	Oil and gas	264	309	—	—	—
4	Bharat Petroleum	Oil and gas	289	914	—	—	—
5	Hindustan Petroleum	Oil and gas	311	1,011	—	—	—
6	Oil & Natural Gas	Oil and gas	402	265	96	32	—
7	National Thermal Power	Utilities	—	486	—	—	—
8	Steel Authority of India	Materials	—	831	—	—	—
9	Tata Consultancy Svcs	Business services and supplies	—	1,167	—	—	—
10	GAIL (India)	Utilities	—	1,250	—	—	—
11	Infosys Technologies	Business services and supplies	—	1,250	—	—	X
12	ITC	Food, drink, and tobacco	—	1,336	—	—	—
13	Wipro	Business services and supplies	—	1,362	—	—	X

Table 10.4 (*cont.*)

	Companies	Industry	Fortune 500 (2009)[a]	Forbes 2000 (2009)[b]	WIR (2008)[c] TNI[d]	WIR (2008)[c] Foreign assets	BCG (2009)[e]
14	Tata Motors	Capital goods	—	1,519	—	—	X
15	Bharti Tele—Ventures	Telecom	—	1,648	—	—	—
16	Mahanagar Telephone Nigam	Telecom	—	1,835	—	—	—
17	Bharat Heavy Electricals	Capital goods	—	1,907	—	—	—
18	Ranbaxy Laboratories	Drugs and biotechnology	—	1,936	36	99	X
19	Hindalco Industries	Materials	—	1,982	—	—	X
20	Larsen & Toubro	Capital goods	—	1,996	—	—	X

[a] Fortune (2009); [b] Forbes (2009); [c] *World Investment Report* (UNCTAD, 2008); [d] Transnationality Index: average of foreign assets to total assets, foreign sales to total sales, and foreign employment to total employment; [e] Boston Consulting Group (2009); X indicates inclusion in BCG's New Global Challengers list.

10.4.3 The Tata case: the most internationalized Indian business house

Tata was established in 1868 by Jamsetji Nusserwanji Tata. Originally a commercial concern, in the early twentieth century it expanded into iron and steel. Up to the early 1960s, its strategy had focused on domestic expansion, through new business acquisitions in the chemical, cosmetics, and automotive sectors. The Boston Consulting Group (2009) lists six Tata enterprises among the 20 Global Challengers from India: Tata Chemicals, Tata Communications, Tata Consultancy Services, Tata Motors, Tata Steel, and Tata Tea.

The Tata group is currently the largest Indian industrial conglomerate, operating in more than eighty-five countries across the six continents, with ninety-six operating companies in seven business sectors: engineering, materials, chemicals, energy, consumer products, services, and IT and communications systems. Back in the 1960s, Tata Consultancy Services (TCS) was established as a division of Tata and Sons and it now competes as an IT supplier. However, it was only from 2000 that the conglomerate's internationalization began, when Tata Tea acquired the Tetley Group, a British enterprise; this was followed by Tata Steel's acquisition of Corus.

Concerning the case of Tata Steel, Indian industry was protected up to the 1990s and focused on its domestic market. After 1991, thanks to the new industrial policy and market deregulation, the Indian producers, encouraged by export possibilities, aimed at improving the quality of their steel, which was manufactured at competitive prices.

The threat of competition from foreign suppliers and competitors encouraged the upgrade of plants and operations. Cost-cutting, quality improvements, Six Sigma programs, productivity increases, and improved marketing and customer service were put in place.

Two specific country factors aided the internationalization process. The first was the size of the Indian market; although the country was poor, there was high absolute demand for certain products, especially once the economy started growing at high rates. This provided local producers with economies of scale. The second was the advantages of the low cost of labor and of raw materials (Ramamurti and Singh, 2009).

In 2005, in Singapore, Tata Steel acquired 100 percent of the shares of NatSteel, the largest steel enterprise in Asia. Thus, Tata Steel combined the latter's network of steel mills in Asia with its own knowledge of how to make steel at competitive prices and its own raw material sources. In April 2006, Tata Steel acquired 67.1 percent of the controlling stock of Millennium Steel, Thailand's largest steel mill. The investment reflected the significant advance of Tata Steel's globalization initiatives and aimed to strengthen its position in the Southeast Asia market. In January 2007, Tata Steel took control of an Anglo-Dutch concern, Corus, acquired with the Tata Group's financial support. In this bid, Tata outdid CSN, a Brazilian steel corporation, after a tough struggle.

For Kumar and Chadda (2009), the acquisition of Western firms that enjoyed cutting-edge technology in steel manufacturing provided Tata with fast access to state-of-the-art steel manufacturing technology. Thus, Tata Steel, a high-cost producer in the 1980s, with investments in cutting-edge technology, labor agreements, and commitments to the community, became one of the steel producers with the lowest costs in the world.

Tata Steel's internationalization process followed the global consolidator model (Ramamurti and Singh, 2009), i.e., it began with horizontal acquisitions in other emerging markets (e.g., NatSteel and Millennium Steel) and culminated with its acquisitions in developed countries (e.g., Corus).

In the automotive field, Tata developed and initiated the production of the innovative Nano, the world's cheapest car to date, which is to be marketed at $2,500. This catapulted Tata Motors to a new level among automakers. The Nano is a product that makes very good sense in the Indian market, where urban traffic is chronically gridlocked and where the so-called "tuk tuks" predominate. These are a type of three-wheeled rickshaw (with polluting two-stroke engines produced by Maruti) that function as taxis. In early 2007, Maruti announced that it too would develop a car similar to the Nano, in partnership with Renault.

It is worth recalling that Brazil also had its Nano, or actually two. The first was the Romi-Isetta, mentioned in the Romi case study in Chapter 8. The second was the Gurgel, a low-cost car, also designed and produced on a small scale, back in the 1970s and 1980s. It ran on a two-cylinder engine, half of a Volkswagen Beetle engine. Gurgel, a new enterprise, did not prosper in the Brazilian market, where it had to compete with the powerful subsidiaries of the automakers already in operation in the country.

That leads to the hypothesis that the Nano's success may be due largely to Tata's power as a business house. Moreover, Tata acquired Jaguar and Land Rover, sophisticated car brands that target the high-income market. Thus, Tata Motors has been building a unique path toward joining the club of the world's largest automakers.

When it comes to producing buses, Tata resorted to a different strategy. Together with Marcopolo, a Brazilian enterprise, they set up a joint venture in 2006 to assemble and market long-distance coaches, urban public transport buses and mini-buses, with a view to serving the Indian market as well as for exporting. The joint venture absorbed an initial investment of $13.3 million, of which 51 percent came from Tata Motors and 49 percent from Marcopolo, management being shared by the two firms. The first plant went on-stream in early 2008. In this joint venture, Tata Motors provides the chassis and markets the end products. Marcopolo provides the bus production processes and systems, as well as project technology and new model development.

The Lucknow plant, the joint venture's first, produces sophisticated urban transport buses, with a low floor and a rear gas-fuelled engine, for use in large urban centers such as New Delhi. The production of smaller models, such as mini-buses and low entry urban models with gas- and diesel-fuelled engines, is concentrated in Dharwad.

The Dharwad plant currently has 1,300 personnel. This should increase gradually until it reaches an output of fifty vehicles a day. It is forecast that by 2011 the second stage will be complete, making this plant the world's largest of its kind, with a capacity to make 25,000 vehicles a year.

10.4.4 *The Wipro case: an innovative business model to move up the IT value chain*

India used its factor endowments very cleverly to enter the global IT market. Besides instating a development policy for this sector, along the lines of the Brazilian information technology policy, it invested heavily in what is now called business process outsourcing (BPO), resorting to people with good education, skilled in the exact sciences (especially mathematics), and fluent in English.

Thus, when corporations from the developed countries embarked upon reengineering, focusing and outsourcing in order to restructure their production, the Indian firms were in an ideal position to become suppliers of IT services. At first, they were essentially "software factories" in that they produced software designed to the specifications of the companies that ordered and bought such programs. Nevertheless, over time, these Indian enterprises escalated the value chain. Today, firms such as Infosys, Wipro, and TCS compete on par with world leaders such as IBM and Accenture. These firms generate spin-offs very fast, which means that the Indian IT industry is constantly renewing itself and progressing thanks to the synergy of what Khanna (2007) sees as "a billion entrepreneurs."

Among the Indian IT enterprises, Wipro's path was distinctive. It was first established in 1945 as the Western Indian Vegetable Products company, a producer of vegetable oil and cleaning products. In 1966, Azim Prenji, then a student at Stanford University in the US, took over the firm following his father's death. Wipro was then in a crisis, as its founder had been more of a politician than a businessman, so that changes had to be implemented in its production system and in the enterprise's culture for it to survive and prosper.

In the late 1970s, Wipro took advantage of the market reserve law and IBM's exit from India to start making computers. In the 1980s, it entered the field of software. When market deregulation came about, the enterprise changed its strategy and specialized in the outsourcing of R&D services for major Western companies, making use of the competence it had developed in computer production.

With growth that resulted from its diversification, Wipro has been betting increasingly on innovation-related products and services, investing heavily in R&D. For instance, its consumer laboratory designed a five-thousand channel digital box that is being marketed in Europe and that enables analog TV sets to operate with digital technologies. At the mobile laboratory, the engineers focus on creating intellectual property in the wireless segment and in the mobile telephone segment with low-cost applications already used in more than 90 million handsets. The enterprise states is it not afraid of moving away from its core business, which is the outsourcing of IT services.

Comparing Wipro's and TCS's strategy and data, we learn that:

• Wipro is large and roughly the same size as TCS; the latter invoices $4.3 million a year and has 100,000 employees, while Wipro invoices $3.47 billion a year and has 80,000 employees;

- the two compete with each other in the Indian IT market;
- both internationalized in order to also compete with Accenture, IBM, Siemens, and Brazilian firms of a similar nature, in Brazil and abroad;
- TCS came into Brazil through a global service contract with the ABN bank; Wipro came into Brazil by acquiring Enabler, a Portuguese enterprise with a Brazilian subsidiary;
- the differences between TCS and Wipro seem to be:

  - TCS internationalizes by means of contracts (such as the ABN one) and is having difficulty in designing its diversification;
  - Wipro is internationalizing by investing in R&D laboratories and creating intellectual property capital; the presence of Wipro R&D is global;

- in this R&D strategy, Wipro works with hardware in addition to services; there is no record of TCS developing hardware.

Thus, TCS is strong when it comes to developing client-oriented software. In other words, it enters into strategic agreements with governments and major corporations. Wipro's strategy involves acquisitions and the development of innovations for clients: their software development is product-oriented. The software is built-in and the firm's distinguishing feature is that it provides innovative technological solutions.

Wipro's international expansion took place through the acquisition of enterprises in developed countries and emerging markets. At present, the billings of these companies derive mainly from their international, rather than from their domestic, sales. According to the testimonials of Wipro directors, confirmed in an interview at the Confederation of Indian Industry, the Indian diaspora (especially the migration of Indian youths to developed nations in pursuit of educational opportunities and employment) helped these firms, because they can resort to fellow countrymen in senior positions in the US and in Europe, which is helpful when it comes to operations and contacts.

India's infrastructure is a routine problem for enterprises. It is estimated that its highways, railways, and power production systems are lagging behind current needs by some ten years. Power cuts for short time spans are common, as well as floods and the extraordinarily difficult traffic in cities such as Bangalore and New Delhi. Another major problem in India is manpower. Even though the country boasts thousands of new software engineering graduates who are fluent in English, the sector's boom is closely related with problems, ironic though this may seem.

10.4.5 Is there an Indian model of international management?

Studies to identify the Indian way of managing have been inconclusive so far. Cultural and religious characteristics, coupled with political and social conditions, plus the family structure of the Indian business houses, lend fairly well-defined contours to this theme.

Some of the approaches developed indicate that the traditional system based on caste, karma (predestination), and dharma (social duty), has been replaced by a modern management model, based on up-to-date approaches to corporate management, as shown in Table 10.5. This presumably results from the opening of the economy, competition from low wage countries, the rising importance of stakeholders, and concern about the environment.

Apparently, conformance and dependence were also found at the middle-management level. Ghoshal *et al.*, (2005), in a study about Indian managers, found that "satisfactory underperformance is pervasive in India," and urged a dramatic improvement in behavior.

As to higher level decision-making, Piramal (1996), when analyzing Indian groups in his book *Business Maharajas*, makes the following statement about them: "management gurus love to talk about strategy and strategic decisions, but the more I learn about business, the more I am convinced that management decisions are based on the personal experience, aims and vision of one person. Usually this is the head of the business house or chairman of the [Indian] company." Therefore, it seems that, so far, each business house professes a particular management model.

10.4.6 The relationship between India and Brazil during global productive restructuring

As mentioned earlier, trade relations between India and Brazil are not strong. India is not ranked among the twenty largest importers of Brazilian goods or exporters to Brazil.

Table 10.5 *Evolution of Indian management*

Management practices	Traditional	Modern
Employee requirements	Family relations and caste of employees must be considered	Objective selection criteria. Training programs and performance related compensation applied
Leadership style	Organizational leaders have a high level of personal involvement with their subordinates. Leaders provide nurturance contingent upon the subordinate's task accomplishment	Increasingly participative management style, in which subordinates' opinions and input are requested. Personal relationship between management and employees reduced
Motivational aspects and rewards	Work is viewed as a means to an end, i.e., to satisfy family needs. Little demand for changing work tasks; only compensation is relevant	Elements such as job rotation, enrichment, autonomy, team work, and competitive salaries are increasingly considered to motivate employees
HRM practices	Nepotism and caste considerations affect selection and compensation. Training less emphasized	Relevant educational background and experience matching task requirements

Source: Chong and Agrawal (in press).

Nevertheless, the number of Indian subsidiaries in Brazil, in the industries in which India specializes, is rising. In pharmaceuticals, there is news that eleven Indian firms have already established themselves in Brazil, albeit on a small scale. In the steel industry,

Arcelor-Mittal is the largest local producer. Mahindra & Mahindra is assembling jeeps in Brazil. Moreover, in IT, the large BPO firms are already in operation: TCS, Infosys, and Wipro, among others.

In the case of Indian BPO firms coming to Brazil, there are some reasons for this. First, they want to be close to North America – the chief source of outsourcing businesses. The Brazilian market has many similarities with North America, which include a similar time zone and cultural empathy. On the other hand, it has not been as heavily exploited and is not as competitive as the Mexican market, which is saturated with US firms and has decades of experience with global service enterprises.

The second factor is the large domestic Brazilian market. The third is that Indian firms are now witnessing a strong trend among their current client base toward minimizing the risk of maintaining all operations in a single country. Clients are beginning to pursue geopolitical diversification and no longer want to depend on the workforce of a single country. Should the Indian enterprises be unable to offer such diversification, they run the risk of losing the client.

This point becomes even more important when one realizes that regulations such as the Sarbanes–Oxley law are beginning to demand better corporate risk management. Moreover, there is great vulnerability in maintaining all outsourced technology operations in a single country, especially in one with outdated infrastructure and a history of natural catastrophes.

On the Brazilian side, there are two IT firms that have internationalized, as we have seen: Stefanini and Bematech. Stefanini follows the conventional BPO model and has recently established an office in Bangalore. The other Brazilian firms operating in India are Marcopolo and Weg, though it is thought that Gerdau is planning to establish operations in India as well.

10.4.7 The international competitiveness of Indian enterprises

Kumar (2007) developed an analytical framework for explaining the probability of an Indian enterprise investing abroad. He finds that Indian firms draw their ownership advantages from their accumulated production experience, from the cost effectiveness of their production processes and from other adaptations of imported technologies achieved with their technological effort, and sometimes with their ability to differentiate products.

Ramamurti and Singh (2009) conclude that Indian firms internationalized after 2000 using more than one strategy, each of which had its own background and consequences. They identified four generic internationalization strategies: local optimizers (firms that optimized products and processes for the local market internationalize toward other emerging markets); low-cost partners (whose core competences – factor cost arbitrage, process excellence, and project management – enabled them to became global suppliers); global consolidators (core competences in engineering processes for operational excellence in mature industries such as steel); and global first-movers (global innovators).

10.5 The internationalization of Russian firms

10.5.1 Russia's transition into a global economy

A territory spanning eleven time zones and covering one-eighth of the Earth's surface, Russia is the largest country in the world and the richest in natural resources. With more than 145 million inhabitants, it is also the country with the largest population in Europe.

Thanks to its abundance of natural resources, particularly energy, Russia has a dominant global position in the energy sector, controlling over 6 percent of the world's oil resources and 27 percent of the world's gas. It supplies 25 percent of Europe's gas needs. It is also a major exporter, maintaining a positive trade balance and strong gold and foreign currency reserves.

As one of the two world superpowers from 1950 to 1990, Russia led what was seen as "the second world" behind the Iron Curtain. After the disintegration of the Soviet Union, complex diplomatic and economic relationships remained with those countries that were formerly part of the same bloc, such as Bulgaria, the Czech Republic, Hungary, Romania, Poland, and Yugoslavia (now broken down into several countries, including Serbia and Montenegro).

On the other hand, Russia maintained strong bonds with the former Soviet republics, now members of the Commonwealth of Independent States (CIS). The organization was founded in December 1991 by the Russian Federation, the Republic of Belarus, and Ukraine. Eight other former Soviet Republics joined later, namely: Armenia, Azerbaijan, Kazakhstan, Kyrgyzstan, Moldova, Turkmenistan, Tajikistan, and Uzbekistan. The Baltic states of Estonia, Latvia, and Lithuania decided not to join. It is also important to recall that the Soviet Union was a role model for and a strong ally of countries such as China and Cuba.

The abundance of natural resources and its militaristic industrial development defined Russia's stakes in the global economy. The privatization period, during which the Russian MNEs emerged, followed the fall of the Berlin Wall. "In the 1990s virtually the entire Russian economy, except for small businesses and the black market sector, was dominated by a relatively small number of businessmen (oligarchs) who gained control of the country's most valuable enterprises (oligarchic capitalism)" (McCarthy *et al.*, 2009: 174). A major fall in production output was the outcome of that period. However, since 1999, the Russian economy has rebounded thanks to favorable international factors related to the prices of its main export products.

During the period of "oligarchic capitalism," the empires built by the oligarchs consisted of firms in several industries, especially in the field of natural resources, with a bank at the centre of the group. McCarthy *et al.*, (2009: 174) argue that "in some ways, they resembled the Korean Chaebol and the Japanese Keiretsu." This period lasted until the mid-2000s, when President Putin's second term began.

Recently, however, a process of renationalization was put in motion and the Russian state has been buying back a majority interest in several enterprises that had been privatized. "President Putin's policies concerning the government's role in the economy have been described as state-managed, network capitalism. Thus, Russia exhibits a form of economic dualism rather than a purer form of Western capitalism" (McCarthy *et al.*, 2009).

Russia's outward FDI has been growing fast: while from 2001 to 2005 the average was $7 billion per year, in the 2006–8 period this figure increased almost five-fold, to $34 billion.

10.5.2 Russian multinationals

"Some 50 to 60 MNEs account for most of the Russian assets abroad, with OFDI among this group dominated by such behemoths as Gazprom, Lukoil, Sberbank, AKF Systema, Norilsk Nickel, Evraz,

Rusal, and Severstal, all of them global players, some of which are part of larger and looser groups" (Panibratov and Kalotay, 2009: 2).

The list of Russian multinationals (Table 10.6) followed different criteria because they are not mentioned in UNCTAD'S *World Investment Report* and only six of them are mentioned as part of the BCG's 100 Global Challengers. Therefore, we have listed the Russian enterprises in the *Fortune* and *Forbes* rankings.

The state has played an important role in the emergence of Russian outward FDI. State-owned enterprises, such as Gazprom, enjoy a set of advantages. Even in fully or partially privatized enterprises, state influence remains.

10.5.3 The paths of Russian multinationals

Acquisition is the preferred mode of entry; as Russian MNEs are essentially in the natural resources area, they pursue scale increases and vertical downstream integration. For example, the largest recent take-over was made by Norilsk Nickel, which acquired Lion Ore Mining in Canada in 2007 to increase resources; on the other hand, Luckoil has bought Getty Oil in the US, where the main activity is distribution. The primary destinations are the CIS, especially Belarus and Ukraine, followed by North America and Italy.

Russia is the tenth largest buyer of Brazilian products (meat is the most important of these) but it is not among the twenty largest exporters into Brazil. The Russian MNEs that compete more directly with Brazilian MNEs are MTS Norilsk Nickel (mining) and Suckoi.

Norilsk Nickel is a nickel and palladium mining and smelting operator headquartered in Moscow. It is also active in gold, platinum, copper, and cobalt. The company is the world's leading producer of nickel and palladium and is Russia's leading gold producer. It is ranked among the top four world platinum producers, in association with the subsidiary Stillwater Mining Company of Billings, Montana. It is ranked among the top ten copper producers.

The company is listed on NASDAQ and the RTS stock exchange. According to the company's English-language website, its activity accounts for as much as 1.5 percent of Russia's current GDP. Norilsk Nickel's production facilities are spread over six countries: Russia, Australia, Botswana, Finland, the US, and South Africa.

Table 10.6 *Russian multinationals in the international rankings*

	Company	Industry	Fortune 500 (2009)[a]	Forbes 2000 (2009)[b]	WIR (2008)[c]		BCG (2009)[e]
					TNI[d]	Foreign assets	
1	Gazprom	Oil and gas	22	13	—	—	X
2	Lukoil	Oil and gas	65	76	—	—	X
3	Rosneft Oil	Oil and gas	158	64	—	—	
4	TNK-BP Holding	Oil and gas	234	211	—	—	
5	Sberbank	Banking	310	172	—	—	
6	SeverStal	Materials	409	450	—	—	X
7	Surgutneftegas	Oil and gas	420	168	—	—	
8	Evraz Group	Metals	454	—	—	—	X
9	MMC Norilsk Nickel	Materials	—	241	—	—	
10	VTB Bank	Banking	—	505	—	—	
11	Tatneft	Oil and gas	—	548	—	—	
12	Transneft	Oil and gas	—	566	—	—	
13	Novolipetsk Steel	Materials	—	570	—	—	
14	Sistema JSFC	Telecom	—	679	—	—	
15	VimpelCom	Telecom	—	682	—	—	
16	Magnitogorsk Iron & Steel	Materials	—	899	—	—	
17	Mechel	Materials	—	1,077	—	—	
18	Novatek	Oil and gas	—	1,177	—	—	
19	Moscow Municipal Bank	Banking	—	1,297	—	—	

			[a]	[b]	[c]	[d]	[e]
20	RusHydro	Utilities	—	1,349	—	—	—
21	TMK	Materials	—	1,676	—	—	—
22	Bashneft	Oil and gas	—	1,708	—	—	—
23	Slavneft Megioneft	Oil and gas	—	1,731	—	—	—
24	Avtovaz	Consumer durables	—	1,802	—	—	—
25	PIK Group	Diversified financials	—	1,832	—	—	—
26	GAZ Group	Consumer durables	—	1,856	—	—	—
27	Polyus Gold	Materials	—	1,866	—	—	—
28	Rostelecom	Telecom	—	1,921	—	—	—
29	Uralkali	Chemicals	—	1,927	—	—	—
30	Sistema	Telecom and high technology	—	—	—	—	X
31	Basic Element (United Company Rusal)	Diversified	—	—	—	—	X

[a] Fortune (2009); [b] Forbes (2009); [c] *World Investment Report* (UNCTAD, 2008); [d] Transnationality Index: average of foreign assets to total assets, foreign sales to total sales, and foreign employment to total employment; [e] Boston Consulting Group (2009); X indicates inclusion in BCG's New Global Challengers list.

The group also encompasses the Gipronickel Institute, an R&D facility in Saint Petersburg, and Norilsk Process Technology, an R&D facility in Australia.

Suckoi, a producer of military jets since 1939, recently announced the launch of a regional jet to compete with Embraer's new line of regional jets for 80 to 120 passengers.

10.6 The internationalization of South African firms

10.6.1 South African industrialization and internationalization

The case of South Africa involves altogether different issues, since the country has a different and highly particular institutional context. Following English rule and apartheid, it is still struggling to stabilize its political regime and to integrate diverse cultures.

Its industrialization was based on the exploitation of natural resources, especially diamonds and gold. Cecil Rhodes' De Beers and the Anglo-American Corporation are the largest producers.

The riches created by these corporations stimulated industrialization in the early twentieth century.

But the rapid development of the English-controlled mineral economy did not result in major growth in Afrikaaner business. This contributed to the rise of the Nationalist government in 1948, which brought with it two profound changes in the South African economy. First, state-owned enterprises became a vehicle for Afrikaaner-focused economic development and, second, full-blown apartheid forcefully removed the non-white population to townships and homelands. [Therefore] two distinct economies developed in South Africa. Goldstein and Prichard (2009: 246).

The characteristics of South African firms are described by those authors as having:

- a rapid unbundling and reorganization of the conglomerates;
- strong ties with the European business community;
- a level of industrialization and business sophistication uncommon in countries with similar income levels;
- strong incentives for rapid international expansion, sanctions having been lifted at the end of the apartheid period.

10.6.2 South African multinationals

South African firms are ranked in the *Forbes* 2000 and also in UNCTAD's *World Investment Report*. The majority of listed companies belongs to natural resources-based industries and market operators providing services for the region (Table 10.7).

10.6.3 The paths of South African multinationals

Three South African MNEs are particularly important to analyze due their similarity and interrelationship with Brazilian cases: South African Brewery (SAB), AngloGold Ashanti, and Naspers.

   SAB is a South African enterprise that has expanded quickly in the last decade and that has added the Miller brand to its name following its acquisition of the Milwaukee brewery from the US in 2002. SAB has followed the strategy of acquiring local brands to add breweries in Europe, Asia, and the US to its operations.

   SABMiller competes with AB/InBev for the title of largest brewery in the world. Six of its brands are among the world's fifty largest beer brands. It is also one of the largest Coca-Cola bottlers. The group posted annual revenues of $21.4 billion in 2008. Recently, SABMiller hired Citibank and Goldman Sachs to negotiate the acquisition of Schincariol, a Brazilian brewery.

   Although beer accounts for 71 percent of its total sales volume, Schincariol expanded into soft drinks in its key stronghold in the northeast of Brazil. Having acquired Bavaria in Colombia in 2005, Schincariol could help SABMiller to improve its market share in Latin America.

   Anglogold Ashanti, headquartered in Johannesburg, South Africa, has twenty-one operations and a number of exploration programs in both the established and the new gold-producing regions of the world. It resulted from the 2004 merger of AngloGold (majority-owned by the Anglo American group from the UK) and the Ashanti Goldfields Corporation (the Ghana government having been the latter's controlling shareholder).

   In 2008, AngloGold Ashanti's operations produced 4.98 million ounces of gold, or some 7 percent of global production. This made it the third largest producer in the world. The bulk of its production came from deep underground mining (40%) and surface mining

Table 10.7 *South African multinationals in the international rankings*

	Company	Industry	Fortune 500 (2009)[a]	Forbes 2000 (2009)[b]	WIR (2008)[c]		BCG (2009)[e]
					TNI[d]	Foreign assets	
1	MTN Group	Telecom	—	382	65	60	—
2	Impala Platinum Holdings	Materials	—	772			—
3	Telkom	Telecom	—	786			—
4	Gold Fields	Metals	—	1,097	80	40	—
5	Bidvest Group	Conglomerates	—	1,102	83	96	—
6	Sanlam	Insurance	—	1,142			—
7	Remgro	Conglomerates	—	1,220			—
8	Naspers	Media	—	1,240	81	44	—
9	AngloGold Ashanti	Materials	—	1,408			—
10	Steinhoff Intl Holdings	Consumer durables	—	1,461	46	47	—
11	ARM–African Rainbow Minerals	Materials	—	1,664			—
12	RMB Holdings	Diversified financials	—	1,740			—
13	Shoprite Holdings	Food	—	1,749			—
14	Harmony Gold Mining	Materials	—	1,958			—

15	Sasol	Chemicals	—	—	—	82	22	—
16	Sappi	Wood and paper products	—	—	—	30	50	—
17	Barloworld	Diversified	—	—	—	68	83	—
18	Datatec	Electronics	—	—	—	6	93	—

[a] Fortune (2009); [b] Forbes (2009); [c] World Investment Report (UNCTAD, 2008); [d] Transnationality Index: average of foreign assets to total assets, foreign sales to total sales, and foreign employment to total employment; [e] Boston Consulting Group (2009); X indicates inclusion in BCG's New Global Challengers list.

(2%) in South Africa. The rest came from Ghana (11%), Mali (8%), Australia (9%), Brazil (8%), Tanzania (6%), the US (5%), Guinea (7%), Argentina (3%), and Namibia (1%). AngloGold Ashanti's global exploration program continued to gain momentum, either directly or in collaboration with exploration partnerships and joint ventures, in Colombia, the Democratic Republic of Congo (DRC), Australia, Russia, China, and the Philippines.

Naspers, a South African media enterprise, acquired the BuscaPé portal in a negotiation worth $342 million. The stake previously belonged to Great Hill Partners, an American investment fund that had acquired a majority stake in BuscaPé in 2005, and to other stakeholders that were individuals. The Brazilian website, whose core activity is to compare product prices in a wide range of segments, may keep its management team despite the acquisition. The South African's group strategy is to expand its operations around the world with a focus in Latin America. As part of its expansion strategy, the firm recently started operating Allegro, a European e-commerce platform, and bought Tradus, a European auction service. In Brazil, the firm owns part of the Editora Abril publishing house and of ComperanTime.

10.7 Diversity within the BRICS

The Goldman Sachs report, "Dreaming with BRIC(S)," by coining this acronym, created the impression that these countries were in some way similar. However, if on one hand they form the bloc of the large emerging economies, on the other they have evident historical, cultural, social, political, and factor endowment differences.

The first point that one must highlight is that "history matters." The internationalization process of enterprises from the BRICS is strongly linked to their individual histories. Back in 1979, China, as part of its attempt to recover its imperial position in the global economy, had already planned to have forty firms among the largest in the world. According to the latest *Fortune* ranking, it currently has twenty-six.

Russia, after overcoming the tough adjustment period that followed the demise of the communist system, is now attempting to maintain the political power that it enjoyed for more than thirty years after the second world war. The expansion and actions of its MNEs are influenced by political decisions that are part of a specific type of capitalism, i.e., oligarchic capitalism, which is strongly tied to the established powers.

India and South Africa, both of them former British colonies, have a different type of legacy as their starting point. India, as a result of its past, accommodated different ethnicities when it became free of British rule, but it did not pursue a nation project such as the Chinese one. Thus, the different ethnicities co-exist in a permanent state of tension, while the Indian state tries to intervene as little as possible in productive activities. In this context, the large family groups and their heads, the business maharajas, have conducted their strategies autonomously since the nineteenth century. Like the South African MNEs, their relationship with the UK is fundamental; it is no coincidence that the major investments made by Tata Steel, Tata Tea, and Tata Auto have targeted the UK. Meanwhile, the South African MNEs have also relocated their offices and core activities to the UK.

Brazil's history, as we have seen, is more recent. It was never an imperial power and Portugal, its colonizer, is a modest player on the world's economic scene. This is the first time Brazil has made an effort to stand out in the global order.

The emergence of these countries and the crises that have arisen since the 1980s among the developed nations have led to a resumption of the discussion about the different types of capitalism. The distinguishing features that set these apart from each other are the financial system, the industrial relations system, the educational system and the system of relations between firms. Amable's typology (2003) identified five types or models of capitalism: Asiatic, continental, market-based, Mediterranean, and social-democratic. Currently, the rise of the emerging countries has generated new questions and insights about this important issue.

The second point is that the BRICS' internationalization dynamics were different. Their opening to the world took place, in Brazil, in the 1950s; in China, in the 1990s; and in India, in the 2000s. As for South Africa, it is yet to become a priority investment destination.

In a way, Brazil pioneered the internationalization process among the BRICS, which enabled the other bloc members to learn from its mistakes. This, in turn, helped them to speed up their respective internationalization processes. Moreover, China and India elected cutting-edge industries that, under the government's auspices, develop and promote the vertical transfer of technology to other enterprises. The aerospace industry in China and the nuclear industry in India are examples of this. In Brazil, for a few years during the 1970s, both the aerospace and the nuclear sectors were prioritized. The latter was soon discontinued whereas in the aerospace sector the only surviving enterprise is Embraer.

The major MNEs started to establish operations in China in the 1980s, but in a gradual manner, controlled by the Chinese government. As for India, they started returning to it in the 1990s. In each of these countries, the rationale for entry was different. In China, for instance, the subsidiaries first focused on manufacturing, beginning to include R&D only more recently. In India, on the other hand, the MNEs set up subsidiaries centered on business process offshoring and gradually increased their R&D investments. Evidently, the profile of these operations is tied to the competitive advantages of each country. This includes both size and the characteristics of the local markets, each of which demands specific products and processes.

Nevertheless, the MNEs from developed countries operating in China and India still face many difficulties. A recent article in *The Economist* describes how hard some firms find it to do business in China, whose market still seems "impenetrable" (*The Economist*, October 17, 2009, p. 73). Certain Brazilian enterprises, such as WEG, Marcopolo, and Embraer, had previously reported this type of difficulty already. In the case of India, the complexity of its cultural, religious, and political context per se constitutes a barrier to the expansion of foreign MNEs.

Finally, the internationalization strategies of the firms from the RICS also differ from those of the Brazilian MNEs. Most Chinese MNEs have some sort of relation with institutions that belong to some sphere of government. A number of these MNEs seek those natural resources needed to guarantee their supply, whereas others, which can be described as local optimizers (Ramamurti and Singh, 2009), have become international as a result of the reengineering of niche products for the mass market, though they concurrently have sought to obtain intangible assets (knowhow and brands) to catch up with their competition.

As for the Indian enterprises, they have different types of internationalization strategies. However, in general, they invest mainly in developed countries, especially in Europe and more particularly in the UK, with which they have historical relations and where they can turn to a substantial base of Indian emigrants.

As for the internationalization of South African enterprises, less is known about it. Except for the cases of SAB and of the mining companies, their internationalization still seems incipient.

11 | *The long journey of emerging country multinationals*

Ithaca

As you set out for Ithaca
hope your road is a long one,
full of adventure, full of discovery.
Laistrygonians, Cyclops,
angry Poseidon – don't be afraid of them:
you'll never find things like that on your way
as long as you keep your thoughts raised high,
as long as a rare excitement
stirs your spirit and your body.
Laistrygonians, Cyclops,
wild Poseidon – you won't encounter them
unless you bring them along inside your soul,
unless your soul sets them up in front of you.
Hope your road is a long one.
May there be many summer mornings when,
with what pleasure, what joy,
you enter harbours you're seeing for the first time;
may you stop at Phoenician trading stations
to buy fine things,
mother of pearl and coral, amber and ebony,
sensual perfume of every kind –
as many sensual perfumes as you can;
and may you visit many Egyptian cities
to learn and go on learning from their scholars.
Keep Ithaca always in your mind.
Arriving there is what you're destined for.
But don't hurry the journey at all.
Better if it lasts for years,
so you're old by the time you reach the island,
wealthy with all you've gained on the way,
not expecting Ithaca to make you rich.

Ithaca gave you the marvelous journey.
Without her you wouldn't have set out.
She has nothing left to give you now.
And if you find her poor, Ithaca won't have fooled you.
Wise as you will have become, so full of experience,
you'll have understood by then what these Ithacas mean.

(Konstantin Kavafis)

11.1 Our journey in this book

The well-known poem by Konstantin Kavafis describes with rare beauty a journey through life. It is a poem that touches us deeply because it expresses an attitude that we value: learning from challenges and living each experience fully. This attitude might be extended to the organizations, in this case the companies from emerging countries, in their journeys toward internationalization. It can also be applied to our journey, in order to unveil this process.

The Brazilian development, in its various dimensions: economic, cultural, and socio-political, as well as the comparison with other Latin American and Asian (Japan, Korea) countries, have always been the subject of our studies – academic studies but also studies that support the development of public policy and actions of companies.

This book aims to understand the process of internationalization of Brazilian companies, having as a background the multinationals of developed countries (first-movers), of Japan (second-movers), and of emerging countries, which are forming the third wave of internationalization.

The analytical framework designed for previous studies (Fleury and Fleury, 2000) proved necessary but not sufficient to account for the phenomenon. In other words, we observed that to analyze the dynamics of multinational companies we must not only understand the relationship between the formation of competences in the company and the competition between companies, but also how the local environment (with its cultural, socio-political, and factor endowment components) influences the development of competences and the management style, at the firm level. We understand that organizational competences are primarily driven by the firm's competitive environment while management style is primarily influenced by the firm's national or local environment, comprising the socio-political and cultural dimensions, as well as the country's or region's factor endowment.

Thus, the analytical framework has been refined, incorporating new dimensions, whose theoretical roots are not only in the field of international business but also in international operations, international management, and competence-based competition. With this choice, it was possible to address, in an integrated manner, "why internationalize?" and "how to internationalize?", two issues that should not be analyzed independently. Using the analogies provided by Kavafis' verse, when the company has reasons to depart for Ithaca, it has to be certain of having the resources and competences "to buy fine things" at "Phoenician trading stations" and cope with Laistrygonians (a tribe of giant cannibals from ancient Greece), Cyclops (in Greek mythology, a member of a primordial race of giants, each with a single eye in the middle of its forehead), and wild Poseidon (the God of the sea and, as "Earth-Shaker," of earthquakes). But, above all, firms won't encounter them if they don't bring them along inside their souls (minds), unless their souls set them up in front of them.

During this journey, the analytical framework was better expressed and exemplified. Its construction, with the identification of core competences and management styles, was made by comparing the model with the empirical reality. In the initial presentation in Chapter 2, we focused the framework on three competences: manufacturing, product development, and marketing. In Chapter 5, we expanded this to nine competences, namely: planning, organizational, technological, production, marketing, human resources management, financial, customer relationship management, and supply chain management competences.

From empirical studies: survey and case studies, we observed how these competences contribute to the process of internationalization of companies. We also found that the human resources management competence has been the most deficient, a true "Achilles' heel." At the same time, we observed that new competences have started to emerge such as corporate social responsibility and environmental sustainability as a sine qua non condition for the strategy of international expansion. Besides the intrinsic value of these competences, they play a key role in overcoming the strong liability of foreignness, much stronger than that faced by early-movers.

The analytical framework is shown on the left side of Figure 11.1, while the right side shows the firm's competitive environment.

The left side of Figure 11.1 represents the influence of the local environment (national/local culture, socio-political infrastructure,

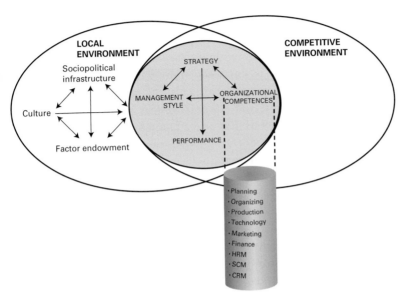

Figure 11.1 The enhanced analytical framework

and factor endowment) and can be understood as generator of the country's competitive advantages and disadvantages. Taken separately, each one of the dimensions has already been extensively used in studies about internationalization. Our contribution was to organize them so as to relate the economic plan, the plan where global industrial competition takes place, and the national or regional plan, where the characteristics related to the location are built. This systemic articulation homogenized the analysis in each country and facilitated the comparison among countries. It is the comparative analysis of the countries that proves to be fruitful to illustrate the usefulness of the framework.

The influence that environmental variables, specific to each country, exert in the development of management style is a known subject. What is new is how environmental variables and management style influence the development of organizational competences, and how both competences and management style are reflected in the processes of internationalization.

In the international action of the Chinese companies, for example, the issue of asset seeking is more important than for Brazilian companies. Since the timing is crucial for Chinese companies to catch up in terms of competences, and there is governmental support, "aggressively setting out on shopping," as formerly mentioned, is justifiable. In the case of Indian multinationals, they are positioning themselves in an outstanding way in knowledge-intensive industries, for having developed distinctive competences. This has occurred in function of the historical, religious, and cultural context that prizes education. In the case of Brazil, as well as other Latin American countries, the "embeddedness factor" nurtured other types of competences that became drivers of their internationalization paths.

As already noted by Ramamurti and Singh (2009: 407), for multinationals from emerging countries, the competences of greater strategic value are, in general, those related to production and operational excellence. However, in the analysis of Brazilian multinationals it became evident that it is necessary to elaborate further to understand how organizational competences justify the movement toward internationalization. There are two points to be stressed in that respect. First, operational excellence must be considered as a "qualifier" for internationalization (a competence that qualifies the company to become international) but not an "order winner." Second, operational excellence might have different meanings because it is developed in the sphere of different industries as, for example, Brazil focused on natural resources-based industries and India focused on knowledge intensive industries.

This point can be extended to companies other than the multinationals from emerging countries. Elaborating on the lessons from the field, the Massechussets Institute of Technology (MIT) Industrial Performance Center's five-year study of 500 international companies suggests that firms "Select on unique capabilities [competences], not industries" (Berger, 2005: 254). In other words, perhaps, the framework we designed for emerging multinationals can be extended to multinationals from developed countries as well.

11.2 The limits of the wave metaphor: dynamic interaction instead of sequential initiatives

Throughout the book we used the image of waves as a metaphor for the internationalization of firms from different regions and countries. However, the analyses that were presented reveal a more complex pattern where there is a dynamic interrelationship and a continuous reconfiguration of multinationals from the first, second, and third waves.

The subsidiaries of multinationals originated in the first and second waves deeply influenced the development of the multinationals from the emerging countries. For the latter, the Japanese case, presented in Chapter 4, was particularly relevant. During the period of reconstruction and catch-up, Japan showed great consistency in the treatment of variables of the national environment (culture, socio-political infrastructure, and factor endowment) with the development of dynamic organizational competences and a management style of its own.

The demonstration effect of the Japanese case was important not only to Brazil but also to other emerging countries: it broke the hegemony enjoyed by models and practices emanated from the first world, especially the US, and it opened the mindset of the then third world to the need of developing competences according to local circumstances and finding the most appropriate models of management.

The impact of the Japanese case was not lower for developed countries, which already held strong positions in the international context, being the role-model from which management models were reconsidered during the so-called period of productive restructuring.

The change that occurred from the 1990s, in emerging countries, is associated with a combination of a series of crisis, internal and external, that overturned presuppositions about development models leading the countries to productive restructuring and effective insertion into the global economy. The disruption with previous standards required a self-knowledge effort and restructuring at both macro and micro level. The development of a new profile of corporate competences and of management style was necessary as soon as the conditions of protection were withdrawn. The companies found out that they had to develop their own organizational models, with a degree of intelligent copying and imitation, that were convenient.

However, it is fundamental to recognize that the rise of emerging country multinationals is influencing the paths of developed country multinationals, and vice-versa.

11.3 Incumbents and emerging country multinationals compete in different lanes

The purchase of the division of IBM Personal Computers by Lenovo is the most paradigmatic case. The purchase of Jaguar by Tata reinforces the point. The presence of Embraer as the third largest aircraft manufacturer in the world is also surprising. But apart from a few other high profile cases, such as Li & Fung, admittedly a global network orchestrator (Fung *et al.*, 2008), the list of other multinationals from emerging countries is not surprising, at least so far, when considering spaces opened by multinationals from emerging countries.

There is a controversy about the competitiveness of multinationals from emerging countries in relation to the competitiveness of companies from developed countries. For us, this is a false controversy since early-movers and late-movers compete in separate lanes.

Table 11.1 has been put together from the tables presented in Chapters 7, 9, and 10; those with the greatest international presence, according to the indicators of the Boston Consulting Group, UNCTAD's *World Investment Report*, and the Columbia Program on International Investment, were favored.

Table 11.1 shows the large concentration of multinationals from emerging countries in the base industries still associated with a particular stage of economic and social development of countries. With the exception of India, which for historical and cultural reasons focused on industries related to information society, the other countries show strength in resource-intensive industries, rather than knowledge-intensive.

In general, there are few emerging multinational companies in downstream positions, linked directly to the buyers in international markets or even sectors considered as high-tech, though we do not totally agree with what is implicit in this designation. Exceptions to this rule are the multilatinas in their regional operations in Latin America and, again, Li & Fung, probably one of the most innovative companies as a network orchestrator in various global production networks (Fung *et al.*, 2008).

What this table does not reveal is the position of early-movers. The effects of productive restructuring and the advent of the information society and knowledge economy changed the profile of activities of the early-movers, which, as noted earlier, began to prioritize the knowledge-intensive activities that gave them command of global production chains. No multinational from an emerging country with the characteristics of a Google or Microsoft has emerged as of yet.

We observe, therefore, two trends: the block of traditional multinationals moving downstream, seeking for the direct relationship with markets and knowledge-intensive activities, and the new multinationals

Table 11.1 *Map of emerging country multinationals according to industry (partial)*

	Brazil	China	India	Russia	South Africa	Others
Retail		Li & Fung				Elektra, Ripley, Falabela
Services – engineering	Odebrecht, Camargo Correa, others	CSCE				
Services – food	Fogo de chão					Bimbo, Gruma
Telecom – Operators		China Mobile	Bharti, Airtel	MTS		América Movil
– Equipment		Huawei	Several	Sistema		
BPO/IT	Stefanini		Several		Dimension Data	
Pharmaceuticals						
Integrators: aircraft	Embraer	China Aviation Industry Corporation (Avic)		Sukhoi		
Durable white goods		Haier, Gree				
Durable goods: comp		Lenovo Acer	Hindalco			
Semiconductors		Taiwan Semi United Micro				
Durable goods: auto	Marcopolo	SAIC, Effa, Cherry	Tata, Marutti			Malaysia

Table 11.1 (*cont.*)

	Brazil	China	India	Russia	South Africa	Others
Durable goods electro	(Gradiente)	TCL, Haier, Galanz				
Autoparts	Sabo	Wangxiang		Alfa (Nemak)		Arcor, 4 Mexican
Consumer goods	AmBev		Tata Tea		SABMiller	
Capital goods	Romi	Nr 1, Dalian	Larsen & Toubro			
Electric goods	WEG	Johnson				
Steel	CSN, Gerdau	Baosteel	Tata Steel	Severstal		Techint
Agribusiness	JBS-Friboi, Brazil Foods					
Resources based	Votorantim, Magnesita		Aditya Birla	Evraz	Sappi	Cemex
Mining	Vale			Norilsk	AngloAmerican Ashanti	
Petrochemicals	Braskem	Sinochem, Formosa				Mexichem
Oil and gas	Petrobras	Sinopec, CNPC, others	Oil & Gas Reliance, others	Lukoil Gazprom, others		Every other country

from emerging countries creating another block upstream, focusing on resource-intensive activities. Any guess on who may exercise the governance of production systems and exercise command positions in decisions of international scope would be pretentious and risky. If, on one hand, the choice of the first multinationals fits a trend that has been observed since the beginning of industrialization, on the other hand, the issue of access to natural resources and the resolution of global problems related to environmental sustainability will become increasingly dependent on the practice of emerging countries and their companies. Interestingly, the MIT Industrial Performance Center's five-year study of 500 international companies also finds a similar lesson from the field. Reviewing a position taken twenty years ago in the report "Made in America", Berger (2005: 255) suggests that "there are no Sunset Industries."

11.4 Emerging country multinationals: integrating different approaches

In Chapter 5, we mentioned two approaches that have been presented in the study of multinationals from emerging countries: Matthews (2006) and Ramamurti and Singh (2009). It is important to evaluate how they could assist and advance in the analysis of the cases presented.

It is appropriate to ask if the analytical framework proposed by Matthews (2006) to study the "dragon multinationals" (the most successful multinationals from the Asian countries) explains the development of Brazilian multinationals. The answer is: in a few cases.

Matthews suggests that the mechanisms mostly used in internationalization would be linking, leveraging, and learning. Undoubtedly, the latter is always relevant. But linking and leveraging, which can be very important for Asian companies due to cultural and social factors, do not stand out in the repertoire of Brazilian companies. The same author states that the movement of the dragon multinationals is fast, involving innovative management models and relying on innovative products. In the case of Brazilian companies, we can argue that the management model should be considered a local innovation, that is, it is the optimal model for local circumstances; it is not necessarily innovative for the cases of companies of any other nations. They induce the Brazilian companies to adopt the strategy of active waiting and to move cautiously due to possible consequences of wrong decisions. It is different from the behavior of Chinese companies which, as we saw, by operating in a different environment, was more aggressive. Besides, as the core competency of Brazilian companies consists of operational excellence, the search for innovative products is not a general practice. Among the Brazilian multinationals, those that have more similarities with the dragon multinationals are Embraer and Ambev. It is also hard to predict that emerging multinationals from different emerging countries will develop similar international management models.

We can still find common ground between Brazilian multinationals and the typology of generic strategies proposed by Ramamurti and Singh (2009: 417). From the five types of internationalization strategy pictured by the authors, three are observed in Brazilian multinationals: global consolidators, local optimizers, and global first-movers. Brazil has neither natural-resource vertical integrators nor low-cost partners. However, it has global value chain climbers.

The global consolidators strategy is illustrated by cases like Vale, Petrobras, AmBev, and Gerdau. They operate in mature industries and their internationalization strategies are based on horizontal acquisitions. Petrobras is revealing a strategy that is different from the majority of its global competitors in the oil and gas industry, so far. The case of AmBev reveals that AB InBev's growth in the global markets is dependent on AmBev's management model and its operational know-how because that is the key factor for expansion in the emerging economies, the only ones in which demand is rising. Finally, Gerdau can be considered a regional consolidator more than a global one to the extent that it focuses its activities on American construction markets only.

Tigre and IBOPE illustrate the strategy of the local optimizers. They are companies that look for regional leadership in markets with regional characteristics. Their positions seem to be sustainable despite threats from other companies from Latin American countries.

Embraer and Marcopolo are representative of global first-movers. They are companies that develop products that are appropriate for local markets and then take them to international markets. Their internationalization strategies are based on a significant number of partnerships, although these two cases are distinct when their products/markets and management models are considered.

Finally, there are various companies that should be considered as global value chain climbers. These are companies that actively participate in the dynamic relationships among companies that operate within global production networks (GPNs). Their processes of internationalization aim to guarantee and extend the scope of their participation in these GPNs and they seek to assume activities where there is greater added value. Among the companies mentioned in the case studies are WEG, Coteminas, and Sabo.

In summary, the proposals by Mathews and Ramamurti and Singh are based on the characteristics of the internationalization process of successful companies. While Mathews seeks common traits, Ramamuti and Singh seek to work with diversity. Our analysis seeks to lay the foundations of diversity and, in this sense, aligns with the second approach. Once more, our findings are not different from the MIT Industrial Performance Center's five-year study of 500 international companies: "many models of success, no silver bullets: we were struck by the diversity of the strategies and capabilities [competences] that companies employed to build profitable and innovative businesses" (Berger, 2005: 251).

11.5 The challenge of the development of international management models

Since the process of internationalization of companies from emerging countries is recent, there are few studies on how they organize their international operations. Studies on internationalization of companies from emerging countries usually focus on the decision to internationalize and on the entry mode. The studies on how they organize the network of subsidiaries look at individual cases in general. In this sense, the survey seeking to understand strategies and competences of Brazilian multinationals was an original contribution of this book.

The framework utilized to discuss headquarters–subsidiary relationships, based on six dimensions, led to a preliminary characterization of a pattern of international management of Brazilian companies, as a possible indication of how multinationals from other emerging countries may be dealing with the issue.

The results of the survey show that, in general, the trend of Brazilian multinationals is to live with different management styles, acknowledging diversity. In principle, this pattern was not new and has already been characterized as a metanational model. But what makes the case of Brazilian multinationals specific is that, in the metanational model, the parent company has legitimacy for being located in a developed country; hence, the headquarters grants initiative of the subsidiary. In the case of Brazilian companies, the legitimacy is questioned and the liability of origin is much more pronounced. The solution that has been adopted is the establishment of an ambiguous relationship in which the headquarters admits to be controlling the activities of the subsidiary but accepts its initiatives without further questioning.

This pattern is consistent with the traits of the Brazilian management model, developed in the context of Brazilian culture, especially over the past twenty years, depending on the incentives and disincentives of the industrial and economic policy, changes in business environment, and new features of international competition.

If, in this way, the operational flexibility of the network of subsidiaries is ensured, the utilization of synergies in the development of competences is impaired. There is a strong impression of the managers of subsidiaries of Brazilian multinationals that they have non-local competences more developed than the headquarters, which have not been examined.

These traits allow us to suggest a first draft of the Brazilian model of international management. This is clearly a model in development based on the first steps of a heterogeneous group of companies in different international trajectories. But it already allows some differentiation with the trajectories of internationalization of multinationals from other countries, whether from developed or emerging countries.

11.6 Poseidon, the crisis, and the sustainability of internationalization

The financial crisis of 2008 and the slower growth in advanced economies, in stark contrast to the rapid expansion of Brazil, Russia, India, and China (the BRICs) and other developing economies are generating different metaphors: flat world, spiky world and even upside-down world. Those who advocate the latter admit that emerging and developing economies will not only become dominant in world exports in a few years, or (via purchasing power parity) outweigh advanced economies; their companies will become major actors in the global economy, challenging the incumbents that dominated the international scene in the twentieth century.

The global financial crisis that was established from 2008 affected differently the emerging countries, their companies, and their internationalization processes. Initially, the country that was most affected by the crisis of 2008 was China, which experienced a strong retraction in demand seen in developed countries, especially in the US, and the shrinking of offshoring strategies. The rapid and efficient work of the Chinese government seems to have reversed this situation. At the same time, the Chinese government announced that it would "use its reserves to expand and support the acquisition of companies abroad by Chinese companies to accelerate the exit strategies and exchange currencies and short-term financial assets by long-term corporate assets" (OESP, July 22, 2009, B1). Indeed, taking advantage of the crisis and of the reduction in the value of assets in developed countries, Chinese companies began to make acquisitions, especially in the sectors of oil and gas and natural resources. North America was a priority target.

For India, the global economic crisis has made Indian firms wary of further expansion abroad. "Indian FDI [foreign direct investment] outflows, which rose to a historic level of nearly $18 billion in 2007, fell by 6% in 2008 to under $17 billion. Consequently Indian Multinationals tread cautiously" (Pradhan, 2009: 1).

From a macro point of view, Brazil is doing well in the current crisis. The best indicator, perhaps, is the substantial increase in the inward FDI, which led the government to introduce a fee to discourage foreign investors in October 2009. Data on outward FDI showed a downward trend in early 2009. But, at the same time, Ernst & Young (2009) announced that the major Brazilian companies have improved their position in the ranking of the 300 largest companies on the planet and were those that had a higher market valuation in the first half of 2009. In the second half, acquisitions of JBS-Friboi and Vale reversed the downward trend of outward FDI. At the same time, the internationalization of small and medium companies is speeding up, especially in the service sector.

Some Brazilian multinationals are taking advantage of the moment of crisis to streamline their international networks, to focus simultaneously on growth and cost reduction. For example,

Marcopolo decided to permanently close its subsidiary in Portugal, which, according to its chairman, "never performed satisfactorily." Marcopolo also gave up on one of two plant projects in Russia in light of problems in the Russian economy because of the financial crisis. But it established a joint venture for a new factory in Egypt. Vale has changed its acquisition strategy, looking for companies that can add knowledge to the business, and strengthening its logistics structure to optimize its new business strategy of direct selling. AmBev, in its trajectory tied to Inbev in 2004 and to Annheuser Busch in 2008, is disposing of subsidiaries in developed countries to focus on growth in emerging countries. Votorantim, both in cement and metals, is expanding considerably its operations in the South and North American markets.

The only Brazilian multinational that suffered due to the crisis was Sadia, which had to propose a merger with its main competitor, Perdigao, with support from Brazil's development bank, BNDES. With this merger, it created Brazil Foods, the largest processed food company in Brazil, the tenth largest in the Americas, number one in the world in poultry processing, and the third largest Brazilian exporter.

There is a consensus among managers and analysts that in the process of internationalization the main bottleneck lies in people, people who have an international mindset and entrepreneurship, or individual international business competence, and that the greatest challenges for sustainable international expansion are in the areas of personnel management, industrial relations, and corporate social responsibility.

If the political and economic changes of the 1990s have changed the pattern of external insertion of the country and redefined its bases and its international interests, this did not occur in a linear and homogeneous way. In contrast, strategies and actions lived side by side, sometimes contradictory, both in governmental and private spheres. As the internationalization progresses, the country must be prepared for increasingly stronger resistance that it will face in relationships and investments with more advanced countries. The liability of foreignness will become increasingly pronounced.

But unlike the other cycles of international insertion of Brazil, the current is, by its very nature, broader and multifaceted and not limited to adjustments of foreign policy. It involves new actors and forums within and outside the country and it involves redefinitions of strategies and international alliances. Brazil is facing a huge challenge: to fully incorporate international variables in the equation of national development and redesign, consistently and creatively, the role it expects to play in the world in coming decades.

References

Abernathy, William and Utterback, James (1975). Dynamic model of process and product innovation. *Omega*, **3** (6): 639–657.

Almeida, André (2007). *Internacionalização de empresas brasileiras: perspectivas e riscos*. Rio de Janeiro: Elsevier.

Almeida, Paulo Roberto (2007). As relações internacionais do Brasil dos anos 1950 a 1980. *Revista Brasileira de Política Internacional*, **50** (2): 60–79.

Amable, Bruno (2003). *The diversity of modern capitalism*. Oxford: Oxford University Press.

América Economia (2009). Ranking: multilatinas – as mais globais da América Latina (www.americaeconomia.com.br).

Amsden, Alice (1989). *Asia's next giant: South Korea and late industrialization*. Oxford: Oxford University Press.

Aoki, Masahiko (1990). Toward an economic model of the Japanese firm. *Journal of Economics Literature*, (March): 1–27.

(2007). Whither Japan's corporate governance? In Masahiko Aoki, G. Jackson, and H. Miyajima (eds.): *Corporate governance in Japan: institutional change and organizational diversity*. Oxford: Oxford University Press.

Aulakh, Preet S. (2006). Global strategies of Brazilian firms in an era of economic liberalization. In Subhash C. Jain (ed.): *Emerging economies and the transformation of international business*. Cheltenham, UK: Edward Elgar.

Aykut, Dilek and Goldstein, Andrea (2008). Multinacionais de países em desenvolvimento: o investimento sul-sul chega a maioridade. *Revista Brasileira de Comércio Exterior*, 95: 66–89.

Barreto, A. and Rocha, Ângela (2003). Porque as empresas brasileiras não se internacionalizam? In Angela Rocha (ed.): *As novas fronteiras: a multinacionalização das empresas brasileiras*. Rio de Janeiro: Mauad Editora.

Barros, Betania T. and Prates, Marco A. (1996). *O estilo brasileiro de administrar*. Sao Paulo: Editora Atlas.

Bartlett, Christopher and Ghoshal, Sumantra (1998). *Managing across borders: the transnational solution* (2nd edn). Harvard Business School Press.

—— (2000). Going global: lessons from late-movers. *Harvard Business Review*, March–April: 132–142.

Bartlett, Christopher, Ghoshal, Sumantra, and Beamish, Paul (2008). *Transnational management: text, cases and readings in cross–border management*. Boston: McGraw-Hill.

Bartlett, Christopher and Wozny, Meg (2005). GE's two-decade transformation: Jack Welch's leadership. Harvard Business School, Case 399–150.

Baumann, Renato (1996). *O Brasil e a economia global*. Rio de Janeiro: Campus.

Beamish, Paul, Delios, Andrew and Makino, Shige (2001). *Japanese subsidiaries in the new global economy*. Cheltenham: Edward Elgar.

Bell, David E. and Ross, Catherine (2008). *JBS Swift & Co*. Harvard Business School N9–509–021, December 12: 21.

Berger, Suzane (2005). *How we compete: what companies around the world are doing to make it in today's global economy*. New York: Currency-Doubleday.

Best, Michael (1990). *The new competition*. Cambridge, UK: Polity Press.

Bielschowsky, Ricardo (1978). Notas sobre a questão da autonomia tecnológica na indústria brasileira. In Wilson Suzigan (ed.): *Industria: políticas, instituições e desenvolvimento*. Rio de Janeiro, Instituto de Pesquisas Econômicas Avançadas (IPEA), Monografia No. 28, 99–136.

Birkinshaw, Julian and Hood, Niel (1998). Multinational subsidiary evolution: capability and charter change in foreign-owned subsidiaries companies. *Academy of Management Review*, **23** (4): 773–795.

Birkinshaw, Julian and Morrison, Allen J. (1995). Configuration of strategy and structure in subsidiaries of multinational corporations. *Journal of International Business Studies*, Fourth Quarter: 729–753.

Birkinshaw, Julian, Hood, Niel, and Jonsson, Stefan (1998). Building firm-specific advantages in multinational corporations: the role of subsidiary initiative. *Strategic Management Journal*, **19** (3): 221–241.

Blomstermo, Anders and Sharma, D. Deo (2003). Three decades of research on the internationalization process of firms. In Anders Blomstermo and D. Deo Sharma (eds.): *Learning in the internationalisation process of firms*. Cheltenham, UK: Edward Elgar.

BNDES (1995). Caracterização do processo de internacionalização de grupos econômicos privados brasileiros. Rio de Janeiro, November (Série Pesquisas Empresariais, 1).

(2002). Desestatização e Reestruturação, 1990–2002. Relatório BNDES, July. (www.bndes.gov.br/publicacoes.)

Bonelli, Regis (1997). *O Brasil na virada do milênio: trajetória de crescimento e desafios do desenvolvimento*. Rio de Janiero: IPEA, June, 2 vols.

(2000). *Fusões e aquisições no Mercosul*. Rio de Janeiro: IPEA, Discussion paper no. 718.

Borini, Felipe (2008). Transferencia, desenvolvimento e reconhecimento de competencias organizacionais em subsidiarias estrangeiras de empresas multinacionais brasileiras. PhD dissertation, School of Economics Business Administration, Universidade de São Paulo, p. 179.

Borini, Felipe, Fleury, Maria T. L., Fleury, Afonso, and Oliveira Jr., Moacir M. (2009). The relevance of subsidiary initiatives for Brazilian multinationals. *Revista de Administração de Empresas*, July–September, 49 (3): 253–265.

Boston Consulting Group (BCG) (2005–9). *The BCG 100 new global challengers*.

Bruche, Gert (2009). A new geography of innovation – China and India rising. Vale Columbia Center on Sustainable International Investment, *Columbia FDI Perspectives*, (April 29).

Buckley, Peter and Casson, Mark (1976). *The future of multinational enterprise*. London: Macmillan.

Caldas, Miguel (2006). Conceptualizing Brazilian multiple and fluid cultural profiles. *Management Research*, 4 (3): 169–180.

Capelli, Peter (2009). The future of the US business model and the rise of competitors. *Academy of Management Perspectives*, May: 5–10.

Cardenas, Enrique, Thorp, Rosemary, and Ocampo, Jose A. (2001). *The economic history of 20th century Latin America: the export Age*. Basingstoke, UK: Palgrave-Macmillan.

Carvalho, Ruy Q., Fleury, Afonso, and Fleury, Maria T. L. (1996). *O papel das subsidiárias japonesas no processo de desenvolvimento tecnológico da indústria brasileira*. Revista de Administração da Universidade de São Paulo (RAUSP), (31) 3: 19–27.

Central Intelligence Agency (CIA). The world factbook. (www.cia.gov/library/publications/the-world-factbook/.)

Chandler, Alfred (1962). *Strategy and structure: chapters in the history of the American industrial enterprise*. Cambridge, Mass: MIT Press.

Chang, Ha-Joon (2002). *Kicking away the ladder: development strategy in historical perspective*. London: Anthem Press.

Chang, Sea-Jin (2003). *Financial crisis and the transformation of Korean business groups*. Cambridge: Cambridge University Press.

Chang, Sea-Jin and Delios, A. (2006). Competitive interactions between global competitors: the entry behavior of Korean and Japanese multinational firms. Conference, Japan Center for Economic Research, Tokyo, June.

Chesnais, François (1995). *A mundialização do capital*. São Paulo, Editora Xamã.

Child, John (2005). *Organization: contemporary principles and practice*. Oxford: Blackwell Publishing.

Child, John and Rodrigues, Suzana B. (2005). The internationalization of Chinese firms: a case for theoretical extension? *Management and Organization Review*, 1 (3): 381–410.

Child, John and Tse, David K. (2001). China's transitions and its implications to international business. *Journal of International Business Studies*, p. 32.

Chong, L. C. and Agrawal, N. M. (eds.) (in press). *Globalisation and Indian management: environmental change and management transition in modern India*.

Chu, Rebeca A. and Wood Jr., Thomas (2008). Cultura organizacional brasileira pós-globalização: global ou local? *Revista de Administração Pública*, 42 (5): 969–991.

Chudnovski, Daniel and Lopez, Andrés (1999a). A third wave of FDI from developing countries: Latin American multinationals in the 1990s. Buenos Aires: Centro de Investigaciones para la Transformación (CENIT), August, p. 34.

(1999b). *As multinacionais Latino-Americanas: Evolução e perspectivas de empresas da Argentina, Brasil, Chile e México*. Rio de Janeiro: Revista Brasileira de Comércio Exterior (RBCE).

Chung, W. (2001). Identifying technology transfer in foreign direct investment: influence of industry conditions and investing firm motives. *Journal of International Business Studies*, 32 (2): 211–229.

Cleveland, Gary, Schroeder, Roger, and Anderson, John (1989). A theory of production competence. *Decision Sciences*, 20: 655–668.

Cole, Robert (1989). *Strategies for learning*. Berkeley: University of California Press.

Collinson, Simon and Rugman, Alan (2008). The regional nature of Japanese multinational business. *Journal of International Business Studies*, 39 (2): 215–230.

Commission Economica para America Latina (CEPAL) (2005). *La inversion estrangera en America Latina y el Caribe*. Santiago de Chile: CEPAL.

Coriat, Benjamin (1993). *Made in France*. Paris: Librairie Générale Française.

Coutinho, Luciano, Hiratuka, Celio, and Sabatini, Rodrigo (2008). O investimento direto no exterior como alavanca dinamizadora da economia brasileira. In Octavio de Barros and Fabio Giambiagi (eds.): *Brasil Globalizado*. Rio de Janeiro: Editora Campus.

Cuervo-Cazurra, Alvaro (2007). Sequence of value-added activities in the internationalization of developing country MNEs. *Journal of International Management*, **13**, 258–277.

(2008). The multinationalization of developing country MNEs: the case of multilatinas. *Journal of International Management*, **14**, 138–154.

Cyert, Richard and March, James (1963). *A behavioral theory of the firm*. New Jersey: Prentice-Hall.

Dahlman, Carl and Frischtak, Cláudio (1993). National systems supporting technical advance in industry: the Brazilian experience. In R. Nelson (ed.): *National innovation systems*. Oxford: Oxford University Press, 414–450.

Dean, Warren (2001). *A industrialização de São Paulo: 1880–1945*. São Paulo: Editora Bertrand Brasil.

Deloitte Consulting (2004). Changing China: will Chinese technology standards reshape your industry? Report Technology, Media and Telecommunications, p. 11.

De Marchi, Frederico (2005). *A logística, o caos e as formigas*. (www.empresario.com.br/artigos/artigos_html/artigo_310503.html.)

Dertouzos, Michael L., Lester, Richard K., and Solow, Robert (1989). *Made in America: regaining the productive edge*. New Baskerville: MIT Press.

Desai, Ashok (1984). Achievements and limitations of India's technological capability. In Martin Fransman and Keneth King (eds.): *Technological capability in the third world*. London: Macmillan.

Dicken, Peter (1992). *Globalshift: industrial change in a turbulent world*. London: Harper and Row.

Doz, Yves and Hamel, Gary (1998). *Alliance advantage: the art of creating value through partnerships*. Harvard Business School Press.

Doz, Yves, Santos, Joe and Williamson, Peter (2001). *From global to metanational: how companies win in the knowledge economy*. Boston: Harvard University Press.

Dunning, John H. (1980). Toward an eclectic paradigm of international production: some empirical tests. *Journal of International Business Studies*, **11** (1): 9–31.

(1993). *Multinational enterprises and the global economy*. Wokingham, UK: Addison-Wesley.

Dunning, John H. and Lundan, S. M. (2008). *Multinational enterprises and the global economy* (2nd edn). Cheltenham, UK: Edward Elgar.

Durand, Thomas (1998). Forms of incompetence. Paper presented at the fourth international conference on competence-based management, Norwegian School of Management, Oslo.

Economic Commission to Latin America and the Caribbean (ECLAC) (2000). *Foreign investment in Latin America and the Caribbean 1999*. Santiago, Chile: United Nations.

(2008). *Foreign investment in Latin America and the Caribbean 2007*. Santiago, Chile: United Nations.

Edmund, John (2007). National financial systems in Latin America: attributes, credit allocation practices and their impact on enterprise development. In Robert Grosse and Luiz F. Mesquita (eds.): *Can Latin American firms compete?* Oxford: Oxford University Press.

Egelhoff, William (1988). Strategy and structure in multinational corporations: a revision of the Stopford and Wells model. *Strategic Management Journal*, 9: 1–14.

Eisenhardt, Kathleen and Sull, Donald (2001). Strategy as simple rules. *Harvard Business Review*, January: 106–116.

Engardio, Pete (2006). The future of outsourcing. *Business Week*, January 30.

Ernst & Young (2009). Market capitalization 2006 to 2009: the top 300 companies worldwide. An international comparison. June 30. (www.ey.com/BR/pt/Issues/Top_100_-_Estudo_EY).

Evans, Peter (1976). Foreign investment and the transformation of Brazilian industry. *Journal of Development Economics*, 3 (4): 119–139.

Ferdows, Kasra (1997). Making the most of foreign factories. *Harvard Business Review*, March: 73–88.

(1998). Made in the world: the global spread of production. *Production and Operations Management*, 6 (2): 102–109.

Ferraz, João C., Kupfer, David and Haguenauer, Lia (1996). *Made in Brazil: desafios competitivos para a indústria*. Rio de Janeiro: Editora Campus.

Ferraz, João C., Kupfer, David, and Serrano, Franklin (1999). Macro/micro interactions: economic and institutional uncertainties and structural change in the Brazilian industry. *Oxford Development Studies*, 27 (3): 279–304.

Fleury, Afonso (1989). The technological behaviour of Brazilian state-owned enterprises. In Jeffrey James (ed.): *The technological behaviour of public enterprises in developing countries*. London: Routledge.

(1999). The changing pattern of operations management in developing countries: the case of Brazil. *International Journal of Operations and Production Management*, 19 (5/6): 565–581.

Fleury, Maria T. L. (1986). O simbólico nas relações de trabalho: um estudo sobre relações de trabalho na empresa estatal. Thesis, School of Economics and Business Administration, University of São Paulo, p. 237.

Fleury, Afonso and Fleury, Maria T. L. (1995). *Aprendizagem e inovação organizacional: as experiências de Japão, Coréia e Brasil.* São Paulo: Editora Atlas.

(2000). *Estratégias empresariais e formação de competências.* São Paulo: Editora Atlas.

(2005). Competitiveness, competences and corporate strategies: Brazil and China catching-up in the global economy. Paper submitted to the Third International Workshop "Globalization and Corporate Strategies for the XXI Century: The Brazilian Innovation Challenge." Rio de Janeiro: BNDES, November 2007, p. 20.

(2007). The evolution of production systems and conceptual frameworks. *Journal of Manufacturing Technology Management,* **18** (8): 949–965.

Fleury, Afonso and Humphrey, John (1993). *Human resources and the diffusion and adaptation of new quality methods in Brazilian manufacturing.* Brighton: Institute of Development Studies, Research Report no. 24.

Forbes (2007, 2008). *The Forbes global 2000.* (www.forbes.com/2009/04/08/worlds-largest-companies-business-global-09-global_land.html.)

Fortanier, Fabienne and vanTulder, Rob (2007). Internationalization strategies of multinational enterprises: 1990–2004. Paper presented at the Internationalization of Indian and Chinese firms conference, Brunel Business School, April 18–19.

Fortune (2008; 2009). *The top 500 global companies.* (money.cnn.com/magazines/fortune/global500/2009/.)

Fransman, Martin (1984). Technological capability in the third world: an overview. In M. Fransman and K. King (eds.): *Technological capability in the third world.* London: Macmillan.

Freeman, Christopher, Clark, John, and Soete, Luc (1982). *Unemployment and technical innovation.* London: Francis Pinter.

Frischtak, C. (2008) O Brasil diante da nova competição global: as empresas brasileiras como vetores internacionais de investimento. Paper presented at the XX Forum Nacional, BNDES, Rio de Janeiro, 28 May.

Fruin, W. Mark (1992). *The Japanese enterprise system: competitive strategies and cooperative structures.* New York: Oxford University Press.

Fundação Dom Cabral (FDC) (2006–9). Ranking das transnacionais brasileiras. (www.fdc.org.br/pt/pesquisa/internacionalizacao/Paginas/publicacoes.aspx.)

Fung, Victor, Fung William K., and Wind Yoram, Jerry (2008). *Competing in a flat world: building enterprises for a borderless world.* Upper Saddle River, New Jersey: Wharton School Publishing.

Furtado, Celso (1999). *Formação Econômica do Brasil*. São Paulo: Companhia Editora Nacional.

Garcez, Mauro and Vasconcellos, Eduardo (2008). Estratégia tecnológica e a internacionalização da braskem – empresa líder no setor petroquímico. In Eduardo Vasconcellos (ed.): *Internacionalização competitiva*. São Paulo: Editora Atlas.

Gereffi, Gary (1994). Capitalism, development and global commodity chains. In Leslie Sklair (ed.): *Capitalism and development*. London: Routledge.

Gereffi, Gary, Humphrey, John, and Sturgeon, Timothy (2005). The governance of global value chains. *Review of International Political Economy*, 12 (1): 78–104.

Ghemawat, Pankaj (2001). Distance still matters: the hard reality of global expansion. *Harvard Business Review*, September.

Ghoshal, Sumantra and Bartlett, Christopher (1997). *The individualized corporation*. New York: Harper-Collins.

Ghoshal, Sumantra, Piramal, Gita, and Bartlett, Christopher (2005). Radical performance improvement is possible. In Julian Birkinshaw and Gita Piramal (eds.): *Sumantra Ghoshall on management*. King's Lynn, UK: Prentice-Hall.

Giambiagi, Fabio and Villela, Andre (2005). *Economia Brasileira Contemporânea*. São Paulo: Editora Campus.

Goldstein, Andréa (2007). *Multinational companies from emerging economies*. New York: Palgrave-Macmillan.

(2008). The internationalization of Indian companies: the case of Tata. Philadelphia, University of Pennsylvania, Center for the Advanced Study of India, CASI Working Paper 08–02, January.

Goldstein, Andréa, and Pritchard, Richard (2009). South African multinationals: building on a unique legacy. In Ravi Ramamurti and Jitendra Singh (eds.): *Emerging multinationals from emerging markets*. Cambridge, UK: Cambridge University Press.

Goldstein, Andréa, and Toulan, Omar (2007). Multilatinas' go to China: two case studies. In Robert Grosse and Luiz F. Mesquita (eds.): *Can Latin American firms compete?* Oxford: Oxford University Press.

Grosse, Robert (2007). The role of economic groups in Latin America. In Robert Grosse and Luiz F. Mesquita (eds.): *Can Latin American firms compete?* Oxford: Oxford University Press.

Grosse, Robert and Mesquita, Luiz F. (2007). *Can Latin American firms compete?* Oxford: Oxford University Press.

Grosse, Robert and Thomas, Douglas (2007). Sources of competitiveness of large Mexican groups. In Robert Grosse and Luiz F. Mesquita (eds.): *Can Latin American firms compete?* Oxford: Oxford University Press.

Guillén, Mauro (2000). Business groups in emerging economies: a resource based view. *Academy of Management Review*, **43** (3): 362–380.

(2001). Is globalization civilizing, destructive or feeble? A critique of five key debates in the social science literature. *American Sociological Review*, **27**: 235–260.

(2007). *Indicators of globalization, 1980–2007.* (www-management.wharton.upenn.edu/guillen/2009_docs/Global_Table_1980–2007.pdf.)

Guillén, Mauro and Garcia-Canal, Esteban (2009). The American model of the multinational firm and the "new" multinationals from emerging economies. *Academy of Management Perspectives*, May: 23–35.

Hamel, Gary (1994). The concept of core competence. In Gary Hamel and Aimé Heene (eds.): *Competence-based competition*. Chichester: John Wiley.

Hammer, Michael and Champy, James (1994). *Reengineering the corporation: a manifesto for business revolution*. New York: Harperbusiness

Hamon, Maurice (1988). *Saint-Gobain 1665–1990: the making of a French multinational*. Paris: Editions Jean-Claude Lattès.

Hayes, Robert and Upton, David (1998). Operations based strategy. *California Management Review*, **40** (4): 8–25.

He, Xiyou (2007). Outgoing strategy of Chinese firms in telecom equipment industry: the case of Huawei. Paper presented at the Conference "The internationalization of Indian and Chinese enterprises," Brunel University, April, p. 51.

Hickson, David and Pugh, Derek (1995). *Management worldwide: the impact of societal culture on organizations around the globe*. Harmondsworth, UK: Penguin Books.

Hill, Charles W. L. (2008). *Global business today* (5th edn.). New York: The McGraw-Hill Company.

Hofstede, Gert (1980). *Culture's consequences: international differences in work-related values*. Beverly Hills, Calif.: Sage.

(2005). *Cultures and organizations: software of the mind* (2nd edn). New York: McGraw Hill

Huang, Y. (2003). One country, two systems: Foreign-invested enterprises and domestic firms in China. *China Economic Review*, **14** (4): 404–416.

Ietto-Gillies, Grazia (2005). *Transnational corporations and international production: concepts, theories and effects*. Cheltenham, UK: Edward Elgar.

Iglesias, R. M. and Veiga, P. M. (2002). *Promoções de exportações via internacionalização de firmas de capital brasileiro.* Rio de Janeiro: BNDES.

Imai, Ken-Ichi (1992). The Japanese pattern of innovation and its evolution. In Nathan Rosenberg, Ralph Landau, and David Mowery (eds.): *Technology and the wealth of nations.* Stanford: Stanford University Press.

Instituto Brasileiro de Geografia e Estatística (IBGE). (www.ibge.gov.br.)

Instituto de Pesquisa Econômica Aplicada (IPEA). IPEADATA: base de dados macroeconômicos, financeiros e regionais do Brasil. (www. ipeadata.gov.br.)

International Monetary Fund (IMF). *World Economic Outlook: Data and Statistics* (several volumes). Washington, DC: IMF.

Jank, M. (2005). Of flying geese and sitting ducks: Brazil stares, East Asia takes off ... *Yaleglobal Online* (yaleglobal.yale.edu/content/flying-geese-and-sitting-ducks-brazil-stares-east-asia-takes-off%E2%80%A6.)

Johanson, Jan and Vahlne, Jan E. (1977). The internationalization process of the firm: a model of knowledge development and increasing foreign market commitment. *Journal of International Business Studies,* 8 (1): 23–32.

 (2003). Building a model of firm internationalisation. In A. Blomstermo and Deo Sharma (eds.): *Learning in the internationalisation process of firms.* Cheltenham, UK: Edward Elgar.

Jones, Geoffrey. (2002) *Merchants to multinationals: British trading companies in the nineteenth and twentieth centuries.* Oxford: Oxford University Press.

 (2005). *Multinationals and global capitalism from the nineteenth to the twenty-first century.* Oxford: Oxford University Press.

Kakabadse, Andrew and Kakabadse, Nada (2002). Trends in outsourcing: contrasting USA and Europe. *European Management Journal,* 20 (2): 189–198.

Kaplinsky, Raphie (2005). *Globalization, poverty and inequality.* Cambridge, UK: Polity Press.

 (2006). The impact of Asian drivers on the developing world. *IDS Bulletin,* 37 (1): 3–11.

Katz, Jorge (1981). *Domestic technology generation in less developed countries: a review of research findings.* Buenos Aires: ECLA/IDB/IDRC/UNDP Research Programme.

 (1994). Industrial organization, international competitiveness and public policy. In Colin Bradford Jr. (ed.): *The new paradigm of systemic competitiveness: toward more integrated policies in Latin America.* Paris: Organization for Economic Co-operation and Development (OECD) Development Centre.

Katz, Jorge and Kosakoff, Bernardo (1983). Multinationals from Argentina: In Lall, Sanjaya (ed.): *The new multinationals: the spread of third world enterprises.* Chichester, UK: John Wiley.

Khanna, Tarum (2007). *Billions of entrepreneurs: how China and India are reshaping their future and yours.* New Delhi: Penguin-Viking.

Khanna, Tarum and Huang, Yasheng (2003). Can India overtake China? *Foreign Policy,* 137: 74–81.

Khanna, Tarun and Palepu, Krishna (1997). Why focused strategies may be wrong for emerging markets. *Harvard Business Review,* 75 (4, July–August): 41–51.

(1999). The right way to restructure conglomerates in emerging markets. *Harvard Business Review,* July/August: 125–134.

Knight, Gary and Kim, Daekwan (2009). International business competence and the contemporary firm. *Journal of International Business Studies,* 40 (2), 255–273.

Kodama, Fumio (1985). Alternative innovation: innovation through technological fusion. Discussion paper, Saitama University.

Kogut, Bruce (1991). Country capabilities and the permeability of borders. *Strategic Management Journal,* 12: 33–47.

Korine, Harry and Gómez, Pierre-Yves (2002). *The leap to globalization.* San Francisco: Jossey-Bass.

Kosacoff, Bernardo (1999). El caso Argentino. In Chudnovsky, Daniel, Kosacoff, Bernardo and Lopez, Andrés (eds.): *Las multinacionales Latinoamericanas: sus estrategias en un mundo globalizado.* Buenos Aires: Fondo de Cultura Económica (FCE).

KPMG (2009). Mergers and acquisitions research 2009 – 1st quarter: mirror of transactions undertaken in Brazil. (www.kpmg.com. br/publicacoes/fusoes_aquisicoes/2009/Fusoes_Aquisicoes_1_trim_2009.pdf.)

Kumar, N. (2007). *India's emerging multinationals.* London: Routledge.

Kumar, N. and Chadda, A. (2009). India's outward foreign direct investments in steel industry in a Chinese comparative perspective. *Industrial and Corporate Change,* 18 (2): 249–267.

Lacerda, Antonio C. (2009). Estoque de IED do Brasil é o maior do BRIC. *Jornal Valor,* October, 13: A4.

Lacerda, Antonio C., Bocchi, João, I., Rego, Jose, M., Borges, Maria A., and Marques, Rosa M. (2006). *Economia Brasileira* (3rd edn). São Paulo: Editora Saraiva.

Lall, Sanjaya (1983). *The new multinationals: the spread of third world enterprises.* Chichester, UK: John Wiley.

(1992). Technological capabilities and industrialization. *World Development,* 20 (2): 165–186.

Laplane, Mariano, Coutinho, Luciano, and Hiratuka Celio (2003). *Internacionalização e desenvolvimento da indústria no Brasil.* Campinas: Editora UNESP.

Leo, Francesco De (1994). Understanding the roots of your competitive advantage: from product/market competition to competition as a multiple-layer game. In Gary Hamel and Aimé Heene (eds.): *Competence-based competition.* Chichester, UK: John Wiley.

Lessard, Donald R., and Lucea, Rafel (2009). Mexican multinationals: insights from Cemex. In Ravi Ramamurti and Jitendra Singh (eds.): *Emerging multinationals from emerging markets.* Cambridge, UK: Cambridge University Press.

Levitt, Theodore (1983). The globalization of markets. *Harvard Business Review*, May (3): 92–102.

Liu, Chuan Z. (2007). Lenovo: an example of globalization. *Journal of International Business Studies*, 38 (4): 573–577.

Lopes, Juarez B. (1964). *Sociedade industrial no Brasil.* São Paulo: Difusão Européia do Livro.

Luo, Yadong and Tung, Rosalie (2007). International expansion of emerging market enterprises: a springboard perspective. *Journal of International Business Studies*, 38: 481–498.

Masiero, Gilmar (2003). As lições da Coréia do Sul. *Revista de Administração de Empresas Executiva*, 1 (2): 16–21.

Matesco, Virene and Hasenclever, Lia (2000). As empresas transnacionais e o seu papel na competitividade industrial e dos países: o caso do Brasil. In Pedro Motta Veiga (ed.): *O Brasil e os desafios da globalização.* São Paulo, SOBEET/Relume Dumara, p. 161–192.

Mathews, John (2006). Dragon multinationals: new players in 21st century globalization. *Asia-Pacific Journal of Management*, 23: 5–27.

Mathews, John and Zander, Ivo (2007). The international entrepreneurial dynamics of accelerated internationalisation. *Journal of International Business Studies* 38 (3): 387–403.

McCarthy, Daniel J., Puffer, Sheila, and Vikhanski, Oleg (2009). Russian multinationals: natural resources champions. In Ravi Ramamurti and Jitendra Singh (eds.): *Emerging multinationals in emerging countries.* Cambridge: Cambridge University Press.

Menzies, Gavin (2002). *1421: the year China discoverd the world.* London: Bantam Books.

MERCOSUL. Departamento do Mercosul (DMSUL) do Ministério das Relações Exteriores do Brasil. (www.mercosul.gov.br/.)

Messner, Dirk (2004). Regions in the "world economic triangle." In Hubert Schmitz (ed.): *Local enterprises in the global economy: issues of governance and upgrading.* Cheltenham, UK: Edward Elgar.

Mills, John, Platts, Ken, Bourne, Mike, and Richards, Huw (2002). *Competing through competences.* Cambridge: Cambridge University Press.

Mishina, Kazuhiro (1998). Making Toyota in America: evidence from the Kentucky transplant, 1986–1994. In Steven Tolliday, Robert Boyer, Elsie Charron and Ulrich Jürgens (eds.): *Between imitation and innovation.* Oxford: Oxford University Press.

Mortimore, M. (1993). Flying geese or sitting ducks? Transnationals and industry in developing countries. *CEPAL Review*, 51: 15–34.

Munday, Max and Peel, Michael (1998). An analysis of the performance of Japanese, US and domestic firms in the UK electronics/electrical sector. In Rick Delbridge and James Lowe (eds.): *Manufacturing in transition.* London: Routledge.

Mytelka, Lyn K. (1993). Rethinking development. *Futures*, 25 (6): 694–711.

Nelson, Richard (1993). *National innovation systems.* Oxford: Oxford University Press.

OESP (2009). Governo chines anuncia apoio a empresas. *Jornal O Estado de São Paulo*, July 22, B1.

Ohmae, Kenichi (1995). *The end of the nation state.* Cambridge, Mass: Free Press.

Oliveira, Marcelo F. (2003). *Mercosul: atores políticos e grupos de interesses brasileiros.* São Paulo: Editora UNESP.

Oliveira, Thais R. S. and de Paula, Germano M. (2006). Estratégia de internacionalização da companhia Vale do Rio Doce. Paper presented at the workshop on internationalization, Instituto de pós-graduação University of Rio de Janeiro, p. 20.

Panibratov, Andrei and Kalotay, Kalman (2009). *Russian outward FDI and its policy context.* New York, Columbia University, Vale Columbia Center, Columbia PDI Profiles, No. 1, October 13, 2009, 9 pp.

Peng, Mike (2001). The resource-based view and international business. *Journal of Management*, 27: 803–829.

(2009). Unbundling the institution-based view of international business strategy. In Alan Rugman (ed.): *The Oxford Handbook of International Business*, 2nd edition. Oxford: Oxford University Press.

Peng, Mike W., Wang, Denis Yi, Jiang, Yi (2008). An institution-based view of international business strategy: a focus on emerging economies. *Journal of International Business Studies*, (2008) 39: 920–936.

Penrose, Edith T. (1959). *The theory of growth of the firm.* London: Basil Blackwell.

Perez, Carlota (1985). Microelectronics, long waves and world structural change: new perspectives for developing countries. *World Development*, 13 (3): 441–463.

Peteraff, Margaret and Barney, Jay (2003). Unraveling the resource-based tangle. *Managerial and Decision Economics*, **24**: 303–329.

Peters, Tom and Waterman, Robert (1982). *In search of excellence: lessons from America's best run companies*. New York: Harper and Row.

Piramal, Gita (1996). *Business Maharajas*. New Delhi: Penguin Books India.

Porter, Michael (1986). Competition in global industries: a conceptual framework. In Michael Porter (ed.): *Competition in global industries*. Boston: Harvard Business School Press, ch. 1.

Pradhan, Jaya Prakash (2009). Indian FDI falls in global economic crisis: Indian multinationals tread cautiously. Vale Columbia Center on Sustainable International Investment. *Columbia FDI Perspectives*, No. 11, August 17.

Prahalad, Coimbatore K., and Hamel, Gary (1990). The core competence of the corporation. *Harvard Business Review*, **90** (3): 79–91.

Price, John and Haar, Jerry (2008). Can Latin America compete? In Jerry Haar and John Price (eds.): *Can Latin América compete? confronting the challenges of globalization*. New York: Palgrave MacMillan.

Proença, Adriano (1999). Dinâmica estratégica sob uma perspectiva analítica: refinando o entendimento gerencial. *ARCHÉ*, **23**: 5–19.

Ramamurti, Ravi (2004). Developing countries and MNEs: extending and enrichening the research agenda. *Journal of International Business Studies*, **35**: 277–283.

(2009). What have we learned about EMNEs? In Ravi Ramamurti and Jitendra Singh (eds.): *Emerging multinationals from emerging markets*. Cambridge, UK: Cambridge University Press.

Ramamurti, Ravi and Singh, Jitendra (2009). Why study emerging market multinationals? In Ravi Ramamurti and Jitendra Singh (eds.): *Emerging multinationals in emerging countries*. Cambridge: Cambridge University Press.

Roberts, John (2004). *The modern firm: organizational design for performance and growth*. Oxford: Oxford University Press.

Rodrigues, Leoncio M. (1970). *Industrialização e atitudes operárias*. São Paulo: Editora Brasiliense.

Rojas, Carlos A. (2004). *América Latina: história e presente*. São Paulo: Editora Papirus.

Ronen, Simcha and Shenkar, Oleg (1985). Clustering countries on attitudinal dimensions: a review and synthesis. *Academy of Management Review*, **10**: 435–454.

Rugman, Alan (1981). *Inside the multinationals*. New York: Columbia University Press (Palgrave Macmillan, 25th anniversary edn, 2006).

(2008) How global are TNCs from emerging markets? In Karl Sauvant (ed.): *The rise of transnational corporations from emerging markets: threat or opportunity?* Cheltenham, UK; Edward Elgar.

Rugman, Alan and Li, Jing (2007). Will China's multinationals succeed globally or regionally? *European Management Journal,* 25 (5): 333–343.

Rugman, Alan and Verbeke, Alain (2001). Subsidiary-specific advantages in multinational enterprises. *Strategic Management Journal,* 22: 237–250.

Ruigrok, Winfried and vanTulder, Rob (1995). *The logic of international restructuring.* London: Routledge.

Rumelt, Richard P. (1994). Foreword. In Gary Hamel and Aimé Heene (edns): *Competence-based competition.* Chichester: John Wiley, pp. xv-xix.

Santiso, Javier (2007). The emergence of Latin Multinationals. OECD Development Centre. (www.oecd.org/dataoecd/4/40/40512615.pdf.)

Sauvant, Karl (2008). The rise of TNCs from emerging markets: the issues. In Karl Sauvant (ed.): *The rise of transnational corporations from emerging markets: threat or opportunity?* Cheltenham, UK: Edward Elgar.

Schein, Edgar H. (1985). *Organizational culture and leadership.* San Francisco: Jossey-Bass.

(2001). *Guia de sobrevivência da cultura corporativa.* Rio de Janeiro: Editora José Olympio.

Schmitz, Hubert and Cassiolato, Jose (1992). *Hi-tech for industrial development: lessons from the Brazilian experience in electronics and automation.* London: Routledge.

Sethi, S. Prakash e Elango, B. (1999). The influence of "country of origin" on multinational corporation global strategy: a conceptual framework. *Journal of International Management,* 5: 285–298.

Shapiro, James (2005). *1599: a year in the life of William Shakespeare.* London: Faber and Faber.

Simonsen, Mario H. (1969). *Brasil 2001.* Rio de Janeiro: APEC Editora.

Skinner, Wickham (1974). The focused factory. *Harvard Business Review,* May–June (4): 113–121.

Sociedade Brasileira de Estudos de Empresas Transnacionais e da Globalização Economica (SOBEET) (2006–8). *Multinacionais Brasileiras: as mais internacionalizadas.* São Paulo: Valor Economico.

Stopford, John and Wells, Louis (1972). *Managing the multinational enterprise.* London: Longmans.

Story, Jonathan (2004). *China: corrida para o mercado.* São Paulo: Editora Futura.

Sturgeon, Timothy (1997). Turnkey production networks: a new American model of industrial organization? Working Paper 92A, Berkeley Roundtable on the International Economy, University of California, August.

Sull, Donald N. (2005a). Active waiting as strategy. *Harvard Business Review*, September: 120–129.

(2005b). *Made in China: what Western managers can learn from trailblazing Chinese entrepreneurs.* Cambridge, Mass.: Harvard Business School Press.

Sull, Donald N. and Escobari, Martin E. (2004). *Sucesso made in Brazil: o segredo das empresas brasileiras que dão certo.* Rio de Janeiro: Elsevier.

Suzigan, Wilson (1986). *Indústria brasileira: origem e desenvolvimento.* São Paulo: Editora Brasiliense.

Tanaka, Yuji and Koike, Yoichi (1995). Transferência de tecnologia para as empresas subsidiarias japonesas no Brasil. *Proceedings of the International Symposium of Business Management, Economics, and Technology: the dynamics of Brazil–Japan relationships*, São Paulo, Universidade de São Paulo, August.

Tanure, Betania (2005). *Gestão à Brasileira: uma comparação entre América Latina, Estados Unidos, Europa e Ásia.* São Paulo: Editora Atlas.

Tavares, Márcia and Ferraz, João Carlos (2007). Translatinas: quem são, por onde avançam e que desafios enfrentam? In Afonso Fleury and Maria T. L. Fleury (eds.): *Internacionalização e países emergentes.* São Paulo: Editora Atlas.

Teece, David, Pisano, Gary, and Shuen, Amy (1997). Dynamic capabilities and strategic management. *Strategic Management Journal*, 18 (7): 509–533.

The Jai Group (2007). *Seven strategic themes: perspectives on Indo-Brazilian engagement to guide CEO thinking.* Delhi: The Jai Group, November, p. 27.

Tolliday, Steven, Boyer, Robert, Charron, Elsie, and Jürgens, Ulrich (1998). Between imitation and innovation: the transfer and hybridization of productive models in the international automobile industry. In Steven Tolliday, Robert Boyer, Elsie Charron, and Ulrich Jürgens (eds.): *Between imitation and innovation.* Oxford: Oxford University Press.

Torta, Maria H. and Reis, Eustaquio (1978). Liderança de crescimento entre as grandes empresas do setor industrial brasileiro. In Wilson Suzigan (ed.): *Industria: políticas, instituições e desenvolvimento.* Rio de Janeiro: IPEA/INPES, Monografia No. 28, 227–281.

Treacy, Michael and Wiersema, Fred (1995). *The discipline of market leaders*. Reading, Mass: Addison-Wesley.

United Nations Conference on Trade and Development (UNCTAD) (2005). *Investment policy review Brazil*. New York and Geneva: United Nations.

   (2006). *World investment report (WIR) 2006: FDI from developing countries and transition economies – implications for development*. New York and Geneva: United Nations.

   (2007). *WIR 2007: transnational corporations, extractive industries and development*. New York and Geneva: United Nations.

   (2008). *WIR 2008: transnational corporations and the infrastructure challenge*. New York and Geneva: United Nations.

United Nations Development Programme (UNDP) (2009). *Human development report*. (hdr.undp.org/en/.)

Vernon, Raymond (1966). International investments and international trade in the product cycle. *Quarterly Journal of Economics*, 80: 190–207.

Wang, Kaimei (2009). Chinese firms' manufacturing internationalization processes. PhD Dissertation, Institute for Manufacturing, University of Cambridge, May.

Warr, P. B. (1980). An introduction to models in psychological research. In A. Chapman and D. Jones (eds.): *Models of man*. Leicester: BPS Publications.

Watanabe, Susumu (2007). Japanese investment in China and India: firm-level impact in automobile and electronics industries. In Afonso Fleury and Maria T. L. Fleury (eds.): *Internacionalização e países emergentes*. São Paulo: Editora Atlas.

Wells, Louis Jr. (1982). *Third world multinationals: the rise of foreign investment from developing countries*. Cambridge, MA: MIT Press.

Wernerfelt, Birger (1984). A resource based view of the firm. *Strategic Management Journal*, 5: 171–180.

Westney, E. (2001). Japan. In Alan Rugman and Thomas Brewer (eds.): *The Oxford handbook of international business*. Oxford: Oxford University Press, 623–651.

Wheelwright, Steve and Hayes, Robert (1985). Competing through manufacturing. *Harvard Business Review*, Jan-Feb: 99–109.

Williams, Karel, Elger, Tony, and Smith, Chris (1994). *Global Japanization: the transnational transformation of the labour process*. London: Routledge.

Williams, Karel, Mitsui, Itsutomo and Haslam, Collin (1994). How far from Japan? In Karel Williams, Tony Elger, and Chris Smith (eds.): *Global Japanization*. London: Routledge.

Wilson, Dominic and Purushothaman, Roopa (2003). Dreaming with BRICs: the path to 2050. Goldman Sachs Report No. 99; reprinted in Subbash Jain (ed.) (2005): *Emerging economies and the transformation of international business*. Cheltenham: Edward Elgar, 3–35.

Winer, Russell S. (2001). A framework for customer relationship management. *California Management Review*, 43 (4): 89–105.

Womack, James P., Jones, Daniel T., and Roos, Daniel (1990). *The machine that changed the world*. New York: Harper Perennial.

Wood Jr., Thomas and Caldas, Miguel P. (1998). Antropofagia organizacional. *Revista de Administração de Empresas*, 38 (4): 6–17.

(2007). Brazilian firms and the challenge of competitiveness. In Robert Grosse and Luiz F. Mesquita (eds.): *Can Latin American firms compete?* Oxford: Oxford University Press.

Woodward, Joanne (1965). *Industrial organisation: theory and practice*. London: Tavistock Publications.

World Bank. *World development indicators*. (www.worldbank.org/indicator.)

World Economic Forum (WEF) (2009). *The Global Competitiveness Report 2009–2010*. (www.weforum.org/documents/GCR09/index.html.)

World Trade Organization (WTO). *Data and statistcs.* (www.wto.org/english/res_e/statis_e/statis_e.htm.)

Yin, Eden and Choi, Chong J. (2005). The globalization myth: the case of China. *International Management Review*, 45 (1): 103–120.

Yu, Abraham and Tromboni, Paulo (2002). The management of product development projects: the cases of Embraer and Natura. Paper presented in the 11th International Conference on the Management of Technology (IAMOT), Vienna, p. 12.

Zarifian, Phillipe (2001). *Mutacao dos sistemas produtivos e competencias profissionais: a producao industrial de servico*. São Paulo: Editora SENAC.

Zeng, Ming and Williamson, Peter (2007). *Dragons at your door*. Boston, MA: Harvard Business School Press.

Index